BELIEF AND UNBELIEF IN THE ANCIENT WORLD

BELIEF *and* UNBELIEF *in the* ANCIENT WORLD

Edited by

Taylor O. Gray, Ethan R. Johnson,
and Martina Vercesi

WILLIAM B. EERDMANS PUBLISHING COMPANY
GRAND RAPIDS, MICHIGAN

Wm. B. Eerdmans Publishing Co.
2006 44th Street SE, Grand Rapids, MI 49508
www.eerdmans.com

© 2025 Taylor O. Gray, Ethan R. Johnson, and Martina Vercesi
All rights reserved
Published 2025
Printed in the United States of America

30 30 29 28 27 26 25   1 2 3 4 5 6 7

ISBN 978-0-8028-7897-7

Library of Congress Cataloging-in-Publication Data

Names: Gray, Taylor O., editor. | Johnson, Ethan R., editor. | Vercesi, Martina, editor.
Title: Belief and unbelief in the ancient world / edited by Taylor O. Gray, Ethan R.
    Johnson, and Martina Vercesi.
Description: Grand Rapids, Michigan : William B. Eerdmans Publishing Company,
    2025. | Includes bibliographical references and index. | Summary: "A collection
    of essays focusing on religious belief in the ancient Mediterranean world"—
    Provided by publisher.
Identifiers: LCCN 2024041731 | ISBN 9780802878977 (hardcover) |
    ISBN 9781467469678 (epub)
Subjects: LCSH: Mediterranean Region—Religious life and customs. |
    Belief and doubt.
Classification: LCC BL687 .B45 2025 | DDC 200.937—dc23/eng/20250113
LC record available at https://lccn.loc.gov/2024041731

Contents

Preface		vii
List of Abbreviations		x
Introduction		1
	Taylor O. Gray, Ethan R. Johnson, and Martina Vercesi	
1.	**Speaking of the Gods**	7
	Religious Belief in Thucydides	
	Edward Armstrong	
2.	**Αἶρε τοὺς ἀθέους (Mart. Pol. 9.2)**	23
	The Relationship between the Accusation of Atheism and a Radical Interpretation of Eschatology in Early Christianity	
	Stefano De Feo	
3.	**The Empiricism of the Apostle Paul**	42
	Belief and Knowledge in the Context of Roman Divination	
	Matthew T. Sharp	
4.	**The Relationship of Faith and Law Observance in Paul**	58
	The One Who Is Weak in Faith in Romans 14:1–15:13	
	David J. Johnston	

v

CONTENTS

5. **Augustine on Faith**   73
   Trust, Acceptance, Credence, and Belief
   Teresa Morgan

6. **The Point of Belief(s)**   98
   Ritual, Explanation, and the Demonstration of the Divine
   Thomas Harrison

7. **From Bar Rakib to Cyrus**   112
   What Do Royal Portrayals of Divinity Have to Do with Belief?
   Theodore J. Lewis

8. **Bad Blood?**   142
   Varying Attitudes on Human Sacrifice in Archaic Greek Art
   Michael Anthony Fowler

9. **"God Is Our King"**   164
   How Beliefs Surrounding the Ptolemaic Monarchy Influenced the Depiction of God in the LXX Pentateuch on a Lexical Level
   Camilla Recalcati

10. **Is Belief (or Is It Faith?) an Ancient Israelite Notion?**   177
    Thinking and/as Seeing, Seeing and/as Thinking . . . and Believing
    Brent A. Strawn

11. **(Be)li(e)ving in a Material World**   225
    What Can Ancient Figurines Teach Us about the Modern Study of Religion?
    Erin Darby

List of Contributors   261

Index of Authors   265

Index of Subjects   273

Index of Scripture   277

Index of Other Ancient Sources   280

Preface

This book is the result of a biblical studies conference entitled "Aspects of Belief in Ancient West Asia and the Mediterranean Basin: 1000 BCE–100 CE," hosted by the University of St Andrews (online) in July of 2021. The University of St Andrews has for several years given PhD students the opportunity to organize a semiannual symposium linked thematically to biblical studies. In the winter of 2018–2019, Taylor Gray became the promoter of this initiative, and he kindly invited Ethan Johnson and Martina Vercesi to be part of the project.

At that time, the three of us were PhD students working in different areas of biblical studies: the Hebrew Bible, the Pauline Epistles, and the book of Revelation, respectively. We spent many bleak, cold Scottish afternoons in the common area of our office discussing our work and drinking copious amounts of coffee. As we talked with each other about the ancient Near East, the interaction between Second Temple Judaism and the broader Greco-Roman world, and Greek and Latin manuscript traditions, we learned not only about the content of one another's research areas but also about the sometimes significantly divergent approaches in each of our areas of biblical studies. Such enlightening conversations left us fascinated by the potential of interdisciplinary conversations. We decided that we wanted to create a conference environment that would encourage discussions of the concept of belief across the fields of ancient history and literature and that would lead to new and creative angles of research. We also hoped to offer an opportunity for early career researchers and established scholars to connect with one another.

The topic of "belief" or "faith" in the ancient world stood out to us as a research space that could benefit from fresh perspectives. Both English words continue to play a pervasive role in Western religious discourse, particularly in relation to

PREFACE

Christianity. Indeed, all three of us were exposed to discussions of belief/faith primarily in Christian contexts.

- I (Taylor) grew up in a predominantly Lutheran context and attended a private, Christian university to study theology and the Bible. Even though I no longer identify with a practicing religion, I continue to find the development of religious ideas in the Hebrew Bible and Southwest Asia to be appropriate objects of study, since these ideas and beliefs still shape human life today. In many respects, the development and evolution of "belief" as a self-conscious expression of religiosity underscores my own conclusion that what one believes and how is a product of human history.

- I (Martina) grew up in a Catholic Italian cultural environment, so I regularly attended church until high school. However, interest in biblical studies developed as a result of my fascination with the historical aspects of the religious phenomenon, particularly Christianity. I find the differences between the early Christian movements and what is now regarded as "Christianity" to be a subject for ongoing reflection, and I continue to attend to how Christianity has played a pivotal role in shaping our Western culture. "Faith" and "belief" have always been closely associated with the Catholic Church in my context, but studying ancient Christianity has opened up new perspectives on these concepts, allowing me to reconsider their meanings and also question my personal understanding of faith.

- I (Ethan) worshiped in rural Christian churches as a child, and I currently pastor a United Methodist Church in Central Appalachia. In my location, "belief" and "faith" are often used synonymously and treated as a necessary step for salvation, by which most mean reaching heaven after death. Both Christians and non-Christians in my context not only assume that faith or belief is a feature of "religion" in general but also understand it to be *the* feature that marks a religious life.

Each of us examines biblical texts through lenses colored by Christian interpretive traditions, and the variances between these traditions and the ways they approach "belief" or "faith" play integral roles in shaping the different analytical starting points, questions, and objectives that guide our respective approaches to the subject.

While we value confessional readings of ancient texts, for the St Andrews conference we wanted to think more critically about belief and, as much as possible, attempt to step outside frameworks of interpretation shaped by Christian theological concerns. This effort to approach faith and belief with a new perspective

viii

Preface

generated an array of insightful questions. What are ancient texts getting at when they use language of belief and faith? Are they talking about these topics in the same way that we talk about them today? What differences or similarities can we discern across text corpora?

In discussing the issues described above, the conference proved fascinating and instructive. The opportunity to interact with scholars from the fields of biblical studies, classics, ancient Near Eastern studies, and the philosophy of religion challenged each of us to consider belief/faith in new ways and from new angles. These conversations and presentations serve as the basis for the chapters comprising the present volume, which examines the topic of belief/faith from a variety of academic perspectives, including those of established scholars and early career researchers alike.

This book would not have seen the light of day without the unwavering support of the University of St Andrews. Not only was this the first conference that any of us had ever organized, but it was also among the first academic meetings to be canceled and then transitioned to an online format due to the COVID-19 pandemic. This was a challenging task, but we were fortunate to receive invaluable assistance from several people in particular. We extend our deepest gratitude to Steve Holmes, whose offer of generous funding from the divinity department made this event possible. We also wish to express our appreciation to William A. Tooman and T. J. Lang, who believed in us and offered numerous valuable suggestions. Thank you for being always available to help us. We would also like to thank Elizabeth O'Keeffe, Susan Miller, and Debbie Smith, who dedicated a significant amount of their time to helping us understand the practical aspects of organizing a conference and offered consistent support throughout the organizational process.

The symposium owes its final form to the dedication of the PhD students at St Andrews as well as colleagues and friends, who expertly moderated the sessions.

Last but not least, we extend our heartfelt thanks to all the scholars, early career researchers, and students who participated in the symposium and contributed to this volume. We hope and trust that this project will be just one of many initiatives that will bring different disciplines together, enhance insightful discussions, and create new friendships, just as it did for each of us.

Taylor O. Gray, State College, PA, USA
Ethan R. Johnson, Tazewell, VA, USA
Martina Vercesi, Leuven, Belgium

Abbreviations

All abbreviations of Scripture follow *The SBL Handbook of Style*, 2nd ed. (Atlanta: SBL Press, 2014).

ANCIENT SOURCES

Abr.	Philo, *De Abrahamo*
Ab urbe cond.	Livy, *Ab urbe condita*
Acad.	Augustine, *Contra Academicos*
Adv. nat.	Arnobius, *Adversus nationes*
Aet.	Philo of Alexandria, *De aeternitate mundi*
Aj.	Sophocles, *Ajax*
Alex.	Lucian, *Alexander* (*Pseudomantis*)
Anab.	Xenophon, *Anabasis*
Ant.	Josephus, *Antiquitates judaicae*
Ant. rom.	Dionysius of Halicarnassus, *Antiquitates romanae*
Apol.	Plato, *Apologia*; Tertullian, *Apologeticus*
1 Apol.	Justin Martyr, *Apologia i*
Aug.	Suetonius, *Divus Augustus*
Bacch.	Euripides, *Bacchae*
Beat.	Augustine, *De vita beata*
Cant.	Origen, *In Canticum canticorum*
Cels.	Origen, *Contra Celsum*
Comm. Gal.	Jerome, *Commentariorum in Epistulam ad Galatas libri III*
Comm. in Luc. hom.	Cyril of Alexandria, *Commentariorum in Lucam, homiliae*

Abbreviations

Comm. Matt.	Origen, *Commentarium in evangelium Matthaei*
Conf.	Augustine, *Confessionum libri XIII*
Cyr.	Xenophon, *Cyropaedia*
Def. orac.	Plutarch, *De defectu oraculorum*
Div.	Cicero, *De divinatione*
El.	Euripides, *Electra*
Enarrat. Ps.	Augustine, *Enarrationes in Psalmos*
Enchir.	Augustine, *Enchiridion de fide, spe, et caritate*
Ep.	Augustine, *Epistulae*; Cyprian, *Epistulae*; John Chrysostom, *Epistulae*; Pliny the Younger, *Epistulae*
Ep. ad Claudiam	Pelagius, *Epistula ad Claudiam*
Ep. fest.	Athanasius, *Epistula festalis*
Ep. Men.	Epicurus, *Epistula ad Menoeceum*
Fid.	Augustine, *De fide rerum quae non videntur*
Fid. symb.	Augustine, *De fide et symbolo*
Fort. rom.	Plutarch, *De fortuna Romanorum*
Fug.	Philo of Alexandria, *De fuga et inventione*
Haer.	Irenaeus, *Adversus haereses*
Hec.	Euripides, *Hecuba*
Her.	Philo of Alexandria, *Quis rerum divinarum heres sit*
Herc. fur.	Euripides, *Hercules furens*
Hipp.	Euripides, *Hippolytus*
Hist.	Herodotus, *Historiae*
Hist. eccl.	Eusebius, *Historia ecclesiastica*
Hist. rom.	Cassius Dio, *Historia romana*
Hom. Eccl.	Gregory of Nyssa, *In Ecclesiasten homiliae*
Hom. Gen.	John Chrysostom, *Homiliae in Genesim*
Hom. Heb.	John Chrysostom, *Homiliae in epistulam ad Hebraeos*
Hom. Jo.	John Chrysostom, *Homiliae in Joannem*
Il.	Homer, *Ilias*
In Matt.	Chromatius, *In Matthaeum*
Leg.	Athenagoras, *Legatio pro Christianis*; Plato, *Leges*
Lib.	Augustine, *De libero arbitrio*
Mart. Pol.	Martyrdom of Polycarp
Mem.	Xenophon, *Memorabilia*
Migr.	Philo of Alexandria, *De migration Abrahami*
Mut.	Philo of Alexandria, *De mutatione nominum*
Nat. d.	Cicero, *De natura deorum*
Oct.	Minucius Felix, *Octavius*
Od.	Homer, *Odyssea*

ABBREVIATIONS

Oed. col.	Sophocles, *Oedipus coloneus*
Or. cat.	Gregory of Nyssa, *Oratio catechetica magna*
Ord.	Augustine, *De ordine*
P.Cair.Zen	Cairo Zenon Papyri
Pers.	Aeschylus, *Persae*
P.Oxy.	Oxyrhynchus Papyri
Phil.	Sophocles, *Philoctetes*
Poet.	Aristotle, *Poetica*
Pol. *Phil.*	Polycarp, *To the Philippians*
Post.	Quintus Smyrnaeus, *Posthomerica*
P.W.	Thucydides, *Historia belli peloponnesiaci*
Pyth. orac.	Plutarch, *De Pythiae oraculis*
Quaest. rom.	Plutarch, *Quaestiones romanae et graecae*
Rep.	Cicero, *De republica*
Rhod.	Dio Chrysostom, *Rhodiaca*
Rom.	Plutarch, *Romulus*
Serm.	Augustine, *Sermones*; Leo, *Sermones*
Solil.	Augustine, *Soliloquiorum libri II*
Spec.	Philo of Alexandria, *De specialibus legibus*
2 *Steph.*	Demosthenes, *In Stephanum ii*
Strom.	Clement of Alexandria, *Stromateis*
Superst.	Plutarch, *De superstitione*
Them.	Plutarch, *Themistocles*
Thuc.	Dionysius of Halicarnassus, *De Thucydide*
Trin.	Augustine, *De Trinitate*
Tro.	Euripides, *Troades*
Ver. rel.	Augustine, *De vera religione*
Vesp.	Suetonius, *Vespasianus*
Virt.	Philo of Alexandria, *De virtutibus*
Vit. Thuc.	Marcellinus, *Vita Thucydides*

SECONDARY SOURCES

AugStud	*Augustinian Studies*
BASOR	*Bulletin of the American Schools of Oriental Research*
CIG	*Corpus Inscriptionum Graecarum.* Edited by August Boeckh. 4 vols. Berlin, 1828–1877
ClAnt	*Classical Antiquity*
CP	*Classical Philology*

Abbreviations

DCH	*Dictionary of Classical Hebrew.* Edited by David J. A. Clines. 9 vols. Sheffield: Sheffield Phoenix, 1993–2014
HSCP	*Harvard Studies in Classical Philology*
ICUR	*Inscriptiones christianae urbis Romae.* Edited by Giovanni B. de Rossi. Rome: Officina Libraria Pontificia, 1857–1888
JBL	*Journal of Biblical Literature*
JHS	*Journal of Hellenic Studies*
JSNT	*Journal for the Study of the New Testament*
JSOT	*Journal for the Study of the Old Testament*
KAI	*Kanaanaische und aramaische Inschriften.* Herbert Donner and Wolfgang Rollig. 2nd ed. Wiesbaden: Harrassowitz, 1966–1969
LCL	Loeb Classical Library
LIMC	*Lexicon Iconographicum Mythologiae Classicae.* Edited by H. Christoph Ackerman and Jean-Robert Gisler. 8 vols. Zurich: Artemis, 1981–1997
LSJ	Liddell, Henry George, Robert Scott, Henry Stuart Jones. *A Greek-English Lexicon.* 9th ed. with revised supplement. Oxford: Clarendon, 1996
MTSR	*Method and Theory in the Study of Religion*
NEA	*Near Eastern Archaeology*
NIDOTTE	*New International Dictionary of Old Testament Theology and Exegesis.* Edited by Willem A. VanGemeren. 5 vols. Grand Rapids: Zondervan, 1997
NTS	*New Testament Studies*
OGIS	*Orientis Graeci Inscriptiones Selectae.* Edited by Wilhelm Dittenberger. 2 vols. Leipzig: Hirzel, 1903–1905
SB	*Sammelbuch griechischer Urkunden aus Aegypten.* Edited by Friedrich Preisigke et al. Vols. 1–21. Wiesbaden: Harrassowitz, 1915–2002
SJT	*Scottish Journal of Theology*
TAPA	*Transactions of the American Philological Association*
TWOT	*Theological Wordbook of the Old Testament.* Edited by R. Laird Harris, Gleason L. Archer Jr., and Bruce K. Waltke. 2 vols. Chicago: Moody, 1980
VC	*Vigiliae Christianae*
WBC	Word Biblical Commentary
ZDPV	*Zeitschrift des deutschen Palastina-Vereins*

xiii

Introduction

TAYLOR O. GRAY, ETHAN R. JOHNSON, AND MARTINA VERCESI

The chapters contained in this anthology are united by an interest in belief in the ancient Mediterranean world. Since this book could not feasibly address all the facets of what and how people believed in the ancient world, the focus of these essays has been narrowed to address the particular subject of religious belief. The reader will find in the following chapters an array of topics related to belief that span approximately one thousand years of human history. Since this volume focuses on the ancient world and various expressions of belief therein, there is minimal theorizing about religious belief. To frame and anticipate the essays to follow, a few introductory words regarding religious belief on a general level seem appropriate.

Any effort to define religious belief faces a series of significant challenges. How does one define the adjective "religious" or its sibling noun "religion"?[1] Is it best explained as a product of our cognitive evolution, the subconscious, or society?[2] What does it mean to believe, and what is a belief? Is the act of belief

---

1. Theories of religion abound. A helpful introduction to the topic and enduring theories can be found in Daniel L. Pals, *Ten Theories of Religion*, 4th ed. (Oxford: Oxford University Press, 2021); Thomas A. Idinopulous and Brian C. Wilson, eds., *What Is Religion? Origins, Definitions, and Explanations* (Leiden: Brill, 1998).

2. Concerning religion from a cognitive-evolutionary perspective, see Pascal Boyer, *Religion Explained: The Evolutionary Origins of Religious Thought* (New York: Basic Books, 2001). Famously on religion and the subconscious is Sigmund Freud, *Die Zukunft einer Illusion* (Vienna: Internationaler Psychoanalytischer Verlag, 1927). Regarding society and religion, see Émile Durkheim, *Les formes élémentaires de la vie religieuse*, 5th ed. (Paris: Les presses universitaires de France, 2003).

representational or dispositional? Are beliefs finely structured propositions or loosely organized?[3] Moreover, what constitutes a religious belief, especially in the remote context of the ancient Mediterranean and Southwest Asia? Indeed, do the categories of "religion," "religious," and "belief" even map onto ancient thought and behavior?[4]

While we, the editors of this volume, certainly have our own opinions regarding these abovementioned issues and the legitimate challenges that confront our contemporary discussion of ancient religious belief, our intention is to let the contributors to this volume deal with these issues as they see fit and avoid our own commentary on the topic. That being said, despite the clear challenges noted above facing scholarly analysis of ancient religious belief, we hold that the enterprise still remains necessary for contemporary historiography. Of course, we cannot represent the past objectively. As we should admit, all historiography is contingent.[5] The paradigms we operate within and the methods we employ are useful only insofar as they serve our ends. So, even though we risk describing the past in ways that are perhaps incompatible with ancient ways of thinking or behaving, the analysis of the ancient world is, as Nietzsche affirms, "necessary to the health of an individual, a community, and a system of culture."[6] The essays that follow should, then, be read as attempts to capture various dimensions of ancient religious belief, however it is conceived. Hopefully, we learn something about our own understanding of belief along the way.

In the first chapter, "Speaking of the Gods: Religious Belief in Thucydides," **Edward Armstrong** discusses the question of the presence of religious themes in the writing of the Greek historian Thucydides. Armstrong explores Thucydides's representation of religion through the analysis of the following speeches, which are usually considered to be free of religious features: the siege and trial at Plataea, the fortification and siege at Delium, the Melian Dialogue, and the Sicilian expedition. Armstrong reevaluates the presence of religious discourse in Thucydides's oeuvre, highlighting the elements that allow us to recognize it. Through the words

---

3. Eric Schwitzgebel, "Belief," *The Stanford Encyclopedia of Philosophy*, last updated November 15, 2023, https://plato.stanford.edu/archives/spr2024/entries/belief/.

4. Consider Talal Asad, *Genealogies of Religion: Discipline and Reasons of Power in Christianity and Islam* (Baltimore: Johns Hopkins University Press, 1993); Brent Nongbri, *Before Religion: A History of a Modern Concept* (New Haven: Yale University Press, 2013).

5. Hayden While, *Metahistory: The Historical Imagination in Nineteenth-Century Europe*, 40th anniversary ed. (Baltimore: Johns Hopkins University Press), 2014.

6. Friedrich Nietzsche, *The Use and Abuse of History*, trans. Adrian Collins (New York: Dover, 2019), 8.

Introduction

of the characters of his *History of the Peloponnesian War*, Thucydides expresses various nuances of Greek religion that are manifested through decisions, actions, and words.

In "Αἶρε τοὺς ἀθέους (Mart. Pol. 9.2): The Relationship between the Accusation of Atheism and a Radical Interpretation of Eschatology in Early Christianity," **Stefano De Feo** reflects on the relationship between charges of atheism against early Christians and a radical idea of eschatology. Through an exploration of the significance of atheism and eschatology in the ancient world, De Feo reassesses the accusation of atheism against ancient Christians within a new framework. He notes that early Christians shared common features with Epicureans about the fate of the world, which led the Roman political authorities to consider both groups to be atheists. Through his examination of ancient sources, De Feo aims to improve our understanding of the reasons behind these accusations and highlights the centrality of eschatology in early Christianity.

In "The Empiricism of the Apostle Paul: Belief and Knowledge in the Context of Roman Divination," **Matthew T. Sharp** examines the relationship between faith and empiricism in the ancient world. Addressing scholarship that contrasts the Romans' "knowledge" of the gods with the Christians' "faith," Sharp considers the extent to which Paul grounds his religious program on empirical observation. From the appearance of the resurrected Jesus to the manifestation of πνεῦμα in Paul's churches and the tangible results of incorrect cult, Sharp draws attention to the ways in which Paul links faith to experiential evidence. While Sharp notes differences between Paul's Christianity and Roman religion(s), he highlights the ways they share underlying, conceptual frameworks.

David J. Johnston approaches the use of πίστις language to designate different members of early Christian groups in "The Relationship of Faith and Law Observance in Paul: The One Who Is Weak in Faith in Romans 14:1–15:13." He examines the issue of divergent practices related to food, wine, and days in Rom 14:1–15:13. While many have argued that the "one who is weak in faith" and "the strong ones" represent a primarily Jewish and primarily gentile group, respectively, Johnston suggests that the controversy surrounding the weak relates to the inclusion of gentiles in the eschatological age. His article challenges not only our reading of the Epistle to the Romans but also the ways in which we understand Paul's gospel in relation to broader issues of law, faith, and ethnicity.

Although language of "faith" appears in even the earliest Christian texts, it is worth considering the ways in which different Christian authors in different eras conceptualize faith. **Teresa Morgan** directs our focus in this direction with her essay, "Augustine on Faith: Trust, Acceptance, Credence, and Belief." Noting how concepts of πίστις and *fides* shifted toward a greater emphasis on belief by the fifth century, Morgan reconsiders how Augustine understands *fides* and asks whether belief is central to his thinking on faith. She urges that Augustine's thinking about faith includes both propositional and relational components.

Thomas Harrison contributes to the discussion about the nature of belief with his chapter "The Point of Belief(s): Ritual, Explanation, and the Demonstration of the Divine," where he deals with the question of what function belief might have had in the ancient world using the evidence of ancient Greek religions. Harrison guides the reader through various examples from Greek literature, reflecting on the ways in which beliefs can impact practices and how belief can provide explanations for tragic and unpredictable events. While Harrison's contribution primarily aims to comprehend what it meant "to believe" in ancient Greece, in the process he also elucidates the implications of religious belief throughout history.

In "From Bar Rakib to Cyrus: What Do Royal Portrayals of Divinity Have to Do with Belief?" **Theodore J. Lewis** raises the long-standing interpretative issue in the Hebrew Bible regarding the relationship between Cyrus of Persia and Yahweh. For Lewis, the issue of belief is integrally tied up in a matrix of internal and external politics, hegemony, ancestral traditions, and royal legitimacy. To unpack the complexities of belief in this context, Lewis presents a case study of Bar Rakib, an Aramean monarch of the eighth century of ancient Sam'al (Zincirli, Syria). He shows how Bar Rakib employed a variety of media (orthostats, inscriptions, and seals) combining textual and visual narratives about divinity in order to shape the perceptions of his local constituents and external powers, namely, the Neo-Assyrian Empire. At times he portrays divinity conservatively, in line with inherited traditions of his royal ancestors and their devotion to a dynastic deity. At other times he innovatively breaks with his royal family's traditions to pragmatically curry more favor with his local constituency due to its hybrid makeup. His boldest move is to play to imperial power by again using both text and image on an imposing orthostat to portray his allegiance not to his local gods but rather to Neo-Assyrian divinity. The takeaway for Cyrus's putative belief in Yahweh is cautionary. Had we more data for Cyrus (similar to what we have for Bar Rakib) we would shun simplistic reconstructions, realizing that all monarchs portray religious belief in ways that are politically, culturally, and sociologically contingent and audience dependent. Without such data, we must be agnostic with regard to reconstructing Cyrus's belief in divinity, Yahweh or otherwise.

Although human sacrifice features in a variety of Greek myths, it is also criticized by Plato and other Greek writers. Did ancient Greeks *believe* human sacrifice

Introduction

was permissible and efficacious? The contribution of **Michael Anthony Fowler**, "Bad Blood? Varying Attitudes on Human Sacrifice in Archaic Greek Art," attempts to answer this question in the context of archaic Greece. Rather than focus on texts, Fowler considers the presence of human sacrifice in visual media. Fowler examines details, motifs, and configurations of the scene of Polyxena's sacrifice to understand how the artwork conveys different ancient attitudes toward human sacrifice. While some ancient Greeks did criticize and condemn the practice, Fowler's essay shows that others appear to have thought that human sacrifice was efficacious and appropriate in extreme circumstances. In other words, the textual and iconographic evidence indicates a "plurality" of beliefs surrounding human sacrifice in archaic Greece.

In the third century BCE, Jewish scribes living in Alexandria undertook the task of translating the scriptures of early Judaism from their native Semitic languages (Hebrew, Aramaic) into Greek. In her chapter, "God Is Our King: How Beliefs Surrounding the Ptolemaic Monarchy Influenced the Depiction of God in the LXX Pentateuch on a Lexical Level," **Camilla Recalcati** discusses how the Septuagint's translators were influenced by concepts of God and kingship in the Ptolemaic period and how these beliefs shaped the translation of divine epithets in the Greek Pentateuch. Recalcati devotes her analysis to several Greek lexemes such as δεσπότης "master, lord," δυνάστης "master, ruler," and εὐεργέτης "benefactor." The result of the analysis, Recalcati argues, is that some epithets (δεσπότης and δυνάστης) reflect specifically Ptolemaic beliefs about the gods and kingship, and these beliefs are reflected in the vocabulary of aulic titles and divine epithets in the Septuagint.

Brent A. Strawn steps into the conversation about belief/faith in ancient Israel with his chapter "Is Belief (or Is It Faith?) an Ancient Israelite Notion? Thinking and/as Seeing, Seeing and/as Thinking . . . and Believing." Strawn addresses three areas. First, he considers the definitions of belief and faith in the Hebrew Bible, arguing that belief and faith represent interrelated phenomena in the Hebrew Bible. Second, he discusses the role of cognition in belief/faith. He notes the inseparability of cognition and emotion as well as explores Israelite theology in relation to what we find in ancient Egypt. Finally, he examines the visual arts as a locus of belief/faith and their relation to cognition. Analyzing three vignettes through the lens of visual studies, Strawn invites us to appreciate that seeing both involves and reflects belief/faith.

In "(Be)li(e)ving in a Material World: What Can Ancient Figurines Teach Us about the Modern Study of Religion?," **Erin Darby** takes up the question, What can material culture teach us about ancient belief? She argues that the most effective way to access ancient believers is to rely on critical theory while attending to objective structures (social institutions and political economies) that shape daily life and believers' identities. Examining Judean pillar figurines in this light not only suggests that the relationship between believers and figurines was affected by changes in the believers' context but also allows Darby to challenge long-standing interpretations that associate these figurines with women and fertility.

1

Speaking of the Gods

Religious Belief in Thucydides

EDWARD ARMSTRONG

Three decades ago, Simon Hornblower observed that "Thucydides' neglect of the religious factor in his narrative" is to some extent counterbalanced by the speeches in the text.[1] In the same article, Hornblower argues that Thucydides excluded religious aspects of the Atheno-Peloponnesian Wars—including its motives and causes—from his narrative.[2] That the speeches of his *History of the Peloponnesian War* are an exception to the general rule of religious silence, for which Hornblower argues, elevates their significance for our understanding of the place of ancient Greek religion in Thucydides's work.

After Hornblower, William D. Furley and Paul Rahe approached the study of religion in Thucydides by analyzing the function of the religious elements of the narrative.[3] Furley contends that Thucydides explored the "psychology of religion"

1. Simon Hornblower, "The Religious Dimension to the Peloponnesian War, or, What Thucydides Does Not Tell Us," *HSCP* 94 (1992): 169.

2. Hornblower, "Religious Dimension," 197.

3. William D. Furley, "Thucydides and Religion," in *Brill's Companion to Thucydides*, ed. Antonis Tsakmakis and Antonios Rengakos (Leiden: Brill, 2006), 413–38; Paul Rahe, "Religion, Politics, and Piety," in *The Oxford Handbook of Thucydides*, ed. Sara Forsdyke, Edith Foster, and Ryan Balot (Oxford: Oxford University Press, 2017), 427–42.

My sincere thanks to Julia Kindt and Jelle Stoop for their comments on very early drafts of this paper. Unless otherwise stated, all translations of Thucydides are from Robert B. Strassler, *The Landmark Thucydides* (New York: Free Press, 1996) with some adaptations.

through his narrative.[4] For Furley, this conception of a religious "mindset" shows an understanding of Greek religion that is more functional than that perpetuated in previous studies.[5] In his study, Rahe argues that the religious elements of the text function to applaud the Spartans' scruple and to chart the Athenians' decline in the war as they withdraw from traditional religion, νόμος, and σωφροσύνη. As the established cultural customs of Greek societies, νόμοι dictated the social expectations that governed politics, personal lives, and (significantly) religious beliefs and practices. The study of religion in Thucydides has greatly benefited from approaches like Furley's and Rahe's that have examined religion using a framework in which concepts such as νόμος have religious connotations and which show that the motivations of Thucydides's characters can provide insight into their religious psychology. Through their respective studies, Furley and Rahe have presented a glimpse at the grander representation of religion in Thucydides, developing some of Hornblower's earlier observations.

Preceding Hornblower, a long tradition attested in both ancient sources and modern classical scholarship has presented Thucydides's own view as either suspect of religion or entirely uninterested in it.[6] And yet, the entrenched sentiment amid classical scholars that Thucydides is largely devoid of religion is slowly eroding.[7] Conceptions of Greek religion applied to Thucydides have since developed beyond ritual-based religion and the *polis* religion model to the breadth displayed by Furley's concept of it as "the world of the gods."[8] Recent scholarly interest in religion in Thucydides coincides with new interest in belief and cognitive religion, which has emerged following the critique of the *polis* model of ancient Greek religion.[9] The focus of earlier studies on a single dimension of religion in Thucy-

4. Furley, "Thucydides and Religion," 424.

5. Furley, "Thucydides and Religion," 429.

6. See, for example, Dionysius of Halicarnassus, *Thuc.* 6–7; Marcellinus, *Vit. Thuc.* 22; Frank E. Adcock, *Thucydides and His History* (Cambridge: Cambridge University Press, 1963), 55–57.

7. Contrast Gregory Crane, *The Blinded Eye: Thucydides and the New Written Word* (Lanham, MD: Rowman & Littlefield, 1996), 164 with Rahe, "Religion, Politics, and Piety," 428. There are exceptions to this trend, such as Tim Whitmarsh, *Battling the Gods: Atheism in the Ancient World* (New York: Knopf, 2015), 146–54.

8. Walter Burkert, *Greek Religion: Archaic and Classical*, trans. J. Raffan (Oxford: Blackwell, 1985); Christiane Sourvinou-Inwood, "What Is *Polis* Religion?," in *Oxford Readings in Greek Religion*, ed. Richard Buxton (Oxford: Oxford University Press, 2000), 13–37; Furley, "Thucydides and Religion," 416. For an in-depth discussion of this trend in more general studies of Greek religion, see Thomas Harrison, "Beyond the *Polis*? New Approaches to Greek Religion," *JHS* 135 (2015): 165–80.

9. See Julia Kindt, *Rethinking Greek Religion* (Cambridge: Cambridge University Press, 2012), 12–35; Esther Eidinow and Julia Kindt, eds., *The Oxford Handbook of Ancient Greek Religion* (Oxford: Oxford University Press, 2015).

Speaking of the Gods

dides, such as ritual or festival, means that their scope is too shallow in content.[10] Conversely, the conception of Greek religion held by Furley suffers from the ambiguity of exhaustive inclusivity.

A broader conception of Greek religion in Thucydides than that of Hornblower, Burkert, and Sourvinou-Inwood is needed, one that obtains greater precision than Furley's approach through a philological analysis of words with religious connotations to expand the definition within contextually appropriate confines. A study of religion in Thucydides that holds such a multidimensional view of Greek religion would contribute to the revision of past conclusions. The implications of such a study would be significant for scholars researching Thucydides, Greek religion, and religious belief in the ancient world.

My purpose in this chapter is to investigate Thucydides's representation of religion in the speeches of his *History of the Peloponnesian War*. I engage with the speeches that Hornblower observed to be a form of redress for an otherwise resounding absence of religion in Thucydides. In doing so, I explore the more subtle dimensions of Greek religion and not only those manifested in obvious forms. For the purposes of this chapter, classical Greek religion is understood as the sum of beliefs and practices pertaining to the conception of the world in which the stories about the Olympian gods are true, and the cosmos is divided into the interactive realms of mortal and divine.[11]

The speeches engaged in this chapter are drawn from four events that sample the representation of religion across Thucydides's *History of the Peloponnesian War*: the siege and trial at Plataea (*P.W.* 2.71–78, 3.52–68), the fortification and siege at Delium (4.76–78, 89–101), the Melian Dialogue (5.84–116), and the Sicilian expedition (6.8–8.1). These four subnarratives feature the most notable peaks in the frequency of religious language and the significance of religious elements to the events therein.[12] Each event also results in military defeat for one of the involved parties. In my analysis of the speeches, I explore the actions and arguments of the relevant characters to deduce an understanding of their religious outlook.

---

10. This is particularly the case with the following studies: Stewart I. Oost, "Thucydides and the Irrational: Sundry Passages," *CP* 70.3 (1975): 186–96; Nanno Marinatos, *Thucydides and Religion* (Königstein: Hain, 1981); Boromir Jordan, "Religion in Thucydides," *TAPA* 116 (1986): 119–47; Michael A. Flower, "Athenian Religion and the Peloponnesian War," in *Art in Athens during the Peloponnesian War*, ed. Olga Palagia (Cambridge: Cambridge University Press, 2009), 1–23.

11. See Herodotus, *Hist.* 8.144.2; Plato, *Leg.* 888c; Julia Kindt, "Religion," in *The Oxford Handbook of Hellenic Studies*, ed. Barbara Graziosi, Phiroze Vasunia, and George Boys-Stones (Oxford: Oxford University Press), 366; Jordan, "Religion in Thucydides," 120.

12. Hornblower, "Religious Dimension," 173 notes that Thucydides has the vocabulary to distinguish the religious from the nonreligious.

To corroborate the contextual accuracy of my identification of Greek religious elements, language, and belief systems, I compare the representation of Greek religion in Thucydides with that of Classical Attic tragedy, because the two were approximately contemporary.[13]

In this chapter, I argue that Greek religion is presented in the speeches through the implied or claimed existence of the gods and supernatural forces as well as by the words that convey religious ideas. Religion functions as a means of sense-making for the characters, rationalizing and justifying their intended actions, and it directs the audience's reading of and reaction to military defeats. Religion is not limited to appearances of the gods or offerings in temples. Instead, religion is made manifest through the words of the narrative's characters, and it is actualized by their actions that respond to religious ideas in speeches. Furthermore, Thucydides presents a complex view of Greek religion through the speeches, in which justice and morality are tested and the audiences are guided to interpret and respond emotionally as they engage with these real disasters.

IDENTIFYING RELIGIOUS BELIEF IN THUCYDIDEAN SPEECHES

Divine invocations in speeches are one expression of the religious beliefs held by the speaker or those whom the speaker represents. For example, in Thucydides's account of the trial of the Plataeans by the Spartans, the representatives of each side use religious arguments to justify their city's actions and intentions. In one instance, the Plataeans use a divine invocation as a form of evocative manipulation in an attempt to justify their actions (*P.W.* 3.58.1–2). In desperation, the Plataeans invoke the gods as witnesses of their past alliance with Sparta, which the former now claim to be evidence of their friendly status. The Plataeans' arguments imply that, given their alliance, the Spartans have no just reason to punish Plataea and to do so would be unjust. The Plataeans claim that their circumstances in the present war forced them to injure Sparta and its allies, and that their part in the war was involuntary. The Plataeans use the word ἀνάγκη "necessity," to convey the impossibility of acting other than they did, which was done in accordance with their understanding of honorable action toward their ally, Athens (3.58.2).[14] The invocation of the gods is intended to intensify the imperative for both sides to honor the alliance. For the Spartans, this would mean showing mercy by making peace with the Plataeans rather than punishing them.

---

13. See John H. Finley, "Euripides and Thucydides," *HSCP* 49 (1938): 25–28.

14. Cf. Gordon S. Shrimpton, "When Did Plataea Join Athens?," *CP* 79.4 (1984): 295–304.

Speaking of the Gods

A speech containing a prayer that invokes the gods is another expression of religious belief because it implies the existence and power of the divine. Thucydides presents Archidamus invoking the gods in his speech to the Plataeans when he prays to the θεοὶ ὅσοι γῆν τὴν Πλαταιίδα ἔχετε καὶ ἥρωες "gods and heroes of Plataean territory" (2.74.2).[15] Archidamus's final speech portrays the Spartan cause as divinely vindicated to justify their siege. Archidamus reacts to the Plataeans' defiance by appealing to the local gods and heroes, by which Pausanias had made oaths to the Plataeans, as witnesses of the rejection of his fair offer (2.74.2). His unique appeal explains the offense against the Spartans and excuses them of religious obligations associated with the old oaths. Reiterating his earlier claim of nonaggressive intent, Archidamus explains his moral justification to seek revenge against Plataea. He follows the Plataean style of recalling the moment when the original oaths were taken, acknowledging that they had been operational until the Plataeans left the alliance.

In a similar way, Euripides's *Hecuba* portrays religious belief through a divine invocation in the dialogue that transpires following the blinding of Polymestor.[16] For Polymestor, the suffering caused by this disaster is multiplied by having to appeal to Agamemnon for justice with a divine invocation: πρὸς θεῶν σε λίσσομαι "I beg you by the gods" (*Hec.* 1127b). The existence of the gods is implied in Polymestor's petition, which suggests not only his own belief in the gods but also his assumption that Agamemnon likewise holds religious beliefs. In both Thucydides's *History* and Euripides's *Hecuba*, a religious belief in the gods is presented in dialogue through divine invocations.

An expression of trust in a god for military aid demonstrates religious belief by suggesting functional involvement of the god in the outcome of the military event. For example, in Pagondas's speech to the Boeotian army before they attack the Athenians' fortification at Delium, his claim of divine support shows that the Boeotians believe their actions are pious.[17] Thucydides presents Pagondas speaking of trust in Apollo, which implies the manifestation of divine justice through a Boeotian victory over the Athenians: "and trusting in the help of the god whose temple has been sacrilegiously fortified, and in the victims which, when we sacrificed, appeared propitious" (*P.W.* 4.92.7).[18] This reference to Apollo supplements

---

15. See also Ernst Badian, *From Plataea to Potidaea: Studies in the History and Historiography of the Pentecontaetia* (Baltimore: Johns Hopkins University Press, 1993), 112–15.

16. For further parallels between Thucydides and Euripides's *Hecuba*, see James C. Hogan, "Thucydides 3.52–68 and Euripides' Hecuba," *Phoenix* 26.3 (1972): 241–57.

17. Simon Hornblower, *A Commentary on Thucydides*, 3 vols. (Oxford: Oxford University Press, 1991–2008), 2:296–97 notes that this is an unusual instance of a divine invocation by a speaker being followed by their victory.

18. The Greek reads πιστεύσαντας δὲ τῷ θεῷ πρὸς ἡμῶν ἔσεσθαι, οὗ τὸ ἱερὸν ἀνόμως τειχίσαντες

Pagondas's earlier call for the Boeotians to match their ancestors in vigor to defend their country (4.92.6–7). Thucydides uses the mention of trust in divine help to demonstrate that Pagondas thought it would embolden the Boeotian soldiers in the fight to believe that Apollo was aiding them. Implied in this belief is the presumption that their fight against the Athenians was pious. Furthermore, by judging the sanctuary fortification to be ἄνομος "impious," Pagondas renders the Boeotian plan to punish and expel the Athenians as an enforcement of νόμος. By their following military action, the Boeotian army demonstrates that they are convinced by Pagondas's accusation of sacrilege against the Athenians (4.93.1).

Furthermore, Pagondas's claim to have Apollo's help in their battle against the Athenians is underpinned by a belief that Apollo seeks to punish the Athenians for fortifying the sanctuary. Belief in divine justice enacted by a god to punish the hubristic actions of mortals was common in Greek religion and is seen repeatedly in Attic tragedies.[19] In Thucydides's *History*, Pagondas's speech relies on this belief about the deliverance of justice to validate the Boeotians' attack on the Athenians at the sanctuary. The implication is that Apollo will aid the Boeotians in battle to enable them to recover the sanctuary at Delium. Clearly, religious belief is a key factor in these speeches and the ensuing military action.

Less obvious than invocations of the gods and threats involving the gods are those manifestations of a religious outlook that involve hope, fortune, and misfortune. In Greek thought, fortune and hope were intimately linked with belief in divine intervention.[20] Throughout the Melian Dialogue, the Melians propound their belief in the influence of fortune on the unfolding of events (5.90, 102, 104, 112). For instance, the Melians invoke the gods as their security in addition to their reliance on the Spartans as allies: "But we trust that the gods may grant us fortune as good as yours, since we are just men fighting against unjust, and that what we want in power will be made up by the alliance of the Lacedaemonians" (5.104).[21] The surety of the Melians' claim to know that fortune can change the odds of victory indicates their confidence in divine favor. Their hope is based on their ability to resist the Athenians long enough for a change in fortune to occur. This

---

νέμονται, καὶ τοῖς ἱεροῖς ἃ ἡμῖν θυσαμένοις καλὰ φαίνεται. Cf. Peter Hunt, *War, Peace, and Alliance in Demosthenes' Athens* (Cambridge: Cambridge University Press, 2010), 230.

19. Burkert, *Greek Religion*, 130; Hugh Lloyd-Jones, *The Justice of Zeus* (Berkeley: University of California Press, 1983), 152–54.

20. See Burkert, *Greek Religion*, 249 on the perceived role of the gods in misfortunes; see also Esther Eidinow, *Luck, Fate and Fortune: Antiquity and its Legacy* (London: I. B. Tauris, 2011), esp. 5–6.

21. The Greek reads ὅμως δὲ πιστεύομεν τῇ μὲν τύχῃ ἐκ τοῦ θείου μὴ ἐλασσώσεσθαι, ὅτι ὅσιοι πρὸς οὐ δικαίους ἱστάμεθα, τῆς δὲ δυνάμεως τῷ ἐλλείποντι τὴν Λακεδαιμονίων ἡμῖν ξυμμαχίαν προσέσεσθαι.

Speaking of the Gods

condition to the Melians' hope demonstrates that they recognize the pragmatic necessity of military resistance. For the Melians, hope in the gods is not a separate category of reality to pragmatic considerations.

However, the Athenians' disarming arguments render as impractical the hope held by the Melians that the gods will send them fortune and that the Spartans will aid them.[22] The Athenians degrade the Melians' reliance on hope by asserting that hope is only valuable to those who have practical and tangible securities (5.103.1). This comment marks the beginning of the Athenians' recurrent dismissal of the Melians' hopes for an unlikely victory delivered by the gods. Their ensuing dismissal of the gods, fortune, and hope anticipates the Melians' defeat. In the Melians' destruction, Thucydides shows that their hopes were misplaced exactly as the Athenians predicted (5.103.1; see also 5.116.3–4).

Furthermore, Thucydides shows the unpredictability of fortune as it manifests in misfortune through speeches and descriptions of suffering.[23] Thucydides's characters only realize their misfortune retrospectively, and moments of such realization are often catalyzed by a cessation in their suffering.[24] Retrospection of this sort is accompanied by emotionally evocative ideas that cause the reader to empathize with the sufferers (e.g., 7.63.4). In Classical Greek thought, misfortune was often perceived as divine intervention in human affairs by which the gods punished those who had wronged them (e.g., Euripides, *Bacch.* 386–394). In Thucydides's *History*, for instance, Nicias provides insight into the religious mind of the Athenians by his explanation for renewed hope in the success of the campaign: "our enemies have had good fortune enough; and if any of the gods was

---

22. Donald Lateiner, "*Elpis* as Emotion and Reason (Hope and Expectation) in Fifth-Century Greek Historians," in *Hope in Ancient Literature, History, and Art*, ed. George Kazantzidis and Dimos Spatharas (Berlin: de Gruyter, 2018), 143–44. On the contrast between the ineffectiveness of hope as a protection from destruction and the positive function of hope as a comforter, see Joel Alden Schlosser, "'Hope, Danger's Comforter': Thucydides, Hope, Politics," *Journal of Politics* 75.1 (2013): 173–76. Lisa Kallet, *Money and the Corrosion of Power in Thucydides: The Sicilian Expedition and Its Aftermath* (Berkeley: University of California Press, 2001), 13–16 argues that the Athenians move the discussion of hope into the realm of economic considerations, by which they portray hope as an expensive commodity; cf. Gregory Crane, *Thucydides and the Ancient Simplicity: The Limits of Political Realism* (Los Angeles: University of California Press, 1998), 289–90.

23. On the centrality of suffering to the tragic plot, see Aristotle, *Poet.* 1452b8–13.

24. Aristotle's definition of the tragic genre notes the necessity of tragedy evoking certain emotions through its function of *mimesis* (*Poet.* 1449b23–28); on issues with Aristotle's restrictive description of the effects of tragedy on the emotions of an audience, see Jonathan Barnes, "Rhetoric and Poetics," in *The Cambridge Companion to Aristotle*, ed. Jonathan Barnes (Cambridge: Cambridge University Press, 1995), 277–81.

offended at our expedition, we have already been amply punished" (*P.W.* 7.77.3).[25] The enemies' state of being fortunate is here linked with the notion of divine favor and divine judgment. Nicias posits the condition under which the Athenians' misfortune would have been the result of their own impiety, the outcome of which is divine judgment in the form of their enemies receiving good fortune in the war against them.

In these examples, fortune and misfortune are subtle religious beliefs that are presented in the speeches of Thucydides's historical characters as they rationalize the prospect or reality of military defeat. In their expressions of hope for good fortune, the characters claim the existence of gods who control the dispensation of fortune and misfortune. It is in these characters' expressions of trust or skepticism in the divine and supernatural realm that the speakers' beliefs can be found.

RELIGIOUS LANGUAGE IN THUCYDIDES AND TRAGEDY

It remains to be seen, however, by what means religious belief is presented in the speeches. That is the purpose of this section. Three Greek words that convey religious ideas in the speeches are the subject of analysis: νόμος, ἐλπίς, and δίκη. Although these words do not represent strictly religious language in all the instances in which Thucydides uses them, in that they are not always naturally connected to an aspect of ancient Greek religion (as defined earlier in this chapter), their semantic ranges include religious concepts such as divine justice. Thucydides uses these words, among others, to present the characters' religious beliefs in the speeches. Comparison with Attic tragedy shows that these words conveyed religious meaning in their context.

In ancient Greek religion, the observance of religious νόμος usually coincided with the will of the gods.[26] In the debate between the Athenians and the Boeotians at Delium, the religious connotations of νόμος are evident. The Athenians respond to the accusations of the Boeotian herald about the morality of the sanctuary fortification with notable references to νόμος (*P.W.* 4.98). For instance, the Athenians invoke the customary rule of Greek law about sanctuaries during war: "The law of the Hellenes was that conquest of a country, whether more or less extensive,

---

25. The Greek reads ἱκανὰ γὰρ τοῖς τε πολεμίοις ηὐτύχηται, καὶ εἴ τῳ θεῶν ἐπίφθονοι ἐστρατεύσαμεν, ἀποχρώντως ἤδη τετιμωρήμεθα.

26. Burkert, *Greek Religion*, 249; see, for example, Xenophon, *Mem.* 1.3.1; 4.3.16; on sacrifices and prayers, see Demosthenes, *2 Steph.* 43.66; on guests, see Plato, *Leg.* 729e; on oaths, see Homer, *Il.* 3.275–280.

Speaking of the Gods

carried with it possession of the temples in that country, with the obligation to keep up the usual ceremonies, at least as far as possible" (4.98.2).[27] This statement outlines νόμος in relation to sanctuary usage during wars. The religious dimension to νόμος is measured by the extent to which it covers religious beliefs and practices. The religious responsibilities that are involved in the conquest of a sanctuary are νόμοι. Through the Athenians' assertion about the customs of the Greeks, then, Thucydides presents the religious dimension of νόμος.

In Attic tragedy, the concept of νόμος carries religious connotations involving both the divine and mortal realm. For example, the Chorus in Sophocles's *Ajax* proclaims the restoration of cosmic order when Ajax acts in accordance with νόμος by making the appropriate sacrifices to the gods: "Now, O Zeus, can the bright light of day shine upon / the swift ships that glide over the sea, now that Ajax / once more forgets his pain, and / has fulfilled the ordinances of the gods with all their sacrifices, doing them reverence with all obedience" (*Aj.* 709–712 [Lloyd-Jones, LCL]).[28] Sophocles crafted the Chorus's words to describe the religious ritual fulfillment by Ajax as εὐνομία "obedience" or "good order," a form of obedience to νόμος that acknowledges the link between Greek customs and divine favor. After a period of impious disdain for the gods, Ajax's sacrifices symbolize his change to reverence for them, which earns him divine favor (666–667). The Chorus's logic reveals the clarity of νόμος in dictating that which is morally right by causally linking Ajax's obedience with renewed divine support. It is necessary to consider the Chorus's proclamation within the context of the impending revelation, upon Ajax's suicide, that his proclaimed change in attitude toward the gods and the sons of Atreus was deceitful (666–667, 837–842, 925–932). However, the context of the Chorus's proclamation does not detract from the analogy because the principle that obedience to νόμος leads to divine favor is unchanged by Ajax's deception.

In Greek thought, ἐλπίς was regularly associated with the belief that the will of the gods was to reward those who pleased them (e.g., Herodotus, *Hist.* 9.61–62; Thucydides, *P.W.* 7.77.4; Euripides, *Herc. fur.* 771–773). To please the gods, mortals were to honor them with animal sacrifices, libations, and financial contributions to their temples.[29] People expected positive outcomes in their life after completing set rituals that swung divine favor toward them. Hope oscillated on a scale

---

27. The Greek reads τὸν δὲ νόμον τοῖς Ἕλλησιν εἶναι, ὧν ἂν ᾖ τὸ κράτος τῆς γῆς ἑκάστης ἤν τε πλέονος ἤν τε βραχυτέρας, τούτων καὶ τὰ ἱερὰ αἰεὶ γίγνεσθαι, τρόποις θεραπευόμενα οἷς ἂν πρὸς τοῖς εἰωθόσι καὶ δύνωνται.

28. The Greek text reads νῦν, ὦ Ζεῦ, πάρα λευκὸν εὐάμερον πελάσαι φάος / θοὰν ὠκυάλων νεῶν, ὅτ᾽ Αἴας / λαθίπονος πάλιν, θεῶν δ᾽ αὖ / πάνθυτα θέσμι᾽ ἐξήνυσ᾽ εὐνομίᾳ σέβων μεγίστᾳ.

29. Burkert, *Greek Religion*, 68–73; Thucydides, *P.W.* 4.98.2; Herodotus, *Hist.* 3.122–123; Euripides, *Bacch.* 313–314; *El.* 624–627; Sophocles, *Phil.* 1031–1036; Homer, *Il.* 11.727–729, 760–761, 772–775.

15

between certain and uncertain expectation. In Thucydides's *History*, the term ἐλπίς denotes a desire for something in the future that is closer to uncertainty (e.g., Thucydides, *P.W.* 2.89.10; 3.56.4).

In Thucydides's work, hope is often linked to fortune, which can be expressed as either benevolent actions from the gods or as divine punishment (i.e., misfortune).[30] For example, in *P.W.* 7.61.3 Nicias exhorts the Athenians and their allies at Syracuse to fight, "with the hope that fortune will not always be against us" (καὶ τὸ τῆς τύχης κἂν μεθ᾽ ἡμῶν ἐλπίσαντες). Nicias leverages the soldiers' belief in fortune as a means to motivate them to renew their vigor for battle. In this statement, the hope about which Nicias speaks is an expectation that the gods may intervene in the future to ensure their military efforts result in a positive outcome. Here, divine intervention is not expected to manifest in the form of a god fighting the battle on their behalf. Rather, as Nicias's practical considerations in the rest of the speech show, fortune was seen as an unquantifiable, supernatural force that mysteriously influenced the outcome of events.[31] However, Nicias's hope in fortune is proven to be misplaced by the reality of their defeat (*P.W.* 7.72).[32]

An analogous treatment of hope is found in the dialogue between Oedipus and Ismene in Sophocles's *Oedipus at Colonus*.[33] Oedipus asks Ismene about his future using the language of hope, linking it directly with the gods: "Have you then attained the hope that the gods / would pay some heed to me, so that I might some day be saved?" (*Oed. col.* 385–386 [Lloyd-Jones, LCL]).[34] Ismene's response assumes the gods' authority over the outcomes of the future: "Yes, father, from the latest prophecies" (387).[35] This exchange reveals Ismene's misplaced hope in

---

30. On links between hope and fortune in Thucydides, see Eidinow, *Luck, Fate and Fortune*, 124–25; see also C. Anton Powell, "Religion and the Sicilian Expedition," *Historia* 28.1 (1979): 24, who notes that good fortune was indicative of divine aid. On τύχη in Thucydides, see Eidinow, *Luck, Fate and Fortune*, 122–42.

31. See Eidinow, *Luck, Fate and Fortune*, 52, 122; on the mystery of fortune, see pp. 8–9.

32. Harry C. Avery, "Themes in Thucydides' Account of the Sicilian Expedition," *Hermes* 101.1 (1973): 1–13 shows that the hope about which Nicias speaks is his own, for the soldiers had already lost their hope.

33. On the positive concept of hope in Euripides's *Hecuba*, *Trojan Women*, and *Heracles*, see Nick Fisher, "Hope and Hopelessness in Euripides," in Kazantzidis and Spatharas, *Hope in Ancient Literature*, 53–84.

34. The Greek text reads ἤδη γὰρ ἔσχες ἐλπίδ᾽ ὡς ἐμοῦ θεοὺς / ὥραν τιν᾽ ἕξειν, ὥστε σωθῆναί ποτε.

35. The Greek reads ἔγωγε τοῖς νῦν γ᾽, ὦ πάτερ, μαντεύμασιν. The parallel between the two instances seems to lessen with the direct influence of oracles on the hope held by Ismene and the apparent absence of support from oracles for the hope held by Nicias. However, the blame ascribed by the Athenians to the oracle-mongers after the events of Sicily indicate that Nicias's hope of success was at least generally, if not specifically, informed by oracles (see Thucy-

Speaking of the Gods

the Delphic oracle to the reader, as she relies on Apollo's pronouncement that her father will be saved, which does not eventuate (413, 1584). Here, Sophocles's characters portray their hope as a desire for the future, one that is acknowledged as uncertain but considered probable. The comparable definitions of hope presented by Sophocles and Thucydides in their characters' speeches show that the word ἐλπίς can imply religious belief.

Justice is a theme that runs throughout Thucydides's account of the Atheno-Peloponnesian Wars, and δίκη is another word that conveys religious belief in the speeches.[36] In the Melian Dialogue, for example, the first response of the Melians implies that they could prove a superior claim to justice than that of the Athenians (*P.W.* 5.86). This claim remains unchanged toward the end of the dialogue in 5.104, as the Melians state: "since we are just men fighting against unjust" (ὅτι ὅσιοι πρὸς οὐ δικαίους ἱστάμεθα). The Melians' unchanging perspective is founded largely on religious beliefs, especially a belief in divine justice (5.90, 112).

In the writings of both Thucydides and Euripides, justice is a divinely upheld principle that warrants fear of retribution if unobserved.[37] In Euripides's *Trojan Women*, Hecuba identifies in her situation the cycle of human success and failure by divine will: "I see the work of the gods: they raise high / what is nothing and destroy what is esteemed" (*Tro.* 612–613 [Kovacs, LCL]).[38] The Melians, too, identify this cycle, implying that the course on which Athens sets itself is success followed by failure (Thucydides, *P.W.* 5.90). Unlike Euripides's overt portrayal, the presence of this tragic cycle in Thucydides is opaque. Melos and Athens disagree about the categorization of that which is just or unjust, which creates some ambiguity. The religious understanding of justice that Melos displays in Thucydides's narrative mirrors that articulated by Euripides's characters.

That Thucydides's work and Attic tragedy offer such closely paralleled conceptions of the religious dimensions of δίκη, ἐλπίς, and νόμος demonstrates that Thucydides presents religious belief in the speeches of the *History of the Peloponnesian War* through religious language. Rather than a "neglect of the religious factor," religion manifests itself in Thucydides's work through the vocabulary of its characters, the beliefs that their words convey to the audience, and their en-

---

dides, *P.W.* 8.1.1). Although the influence of oracles on the hopes of Ismene and Nicias differs in strength, the analogy clearly illustrates that the theme of misplaced hope is present in both texts.

36. See Malcolm Heath, "Justice in Thucydides' Athenian Speeches," *Historia* 39.4 (1990): 385–400.

37. For the role of the gods in meting justice, see Lloyd-Jones, *Justice of Zeus*, 152.

38. The Greek reads ὁρῶ τὰ τῶν θεῶν, ὡς τὰ μὲν πυργοῦσ᾽ ἄνω / τὸ μηδὲν ὄντα, τὰ δὲ δοκοῦντ᾽ ἀπώλεσαν.

suing actions in the war.[39] For the study of ancient Greek religion, especially in Thucydides, there is no longer any excuse for "the exclusion of belief" that was so prevalent in recent decades.[40]

THE FUNCTIONS OF RELIGION IN THE SPEECHES

Finally, we turn to the role of religion in the speeches of the *History of the Peloponnesian War* in directing Thucydides's audience's reading of and reaction to military defeats. Thucydides uses the speeches as a platform for his audience to consider their own conceptions of justice and morality by drawing on the concept of divine justice. For example, the Melians contend that their only chance to convince the Athenians to relent is to use abstract arguments concerning justice and morality (*P.W.* 5.88).[41] Through a discussion of abstract concepts, rather than expedience, the Melians seek to show the Athenians that their violent purpose is morally unjust (5.90). The first part of the Melians' response to the sophistry of the Athenians contains no explicit threats about the ramifications the Athenians will suffer for violating νόμος. Only in the second half of their response do they mention the μεγίστη τιμωρία "great vengeance" that would await the downfall of Athens (5.90).[42] This threat assumes that justice in the situation is upheld only by Melos, and it implies that the Athenians are acting contrary to laws upheld by divine justice. The dispute between Athens and Melos over the justice of the Athenian conquest directs the reader to judge which side is morally right. Through the dialogue, Thucydides presents the arguments of the Melians to both the internal narrative audience (the Athenians) and the external audience (his readers). As the two sides expound their arguments, Thucydides's reader is presented with the religious perspective of Melos and the Athenians' esteem for natural law. The reader cannot help but make a judgment or feel partial to one side.[43]

39. Hornblower, "Religious Dimension," 169.

40. Harrison, "Beyond the *Polis*," 168.

41. Hornblower, *Commentary on Thucydides*, 3:234 notes that the Melians use the impersonal language of "falling short of exactness" to describe these abstract arguments rather than entreating for the pity that they truly seek.

42. Hornblower, *Commentary on Thucydides*, 3:242 explains that the Greeks believed the gods to be concerned with justice, especially Zeus.

43. An example of those partial to Athens is Albert B. Bosworth, "The Humanitarian Aspect of the Melian Dialogue," *JHS* 113 (1993): 30–44. Examples of those partial to Melos include Colin W. Macleod, *Collected Essays* (Oxford: Oxford University Press, 1983), 52–67; Jordan, "Religion in Thucydides," 139–40; Rahe, "Religion, Politics, and Piety," 433–34; Jesse James, "Indicting the Athenians in the Melian Dialogue," *JHS* 144 (2024): 1–18.

Speaking of the Gods

Thucydides also mobilizes the religious aspect of speeches to direct the emotions of his audience. For example, he uses religious themes during the Sicilian expedition narrative to portray the Athenians' disastrous defeat in a way that evokes pity in his audience. For example, Nicias says that the Athenians deserve pity from the gods in their defeat: "Others before us have attacked their neighbours and have done what men will do without suffering more than they could bear; and we may now justly expect to find the gods more kind, for we have become fitter objects for their pity than their jealousy" (7.77.4).[44] Here, the audience is guided to react in the same way that Nicias hopes for the gods to react—with pity for the defeated Athenians. For an audience that has followed the Athenians' preparations for the Sicilian expedition, including their immensely ritualistic send-off at the Piraeus, their defeat seemed impossible (6.32.1–2). With the convincing voice of Alcibiades and the reluctant consent of the trusted Nicias at the beginning of Thucydides's sixth book, the audience is guided to expect either great victory or great defeat. When the latter materializes, the speeches of Nicias, which utilize religious language, direct the audience to feel the suffering of the defeated Athenians.

Conclusion

In this chapter, I investigated the way religion features in the speeches of Thucydides's *History*. Inspired by Simon Hornblower's article, I sampled speeches across four events depicted in the narrative—the siege and trial at Plataea, the fortification and siege at Delium, the Melian Dialogue, and the Sicilian expedition—in order to push back against the traditional view that religion is understated in Thucydides's *History*, a perspective that was the result of a narrow conception of Greek religion and a disregard for religious themes and words in these speeches. By the religious language and themes concentrated in these speeches, I have shown that religion is actually a salient feature of them. Thucydides presents his characters using religion in the speeches to justify and make sense of their decisions and actions. The religious dimension of the speeches guides how the reader interprets and responds to the defeated party of a military conflict. Religious belief promises justice for the Melians threatened with destruction, hope for the Athenians facing defeat in Sicily, and laws by which the Athenians justify their occupation of the Delium sanctuary. It is thereby worth considering Thucydides's *History* in light

---

44. The Greek reads ἦλθον γάρ που καὶ ἄλλοι τινὲς ἤδη ἐφ᾽ ἑτέρους, καὶ ἀνθρώπεια δράσαντες ἀνεκτὰ ἔπαθον. καὶ ἡμᾶς εἰκὸς νῦν τά τε ἀπὸ τοῦ θεοῦ ἐλπίζειν ἠπιώτερα ἕξειν—οἴκτου γὰρ ἀπ᾽ αὐτῶν ἀξιώτεροι ἤδη ἐσμὲν ἢ φθόνου.

of the religious belief held by the characters that plays such a prominent role in many of its speeches.

Greek religion manifested itself not only in festivals and animal sacrifice; it was expressed in decisions, actions, and words by the people whose conception of the cosmos it influenced. For Thucydides, religious belief made the Spartans justify their conquest of Plataea to the local gods. Thucydides portrays religious belief as the reason that the Boeotians responded in anger to the fortification of Apollo's sanctuary at Delium by the Athenians. Through dialogue, Thucydides suggests that the Melians were defeated partly due to their hope in the gods. Indeed, as Thucydides portrays it, the Athenians failed the Sicilian expedition, at least in part, because they expected endless good fortune from the gods.

To investigate ancient Greek religion, it is essential to delve into the outlook of the historical characters. When do they draw on religious beliefs? How do they frame those beliefs in different contexts? How does it affect their decision-making? How do they view the world in light of their beliefs about the gods, fortune, and justice? These are questions that can be answered only by considering an ancient Greek religious outlook from the perspective of those whose world it shaped.

Works Cited

Adcock, Frank E. *Thucydides and His History*. Cambridge: Cambridge University Press, 1963.

Avery, Harry C. "Themes in Thucydides' Account of the Sicilian Expedition." *Hermes* 101.1 (1973): 1–13.

Badian, Ernst. *From Plataea to Potidaea: Studies in the History and Historiography of the Pentecontaetia*. Baltimore: Johns Hopkins University Press, 1993.

Barnes, Jonathan. "Rhetoric and Poetics." Pages 259–86 in *The Cambridge Companion to Aristotle*. Edited by Jonathan Barnes. Cambridge: Cambridge University Press, 1995.

Bosworth, Albert B. "The Humanitarian Aspect of the Melian Dialogue." *JHS* 113 (1993): 30–44.

Burkert, Walter. *Greek Religion: Archaic and Classical*. Translated by J. Raffan. Oxford: Blackwell, 1985.

Crane, Gregory. *The Blinded Eye: Thucydides and the New Written Word*. Lanham, MD: Rowman & Littlefield, 1996.

———. *Thucydides and the Ancient Simplicity: The Limits of Political Realism*. Los Angeles: University of California Press, 1998.

Eidinow, Esther. *Luck, Fate and Fortune: Antiquity and Its Legacy*. London: I. B. Tauris, 2011.

Eidinow, Esther, and Julia Kindt, eds. *The Oxford Handbook of Ancient Greek Religion.* Oxford: Oxford University Press, 2015.

Euripides. *Trojan Women. Iphigenia among the Taurians. Ion.* Edited and translated by David Kovacs. LCL 10. Cambridge: Harvard University Press, 1999.

Finley, John H. "Euripides and Thucydides." *HSCP* 49 (1938): 23–68.

Fisher, Nick. "Hope and Hopelessness in Euripides." Pages 53–84 in *Hope in Ancient Literature, History, and Art.* Edited by George Kazantzidis and Dimos Spatharas. Berlin: de Gruyter, 2018.

Flower, Michael A. "Athenian Religion and the Peloponnesian War." Pages 1–23 in *Art in Athens during the Peloponnesian War.* Edited by Olga Palagia. Cambridge: Cambridge University Press, 2009.

Furley, William D. "Thucydides and Religion." Pages 413–38 in *Brill's Companion to Thucydides.* Edited by Antonis Tsakmakis and Antonios Rengakos. Leiden: Brill, 2006.

Harrison, Thomas. "Beyond the *Polis*? New Approaches to Greek Religion." *JHS* 135 (2015): 165–80.

Heath, Malcolm. "Justice in Thucydides' Athenian Speeches." *Historia* 39.4 (1990): 385–400.

Hogan, James C. "Thucydides 3.52–68 and Euripides' Hecuba." *Phoenix* 26.3 (1972): 241–57.

Hornblower, Simon. *A Commentary on Thucydides.* 3 vols. Oxford: Oxford University Press, 1991–2008.

———. "The Religious Dimension to the Peloponnesian War, or, What Thucydides Does Not Tell Us." *HSCP* 94 (1992): 169–97.

Hunt, Peter. *War, Peace, and Alliance in Demosthenes' Athens.* Cambridge: Cambridge University Press, 2010.

James, Jesse. "Indicting the Athenians in the Melian Dialogue." *JHS* 144 (2024): 1–18.

Jordan, Boromir. "Religion in Thucydides." *TAPA* 116 (1986): 119–47.

Kallet, Lisa. *Money and the Corrosion of Power in Thucydides: The Sicilian Expedition and its Aftermath.* Berkeley: University of California Press, 2001.

Kindt, Julia. "Religion." Pages 364–77 in *The Oxford Handbook of Hellenic Studies.* Edited by Barbara Graziosi, Phiroze Vasunia, and George Boys-Stones. Oxford: Oxford University Press, 2009.

———. *Rethinking Greek Religion.* Cambridge: Cambridge University Press, 2012.

Lateiner, Donald. "*Elpis* as Emotion and Reason (Hope and Expectation) in Fifth-Century Greek Historians." Pages 131–50 in *Hope in Ancient Literature, History, and Art.* Edited by George Kazantzidis and Dimos Spatharas. Berlin: de Gruyter, 2018.

Lloyd-Jones, Hugh. *The Justice of Zeus.* Berkeley: University of California Press, 1983.

Macleod, Colin W. *Collected Essays.* Oxford: Oxford University Press, 1983.

Marinatos, Nanno. *Thucydides and Religion*. Königstein: Hain, 1981.

Oost, Stewart I. "Thucydides and the Irrational: Sundry Passages." *CP* 70.3 (1975): 186–96.

Powell, C. Anton. "Religion and the Sicilian Expedition." *Historia* 28.1 (1979): 15–31.

Rahe, Paul. "Religion, Politics, and Piety." Pages 427–42 in *The Oxford Handbook of Thucydides*. Edited by Sara Forsdyke, Edith Foster, and Ryan Balot. Oxford: Oxford University Press, 2017.

Schlosser, Joel Alden. "'Hope, Danger's Comforter': Thucydides, Hope, Politics." *Journal of Politics* 75.1 (2013): 169–82.

Shrimpton, Gordon S. "When Did Plataea Join Athens?" *CP* 79.4 (1984): 295–304.

Sophocles. *Ajax. Electra. Oedipus Tyrannus*. Edited and translated by Hugh Lloyd-Jones. LCL 20. Cambridge, MA: Harvard University Press, 1994.

————. *Antigone. The Women of Trachis. Philoctetes. Oedipus at Colonus*. Edited and translated by Hugh Lloyd-Jones. LCL 21. Cambridge: Harvard University Press, 1994.

Strassler, Robert B. *The Landmark Thucydides*. New York: Free Press, 1996.

Sourvinou-Inwood, Christiane. "What Is *Polis* Religion?" Pages 13–37 in *Oxford Readings in Greek Religion*. Edited by Richard Buxton. Oxford: Oxford University Press, 2000.

Whitmarsh, Tim. *Battling the Gods: Atheism in the Ancient World*. New York: Knopf, 2015.

2

Αἷρε τοὺς ἀθέους (Mart. Pol. 9.2)

The Relationship between the Accusation of Atheism and a Radical Interpretation of Eschatology in Early Christianity

STEFANO DE FEO

The relationship between the concepts of "Christian" and "atheist"—an intriguing and ostensibly paradoxical connection—has historical roots extending back to antiquity. This complex interrelation has been vividly illustrated in an exchange between the Marxist philosopher Ernst Bloch and the theologian Jürgen Moltmann. Moltmann recounts the event: "At that time, Bloch was living in Tübingen, and I arrived there in 1967. During a discussion with a group of theologians, Bloch asserted, 'Only an atheist can be a good Christian,' to which I replied, 'And only a Christian can be a good atheist.'"[1]

By highlighting this paradox, Bloch and Moltmann draw attention to the intricate, often misunderstood relationship between belief and unbelief—a tension echoed in the accusations of atheism directed at early Christians.

This essay reflects on the relationship between the accusations of atheism against the early Christians and a radical idea of eschatology. After briefly exam-

---

1. E. Bloch, *Ateismo nel cristianesimo: Per la religione dell'Esodo e del Regno; "Chi vede me vede il Padre,"* trans. Francesco Coppellotti (Milan: Feltrinelli, 2005), 355 (my translation).

I extend my sincere gratitude to Gabriele Pelizzari for his unwavering trust and the honor of being counted among his friends and students in the "Milan School." I am also grateful to the editors for their insightful comments. This work is dedicated to the cherished memory of Remo Cacitti, a true *magister magistrorum*.

ining the different notions of atheism found in the Greco-Roman world, particular attention will be devoted to the correlation between charges of atheism, the denial of divine providence, and eschatological ideas. The final section of this chapter will explore the intriguing juxtaposition of Christians and Epicureans in two concise passages (sections 25 and 38) within Lucian's work *Alexander the False Prophet*. This analysis seeks to uncover the primary motives for this association, elucidate the context behind the use of the term ἄθεος in *Alex.* 38, and identify any theoretical or practical commonalities that may have existed between Epicureans and Christians in the eyes of their accusers.

THE CONCEPT OF ATHEISM IN THE GRECO-ROMAN WORLD

First, it is important to stress that the concept of atheism in antiquity differed from the current public perception.[2] According to Marek Winiarczyk, there are two main interpretations of atheism in antiquity.[3] On the one hand, especially in the first half of the twentieth century, scholars argued that ancient atheism should be understood in terms of the connection between religion and politics. On the other hand, more recently scholars have argued for the existence of a more radical form of atheism in antiquity. According to this latter stance, ancient philosophers questioned the very existence of the gods, claiming expressively that the gods did not exist or maintaining a skeptical approach to the matter.[4] Unfortunately, it is not possible to dive any deeper into this debate here.[5] However, it is sufficient, in

2. See also N. P. Roubekas, "Ancient Greek Atheism? A Note on Terminological Anachronisms in the Study of Ancient Greek 'Religion,'" in *Ciências da Religião: história e sociedade* 12.2 (2014): 224–41.

3. See Marek Winiarczyk, *Diagoras of Melos: A Contribution to the History of Ancient Atheism* (Berlin: de Gruyter, 2016), 66–74.

4. For the sake of argument, cf. Tim Whitmarsh, *Battling the Gods: Atheism in the Ancient World* (New York: Knopf, 2015). In this perspective, as Jan N. Bremmer claims: "All we have in antiquity is *the exceptional individual* who dared to voice his disbelief." See "Atheism in Antiquity," in *The Cambridge Companion to Atheism*, ed. Michael Martin (New York: Cambridge University Press 2007), 11 (my emphasis).

5. Generally, I would share the conclusion of Winiarczyk: "I consider false the two diametrically opposite views of scholars of ancient Greek philosophy and religion: 1) atheism never existed in pre-Christian Greece, 2) already in the 6th century BC Presocratic philosophers supported atheism. On the other hand, the theory that atheism, as the rejection of all gods and supernatural phenomena, appeared in Athens towards the end of the 5th century BC does seem probable, as this is testified in book X of Plato's Νόμοι. Nevertheless, this atheism was limited to a small group of people and the majority of society remained faithful to the religion of their polis" (*Diagoras of Melos*, 74). For a recent discussion on scholarly interpretations of atheism

Αἶρε τοὺς ἀθέους (*Mart. Pol. 9.2*)

my opinion, to stress that Hellenistic and early imperial sources generally bind the charge of atheism to a political charge.[6] This last aspect is particularly relevant in the case of the accusation against Christians because, as Xavier Levieils puts it, "The Romans regarded atheism solely in its practical aspect, and for this very reason, it was entirely conflated with the accusation of impiety."[7] In this perspective, being an atheist is equivalent to being a political opponent because, as underlined by Levieils: "Criticizing the existence of the gods posed the danger of dissolving the religious bond that cemented the civic community."[8]

TRANSCENDENCE VERSUS IMMANENCE

One further clarification regarding how to understand correctly the phenomenon of atheism in antiquity and not undertake an anachronistic analysis is still

---

in the ancient world, see James C. Ford, *Atheism at the Agora: A History of Unbelief in Ancient Greek Polytheism* (New York: Routledge 2024), 1–17, who defines atheism as "the various forms of unbelief in the right gods and/or the failure to worship them in appropriate ways" (17).

6. In this regard, one of the most exemplar texts is Cassius Dio, *Hist. rom.* 52.36. This section is particularly meaningful because it represents the discourse of Mecenate, who received the request from Augustus to undertake an apology of the monarchic system. In doing so, he expressively states the direct connection between political disorders and disregard toward the official cult of the Roman State. In this regard, see also Remo Cacitti, "'Athei in Mundo': Il carattere della diversità cristiana nel giudizio della società antica," in *Il cristianesimo e le diversità: Studi per Attilio Agnoletto*, ed. Remo Cacitti, Giovanni G. Merlo, and Paola Vismara (Milan: Biblioteca Francescana, 1999), 58–59. Against Winiarczyk, *Diagoras of Melos*, 67. I would consider still acceptable the words of Karl Löwith: "The distinctions between true belief [Rechtgläubigkeit], erroneous belief [Irrglauben], and unbelief [Ungläubigen] have no equivalent in antiquity. Heresies [Häresien] can exist only where there is orthodoxy [Orthodoxien], and atheists only where there are believers. In antiquity, atheism was not a religious difference from belief but rather a political form of heresy in relation to the religious foundations of the *polis*. Atheism was *asebeia*, an act of sacrilege punishable by the *polis*." See *Wissen, Glaube und Skepsis* (Göttingen: Vandenhoeck & Ruprecht, 1956), 14 (my translation).

7. Xavier Levieils, *Contra Christianos: La critique sociale et religieuse du christianisme des origines au concile de Nicée (45–325)* (Berlin: de Gruyter, 2007), 335 (my translation). According to Manuel Galzerano, the condemnation already expressed by Plato in the *Laws* against the Presocratic philosophers accused of atheism and impiety for their denial of the divine and providential character of the cosmos paves the way for this identification: "This condemnation is significant and adds a new dimension to the debate on the eternity of the world, portraying the enemies of cosmic theology as subversive thinkers." See *La fine del mondo nel De rerum natura di Lucrezio* (Berlin: de Gruyter, 2019), 8 (my translation).

8. Levieils, *Contra Christianos*, 336 (my translation). For an analysis of the relationship between Christian atheism and the Roman Empire, see William R. Schoedel, "Christian 'Atheism' and the Peace of the Roman Empire," *Church History* 42.3 (1973): 309–19.

needed. After more than two millennia of philosophical research, it is customary to think about atheism as a matter of opposition between transcendence and immanence, according to which the former is negated in favor of the latter. From this perspective, the radical atheists are those who sharply negate a further, transcendent reality or generally a transcendent dimension. In my opinion, however, this clear-cut opposition between transcendence and immanence was foreign to ancient thought, insofar as what modern people consider "transcendent" is often what cannot be demonstrated by experience, that is, by the scientific method (a notion that had been formed in a systematic way only starting with Bacon and Galileo). Instead, the chief concern in the ancient world regarding the divine was its direct relationship with the world, especially through religious practice, rather than a dichotomy between transcendence and immanence.[9] For this main reason, it is not surprising that accusations of atheism in antiquity arose less from the theoretical denial of a transcendent divine existence than from a rejection of divine providence.[10] Only very rarely—and solely within the confines of strictly philosophical debates[11]—were the Stoic philosophers accused of atheism for as-

9. This is exemplified by the relative importance of the ritual aspects of religion over "faith." Orthopraxy, that is, the correct way to act (i.e., to perform a rite), was an essential aspect of Roman religion. See, e.g., John Scheid, *Quand faire c'est croire: Les rites sacrificiels des Romains* (Paris: Aubier, 2005) and also Charles King, "The Organization of Roman Religious Beliefs," *ClAnt* 22.2 (2003): 275–318. See also the programmatic statement of Jörg Rüpke: "I suggest that ancient religion enabled leaps between disparate social, material, and transcendent relationships with the world." See *Pantheon. A New History of Roman Religion* (Princeton: Princeton University Press, 2018), 215.

10. See, for example, Cicero, *Nat. d.* 1.1.2 and especially 1.43.121. As claimed by Matthew A. Fox, "Disbelief in Rome: A Reappraisal," in *Sceptic and Believer in Ancient Mediterranean Religions*, ed. Babett Edelmann-Singer et al. (Tübingen: Mohr Siebeck, 2020), 78: "He [i.e., Cicero] points out, indeed, that those few who claim that there are no gods are greatly outnumbered by those who agree they do exist. *Absolute disbelief is an exceptional position.* But a great deal of attention is paid to the less extreme view—one familiar from Epicureanism—that, once their existence is granted, the gods are disconnected from human affairs" (my emphasis).

11. To my knowledge, this accusation in direct connection with the term "atheism" appears only twice in Plutarch; see *Amatorius* 757b–c; *De Iside et Osiride* 377e. The fact that the central point of contention in the critique of religion was the denial of providence—rather than primarily the negation of divine transcendence or the denial of the existence of the gods, which seems instead to follow as a consequence of this initial rejection—is clearly illustrated in a text by Lucian of Samosata. In this work, a Stoic character (Timocles), as representative of religious tradition, is explicitly contrasted with an Epicurean one (Damis). See Lucian, *Juppiter tragoedus* 17: "That confounded Damis asserted that we do not exercise any providence in behalf of men and do not oversee what goes on among them, saying nothing less than that we do not exist at all (for that is of course what his argument implied), and there were some who applauded him. The other, however, I mean Timocles, was on our side and fought for us and got angry and took our

Αἶρε τοὺς ἀθέους (*Mart. Pol. 9.2*)

serting that God was primarily the immanent principle governing the world and, indeed, could even be identified with the world itself.[12] From this perspective, one of the most dangerous enemies of the traditional conception of the divine in antiquity was a materialistic philosophy able to explain how the phenomena of the world worked and "out of what the world was formed without referring to the intervention of the gods."[13] As an example, consider the ancient atomistic doctrine, a pivotal stance in the philosophy of Epicurus. The ancient atomists *imagined* the existence of the atom. Democritus, for example, did not properly discover the atom in the scientific sense of the term; rather he hypothesized it.

This shows that a definition of atheism based on the opposition between transcendence and immanence, as conceived by modern philosophy, cannot be applied uncritically to the ancient world. The modern skepticism toward "what is not seen" is a relatively recent development, rooted in the Kantian distinction between "noumenon" (the reality beyond perception) and "phenomenon" (the reality as perceived).[14]

The Charge of Atheism against Epicureans

The very character of the stereotypical accusations against Epicurean atheism shows that what is at stake is the radical negation of divine providence more

---

part in every way, praising our management and telling how we govern and direct everything in the appropriate order and system; and he too had some who applauded him" (Harmon, LCL).

12. As is well known, many centuries later Baruch Spinoza would repeatedly face accusations of atheism for similar ideas. See M. A. Rosenthal, "Why Spinoza Is Intolerant of Atheists: God and the Limits of Early Modern Liberalism," *Review of Metaphysics* 65.4 (2012): 818–39, in particular 815–23.

13. Winiarczyk, *Diagoras of Melos*, 73. See also Levieils, *Contra Christianos*, 333: "Philosophical speculations and various attempts to provide scientific explanations for meteorological or geological phenomena were therefore regarded as a threat to the state, as they diminished the ability of the gods acknowledged by the city to act in the world" (my translation). In this regard, Winiarczyk claims that with the Presocratic philosophers "the gods were removed from the world" (*Diagoras of Melos*, 73). However, the fact that world phenomena are necessary or even governed by a mechanistic and materialistic law does not in itself exclude the transcendence of a first principle or God. Just think, for example, of Aristotle's unmoved mover that transcends the world despite presiding over his structural order.

14. From this perspective, it is worth noting that even Carl Gustav Jung regarded the phenomenon of unsophisticated atheism as intrinsically tied to modernity, aptly referring to it as "*die Großstädterneurose des Atheismus*" ('the urban neurosis of atheism')." See *Psychologie und Religion* (Zurich: Rascher, 1962), 101.

than the theoretical refusal of the transcendent existence of the divine.[15] In fact, Epicurus never denies the existence of the gods.[16] Instead, he claims that they do not care about the world and human beings. As already stated by Simpson: "Popular repetition of the charge of Epicurean impiety and atheism was probably due to the emphasis on the complete indifference of the gods to human welfare."[17]

As a possible proof of this, one can consider Plutarch's treatise *De superstitione*, which was composed in the second half of the first century.[18] In this text, Plutarch opposes two contrasting and extreme perils: that of δεισιδαιμονία "superstition," and that of ἀθεότης "atheism." As a Platonist and a defender of the Greek tradition of lived religion, Plutarch cannot accept either of those positions, which are both caused, in his opinion, by ἄγνοια "ignorance."[19] However, what matters the most is that Plutarch's description of the atheist's character represents most likely the position of the Epicureans.[20] In this portrayal of atheism as an Epicurean's stance, Plutarch points that the major risk of this position is not primarily the theoretical negation of the gods but rather the denial of how they act (providentially) for the good. This position would lead human beings to indifferent opinions (εἰς ἀπάθειάν) toward the divine (*Superst.* 165b).

In the accusation of atheism, what is at stake is not the gods' existence but their relationship with the world. From this perspective, the materialistic philosophy of the garden negates this connection by affirming the rule of chance, and in doing so it seems to endanger the general well-being of the civic organization, which is guaranteed by the proper worship of the gods. Therefore, the refusal to

---

15. As significantly claimed by Whitmarsh: "For most of antiquity, if you had asked anyone 'Who are the *atheoi*?' the answer would have been immediate: the Epicureans. The modern Hebrew word for 'atheist,' *apikoros*, testifies to the enduring nature of this association" (*Battling the Gods*, 173). For the unjustified nature of this motif, see p. 209.

16. Epicurus, in fact, expressly affirms the existence of the gods: θεοὶ μὲν γὰρ εἰσίν (*Ep. Men.* 123). See also Dirk Obbink, "The Atheism of Epicurus," *Greek, Roman, and Byzantine Studies* 30 (1989): 194–202.

17. Adelaide D. Simpson, "Epicureans, Christians, Atheists in the Second Century," *TAPA* 72 (1941): 373.

18. Notably, this text is listed in the Lamprias Catalogue (entry no. 155) under the title "On Superstition against Epicurus."

19. See *Superst.* 165c: ἡ γὰρ ἄγνοια τῷ μὲν ἀπιστίαν τοῦ ὠφελοῦντος ἐμπεποίηκε.

20. So already André-Jean Festugière, *Epicuro e i suoi dèi*, trans. Luisa Moscardini (Rome: Castelvecchi, 2015), 54 and Morton Smith, "De Superstitione (Moralia 164E–171F)," in *Plutarch's Theological Writings and Early Christian Literature*, ed. Hans D. Betz (Leiden: Brill, 1975), 6. See also recently Tim Whitmarsh, "Plutarch on Superstition, Atheism, and the City," in *Plutarch's Cities*, ed. Lucia Athanassaki and Frances Titchener (Oxford: Oxford University Press, 2022), 293–309.

Αἶρε τοὺς ἀθέους (*Mart. Pol. 9.2*)

worship the traditional gods—because they do not care about human affairs for Epicureans, and for Christians because they are not "true gods" at all[21]—constitutes the first general element held in common between Christians and Epicureans. While for Christians, on the one hand, the awareness of being at the end of history (e.g., 1 Cor 10:11b; Heb 1:2) prevented them from considering the existence of a benevolent providence designed to guarantee the orderly continuation of the old aeon (cf. Mark 1:15; 1 Cor 2:6), for the Epicureans, on the other hand, the random generation of the world from atoms and the existence of the gods in the empty spaces between the infinite numbers of worlds (the so-called *intermundia*) made the existence of divine providence superfluous.[22]

The Charge of Atheism against Christians during the First Two Centuries CE

At first glance, it may seem surprising that the charge of atheism was made against Christians, who, like the Jews, were fierce advocates of the existence of one God.[23] However, this accusation of an apparently "philosophical" character concealed a sociopolitical judgment. Christians, who did not worship the gods of Rome, placed themselves outside the *opinio communis* regarding religious matters.

This charge was "on their non-compliance with socio-religious conventions across the empire," which was, in turn, a pragmatic consequence of their radical idea of eschatology.[24] In fact, the Christians' "good news," which assumed that the world history was going to come to an ultimate end (e.g., Mark 1:15; 1 Cor 7:29–31), set the kingdom of God and Christ in opposition to any other worldly power (1 Cor 15:23–26).[25]

---

21. In this regard, paradigmatic is the following passage by Tertullian, *Apol.* 10.2: *Deos vestros colere desivimus, ex quo illos non esse cognovimus* "Your gods, then, we cease to worship, from the moment when we recognize that they are not gods" (Glover, LCL).

22. See in particular Plutarch, *Def. orac.* 420b: Ἐπικουρείων δὲ χλευασμοὺς καὶ γέλωτας οὔ τι φοβητέον, οἷς τολμῶσι χρῆσθαι καὶ κατὰ τῆς προνοίας μῦθον αὐτὴν ἀποκαλοῦντες "As for the scoffing and sneers of the Epicureans which they dare to employ against Providence also, calling it nothing but a myth, we need have no fear" (Babbitt, LCL). See also Minucius Felix, *Oct.* 5.

23. On this general issue, see Pier Franco Beatrice, "L'accusation d'athéisme contre les chrétiens," in *Hellénisme et christianisme*, ed. Michel Narcy and Éric Rebillard (Villeneuve d'Ascq: Presses universitaires du Septentrion, 2004), 133–52, with further bibliography.

24. William H. C. Frend, "Persecutions: Genesis and Legacy," in *Origins to Constantine*, ed. Margaret M. Mitchell and Frances M. Young, vol. 1 of *The Cambridge History of Christianity* (New York: Cambridge University Press, 2006), 505.

25. Cf. Adolf M. Ritter: "The *eschatological* orientation of early Christianity could only with great difficulties, if at all, be harmonised with those interpretations of the established Roman

STEFANO DE FEO

From this perspective, it is significant that one of the earliest occurrences of the accusation of atheism can be found in the Martyrdom of Polycarp, a text originating from the middle of the second century. The Martyrdom of Polycarp is a great example of the pivotal role played by eschatology in the early Christian traditions of Asia Minor. During the prosecution of Polycarp, the highest Christian authority of that region, the Roman proconsul L. Statius Quadratus orders him to assert publicly the words αἶρε τοὺς ἀθέους "away with the atheists." The bishop, while looking at the hostile crowd that had reached the stadium, raises his arm against them and, eyeing the sky, repeats the phrase (Mart. Pol. 9.2). Remo Cacitti highlights the amphibological (i.e., mirror image) function of that accusation: "It is absolutely clear that, in the use of the noun *atheos*, proconsul and bishop, the pagan and the Christian, refer to two conceptual universes which, although defined by the same term, are in a relationship of clear and frontal opposition to each other."[26]

Regardless of the historical or purely literary consideration of the episode, this passage witnesses to a perception that, already in the second century, pagans and Christians had distinct conceptual universes.[27] As also reported by Lucian of Samosata (see *Alex.* 25, 38; see also *De morte Peregrini* 21), the consideration of Christians as atheists and impious people was quite widespread among the Greco-Roman elites.[28]

It has been noted that the charge of atheism against Christians emerged only at the beginning of the second century.[29] Besides the Martyrdom of Polycarp, the

---

empire which placed, together with Rome's own persistence (*Roma aeterna*), the continuance of the world in the foreground." See "Church and State Up to c. 300 CE," in Mitchell and Young, *Origins to Constantine*, 527.

26. Cacitti, "Athei in Mundo," 38 (my translation).

27. E.g., Whitmarsh, *Battling the Gods*, 240, negates the historical nature of this episode without giving any compelling reason for it. In any case, the Martyrdom of Polycarp witnesses to a perception that pagans and Christian had distinct conceptual universes whether this particular incident happened or not.

28. Cf. also Cassius Dio, *Hist. rom.* 67.14. This accusation of atheism (ἀθεότητος) seems to oppose the conclusion of Whitmarsh, *Battling the Gods*, 240, according to which "the violent 'othering' as atheists of those who hold different religious views was overwhelmingly a Judeo-Christian creation, which was then projected back onto the polytheists." As Whitmarsh also notes, the charge of atheism against Christians witnessed by Lucian is also important because it constitutes an unequivocal accusation held by a pagan (239). If it has been suggested that well-known accusations such as child sacrifices, Thyestean meals, or Oedipal intercourse were rhetoric invented by the Christians themselves (see Lautaro Roig Lanzillotta, "The Early Christians and Human Sacrifice," in *The Strange World of Human Sacrifice*, ed. Jan N. Bremmer [Leuven: Peeters, 2007], 81–102), the same cannot be easily claimed for the charge of atheism.

29. See, e.g., Joseph J. Walsh, "On Christian Atheism," *VC* 45.3 (1991): 268.

Αἶρε τοὺς ἀθέους (Mart. Pol. 9.2)

writings of Justin Martyr (*1 Apol.* 6; 13; 25), Tertullian (*Apol.* 10), and Athenagoras (*Leg.* 4) all reference such charges of atheism (see Eusebius, *Hist. eccl.* 5.1.9). The rationale behind these Roman imputations of early Christians might be explained by focusing on the synthetic character of this accusation. The ancient Roman concept of atheism is most likely being used here to summarize several different accusations leveled against Christians, most notably the Christian negation of the providence of the Roman gods and the refusal of Christians to participate in traditional cults because of their radical idea of eschatology. In this manner, the Roman concept of atheism was employed to sum up the Christian opposition to the *saeculum*. From this perspective, the amphibological character of Polycarp's harsh expression acquires its full value.

Moreover, it is important to notice that Philo of Alexandria, while commenting on two Stoic philosophers, also attests this connection between the idea of a world that will come to an end and an (im)pious conception, which should imply the incorruptibility of the cosmos: "Thus Boethus of Sidon and Panaetius, powerful supporters of the Stoic doctrines, did under divine inspiration abandon the conflagrations and regenerations and deserted to the more religious doctrine that the whole world was indestructible" (*Aet.* 15 [Colson, LCL]).[30] Here, the idea of an infinite cycle of "conflagrations" (τὰς ἐκπυρώσεις), which was a proper Stoic doctrine, is expressively identified as an impious one.[31]

REFLECTIONS ABOUT ESCHATOLOGY IN THE PAGANS' EYES

That the Christian idea of living in the last days scandalized most pagans can be inferred by two brief passages in the *Apology* by Tertullian, a text written at the end of the second century CE.[32] The early Christian documents collected in the

---

30. The Greek text reads Βοηθὸς γοῦν ὁ Σιδώνιος καὶ Παναίτιος, ἄνδρες ἐν τοῖς Στωικοῖς δόγμασιν ἰσχυκότες, ἅτε θεόληπτοι, τὰς ἐκπυρώσεις καὶ παλιγγενεσίας καταλιπόντες πρὸς ὁσιώτερον δόγμα τὸ τῆς ἀφθαρσίας τοῦ κόσμου παντὸς ηὐτομόλησαν. Text from Leopold Cohn and Siegfried Reiter, eds., *Philonis Alexandrini opera quae supersunt* (Berlin: Reimer, 1915).

31. For the direct link between atheism and impiety, see Leveils, *Contra Christianos*, 331–41 and Marco Zambon, *"Nessun dio è mai sceso quaggiù": La polemica anticristiana dei filosofi antichi* (Rome: Carocci, 2019), 77–87. For Plutarch's criticism of the theory of ἐκπύρωσις, see R. Hirsch-Luipold, "The Dividing Line: Theological/Religious Arguments in Plutarch's Anti-Stoic Polemics," in *A Versatile Gentleman: Consistency in Plutarch's Writings*, ed. Jan Opsomer, Gerd Roskam, and Frances B. Titchener (Leuven: Leuven University Press, 2016), 31–32.

32. As stated by Petr Kitzler: "Tertullian's denying of the charge of atheism has only seemingly nothing to do with the Roman state. Its brisance emerges when looking closely to the wider context whose the Roman gods were part of. To deny their existence meant at the same time to

New Testament suggest that (1) believers understood themselves to be living in the "time of the end" (cf., e.g., Mark 1:15; 1 Cor 10:11; Heb 1:2), such that history itself was approaching its ultimate conclusion (cf. 1 Cor 15:24a; 1 Pet 1:5); and that (2) before this final end, the Messiah will return to the world (cf., e.g., 1 Thess 4:16; 1 Cor 15:23, 51; 16:22b)—establishing his kingdom (cf. 1 Cor 15:24; Rev 20:4–6)—and the world must undergo the final judgment (cf. 1 Cor 4:3–5; Rev 20:11–15). These two beliefs can be considered fundamental for all variations of early Christian eschatological expectation.[33] Both aspects of this idea must have appeared threatening to the Romans. In the first instance, the idea of a "kingdom" could well have been interpreted as a political threat (see, e.g., Acts 1:3, 6–8[34]); in the second instance, the idea of judgment was expressively provocative because it implied a competing standard between God's criteria for judgment and those established by human authorities—namely, the *ius* of Rome and the structures of power it had built (cf., e.g., 1 Cor 2:6; 6:2; 15:24b–25; Rom 8:31–39; Rev 18:1–10).[35]

In a brief passage in the *Apology* by Tertullian, we find one exemplary reaction of the pagans toward the common presentation of the early Christian eschatology, one of a rather humorous nature. Indeed, as Tertullian significantly claims in *Apol.* 18.6: "Yes! We too laughed at this in the past! We are from among yourselves. Christians are made, not born!" (Glover, LCL).[36] The leading cause for the pagans' hostility toward Christians, Tertullian implies, is their conception of eschatology. From this perspective, it is significant that the first element that causes the pagans'

---

deny entirely the Roman *pietas*, a virtue which was one of the foundation stones of the Roman society and Roman state alike." See "Christian Atheism, Political Disloyalty, and State Power in the Apologeticum: Some Aspects of Tertullian's 'Political Theology,'" *Vetera Christianorum* 46 (2009): 245–59.

33. For different scholarly definitions of "eschatology," see Stefanos Mihalios, *The Danielic Eschatological Hour in the Johannine Literature* (London: T&T Clark, 2011), 10–12. The insightful advice and definition proposed by Mihalios is as follows: "The term eschatology should not be defined in terms that merely reflect the very end of history. The eschaton as it is described in the Old and New Testaments has primarily to do with God's intervening act in history in order to transform it. . . . Eschatology, therefore, is the transforming act of God in history, towards a progression that leads to the final consummation of all things" (12).

34. On this text, see particularly Peter-Ben Smit, "Negotiating a New World View in Acts 1.8? A Note on the Expression ἕως ἐσχάτου τῆς γῆς," *NTS* 63 (2017): 1–22.

35. As succinctly expressed by Dieter Georgi, "God Turned Upside Down," in *Paul and Empire: Religion and Power in Roman Imperial Society*, ed. Richard A. Horsley (Harrisburg: Trinity Press International, 1997), 155: "Salvation is opposed to power and authority." See also Richard A. Horsley, "I Corinthians: A Case Study of Paul's Assembly as an Alternative Society," in *Paul and Empire: Religion and Power in Roman Imperial Society*, 242–52, particularly 243–44.

36. The Latin reads *Haec et nos risimus aliquando. De vestris sumus: fiunt, non nascuntur Christiani.*

hostile irony is the idea of a worldly judgment, as reaffirmed in the final part of the apology: "So comes it that we are laughed at for proclaiming that God will be judge" (*Itaque ridemur praedicantes Deum iudicaturum*; 47.12).

The cosmological feature of this threat, which permeates early Christian eschatology, is clearly expressed also in the discourse of Cecilius, the pagan character of the *Octavius* by Minucius Felix. Cecilius actually claims, "Further, they threaten the whole world and the universe and its stars with destruction by fire, as though the eternal order of nature established by laws divine could be put to confusion, or as though the bonds of all the elements could be broken, the framework of heaven be split in twain, and the containing and surrounding mass be brought down in ruin" (*Oct.* 11 [Rendall, LCL]).[37] Here, the Roman intellectual Cecilius feels threatened by the Christians' eschatological ideas. With their conceptions, he claims, they break the relationship between worldly elements (*elementorum omnium*) and supernatural, metaphysical ones (*caelesti conpage*). The specific meaning of the term *religio*—a noun that is most likely based on the verb *ligare* "to bind, connect" with the prefix *re* "again"—has been radically altered. The Christians' anticipation of judgment, which should have brought the world to an ultimate end, was a dangerous conception in the eyes of the Greco-Roman elites (cf. Acts 17:31).[38]

The Connection between Christians and Epicureans

Recently, scholars have reevaluated the importance of Epicurean ideas of the end.[39] Consistently with this reevaluation of the role played by cosmic eschatolog-

---

37. The Latin reads *Quid quod toto orbi et ipsi mundo cum sideribus suis minantur incendium, ruinam moliuntur, quasi aut naturae divinis legibus constitutus aeternus ordo turbetur, aut, rupto elementorum omnium foedere et caelesti conpage divisa, moles ista, qua continetur et cingitur, subruatur.*

38. It is relevant to note that the idea of the "end of the world" has been interpreted as a sign of the absence of the gods in relation to one of the most famous catastrophes of the ancient world: the eruption of Vesuvius in 79 CE. See Pliny the Younger, *Ep.* 6.20: *multi ad deos manus tollere, plures nusquam iam deos ullos aeternamque illam et* novissimam *noctem mundo interpretabantur* "Many were raising their hands to the gods, but more took the view that no gods now existed anywhere, and that that night was eternal and *the last* for the universe" (my translation and emphasis).

39. In this regard, the primary witness for a possible reconstruction of this stance is a text written in the first half of the first century BCE, namely the *De rerum natura* by Lucretius. For a comprehensive analysis of the role played by cosmic eschatology in this text, see especially Galzerano, *La fine del mondo*. See also Alessandro Schiesaro, "Lucretius *On the Nature of Things:*

ical ideas in the philosophy of Epicurus, it is important to note that the *Octavius* by Minucius Felix attests such a distinct and powerful connection between Epicureanism and the material end of the world. While considering the destruction of the world, Octavius (the Christian character in the dialogue) replies to his pagan accuser Cecilius:

> As for the destruction of the world by fire, it is a vulgar error to regard a sudden conflagration, or a failure of moisture as incredible. What philosopher doubts, or does not know, that all things which have come into being die, that all things created perish, that heaven and all things contained therein cease as they began. So too the universe, if sun, moon and stars are deprived of the fountains of fresh water and the water of the seas, will disappear in a blaze of fire. The Stoics firmly maintain that when the moisture is dried out, the universe must all take fire. *And Epicureans hold the same about the conflagration of the elements and the destruction of the universe.* (*Oct.* 34 [Rendall, LCL; emphasis mine])[40]

In this context, it is evident that Epicureans hold the belief that the world is not eternal; quite the contrary, they maintain that the entire universe will ultimately face destruction.[41]

As already noted, one can find another text from the second century CE that states a connection between Christians, atheists, and Epicureans.[42] In the work

---

Eschatology in an Age of Anxiety," in *Eschatology in Antiquity: Forms and Functions*, ed. Hilary Marlow, Karla Pollmann, and Helen Van Norden (New York: Routledge, 2021), 280–93 and Schiesaro, "Lucretius' Apocalyptic Imagination," *Materiali e discussioni per l'analisi dei testi classici* 84.1 (2020): 27–93. Cf. also Christopher Star, *Apocalypse and Golden Age: The End of the World in Greek and Roman Thought* (Baltimore: Johns Hopkins University Press, 2021), 75–126 and F. G. Downing, "Cosmic Eschatology in the First Century: 'Pagan', Jewish and Christian," *L'Antiquité Classique* 64 (1995): 102–3.

40. The Latin reads *Ceterum de incendio mundi, aut improvisum ignem cadere aut deficere umorem non credere, vulgaris erroris est. Quis enim sapientium dubitat, quis ignorat, omnia quae orta sunt occidere, quae facta sunt interire, caelum quoque cum omnibus quae caelo continentur, ita ut coepisse, desinere. Omnem adeo mundum, si solem lunam reliqua astra desierit fontium dulcis aqua et aqua marina nutrire, in vim ignis abiturum, Stoicis constans opinio est, quod consumto umore mundus hic omnis ignescet. Et Epicureis de elementorum conflagratione et mundi ruina eadem ipsa sententia est.* The key term here (as well as in *Oct.* 11, for which see note 37) is *ruina*. This same word occurs in descriptions of the end of the world throughout Lucretius's *De rerum natura* (see in particular 1.1107; 6.607). For the relevance of this term in Lucretius's *De rerum natura*, see Schiesaro, "Eschatology," 282–87.

41. From this perspective, the analysis of *De rerum natura* (particularly of book 5) by Galzerano, *La fine del mondo* is important.

42. For the persistence of this association until the fourth century, see in particular Cacitti,

Αἶρε τοὺς ἀθέους (*Mart. Pol.* 9.2)

Alexander the False Prophet by Lucian of Samosata, the self-proclaimed prophet Alexander, who establishes a cult of Asclepius in the north of Asia Minor, considers Christians to be a hindrance to the very effectiveness of divination and healing. The text articulates this perspective as follows:

> When at last many sensible men, recovering, as it were, from profound intoxication, combined against him, especially all the followers of *Epicurus*, and when in the cities they began gradually to detect all the trickery and buncombe of the show, he issued a promulgation designed to scare them, saying that Pontus was full of *atheists and Christians* who had the hardihood to utter the vilest abuse of him; these he bade them drive away with stones if they wanted to have the god gracious. (*Alex.* 25 [Harmon, LCL; emphasis mine])[43]

As becomes evident, the incendiary nature of the counsel provided to Alexander's adherents (i.e., urging them to repel disruptors of the rituals with stones) can be attributed to the presence of Christians and Epicureans. These two groups, due to their skepticism regarding Greco-Roman religious practices, posed a hindrance to the efficacy of the rituals and, consequently, undermined Alexander's credibility. The text continues by specifying that Epicurus (i.e., his followers) was the primary target of Alexander, stating that he conducted a war against Epicurus without truce or parley (Ὅλως δὲ ἄσπονδος καὶ ἀκήρυκτος αὐτῷ ὁ πόλεμος πρὸς Ἐπίκουρον ἦν). It is critical to notice how Lucian's *Alexander* represents a pagan intellectual from the second century CE who considered Christians as the new exemplar atheists because of their negation of God's providential care for the world. This is the element upon which the parallelism between Christians and Epicureans is properly established.

Moreover, as Lucian states later in the work, Alexander also created a formula in order to preserve the forcefulness of the mystery he was going to establish. Significantly, in this formula Christians, Epicureans, and atheists are connected once again:

> He established a celebration of mysteries, with torchlight ceremonies and priestly offices, which was to be held annually, for three days in succession,

---

"Le ceneri di Epicuro: Eversione religiosa, provvidenzialismo politico e polemica antieriticale nel cristianesimo delle origini," *Annali di Scienze Religiose* 4 (1999): 329–40.

43. The Greek reads Ἐπεὶ δὲ ἤδη πολλοὶ τῶν νοῦν ἐχόντων ὥσπερ ἐκ μέθης βαθείας ἀναφέροντες συνίσταντο ἐπ᾽ αὐτόν, καὶ μάλιστα ὅσοι Ἐπικούρου ἑταῖροι ἦσαν, καὶ ἐν ταῖς πόλεσιν ἐπεφώρατο ἠρέμα ἡ πᾶσα μαγγανεία καὶ συσκευὴ τοῦ δράματος, ἐκφέρει φόβητρόν τι ἐπ᾽ αὐτούς, λέγων ἀθέων ἐμπεπλῆσθαι καὶ Χριστιανῶν τὸν Πόντον, οἳ περὶ αὐτοῦ τολμῶσι τὰ κάκιστα βλασφημεῖν· οὓς ἐκέλευε λίθοις ἐλαύνειν, εἴ γε θέλουσιν ἵλεω ἔχειν τὸν θεόν.

in perpetuity. On the first day, as at Athens, there was a proclamation, worded as follows: "*If any atheist or Christian or Epicurean* has come to spy upon the rites [τῶν ὀργίων], let him be off, and let those who believe in the god perform the mysteries [τελείσθωσαν], under the blessing of Heaven." Then, at the very outset, there was an "expulsion," in which he took the lead, saying: "*Out with the Christians*," and the whole multitude chanted in response, "*Out with the Epicureans!*" (*Alex.* 38 [Harmon, LCL; emphasis mine])

Conclusion

Understanding the intricate relationship between religion and politics in the ancient world underscores the gravity of the accusation of impiety, which was often even more perilous than that of atheism.[44] A critical analysis of ancient sources reveals that the dichotomy between "true *religio*" and "false *superstitio*" was already widespread in the Greco-Roman world.[45] The terms ἄθεος and ἀθεότης were particularly employed as accusations against adversaries deemed politically threatening, a practice with roots traceable back to the notorious trial of Socrates.[46]

The accusation of atheism against early Christians was not coincidental. From a Christian perspective, the radical ideas associated with Christian eschatology entailed the refusal to worship the traditional gods and, consequently, to take part in the official cultic practices. From a Roman perspective, their lack of participation

44. As claimed by Ernst Sandvoss: "Jeder ἄθεος ist ἀσεβής, nicht jeder ἀσεβής dagegen ἄθεος. 'Asebie' ist der weitere Begriff." See "Asebie und Atheismus im klassischen Zeitalter der griechischen Polis," *Saeculum* 19 (1968): 314.

45. Contra Whitmarsh, *Battling the Gods*, 238, who bases his analysis on Jan Assmann's distinction in *Die Mosaische Unterscheidung oder der Preis des Monotheismus* (Munich: Hanser, 2003). As proof of this hermeneutical debt, Whitmarsh writes: "Pre-Christian atheism was certainly not uncontroversial, and there were periods of severe repression. But as a rule, polytheism—the belief in many gods—was infinitely more hospitable toward disbelievers than monotheism. Under Christianity, by contrast, there was no good way of being an atheist. Atheism was the categorical rejection of the very premise on which Christians defined themselves" (11). For a critique of the supposed idea of (religious) tolerance within the Greco-Roman world, see Daniel Timmer, "Is Monotheism Particularly Prone to Violence? A Historical Critique," *Journal of Religion and Society* 15 (2013): 1–15.

46. See Plato, *Apol.* 26c. For the importance of the expression νομίζειν θεούς/θεία in Greek thought, see W. Fahr, *ΘΕΟΥΣ NOMIZEIN: Zum Problem der Anfänge des Atheismus bei den Griechen* (Hildesheim: Olms, 1969) and, more recently, Tim Whitmarsh, "The Invention of Atheism and the Invention of Religion in Classical Athens," in *Sceptic and Believer in Ancient Mediterranean Religions*, ed. Babett Edelmann-Singer, Tobias Nicklas, Janet E. Spittler, and Luigi Walt (Tübingen: Mohr Siebeck, 2020), 47–51.

Αἶρε τοὺς ἀθέους (*Mart. Pol. 9.2*)

in the cult was viewed (especially by Roman authorities) as a threat to political stability, given the strong and nearly inseparable connection between religion and politics.[47] Despite differing from Christians in their philosophical foundations—particularly in their materialism—Epicureans shared with Christians the belief in the noneternal nature of the world and also rejected divine interference in worldly affairs. The clear rejection of divine providence likely explains the association of Christians and Epicureans in Roman uses of the label "atheism" and their identification of both groups as "subversive thinkers."[48]

In the eyes of pagan intellectuals, the Christians' refusal to worship the traditional gods and participate in official cults represented a "fight against God," a sentiment echoed by Porphyry in the late third century CE in his *Against the Christians*. In many ways, Porphyry's words serve as an apt and conclusive summary of the connection between the Greco-Roman charge of atheism and political allegations: "How could they not be impious and atheists [δυσσεβεῖς . . . καὶ ἄθεοι] who have forsaken the ancestral gods[(οἱ τῶν πατρῴων θεῶν ἀποστάντες], by which the whole race and the whole state are held together? What good could reasonably be expected from those who have become enemies and adversaries of their saviors, rejecting their benefactors? What else but that they fight against God [θεομαχοῦντας]?"[49]

---

47. For the strict link between cult and politics, see Cicero, *Nat. d.* 3.5. On the implications of this link for Christians, see in particular Cacitti, "Athei in Mundo," 312–24.

48. Moreover, as was kindly suggested to me during the discussion following my paper at the St Andrews symposium, the negation of providence could also be the main feature of the occurrences of the term "Epicurean" in the Mishnah. From this perspective, see Jenny R. Labendz, "'Know What to Answer the Epicurean': A Diachronic Study of the ʾApiqoros in Rabbinic Literature," *Hebrew Union College Annual* 74 (2003): 175–214, who precisely claims that: "The term Epicurean is used to signal a similarly specific point of denial. One may therefore speculate that, among the salient characteristics of Epicureanism, the Rabbis seem to focus on its outright denial of providence rather than upon its missionizing, hedonism, or metaphysical theories" (182).

49. Translation my own. For the Greek text, see Matthias Becker, *Porphyrios, 'Contra Christianos': Neue Sammlung der Fragmente, Testimonien und Dubia mit Einleitung, Übersetzungen und Anmerkungen* (Berlin: de Gruyter, 2016). Again, the political nature of this charge is directly dependent on the negation of the providence, that is, the direct and benevolent influence of divinity toward the world. In this regard, an exemplary text is Plutarch, *Pyth. orac.* 402e: δεῖ γὰρ μὴ μάχεσθαι πρὸς τὸν θεὸν μηδ' ἀναιρεῖν μετὰ τῆς μαντικῆς ἅμα τὴν πρόνοιαν καὶ τὸ θεῖον, ἀλλὰ τῶν ὑπεναντιοῦσθαι δοκούντων λύσεις ἐπιζητεῖν τὴν δ' εὐσεβῆ καὶ πάτριον μὴ προΐεσθαι πίστιν "For we must not *fight against the god*, nor do away with his providence and divine powers together with his prophetic gifts; but we must seek for explanations of such matters as seem to stand in the way, and not relinquish the reverent faith of our fathers" (my translation).

Works Cited

Assmann, Jan. *Die Mosaische Unterscheidung oder der Preis des Monotheismus.* Munich: Hanser, 2003.

Beatrice, P. Franco. "L'accusation d'athéisme contre les chrétiens." Pages 133–52 in *Hellénisme et christianisme.* Edited by Michel Narcy and Éric Rebillard. Villeneuve d'Ascq: Presses universitaires du Septentrion, 2004.

Becker, Matthias. *Porphyrios, 'Contra Christianos': Neue Sammlung der Fragmente, Testimonien und Dubia mit Einleitung, Übersetzungen und Anmerkungen.* Berlin: de Gruyter, 2016.

Bloch, E. *Ateismo nel cristianesimo: Per la religione dell'Esodo e del Regno; "Chi vede me vede il Padre."* Translated by Francesco Coppellotti. Milan: Feltrinelli, 2005.

Bremmer, Jan N. "Atheism in Antiquity." Pages 11–26 in *The Cambridge Companion to Atheism.* Edited by Michael Martin. New York: Cambridge University Press, 2007.

Cacitti, Remo. "'Athei in Mundo': Il carattere della diversità cristiana nel giudizio della società antica." Pages 37–68 in *Il cristianesimo e le diversità: Studi per Attilio Agnoletto.* Edited by Remo Cacitti, Grado Giovanni Merlo, and Paola Vismara. Milan: Biblioteca Francescana, 1999.

———. "Le ceneri di Epicuro: Eversione religiosa, provvidenzialismo politico e polemica antieriticale nel cristianesimo delle origini." *Annali di Scienze Religiose* 4 (1999): 307–41.

Cohn, Leopold, and Siegfried Reiter, eds. *Philonis Alexandrini opera quae supersunt.* Berlin: Reimer, 1915.

Downing, F. G. "Cosmic Eschatology in the First Century: 'Pagan', Jewish and Christian." *L'Antiquité Classique* 64 (1995): 99–109.

Fahr, Wilhelm. *ΘΕΟΥΣ ΝΟΜΙΖΕΙΝ: Zum Problem der Anfänge des Atheismus bei den Griechen.* Hildesheim: Olms, 1969.

Festugière, André-Jean. *Epicuro e i suoi dèi.* Translated by Luisa Moscardini. Rome: Castelvecchi, 2015.

Ford, James C. *Atheism at the Agora: A History of Unbelief in Ancient Greek Polytheism.* New York: Routledge, 2024.

Fox, Matthew A. "Disbelief in Rome. A Reappraisal." Pages 69–91 in *Sceptic and Believer in Ancient Mediterranean Religions.* Edited by Babett Edelmann-Singer, Tobias Nicklas, Janet E. Spittler, and Luigi Walt. Tübingen: Mohr Siebeck, 2020.

Frend, William H. C. "Persecutions: Genesis and Legacy." Pages 503–23 in *Origins to Constantine.* Edited by Margaret M. Mitchell and Frances M. Young. Vol. 1 of *The Cambridge History of Christianity.* New York: Cambridge University Press, 2006.

Αἶρε τοὺς ἀθέους (*Mart. Pol. 9.2*)

Galzerano, Manuel. *La fine del mondo nel* De rerum natura *di Lucrezio*. Berlin: de Gruyter, 2019.

Georgi, Dieter. "God Turned Upside Down." Pages 148–57 in *Paul and Empire: Religion and Power in Roman Imperial Society*. Edited by Richard A. Horsley. Harrisburg: Trinity Press International, 1997.

Hirsch-Luipold, Rainer. "The Dividing Line: Theological/Religious Arguments in Plutarch's Anti-Stoic Polemics." Pages 17–36 in *A Versatile Gentleman: Consistency in Plutarch's Writings*. Edited by Jan Opsomer, Gerd Roskam, and Frances B. Titchener. Leuven: Leuven University Press, 2016.

Horsley, Richard A. "I Corinthians: A Case Study of Paul's Assembly as an Alternative Society." Pages 242–52 in *Paul and Empire: Religion and Power in Roman Imperial Society*. Edited by Richard A. Horsley. Harrisburg: Trinity Press International, 1997.

Jung, Carl G. *Psychologie und Religion*. Zurich: Rascher, 1962.

King, Charles. "The Organization of Roman Religious Beliefs." *ClAnt* 22.2 (2003): 275–318.

Kitzler, Petr. "Christian Atheism, Political Disloyalty, and State Power in the Apologeticum: Some Aspects of Tertullian's 'Political Theology.'" *Vetera Christianorum* 46 (2009): 245–59.

Labendz, Jenny R. "'Know What to Answer the Epicurean': A Diachronic Study of the *Ἀpiqoros* in Rabbinic Literature." *Hebrew Union College Annual* 74 (2003): 175–214.

Lanzillotta, Lautaro Roig. "The Early Christians and Human Sacrifice." Pages 81–102 in *The Strange World of Human Sacrifice*. Edited by Jan N. Bremmer. Leuven: Peeters, 2007.

Levieils, Xavier. *Contra Christianos: La critique sociale et religieuse du christianisme des origines au concile de Nicée (45–325)*. Berlin: de Gruyter, 2007.

Löwith, Karl. *Wissen, Glaube und Skepsis*. Göttingen: Vandenhoeck & Ruprecht, 1956.

Mihalios, Stefanos. *The Danielic Eschatological Hour in the Johannine Literature*. London: T&T Clark, 2011.

Minucius Felix. *Octavius*. Translated by Gerald H. Rendall. LCL 250. Cambridge: Harvard University Press, 1931.

Obbink, Dirk. "The Atheism of Epicurus." *Greek, Roman, and Byzantine Studies* 30 (1989): 187–223.

Philo. *Every Good Man Is Free. On the Contemplative Life. On the Eternity of the World. Against Flaccus. Apology for the Jews. On Providence*. Translated by F. H. Colson. LCL 363. Cambridge: Harvard University Press, 1941.

Plutarch. *Moralia, Volume V: Isis and Osiris. The E at Delphi. The Oracles at Delphi No*

Longer Given in Verse. The Obsolescence of Oracles. Translated by Frank Cole Babbitt. LCL 306. Cambridge: Harvard University Press, 1936.

Ritter, Adolf M. "Church and State Up to c. 300 CE." Pages 524–37 in *Origins to Constantine.* Edited by Margaret M. Mitchell and Frances M. Young. Vol. 1 of *The Cambridge History of Christianity.* New York: Cambridge University Press, 2006.

Rosenthal, M. A. "Why Spinoza Is Intolerant of Atheists: God and the Limits of Early Modern Liberalism." *Review of Metaphysics* 65.4 (2012): 818–39.

Roubekas, Nickolas P. "Ancient Greek Atheism? A Note on Terminological Anachronisms in the Study of Ancient Greek 'Religion.'" *Ciências da Religião: história e sociedade* 12.2 (2014): 224–41.

Rüpke, Jörg. *Pantheon: A New History of Roman Religion.* Princeton: Princeton University Press, 2018.

Sandvoss, Ernst. "Asebie und Atheismus im klassischen Zeitalter der griechischen Polis." *Saeculum* 19 (1968): 312–29.

Scheid, John. *Quand faire c'est croire: Les rites sacrificiels des Romains.* Paris: Aubier, 2005.

Schiesaro Alessandro, "Lucretius' Apocalyptic Imagination." *Materiali e discussioni per l'analisi dei testi classici* 84.1 (2020): 27–93.

―――. "Lucretius *On the Nature of Things*: Eschatology in an Age of Anxiety." Pages 280–93 in *Eschatology in Antiquity: Forms and Functions.* Edited by Hilary Marlow, Karla Pollmann, and Helen Van Norden. New York: Routledge, 2021.

Schoedel, William R. "Christian 'Atheism' and the Peace of the Roman Empire." *Church History* 42.3 (1973): 309–19.

Simpson, Adelaide D. "Epicureans, Christians, Atheists in the Second Century." *TAPA* 72 (1941): 372–81.

Smit, Peter-Ben. "Negotiating a New World View in Acts 1.8? A Note on the Expression ἕως ἐσχάτου τῆς γῆς." *NTS* 63 (2017): 1–22.

Smith, Morton. "De Superstitione (Moralia 164E–171F)." Pages 1–35 in *Plutarch's Theological Writings and Early Christian Literature.* Edited by Hans D. Betz. Leiden: Brill, 1975.

Star, Christopher. *Apocalypse and Golden Age: The End of the World in Greek and Roman Thought.* Baltimore: Johns Hopkins University Press, 2021.

Tertullian. *Apology. De Spectaculis.* Translated by T. R. Glover. LCL 250. Cambridge: Harvard University Press, 1931.

Timmer, Daniel. "Is Monotheism Particularly Prone to Violence? A Historical Critique." *Journal of Religion and Society* 15 (2013): 1–15.

Walsh, Joseph J. "On Christian Atheism." *VC* 45.3 (1991): 255–77.

Whitmarsh, Tim. *Battling the Gods: Atheism in the Ancient World.* New York: Knopf, 2015.

Αἶρε τοὺς ἀθέους (*Mart. Pol. 9.2*)

———. "The Invention of Atheism and the Invention of Religion in Classical Athens." Pages 37–51 in *Sceptic and Believer in Ancient Mediterranean Religions*. Edited by Babett Edelmann-Singer, Tobias Nicklas, Janet E. Spittler, and Luigi Walt. Tübingen: Mohr Siebeck, 2020.

———. "Plutarch on Superstition, Atheism, and the City." Pages 293–309 in *Plutarch's Cities*. Edited by Lucia Athanassaki and Frances Titchener. Oxford: Oxford University Press, 2022.

Winiarczyk, Marek. *Diagoras of Melos: A Contribution to the History of Ancient Atheism*. Berlin: de Gruyter, 2016.

Zambon, Marco. *"Nessun dio è mai sceso quaggiù": La polemica anticristiana dei filosofi antichi*. Rome: Carocci, 2019.

3

The Empiricism of the Apostle Paul

Belief and Knowledge in the Context of Roman Divination

MATTHEW T. SHARP

In *The Matter of the Gods: Religion and the Roman Empire*, Clifford Ando theorizes what he calls the "empiricist epistemology" of Roman religion. "In contrast to ancient Christians, who had faith," he argues that "the Romans had knowledge; and their knowledge was empirical in orientation."[1] That is to say, "they sought information through observation of the actions of the gods in the world."[2] In contrast to modern scientific empiricism, this observation usually occurred through the various methods of divination employed by the Roman state. As an example, Ando adduces an episode recounted by Livy, in which Rome had suffered a number of military defeats. On top of these defeats, two vestals had been charged with sexual misconduct.

> Occurring as it did along with all the other calamities, this piece of sacrilege was, as usual, interpreted as a portent. The decemvirs were therefore instructed to consult the books and Quintus Fabius Pictor was sent to the oracle in Delphi to find out with what prayers and acts of supplication they could appease the gods, and to ask what end there would be to their great disasters. (Livy, *Ab urbe cond.* 22.57.4–6 [Yardley, LCL])

1. Clifford Ando, *The Matter of the Gods: Religion and the Roman Empire* (Berkeley: University of California Press, 2008), ix.
2. Ando, *Matter of the Gods*, xvi.

The Empiricism of the Apostle Paul

A portent or prodigy was an observable sign that was believed to have originated with the gods. In the ancient Roman world, these signs were often aberrations in the natural order (e.g., plagues, hermaphrodite births, rains of blood) that signaled the gods' wrath.[3] The sighting of a prodigy usually led to the consultation of an oracular source to determine how to appease the gods and avert the prodigy. In the example cited above, the Roman Senate consulted both the Sibylline books and the Delphic oracle. Describing this process, Ando writes:

> Having learned from Delphi how to placate the gods, the Senate will have acted; those instructions, their performance, and their results will have been recorded; and the rites will have been repeated in analogous situations, so long as they were judged efficacious. Roman religion was thus founded upon an empiricist epistemology: cult addressed problems in the real world, and the effectiveness of rituals—their tangible results—determined whether they were repeated, modified, or abandoned.[4]

For Ando, the empiricist epistemology of Roman religion stands in sharp contrast to the religious epistemology of ancient Christians (primarily represented by Augustine for Ando), who merely believed things about their God and then doggedly clung to these beliefs. The Romans, however, "knew" about their gods, because their knowledge was based on empirical observation. This in turn meant that Roman rituals needed to be either scrupulously maintained or adapted whenever new information came to light.

The starkness of Ando's thesis leaves it open to a number of critiques, the foremost of which is the way that he leaves the concept of "belief" underdefined.[5] Our understanding of the nature of both Roman and early Christian belief has been considerably refined in recent years, and neither can be said to operate entirely without evidence or "foundations."[6] My purpose in this chapter is not to reassess

---

3. For differing views on the precise function of prodigies and their relation to divine anger and absence, see Susan Satterfield, "Prodigies, the Pax Deum and the Ira Deum," *Classical Journal* 110 (2015): 431–45; Miguel Requena Jiménez, "Prodigies in Republican Rome: The Absence of God," *Klio* 100 (2018): 480–500.

4. Ando, *Matter of the Gods*, 13.

5. Brent Nongbri, review of *The Matter of the Gods*, by Clifford Ando, *Classical Bulletin* 84 (2008): 125–27; Teresa Morgan, *Roman Faith and Christian Faith:* Pistis *and* Fides *in the Early Roman Empire and Early Churches* (Oxford: Oxford University Press, 2015), 126–27.

6. See especially Morgan, *Roman Faith*, 145–51, 508; George H. van Kooten, "A Non-Fideistic Interpretation of πίστις in Plutarch's Writings: The Harmony between πίστις and Knowledge," in *Plutarch in the Religious and Philosophical Discourse of Late Antiquity*, ed. Lautaro Roig Lanzillotta and Israel Muñoz Gallarte (Leiden: Brill, 2012), 215–33; Jennifer Eyl, "Philo and Josephus

directly the meaning of "belief" in Paul's Letters or in Roman religion. This work is already proceeding apace.[7] Rather, I want to focus attention on the other side of Ando's equation: empiricism. The recognition of empiricism as a foundational aspect of Roman religion is, I think, an important observation capable of shedding light on a neglected aspect of ancient religion in general, Christianity included.

The apostle Paul is a particularly interesting figure to study in this regard, as he occupies multiple overlapping categories and contexts that scholars still too often hold apart. Because he was (to use anachronistic categories) both ethnically and religiously a Jew who proclaimed a message about a Jewish messiah, he forms valuable evidence for varieties of Judaism in the first century CE. As one who identified this messiah as Jesus, he also provides evidence for the earliest stages of what would later be called Christianity. He is historically and geographically situated in the Greek-speaking regions of the early Roman Empire, so his writings are also evidence of the work of freelance religious experts in the "Greco-Roman" world more generally. Amid these scholarly categories, Heidi Wendt urges us to "imagine a kaleidoscope of potential relationships, with new patterns in the evidence crystallizing as we rotate the angles of our mirrors."[8] Allow me, then, to angle my mirror to focus on Paul in the context of Roman religion. To what extent does a figure like Paul ground his religious program on beliefs, creeds, and doctrines, and to what extent does he ground it on empirical observation of the actions and will of the divine in the world? This is not the same as the apologetic question whether Christianity is founded on "reliable historical evidence." Rather, I am asking how Paul's Letters relate to the sort of divinatory empiricism that Ando has highlighted in the Roman world, and how this interacts with aspects of belief.

The Empirical Basis of the Gospel

The closest we get to a creed or statement of faith in Paul is in 1 Cor 15:3–8. This is the "good news" that Paul proclaimed to the Corinthians: that Christ died for sins,

---

on the Fidelity of Judeans," *Journal of Ancient Judaism* 12 (2021): 94–121. On Greek belief and evidence, see Robert Parker, *On Greek Religion* (Ithaca: Cornell University Press, 2011), 1–39.

7. In addition to the works noted above, see Jacob L. Mackey, *Belief and Cult: Rethinking Roman Religion* (Princeton: Princeton University Press, 2022); Nijay K. Gupta, *Paul and the Language of Faith* (Grand Rapids: Eerdmans, 2020); Jennifer Eyl, *Signs, Wonders, and Gifts: Divination in the Letters of Paul* (New York: Oxford University Press, 2019), 170–212; Jeanette Hagen Pifer, *Faith as Participation: An Exegetical Study of Some Key Pauline Texts* (Tübingen: Mohr Siebeck, 2019). Most recent research on πίστις language emphasizes its relational aspect.

8. Heidi Wendt, *At the Temple Gates: The Religion of Freelance Experts in the Roman Empire* (New York: Oxford University Press), 216.

The Empiricism of the Apostle Paul

was buried, raised, and seen by a number of witnesses, including Paul himself. This good news has been "believed" by the Corinthians (15:11), and through this belief they are being "saved" (15:2; cf. Rom 10:9). This emphasis on the acceptance of and dedication to a message is what historians of Roman religion might single out as unusual. It is immediately notable, though, that the message itself is a thoroughly empirical one. Especially what one might take to be the most significant aspect of the message—that Christ was raised—is specifically supported by the evidence of witnesses. While Paul's Corinthians are indeed asked to "believe" or "trust" this message, they are asked to do so because of the empirical experiences of Paul and several others. In Ando's framework, Paul himself does not *believe* that Christ was risen from the dead; he *knows* it because he has seen him.

Although direct divine communication involving the seeing of a god is absent from Ando's account of Roman empiricism, the epiphany of a god or hero was an important factor in Roman religion, especially in the introduction of new cults. To take Romulus as a prominent example, several Roman sources say he was accepted as a god by the Roman Senate on the testimony of Julius Proculus, who claimed to have seen Romulus after his mysterious disappearance in a storm cloud.[9] According to Rome's own legends, then, the cultic worship of Romulus began by the senate believing the testimony of a particular person who said he saw Romulus as a god, or at least on his way to becoming one. The Stoic Balbus in Cicero's *De natura deorum* argues that the appearance and popularity of a cult is not "unaccountable or accidental; it is the result, firstly, of the fact that the gods often manifest their power in bodily presence" (2.6 [Rackham, LCL]). Later in *De natura deorum*, the academic Cotta goes on to dismiss such stories (3.11–13), but it is safe to assume that most of the Roman populace would have agreed with Balbus. In the words of Fritz Graf, "To the Greek and Roman mind, epiphanies were real, and they were vital. Gods were irrelevant if they could not manifest themselves to humans."[10] These manifestations provided empirical evidence of a god's power and will, which regularly resulted in the introduction of cultic worship. If the god did not appear in person, he or she might communicate the same information

---

9. E.g., Cicero, *Rep.* 2.17–20; Livy, *Ab urbe cond.* 1.16.1–8; Dionysius of Halicarnassus, *Ant. rom.* 2.56.1–6; 2.63.3; Plutarch, *Rom.* 27–28.

10. Fritz Graf, "Trick or Treat: On Collective Epiphanies in Antiquity," *Illinois Classical Studies* 29 (2004): 113. Graf observes a pattern in which epiphanies to individuals were generally believed quite readily by contemporaries, whereas reports of collective epiphanies only tend to develop later in fictionalized accounts. He treats early Christianity as unexceptional in this regard, as he contrasts later accounts of collective epiphanies in the gospels (such as on the road to Emmaus) to the earlier testimony of the individual epiphany to Paul. In doing so, he curiously neglects Paul's report of Jesus's appearance to more than five hundred brothers at once in 1 Cor 15:6.

through other means, such as dreams or oracles.[11] Likewise, Paul does not ask his converts to believe a doctrine without evidence, but instead he calls for them to adjust their cultic behavior in line with what he and others have observed according to the contemporary standards of epiphanies and divination.

The core of Paul's "good news" rests on an empirical foundation. But epiphany or resurrection is not the only empirical basis for his message. Paul also draws attention to the accompanying signs that verify this message. Earlier in 1 Corinthians he says, "My speech and my proclamation were not with plausible words of wisdom, but with a demonstration of πνεῦμα and of power" (1 Cor 2:4–5).[12] The Greek word πνεῦμα in this passage and its adjectival form πνευματικός are normally translated "spirit" and "spiritual." In modern English, these terms have come to refer to things that are immaterial, subjective, and exclusively religious or otherworldly. "Spiritual," in modern usage, often means the opposite of empirical. Paul's pneumatology, by contrast, coheres with other ancient texts that understand πνεῦμα as a material substance that physically interacts with the body and produces tangible results.[13] In 1 Cor 2:4–5 the effects of πνεῦμα can be demonstrated (ἀπόδειξις) and are associated with power (δύναμις). The same sentiment is expressed in Romans and 2 Corinthians with the divinatory language of "signs and omens."[14] In Rom 15:18–19, Paul states that he won "obedience from the gentiles, by word and deed, by the power of signs and omens, by the power of God's πνεῦμα." In 2 Cor 12:12, he recalls how "the signs of a true apostle were performed among you with utmost patience, signs and omens and mighty works."

Paul never says precisely what these signs were. The presence and operation of πνεῦμα in these passages might lead one to look to the various ways πνεῦμα becomes "manifest" in 1 Cor 12:7–11 (v. 7: ἡ φανέρωσις τοῦ πνεύματος): words of wisdom and knowledge, healings, works of power, prophecies, speaking in other languages.[15] The way Paul uses these signs rhetorically suggests they fulfill the

11. Sarah E. Rollens, "The God Came to Me in a Dream: Epiphanies in Voluntary Associations as a Context for Paul's Vision of Christ," *Harvard Theological Review* 111 (2018): 41–65. In the Greek context, see Georgia Petridou, *Divine Epiphany in Greek Literature and Culture* (Oxford: Oxford University Press, 2015), 318–34.

12. All translations of the New Testament are my own, unless otherwise stated.

13. See, especially Troels Engberg-Pedersen, *Cosmology and Self in the Apostle Paul: The Material Spirit* (Oxford: Oxford University Press, 2010); Paul Robertson, "De-Spiritualizing Pneuma: Modernity, Religion, and Anachronism in the Study of Paul," *MTSR* 26 (2014): 365–83.

14. The next paragraph draws from Matthew T. Sharp, *Divination and Philosophy in the Letters of Paul* (Edinburgh: Edinburgh University Press, 2022), 168–71. Cf. Eyl, *Signs, Wonders, and Gifts*, 87–91, 119–22.

15. On the different ways to understand the gift of "tongues" in Paul, see Sharp, *Divination and Philosophy*, 101–3.

same function as divine signs and omens in the ancient world. In the *Iliad*, when Ajax challenges Hector and predicts the sack of Troy, the Achaeans are encouraged by a bird flying by on the right. They take this as divine confirmation of the truth of Ajax's words (13.815–823). In the Roman imperial context, Suetonius records various signs that accompany the rise to power of certain Roman emperors: trees with enormous and unnatural growth, a rainbow-like circle around the sun, lightning strikes, and extraordinary auspices (Suetonius, *Aug.* 94–95; *Vesp.* 5.2–3). These signs indicate both divine favor for the emperor and a "great and happy future" for Rome under his rule. Likewise, signs of pneumatic activity for Paul verify both the truth and the efficacy of his message, "so that your trust might rest not on human wisdom but on the power of God" (1 Cor 2:4–5).[16]

The empirical efficacy of Paul's message comes to the fore in Gal 3. Here Paul points to the visible presence of πνεῦμα and works of power to argue that the Galatians should continue the religious practices they had begun rather than abandon them in favor of a different ritual that has not yielded the same results for them: "Does [God] supply you with the πνεῦμα and work miracles among you by the works of the law or by the message of trust?" (Gal 3:5). Only one of these options provides tangible results according to Paul, and it is on this path that the Galatians should continue, if they want to continue experiencing the desired results: "Having started with the πνεῦμα, are you now ending with the flesh? Did you experience so much for nothing?" (3:3–4). This is similar to what Ando observes about how the "effectiveness of rituals—their tangible results—determine whether they were repeated, modified, or abandoned."[17]

If positive tangible results accompany correct ritual, getting rituals wrong also carries tangible results. This much was clear to the Romans, for whom prodigies signaled the wrath of the gods and required ritual expiation to secure the desired peace and protection of the gods. In 1 Cor 11:27–30, Paul traces sickness and death among the Corinthians to the failure to observe the ritual meal properly. Paul interprets these smaller scale judgments as acts of divine discipline. The tangible results of this error alert the Corinthians to problems with their ritual observance so that they can rectify their errors and avoid a fuller final judgment "with the cosmos" (11:32). Paul divines the consequences for the even graver ritual error of idolatry by interpreting sacred books. In the preceding chapter of 1 Corinthians, Paul reminds his audience of the pentateuchal wilderness narratives, and how the

---

16. For the idea that πίστις might have stronger or weaker foundations, see van Kooten, "Non-Fideistic," 223–24. Paul sees visible signs of divine power as deserving of more trust than human wisdom.

17. Ando, *Matter of the Gods*, 13.

Israelites in the wilderness participated in comparable rituals to the Corinthians: "They were all baptized into Moses in the cloud and the sea, and they all ate the same pneumatic bread, and all drank the same pneumatic drink" (1 Cor 10:2–4).[18] Nevertheless, the positive effects of these rituals were overridden by the empirically negative effects of their idolatry: "Twenty-three thousand fell in a single day . . . they were destroyed by serpents . . . they were destroyed by the destroyer" (10:8–10).[19] Like the Romans who recorded prodigies and their ritual expiations, Paul says that these empirical results were also recorded so that future generations could perceive the patterns (v. 6: τύποι) of divine response to idolatry and avoid similar results for themselves.

Prodigy and Expiation in Romans 1–3

Paul takes up the negative results of incorrect cult on a much larger scale in Rom 1–3. These chapters are particularly replete with empirical observations about God's character, disposition, and actions in the world.

Paul begins this section of Romans at 1:18 with the observation that "God's wrath is being revealed from heaven on all the impiety [ἀσέβεια] and unrighteousness [ἀδικία] of people who by unrighteousness suppress the truth." While ἀδικία refers to general injustice and wrongdoing toward other people, ἀσέβεια is usually reserved for irreverence and impiety toward the gods (e.g., Xenophon, *Cyr.* 8.8.7; Dio Chrysostom, *Rhod.* 13).[20] Plutarch equates a Roman priest neglecting his cultic duties with an act of impiety against the gods (ἀσεβεῖν τοὺς θεούς; *Quaest. rom.* 291c). Likewise, Cicero worries about the charge of impiety (*impia fraude*) that would result from neglecting the "auspices," "sacred rites," and "religious observances" of Roman *religio* (*Div.* 1.7). In *De natura deorum*, Cotta defines Roman piety as *scientia colendorum deorum*, "the knowledge of giving gods their due" (1.116) and, as Ando remarks, this knowledge "was grounded upon observation."[21]

---

18. The comparability of rituals is possible because of Paul's identification of Christ's presence to the Israelites in the rock that followed them (1 Cor 10:4). See further Matthew Thiessen, "'The Rock Was Christ': The Fluidity of Christ's Body in 1 Corinthians 10:4," *JSNT* 36 (2013): 103–26. Cf. Wendt, *At the Temple Gates*, 151–52.

19. Paul cites specific violations that led to these outcomes: sexual immorality (v. 8), putting Christ to the test (v. 9), and grumbling (v. 10). They are all framed, however, by the initial error of idolatry (v. 7), and Paul's concluding application of these examples to the Corinthians also singles out idolatry as the main issue: "Therefore [διόπερ] . . . flee from idolatry" (v. 14).

20. Robert Jewett, *Romans: A Commentary* (Minneapolis: Fortress, 2007), 152.

21. Ando, *Matter of the Gods*, 13.

The Empiricism of the Apostle Paul

Paul, it seems, would entirely agree, as he argues in Rom 1:19–21 that quite apart from any creeds or doctrines, people do know all that they need to know about the deity in order to give God what God is due. God's eternal power and divinity, though invisible, have been revealed to them (v. 19: ἐφανέρωσεν). The participle νοούμενα in the following clause in v. 20 suggests that this knowledge takes the form of a mental perception.[22] But it is equally clear from the context that this perception is gained by observation (καθορᾶται) of the natural world (τοῖς ποιή-μασιν).[23] The knowledge gained from observation at this point is at quite a high level of generality because the cultic action required is at an equally general level. It simply concerns whether humans give cultic honor to the one true creator God or to images and imitations (v. 23). If piety is "the knowledge of giving gods their due," then impiety (ἀσέβεια) is having the requisite knowledge but not honoring the one true God accordingly. This is the scenario Paul describes in vv. 21–23. There is a clash with Roman ideology at this point, as the very thing the Romans would consider piety—the worship of their gods—Paul labels impiety. At a deeper level, though, there is a coherence of thought, as both parties agree that correct worship can be discerned through observation. For Paul, correct observation of God's works in creation should lead to monolatrous, aniconic cult.[24]

If correct cult can be discerned through observation, then so can incorrect cult, and it is this impiety of iconic worship against which Paul now says God's wrath is revealed—which is to say it is empirically observable. In Rom 1:24–31, Paul lists the observable effects or consequences of this impiety: "Therefore, God gave them up in the desires of their hearts to impurity, to the dishonoring of their bodies among themselves, because they exchanged the truth about God for a lie and honored and gave cult to [ἐσεβάσθησαν καὶ ἐλάτρευσαν] the creature rather than the creator" (vv. 24–25). This "giving up" is evidenced by the sexual and social behaviors that Paul goes on to list.[25] Just as Roman prodigies are aberrations in the natural order that signal God's displeasure, so too Paul points to aberrations

22. James Dunn describes "a realm of reality, invisible to sense perception, which can be known only through the rational power of the mind." See *Romans 1–8*, WBC 38A (Dallas: Word, 1988), 58.

23. This is a common idea in Greco-Roman philosophical discourse: see Niko Huttunen, *Paul and Epictetus on Law: A Comparison* (London: T&T Clark, 2009), 48–49; George H. van Kooten, *Paul's Anthropology in Context: The Image of God, Assimilation to God, and Tripartite Man in Ancient Judaism, Ancient Philosophy, and Early Christianity* (Tübingen: Mohr Siebeck, 2008), 344–47.

24. As van Kooten, *Paul's Anthropology*, 347–56 has documented, Romans such as Varro and Plutarch also told the story of Roman religion as one of decline from an aniconic cult discernible by the intellect to the later worship of images.

25. Marcus A. Mininger, *Uncovering the Theme of Revelation in Romans 1:16–3:26* (Tübingen: Mohr Siebeck, 2017), 146–51.

in what he deems normal social and sexual relations (v. 26: παρὰ φύσιν) to signal God's displeasure against idolatry.[26]

In the example from Livy cited above, the vestals' sexual misconduct incurred its own traditional penalty—one was buried alive and the other committed suicide (Livy, *Ab urbe cond.* 22.57.2–3)—but, in the context of all the other prodigies and misfortunes, the sexual behavior also served as a broader portent of divine wrath, which the community needed to expiate. So too, Paul points to specific penalties for the actions he condemns (Rom 1:27, 32) but also links all the behaviors together as expressions of God's wrath (1:18). In Livy, the Sibylline books prescribed that two Gauls and two Greeks be buried alive. Livy describes this as a most un-Roman rite, but he also says that it was nevertheless carried out as prescribed in order to placate the gods (*Ab urbe cond.* 22.57.6).[27] If we follow Paul's line of reasoning through to Rom 3, we see that he, too, prescribes a propitiation (v. 25: ἱλαστήριον) for his audience in the form of Jesus's blood.[28] The revelation of this propitiation is also connected to oracular texts, as it was witnessed by the law and the prophets (3:21). In Paul's case, though, the propitiation does not lie in the performance of what the text prescribes but in an event the text predicts. Paul, as an authoritative interpreter of oracular texts, identifies this event as the death of Jesus.

The blood of Jesus is a propitiation that God has provided as a gift (v. 24: δωρεάν) in order to demonstrate God's justice (v. 26). If we read still further to Rom 6, it seems that the actual ritual prescribed in response to this is baptism, in which believers ritually share in Christ's death (Rom 6:1–11). In Rom 3:21–26

---

26. "How is God's wrath revealed from heaven? There has been no earthly catastrophe, such as a devastating earthquake or the destruction of a city or enslavement of a people that might be called a sign of God's wrath. . . . God's wrath is revealed through the human behavior described in vv. 24–32. This would mean that God's handing idolaters over to wretched deeds is the revelation of God's wrath." Bernadette J. Brooten, *Love between Women: Early Christian Responses to Female Homoeroticism* (Chicago: University of Chicago Press, 1996), 221. See further Sharp, *Divination and Philosophy*, 179–83.

27. On human sacrifice in Rome, see Celia E. Schultz, "The Romans and Ritual Murder," *Journal of the American Academy of Religion* 78 (2010): 516–41; Gaius Stern, "Devotio and Human Sacrifice in Archaic Italy and Rome," *Acta Antiqua Academiae Scientiarum Hungaricae* 60 (2021): 363–98.

28. The term ἱλαστήριον may carry some resonances to the "mercy seat" in the Greek Bible, but its most obvious meaning to Paul's gentile Roman audience would simply be as a propitiatory offering. See Leon Morris, "The Meaning of ἱλαστήριον in Romans 3:25," *NTS* 2 (1955): 33–43; Adela Yarbro Collins, "The Metaphorical Use of ἱλαστήριον in Romans 3:25," in *Sōtēria: Salvation in Early Christianity and Antiquity; Festschrift in Honour of Cilliers Breytenbach on the Occasion of His 65th Birthday*, ed. David S. du Toit, Christine Gerber, and Christiane Zimmermann (Leiden: Brill, 2019), 273–86.

The Empiricism of the Apostle Paul

though, Paul provides a proliferation of evidentiary terminology to claim that the propitiation available in Christ's death is empirically observable and further reveals God's justice: Christ was publicly set forth (v. 25: προέθετο) as a propitiation to serve as evidence (vv. 25–26: ἔνδειξιν) of God's justice, and so God's justice has been manifested (v. 21: πεφανέρωται).[29]

These evidentiary terms conclude the section spanning Rom 1:16–3:26, which is positively awash with empiricism that would be very familiar to a participant in Roman religion. Correct cult is observable in the physical world. The empirical consequences of incorrect cult are observable in the behavior of idolaters. The propitiation needed to address these consequences is revealed in the death of Jesus, as predicted by prophetic texts. And all of this is empirical evidence of God's justice toward idolaters.

THE LIMITS OF EMPIRICISM?

So far, I have discussed some irreducibly empirical aspects of Paul's *religio* in the context of Roman religion. In this decidedly empirical context, I finish by considering a group of Paul's most anti-empirical statements. These statements occur predominantly in 2 Cor 4:13–5:10 and Rom 8:18–30. Both passages seem to denigrate visible observable realities in favor of the invisible and in favor of belief or "faith."

> Now hope that is seen is not hope. For who hopes for what is seen? But if we hope for what we do not see, we wait for it with patience. (Rom 8:24–25)

> So we fix our eyes not on what is seen, but on what is unseen. For the things that are seen are transient, but the things that are unseen are eternal. (2 Cor 4:18)

> We walk by faith, not by sight. (2 Cor 5:7 NRSV)

Denigration of what one can see is not necessarily at odds with divinatory empiricism. Indeed, divination relies on the assumption that there are hidden realities that are normally inaccessible to human sight. This inaccessibility may be because of temporal or spatial distance (e.g., in the past or future; in the heavens or the

---

29. Rom 3:21–26 is, of course, a dense passage, and there is much disagreement over how to interpret many of these key claims. The proliferation of evidentiary terminology is noted by, among others, Markus N. A. Bockmuehl, *Revelation and Mystery in Ancient Judaism and Pauline Christianity* (Tübingen: Mohr Siebeck, 1990), 134; Mininger, *Revelation*, 350–54.

underword) or because of the nature of the realities themselves (souls, ghosts, daimons). Divination provides glimpses into these hidden realities by means of signs. Chrysippus defines divination as "the power to see, understand, and explain premonitory signs given to men by the gods" (Cicero, *Div.* 2.130). Plutarch also cites a line from Heraclitus that states how Apollo "neither tells nor conceals but gives signs [σημαίνει]" (*Pyth. orac.* 404e). These signs are not the thing itself, but they point toward something that would otherwise be invisible. The same logic applies in contexts like Rom 1:20, where the visible things in creation are signs of the invisible qualities of God. Paul recognizes the partial nature of these signs in 1 Cor 13:12, where he compares current prophetic knowledge to riddles seen in a mirror (δι' ἐσόπτρου ἐν αἰνίγματι) but points to a future in which these things will be fully known.[30]

Second Corinthians 4:13–5:10 and Rom 8:18–30 are both passages in which Paul is looking to the future. Both begin with an acknowledgment of "present sufferings" for himself and his audience. Paul does not, as in 1 Cor 11:29–30, interpret these sufferings as evidence of cultic error that needs rectification. Instead, he contrasts these visible, temporary afflictions with future, eternal glory (δόξα; Rom 8:18; 2 Cor 4:17–18).[31] This glory is still invisible because it is currently located spatially in the heavens (2 Cor 5:1; cf. Phil 3:19–21) and in the inner person (2 Cor 4:16). Its full realization is located temporally in the future (Rom 8:24–25; 2 Cor 5:10). Paul links the temporary afflictions his audience is suffering to the perishability of the natural world and human mortality, and he encourages hope and patience for the currently invisible but imminent transformation of their mortal bodies into immortal bodies (Rom 8:20–23; 2 Cor 5:4; cf. Phil 3:10–21; 1 Cor 15:50–57).[32] Paul's focus on the hope of immortality distinguishes his concerns from the more mundane concerns of Roman civic religion. Instead, Paul's concerns just described are closer to the domain of philosophers and mystery cults.[33]

While the realities that Paul hopes for are currently invisible, he infers them on the basis of the same visible signs discussed above. First, his empirical vision of the resurrected Christ guarantees the resurrection of Christ's followers. Paul ex-

30. Plutarch also compares the semiotic nature of prophecy to the distortions created by seeing in a mirror (*Pyth. orac.* 404c–d). On the link between αἴνιγμα and oracles in antiquity, see Peter T. Struck, *Birth of the Symbol: Ancient Readers at the Limits of Their Texts* (Princeton: Princeton University Press, 2004), 171–77.

31. In Phil 1:27–30 and 2 Thess 1:5, the endurance of the faithful in the face of visible afflictions is itself evidence (ἔνδειξις; ἔνδειγμα) of their future salvation.

32. For a broader discussion of this topic, see Matthew V. Novenson, *Paul and Judaism at the End of History* (Cambridge: Cambridge University Press, 2024), esp. 187–208.

33. See A. G. Long, *Death and Immortality in Ancient Philosophy* (Cambridge: Cambridge University Press, 2019); Walter Burkert, *Ancient Mystery Cults* (Cambridge: Harvard University Press, 1987), 21–29; Wendt, *At the Temple Gates*, 188–89.

The Empiricism of the Apostle Paul

presses this guarantee as knowledge that forms the ground for trust: "We also trust [πιστεύομεν], therefore we also speak, because we know [εἰδότες] that the one who raised the Lord Jesus will also raise us with Jesus" (2 Cor 4:13–14; cf. 1 Cor 15:20). The same logic is expressed in 1 Thess 4:14 solely with the language of trust, which suggests Paul did not see an important distinction between these two terms: "For if we trust [πιστεύομεν] that Jesus died and was raised, in this way also God will bring with him, through Jesus, those who have fallen asleep."

The second sign of this imminent future is the reception of πνεῦμα, which Paul describes as empirically observable in the signs, omens, and works of power that he and others have performed. In Rom 8 and 2 Cor 5, Paul describes πνεῦμα as a deposit (ἀρραβών; 2 Cor 5:5; cf. 1:22) or the first fruits (ἀπαρχή; Rom 8:23) of what is to come. These images, drawn from commercial and cultic contexts, reinforce both the empirical nature of the πνεῦμα's current activity and its function as a sign, which points to a (currently invisible) future transformation into pneumatic bodies.[34] These two streams of evidence are mutually reinforcing as Paul combines them in Rom 8:11: "If the πνεῦμα of the one who raised Jesus from the dead dwells in you, the one who raised Christ from the dead will also give life to your mortal bodies through his πνεῦμα that is dwelling in you."

In Rom 8, the twin signs of Christ's resurrection and the presence of πνεῦμα in Christ's followers becomes a basis for hope (vv. 24–25: ἐλπίς) in what is currently unseen. In 2 Cor 5, the deposit of the πνεῦμα in v. 5 leads directly to the pivotal phrase of v. 7: "for we walk by faith, not by sight" (NRSV). Verse 7 is a parenthesis between two assertions of Paul's confidence (θαρροῦντες in v. 6; θαρροῦμεν in v. 8). The first statement of confidence is directly linked to the deposit of πνεῦμα by the inferential particle οὖν. The πνεῦμα is the reason for confidence. The next phrase introduces a concession to this confidence: "Although we know that while at home in the body, we are absent from the Lord" (v. 6). Verse 7 then interrupts Paul's flow to explain why he still retains confidence despite this concession: διὰ πίστεως γὰρ περιπατοῦμεν, οὐ διὰ εἴδους.

The word εἶδος does not denote the act of sight itself but the outward form or shape of what is seen.[35] In this context, it most naturally refers to the mortal

---

34. On the nuances of ἀρραβών, see Yong-Gyong Kwon, "Ἀρραβών as Pledge in Second Corinthians," *NTS* 54 (2008): 525–41. An ἀρραβών could either refer to a "deposit" (a first installment of what is to come) or a "pledge" (a security or guarantee against the future payment of something else). Both are equally empirical, but pace Kwon the πνεῦμα makes most sense as a deposit here. Paul elsewhere explicitly describes the future resurrection as the bestowal of pneumatic bodies (1 Cor 15:35–57). The present bestowal of πνεῦμα as an ἀρραβών in fleshly bodies expressly prepares (κατεργάζομαι; 2 Cor 5:5) mortal humans for their fully pneumatic future existence. On ἀπαρχή, see Joel R. White, "Christ's Resurrection Is the Spirit's Firstfruits (Romans 8:23)," in *Resurrection of the Dead: Biblical Traditions in Dialogue*, ed. Geert van Oyen and Tom Shepherd (Leuven: Peeters, 2012), 289–303.

35. LSJ, s.v. "εἶδος."

body or the "outer person" (ὁ ἔξω ἡμῶν ἄνθρωπος; 2 Cor 4:16), which is decomposing and is evidence of separation from the Lord.[36] In contrast to this outer form, Paul introduces trust. Given the direct relation Paul has already posited between his confidence and the evidence of the πνεῦμα, it is best to understand this trust or "belief" not as a general epistemological principle but as a further explication of his confidence. David Hay notes that the word πίστις often means "'assurance' or 'pledge' in the sense of a guarantee creating the possibility for trust."[37] He does not discuss 2 Cor 5:7 in this regard, but since Paul presents πίστις and τὸν ἀρραβῶνα τοῦ πνεύματος as parallel reasons for his confidence in a future immortal body, we might translate 2 Cor 5:7 thus: "for we walk by assurance [i.e., trust in the evidence of πνεῦμα], not by outer form [of the perishable body]."[38] "Belief" or "faith" (πίστις) in these seemingly anti-empirical contexts actually refers to the trustworthiness of an inference drawn from the empirical signs of divine activity.

Conclusion

When we read Paul's Letters through the lens of Roman empiricism, he appears much closer to the divinatory observations of the early Roman Empire than to the creeds, doctrines, and councils of later Christianity. The Christ-cult is founded on the empirical evidence of epiphany. The efficacy of the Christ-cult is founded on the empirical evidence of signs, omens, and the work of πνεῦμα. Negative tangible results demonstrate the dangers of iconic worship, but the empirical death of Jesus reveals the required propitiation for God's observable wrath. While texts such as 1 Cor 15:1–11 and Rom 10:9–10 emphasize the adherence to a message, other texts are concerned with how that message is practically enacted in cultic and ritual contexts.

I have avoided a full treatment of Paul's πίστις language, but certainly the most anti-empirical statements he makes—where he valorizes believing and hoping

---

36. Some commentators understand εἶδος as the visible form of Christ (e.g., Gupta, *Language of Faith*, 130). In the broader context of 2 Cor 4–5, I submit it is more likely that outward form refers to the visible form of the mortal body.

37. David M. Hay, "Pistis as 'Ground for Faith' in Hellenized Judaism and Paul," *JBL* 108 (1989): 461–76.

38. I find this reading more contextually coherent and exegetically satisfying than that offered by Morgan (*Roman Faith*, 255), "we walk by the power of our gift of pistis rather than by our own sense of sight." Gupta (*Language of Faith*, 130–31) is closer to the mark: "To live by πίστις means to live in hope and to see with new eyes, to see through the outward appearance of things and to perceive and anticipate what is eternal." But he misses the empirical basis for this perception in the reception of πνεῦμα, which makes his reading as a whole decidedly anti-empirical.

The Empiricism of the Apostle Paul

for things that are not seen—are still based on empirical signs of these hoped-for realities. Hope and trust are inferences drawn from the interpretation of empirical signs, most notably the epiphany of the resurrected Christ and the divinatory signs wrought by the possession of πνεῦμα. In other passages, Paul supports and expounds the promise of resurrection and immortal bodies by the revelation of mysteries (1 Cor 15:50–57) and words of the Lord (1 Thess 4:15–18). Paul's appeal to these oracular sources is comparable to the Romans, who interpret their observation of divinatory signs with the aid of the Sibylline books and the Delphic oracle. Paul likewise uses prophetic texts and new oracles to interpret and extrapolate from the empirical observations of Christ's resurrection and the presence of πνεῦμα to a future state that one can hope for, believe in, and await with patience. The eschatological focus is a departure from the short-term concerns of Roman *civic* religion but not Roman religious or philosophical concerns in general.[39]

Like Roman believers, Christian believers would also adapt their rituals and expectations to changed circumstances. Later readers of Paul would find their own ways of dealing with how to live in the widening gap between empirical sign and promised fulfillment (e.g., 2 Pet 3:3–16).[40] In Paul's presentation, however, the beliefs he urges are simply the divinely ordained (and thus inevitable) result of what he has seen.

WORKS CITED

Ando, Clifford. *The Matter of the Gods: Religion and the Roman Empire*. Berkeley: University of California Press, 2008.

Bockmuehl, Markus N. A. *Revelation and Mystery in Ancient Judaism and Pauline Christianity*. Tübingen: Mohr Siebeck, 1990.

Brooten, Bernadette J. *Love between Women: Early Christian Responses to Female Homoeroticism*. Chicago: University of Chicago Press, 1996.

Burkert, Walter. *Ancient Mystery Cults*. Cambridge: Harvard University Press, 1987.

Dunn, James. *Romans 1–8*. WBC 38A. Dallas: Word, 1988.

Engberg-Pedersen, Troels. *Cosmology and Self in the Apostle Paul: The Material Spirit*. Oxford: Oxford University Press, 2010.

---

39. See, e.g., book 1 of Cicero's *Tusculan Disputations* or his *Dream of Scipio*. On afterlife concerns in the context of freelance religious experts, see Wendt, *At the Temple Gates*.

40. It is the lack of precisely such signs in his eighteenth-century context that G. E. Lessing laments in "On the Proof of the Spirit and of Power," in *Lessing: Philosophical and Theological Writings*, ed. and trans. H. B. Nisbet (Cambridge: Cambridge University Press, 2012), 83–88.

Eyl, Jennifer. "Philo and Josephus on the Fidelity of Judeans." *Journal of Ancient Judaism* 12 (2021): 94–121.

———. *Signs, Wonders, and Gifts: Divination in the Letters of Paul*. New York: Oxford University Press, 2019.

Graf, Fritz. "Trick or Treat: On Collective Epiphanies in Antiquity." *Illinois Classical Studies* 29 (2004): 111–30.

Gupta, Nijay K. *Paul and the Language of Faith*. Grand Rapids: Eerdmans, 2020.

Hay, David M. "Pistis as 'Ground for Faith' in Hellenized Judaism and Paul." *JBL* 108 (1989): 461–76.

Huttunen, Niko. *Paul and Epictetus on Law: A Comparison*. London: T&T Clark, 2009.

Jewett, Robert. *Romans: A Commentary*. Minneapolis: Fortress, 2007.

Jiménez, Miguel Requena. "Prodigies in Republican Rome: The Absence of God." *Klio* 100 (2018): 480–500.

Kooten, George H. van. "A Non-Fideistic Interpretation of πίστις in Plutarch's Writings: The Harmony between πίστις and Knowledge." Pages 215–33 in *Plutarch in the Religious and Philosophical Discourse of Late Antiquity*. Edited by Lautaro Roig Lanzillotta and Israel Muñoz Gallarte. Leiden: Brill, 2012.

———. *Paul's Anthropology in Context: The Image of God, Assimilation to God, and Tripartite Man in Ancient Judaism, Ancient Philosophy, and Early Christianity*. Tübingen: Mohr Siebeck, 2008.

Kwon, Yong-Gyong. "Ἀρραβών as Pledge in Second Corinthians." *NTS* 54 (2008): 525–41.

Lessing, G. E. *Lessing: Philosophical and Theological Writings*. Edited and translated by H. B. Nisbet. Cambridge: Cambridge University Press, 2012.

Livy. *History of Rome. Books 21–22*. Translated by John Yardley. LCL 233. Cambridge: Harvard University Press, 2019.

Long, A. G. *Death and Immortality in Ancient Philosophy*. Cambridge: Cambridge University Press, 2019.

Mackey, Jacob L. *Belief and Cult: Rethinking Roman Religion*. Princeton: Princeton University Press, 2022.

Mininger, Marcus A. *Uncovering the Theme of Revelation in Romans 1:16–3:26*. Tübingen: Mohr Siebeck, 2017.

Morgan, Teresa. *Roman Faith and Christian Faith:* Pistis *and* Fides *in the Early Roman Empire and Early Churches*. Oxford: Oxford University Press, 2015.

Morris, Leon. "The Meaning of ἱλαστήριον in Romans 3:25." *NTS* 2 (1955): 33–43.

Nongbri, Brent. Review of *The Matter of the Gods*, by Clifford Ando. *Classical Bulletin* 84 (2008): 125–27.

Novenson, Matthew V. *Paul and Judaism at the End of History*. Cambridge: Cambridge University Press, 2024.

Parker, Robert. *On Greek Religion*. Ithaca: Cornell University Press, 2011.

Petridou, Georgia. *Divine Epiphany in Greek Literature and Culture*. Oxford: Oxford University Press, 2015.

Pifer, Jeanette Hagen. *Faith as Participation: An Exegetical Study of Some Key Pauline Texts*. Tübingen: Mohr Siebeck, 2019.

Robertson, Paul. "De-Spiritualizing Pneuma: Modernity, Religion, and Anachronism in the Study of Paul." *MTSR* 26 (2014): 365–83.

Rollens, Sarah E. "The God Came to Me in a Dream: Epiphanies in Voluntary Associations as a Context for Paul's Vision of Christ." *Harvard Theological Review* 111 (2018): 41–65.

Satterfield, Susan. "Prodigies, the Pax Deum and the Ira Deum." *Classical Journal* 110 (2015): 431–45.

Schultz, Celia E. "The Romans and Ritual Murder." *Journal of the American Academy of Religion* 78 (2010): 516–41.

Sharp, Matthew T. *Divination and Philosophy in the Letters of Paul*. Edinburgh: Edinburgh University Press, 2022.

Stern, Gaius. "*Devotio* and Human Sacrifice in Archaic Italy and Rome." *Acta Antiqua Academiae Scientiarum Hungaricae* 60 (2021): 363–98.

Struck, Peter T. *Birth of the Symbol: Ancient Readers at the Limits of Their Texts*. Princeton: Princeton University Press, 2004.

Thiessen, Matthew. "'The Rock Was Christ': The Fluidity of Christ's Body in 1 Corinthians 10:4." *JSNT* 36 (2013): 103–26.

Wendt, Heidi. *At the Temple Gates: The Religion of Freelance Experts in the Roman Empire*. New York: Oxford University Press, 2016.

White, Joel R. "Christ's Resurrection Is the Spirit's Firstfruits (Romans 8:23)." Pages 289–303 in *Resurrection of the Dead: Biblical Traditions in Dialogue*. Edited by Geert van Oyen and Tom Shepherd. Leuven: Peeters, 2012.

Yarbro Collins, Adela. "The Metaphorical Use of ἱλαστήριον in Romans 3:25." Pages 273–86 in Sōtēria: *Salvation in Early Christianity and Antiquity; Festschrift in Honour of Cilliers Breytenbach on the Occasion of His 65th Birthday*. Edited by David S. du Toit, Christine Gerber, and Christiane Zimmermann. Leiden: Brill, 2019.

4

The Relationship of Faith and Law Observance in Paul

The One Who Is Weak in Faith in Romans 14:1–15:13

DAVID J. JOHNSTON

Much of the exegesis of Rom 14:1–15:13 is dominated by the argument that the divergent practices around food, wine, and days between two groups in the Roman communities—the weak and the strong—are the result of each group's ethnicity.[1] In this chapter, I argue that it is not ethnicity that lies at the root of these divergent practices. The two groups personified in the "one who is weak in faith" (ὁ ἀσθενῶν τῇ πίστει) and "the strong ones" (οἱ δυνατοί) represent two different positions on the way in which gentiles should be included in the people of God in the escha-

---

1. As an illustration of this dynamic, see Douglas Moo, *The Epistle to the Romans*, 2nd ed., New International Commentary on the New Testament (Grand Rapids: Eerdmans, 2018), 844–45, who presents seven possible situations that could account for Rom 14 from the history of scholarship. All but one identifies the ethnicity of the believers as a contributing factor. Only the one that he attributes to Murray and Achtemeier concerns "Christians, perhaps both Jewish and Gentile, who practiced an ascetic lifestyle" (844). However, if this possible situation occurred, Moo reports, it would be "for reasons that we cannot determine" (844). The ethnicities of the two groups, suggests Moo's account of the scholarship, explain their actions in Rome.

I have presented versions of this paper at the Aspects of Belief in Ancient West Asia and the Mediterranean Basin (1000 BCE–100 CE) symposium and the Biblical Studies Faculty and Postgraduate research seminar, both in St Andrews. In the subsequent revisions I have drawn on much of the feedback that I received. I am also grateful to the editors for their perceptive comments.

The Relationship of Faith and Law Observance in Paul

tological age.[2] This diversity of opinion does not arise from different ethnicities. Indeed, any equation of Jewish ethnicity with a lack of πίστις—whether that word is interpreted as belief, conviction, or faithfulness—places the scholar in danger of reactivating an anachronistic and potentially harmful conception of Paul's gospel that is dependent on opposition between the Mosaic law and faith. This danger becomes apparent when we read Rom 14:23, where Paul states πᾶν δὲ ὃ οὐκ ἐκ πίστεως ἁμαρτία ἐστίν. Although Paul is typically understood as being sympathetic in these particular circumstances (i.e., if the weak were to eat, they would be acting contrary to their convictions), the association of an ethnically Jewish person with a lack of πίστις almost inevitably draws in the wider question of law observance and associates it with sinfulness.[3] In order to refocus the discussion away from ethnic divisions, I shall argue that the negated prepositional phrase οὐκ ἐκ πίστεως in Rom 14:23 activates a different argument than one concerning the relationship between two ethnic groups in one community. Consequently, law observance by a believer should not be considered a sinful relic of a past life.

THE ROLE OF ETHNICITY IN ROMANS 14:1–15:13

Nothing in Rom 14:1–15:13 explicitly identifies the ethnicity of either group in Rome.[4] The reader's first introduction to one of the groups occurs in Rom 14:1

---

2. I follow the majority of the commentary tradition in identifying two groups in Rom 14, rather than the five identified by Paul S. Minear, *The Obedience of Faith: The Purposes of Paul in the Epistle to the Romans* (London: SCM, 1971). This should not lead to the claim that there are only two groups in Rome. Francis Watson, *Paul, Judaism, and the Gentiles: A Sociological Approach* (Cambridge: Cambridge University Press, 1986), 97, suggests that "Paul's argument . . . presupposes two congregations, separated by mutual hostility and suspicion over the question of the law, which he wishes to bring together into one congregation." Rather than this picture of a bifurcated congregation, the nature of the communities in Rome is best captured by Peter Lampe, *From Paul to Valentinus: Christians at Rome in the First Two Centuries*, ed. Marshall D. Johnson, trans. Michael Steinhauser (Philadelphia: Fortress, 2003), 385, who describes a "fractionation into topographically separate house communities." Within these diverse communities is a congregation that Paul terms the weak.

3. See, inter alia, Moo, *Romans*, 879, who states with reference to the weak in v. 23 that "such Christians . . . do not have a strong enough faith to believe that they can ignore the ritual elements of the OT law."

4. Thomas R. Schreiner, *Romans*, Baker Exegetical Commentary on the New Testament (Grand Rapids: Baker Academic, 1998), 707n7, suggests that the reason that ethnic terms are avoided is that "the 'strong' and the 'weak', although primarily consisting of Gentiles and Jews, respectively, were not exclusively confined to Gentiles and Jews." This takes into account that Paul, a Jewish believer in the messiah, aligns himself with the gentile strong group. Nevertheless,

through the designation "weak in faith" (ὁ ἀσθενῶν τῇ πίστει). Another group (ἡμεῖς οἱ δυνατοί) is only named in Rom 15:1, but it is clearly the same group that eats all things in Rom 14:2 and is the subject of Paul's encouragement to welcome the one who is weak in faith in Rom 14:1. Both groups are primarily characterized by their behavior: what they eat and drink, which days they esteem, and how they act toward one another. Language of judgment is associated with the first group (i.e., the weak), while language of despising is associated with the second group (i.e., the strong). Scholars have failed to identify which particular form of Judaism is characterized by the practices of vegetarianism, avoidance of wine, and esteem of certain days. Byrne rightly notes that the law "did not prescribe abstention from meat nor forbid the consumption of wine" and that, as a result, "what is alluded to in Romans 14 goes well beyond normal Jewish practice."[5] Nevertheless, the use of κοινός—which he calls a "technical Jewish legal term"—to describe the practices in Rom 14:14 leads him to argue that "it is hard to explain this allusion on any basis other than Jewish religious sensitivities."[6] Although there is therefore some doubt as to how representative these practices are of the typical Jewish cult, it seems likely that they should still be identified as Jewish practices. However, the interpretative path from this broad identification of the practices of the weak as Jewish to an understanding of the group's ethnicity and an account of the problem in Rome is not quite as smooth as one might at first expect.

The only section of Rom 14:1–15:13 where ethnicity is undoubtedly present is the scriptural catena of Rom 15:9–12. This speaks in ethnic terms of an eschatological vision where gentiles worship Israel's God. After the blessing of vv. 5–6, where Paul prays that the weak and the strong might be given "the same thinking" in order that they might glorify God "with one voice," Paul repeats the injunction to welcome one another in v. 7: "just as the messiah also welcomed [the strong and the weak] for the glory of God" (καθὼς καὶ ὁ Χριστὸς προσελάβετο ὑμᾶς εἰς δόξαν

Moo, *Romans*, 845, argues that the dominant reading of Rom 14 identifies the weak as "Jewish Christians who refrained from certain kinds of food and observed certain days *out of continuing loyalty to the Mosaic law*" (emphasis mine). See also the summary of the secondary literature by Mark D. Nanos, *The Mystery of Romans: The Jewish Context of Paul's Letter* (Minneapolis: Fortress, 1996), 87: "There is almost universal agreement (it appears to be an almost unquestioned fact) that the 'weak' were Christian Jews who still practiced the Law and Jewish customs."

5. Brendan Byrne, *Romans*, Sacra Pagina (Collegeville, MN: Liturgical, 2007), 404. See also Moo, *Romans*, 846–47, who says that "abstention from food and wine is, of course, not required by the Mosaic law. But scrupulous Jews would *sometimes* avoid all meat.... And Jewish Christians in Rome ... *may* have been in precisely this kind of environment. Similarly, Jews would *sometimes* abstain from wine" (emphasis mine).

6. Byrne, *Romans*, 404.

The Relationship of Faith and Law Observance in Paul

τοῦ θεοῦ).[7] This is substantiated by a reference to how the nations (τὰ ἔθνη) might glorify God, as a result of the messiah having become a servant of the circumcision (ἡ περιτομή). The περιτομή and the ἔθνη are undoubtedly ethnic references. However, a direct link between these two groups in the eschatological vision and the two groups in Rome is weaker than typically understood. It has merely been assumed that the Jews and gentiles identified in 15:8 and pictured in 15:9–12 correspond to the weak and the strong in 14:1–15:7. Although we should clearly not break the link between the scriptural catena of 15:9–12 and the tensions between the weak and the strong in Rom 14, this does not mean that ὁ περιτομή should be directly identified with ὁ ἀσθενῶν τῇ πίστει and τὰ ἔθνη with οἱ δυνατοί.[8] The nature of the link between the eschatological vision and the situation in Rome should be reexamined.

Two "distinct but equal identities" are indeed present in the catena, but the prior interpretative decision regarding a mixed, dysfunctional community of two ethnicities in Rome has led scholars to misinterpret the purpose of the catena.[9] Kujanpää suggests that vv. 9–12 "form a catena that is bound together by the catchword ἔθνη and the idea of gentiles praising the Lord."[10] As a result, Witherington determines that "one purpose of these Scripture citations is to make clear that including Gentiles in the people of God was not just a happy afterthought of God."[11] Scholars therefore tend to identify the purpose of the scriptural catena as a recognition of the gentiles' status as worshipers of Israel's God, but then they shy away from the implication that this is the issue at stake in Rome rather than relations in a mixed community of Jews and gentiles. As an example, Kujanpää notes the focus of these four scriptural citations while denying the implication: "Although the catena effectively shows that including gentiles in the worshipping community fulfils scriptural prophecies, it is hardly the reason why Paul created the catena and situated it at the end of the letter. In Paul's argumentation the gen-

---

7. All biblical translations, unless otherwise noted, are my own.

8. The γάρ of verse 8 draws the ethnic references of the scriptural catena together with the discussion of welcoming the other that marks Rom 14:1–15:7.

9. Cf. Scott J. Hafemann, "The Redemption of Israel for the Sake of the Nations," in *Introduction to Messianic Judaism: Its Ecclesial Context and Biblical Foundations*, ed. David Rudolph and Joel Willitts (Grand Rapids: Zondervan, 2013), 208, who states that "the current experience of Jews and Gentiles as distinct but equal identities within the Church therefore takes on significance precisely because it is a foretaste of this consummation yet to come for both Israel and the nations."

10. Katja Kujanpää, *The Rhetorical Functions of Scriptural Quotations in Romans: Paul's Argument by Quotations* (Leiden: Brill, 2019), 279.

11. Ben Witherington III, *Paul's Letter to the Romans: A Socio-Rhetorical Commentary* (Grand Rapids: Eerdmans, 2004), 344.

DAVID J. JOHNSTON

tile mission does not necessitate profound legitimatizing."[12] Longenecker follows the same line of thought: "Paul's purpose in quoting these four biblical passages here seems not to have been to support his mission and message to pagan Gentiles."[13] However, this conclusion is difficult to sustain when the catena is followed in vv. 14–21 with another of Paul's defenses concerning his gentile mission.[14] The scriptural catena is indeed an eschatological portrait of a mixed community of different ethnicities, but its purpose is to depict the gentiles' status as worshipers of Israel's God. The resonance with the current situation in Rome is not necessarily a positive eschatological vision that acts as a comparison to the negative picture in Rome. Rather, the catena captures Paul's vision for his ministry. The problematic situation in Rome that is depicted in Rom 14:1–15:7 might therefore also concern the obedience of gentiles (cf. Rom 15:18).

PAUL'S GOSPEL AND ETHNICITY

The starting point for much of the interpretation of Paul is that both he and his gospel are law-free. This Paul, who considers the law to be the "law of sin and death" (cf. Rom 8:2), stands in opposition to another group, led by Jewish believers, who had a law-observant mission to the gentiles.[15] Jewish practices therefore differentiate both the missional preaching and the behavior of Paul from his opponents. However, Paula Fredriksen has argued that Paul's gospel is not law-free. Rather, it is characterized by Jewish practices and ethics.[16] The divide between Paul and his

---

12. Kujanpää, *Rhetorical Functions*, 290.

13. Richard N. Longenecker, *The Epistle to the Romans*, New International Greek Testament Commentary (Grand Rapids: Eerdmans, 2016), 1015.

14. Cf. Rom 15:16: εἰς τὸ εἶναί με λειτουργὸν Χριστοῦ Ἰησοῦ εἰς τὰ ἔθνη, ἱερουργοῦντα τὸ εὐαγγέλιον τοῦ θεοῦ, ἵνα γένηται ἡ προσφορὰ τῶν ἐθνῶν εὐπρόσδεκτος, ἡγιασμένη ἐν πνεύματι ἁγίῳ.

15. See the standard portrayal of these so-called opponents in J. Louis Martyn, "A Law-Observant Mission to Gentiles: The Background of Galatians," *SJT* 38 (1985): 307–24. I am persuaded that this same mission accounts for certain elements of Romans, including Rom 16:17–20. See Douglas A. Campbell, *The Deliverance of God: An Apocalyptic Rereading of Justification in Paul* (Grand Rapids: Eerdmans, 2009), 469–518.

16. See the argument of Paula Fredriksen, "Judaizing the Nations: The Ritual Demands of Paul's Gospel," *NTS* 56 (2010): 232–52. See also Fredriksen, *Paul: The Pagans' Apostle* (New Haven: Yale University Press, 2017), 147, where she states that "everyone seems to have been required to commit to these twinned, most singularly Jewish behaviors, shunning public cult and worshipping Israel's god alone." She also sets out the Jewish demands that Paul makes of his gentile believers: "no more λατρεία to other, lower gods," and they should "live as *hagioi* ... according to standards of community behavior described precisely in 'the Law'" (111). Douglas A. Campbell,

The difference between Paul and his opponents concerns how gentiles might be included in the worshiping communities of Israel's God. In Fredriksen's view, Paul's gospel cohered with standard Jewish practice. Although one might be attracted to the God of the Jewish people and might decide to worship this God through taking on certain practices, it would be rare to change one's ethnicity.[18] Even in the eschatological age gentiles would remain gentiles, although they would no longer worship idols and might follow some Jewish practices.[19] In effect, they would become "ex-pagan pagans."[20] Fredriksen therefore distinguishes between acting "Jewishly" and becoming Jewish.[21] Jewish behaviors might be found among Paul's gentiles, but conversion through circumcision was not.

opponents is not about whether gentile believers should avoid the law. Indeed, "the gentile-in-Christ *should* Judaize," according to Fredriksen's account of Paul.[17]

Framing Paul: An Epistolary Biography (Grand Rapids: Eerdmans, 2014), 215, also reminds us that "most of the early Christian leaders were Jews, and most early Christian ethics is recognizably Jewish, including much of Paul's." By contrast, the opponents represent "another group whom Paul regards as dangerous in their advocacy of certain additional traditional Jewish practices" (217). With regard to this group, Campbell states, "Certain Jewish practices are in view, which Paul bitterly opposes being foisted on his pagan converts—notably, circumcision and comprehensive Torah observance" (220).

17. Fredriksen, *Paul*, 125.

18. Paula Fredriksen, "The Question of Worship: Gods, Pagans, and the Redemption of Israel," in *Paul within Judaism: Restoring the First-Century Context to the Apostle*, ed. Mark D. Nanos and Magnus Zetterholm (Minneapolis: Fortress, 2015), 182, says that "to fully change gods was tantamount to changing ethnicity: a pagan's 'becoming' a Jew in effect altered his own past, reconfigured his ancestry, and cut his ties to his own pantheon, family, and *patria.*" This is not to say that conversion did not occur. See Paula Fredriksen, "Judaism, the Circumcision of Gentiles, and Apocalyptic Hope: Another Look at Galatians 1 and 2," *Journal of Theological Studies* 42.2 (1991): 535–40, where she argues that, although there was no Jewish mission to the gentiles, converts were accepted. She says: "According to both Juvenal and Josephus, the decision to receive circumcision is what distinguishes, quite precisely, the sympathizer from the convert" (536).

19. Fredriksen, *Paul*, 88, indicates that these "eschatological gentiles ... turn to make an exclusive commitment to the god of Israel, and ... do *not* assume (other) Jewish practices, a.k.a. 'the Law' (circumcision, food laws, Sabbath, and so on)." However, she later states that "Paul's *ethnē*-in-Christ are not only enjoined to Judaize to the extent that they commit to the worship of Israel's God alone and eschew idol-worship. They also, according to Paul, must behave toward each other in such a way that they fulfill the Law" (117). It seems that it would not be unexpected for gentile believers to act in ways that appear like law observance.

20. Fredriksen, *Paul*, 34. Although Denys N. McDonald, "'Ex-Pagan Pagans'? Paul, Philo, and Gentile Ethnic Reconfiguration," *JSNT* 45.1 (2022): 25, is correct that "people can have multiple and/or hybrid ethnic identities," I am unconvinced that the language of "ex-pagan pagans" masks this.

21. Paula Fredriksen, "Why Should a 'Law-Free' Mission Mean a 'Law-Free' Apostle?," *JBL* 134.3 (2015): 637.

While Paul's opponents pushed for gentile conversion, thereby effectively excluding gentiles from the worshiping community, Paul himself was convinced that the presence of gentiles as gentiles was a necessary indication of the eschatological age: "Gentiles needed to remain Gentiles."[22] Fredriksen states that "the very existence of such gentiles who had turned from their idols and who had made an exclusive commitment to the god of Israel was a profound and ongoing validation of Paul's work."[23] The dominant motif of the scriptural catena of Rom 15:9–12 therefore witnesses to Paul's vision of the eschatological age, where gentiles are included as gentiles in the worshiping community.[24] We can see how Fredriksen has reframed the dispute between Paul and his opponents around the question of gentile inclusion in the people of Israel's God now that the eschatological age has come. Ethnicity thus plays a role—the question concerns whether gentiles must, or could, change ethnicity—but the two groups in this dispute are not determined by their ethnicities. On the question of the composition of the people of God in the eschatological age, there is not a Jewish position and a gentile position. Instead, there are (at least) two different positions that, at their heart, represent (at least) two Jewish interpretative possibilities. This dispute is an intra-Jewish dispute concerning the inclusion of gentiles.[25]

22. Fredriksen, *Paul*, 164.

23. Paula Fredriksen, "How Later Contexts Affect Pauline Content, or: Retrospect Is the Mother of Anachronism," in *Jews and Christians in the First and Second Centuries: How to Write Their History*, ed. Peter J. Tomson and Joshua Schwartz (Leiden: Brill, 2014), 51.

24. Fredriksen, *Paul*, 163, identifies Rom 15:9–12 as a "catena of biblical verses that celebrate the nations turning to Israel's god."

25. The work of Raymond E. Brown, "Not Jewish Christianity and Gentile Christianity but Types of Jewish/Gentile Christianity," *Catholic Biblical Quarterly* 45 (1983): 74–79, is instructive and necessary. He argues that different theological positions do not represent different ethnicities. Recognizing the diversity within Judaism, Brown identifies a minimum of four missions to the gentiles, ranging from a more conservative position associated with Paul's opponents to a more radical position found in Hebrews. All four orientations to Judaism and the law originate from Jewish Christ believers. The value of Brown's work lies in his description of the ethnicity of the four diverse groups in Raymond E. Brown and John P. Meier, *Antioch and Rome: New Testament Cradles of Catholic Christianity* (London: Chapman, 1983), 2–6: each group is composed of "Jewish Christians and their Gentile converts." As he acknowledges in Raymond E. Brown, "Further Reflections on the Origins of the Church of Rome," in *The Conversation Continues: Studies in Paul and John in Honor of J. Louis Martyn*, ed. Robert T. Fortna and Beverly Roberts Gaventa (Nashville: Abingdon, 1990), 98–115, some details have been criticized by reviewers. However, these criticisms do not negate the key insight of Brown's analysis, which New Testament scholarship has failed to fully grasp. An interesting example is Richard N. Longenecker, *Introducing Romans: Critical Issues in Paul's Most Famous Letter* (Grand Rapids: Eerdmans, 2011), 81–84, who quotes Brown approvingly and at length, criticizing the tendency to move "from

The Relationship of Faith and Law Observance in Paul

The inclusion of gentiles is not the only intra-Jewish argument that concerns Paul. The position of Jewish nonbelievers in God's economy of salvation is clearly a central concern for Paul (cf. the argument of Rom 9–11, particularly Rom 9:3: ηὐχόμην γὰρ ἀνάθεμα εἶναι αὐτὸς ἐγὼ ἀπὸ τοῦ Χριστοῦ ὑπὲρ τῶν ἀδελφῶν μου τῶν συγγενῶν μου κατὰ σάρκα). Another concern is undoubtedly the relationship of Jewish believers and gentile believers in the one people of God (cf. the collection for Jerusalem; see Rom 15:26: εὐδόκησαν γὰρ Μακεδονία καὶ Ἀχαΐα κοινωνίαν τινὰ ποιήσασθαι εἰς τοὺς πτωχοὺς τῶν ἁγίων τῶν ἐν Ἰερουσαλήμ).[26] Neither of these arguments is entirely discrete: how one views a Jewish person who does not believe in Jesus as the messiah might affect how one treats a Jewish Christ believer in the community. But they are different discussions. In addition to these, Paul is in dispute with his opponents regarding the inclusion of gentiles.[27]

We must therefore recognize that Paul has at least three arguments in view: an intra-Jewish dispute with his opponents concerning how gentiles are included in the people of God; the relationship of Jewish nonbelievers to the Christ-believing communities; and the relationship of Jewish believers and gentile believers within the same community. All three of these arguments include incidences of Jewish practices, but the mere presence of Jewish practices in a particular passage should neither automatically activate any one of these three arguments nor necessarily signal Jewish ethnicity. Jewish practices could be carried out by Jewish Christ believers, Jewish nonbelievers, or gentiles. If the interpreter does not identify which of these arguments is Paul's primary concern at a particular point in his letters, then there is the danger of activating the wrong schema. The "one who is weak in

---

ethnic origin to theological tendency" (82) and identifying a dominant theological stance in Rome "congenial to Jewish Christianity" from a community that comprised "Gentile believers as well as Jewish believers in Jesus" (83). Despite this, he reverts back to the traditional ethnic account of diversity, saying in his commentary that "it may also reasonably be conjectured ... that 'the Strong' group was largely (if not entirely) made up of Gentile Christians ... whereas the group that 'the Strong' identified as 'the Weak' was composed mainly (if not entirely) of Jewish believers in Jesus" (Longenecker, *Epistle to the Romans*, 995–96). I propose that we should follow Brown in recognizing that "each of these Groups present in the Roman church would have had both Jews and Gentiles [and as a result] a division of Roman Christianity into Jewish and Gentile would not be a meaningful theological description" (Brown, "Further Reflections," 106). If we are to accept that different theological positions are presented in Romans, then it does not necessarily follow that they originate from an ethnic conflict.

26. This has often been seen as the "leitmotif of Romans"; cf. Moo, *Romans*, 845.

27. E. P. Sanders, *Paul, the Law, and the Jewish People* (Philadelphia: Fortress, 1983), 4, has argued that "the different things which Paul said about the law depend on the question asked or the problem posed." Whereas his focus is Paul's coherent account of the law, mine is which contingent situation is in view when Paul talks about Jewish practices.

faith" might be misidentified as Jewish rather than gentile, with all of the implications that might entail.

Scholars debate whether the designation "weak in faith" is emic or etic, but few suggest that the designation is Paul's own characterization of this group of believers who carry out Jewish practices.[28] It is too harsh a term, particularly since Paul does not explicitly condemn such practices. The weak's lack of faith tends to be seen as the group's inability to move on from Jewish practices, with the implication that Jewish Christ believers are in view. We can see this dynamic in Kruse, who identifies the weak as "Jewish Christians (including possibly proselytes) who practiced essentially Jewish customs."[29] He then characterizes them, on the basis of the language of "weak in faith," as "people whose grasp of the implications of the gospel is limited."[30] Thus, it is assumed that practices associated with Judaism imply that the weak are Jewish, and these same practices are determined to represent a failure to recognize the full assurance that comes with the gospel of faith. Hence, we find the designation "weak in faith" for this group.[31] However, it is not enough for the presence of apparently Jewish practices in Rom 14 to activate either of the two arguments that the secondary literature tends to consider. Ethnic Jews might be in view, whether they consist of believing ones in the community or nonbelieving ones in the synagogues.[32] But gentiles who carry out Jewish practices might instead lie behind the argument. Any critique or validation of the weak would not be an argument targeted at those who are Jewish but rather at those who are gentile. It would concern the discussion concerning the inclusion of the gentiles rather than tell us anything directly concerning Paul's view of Jews or Judaism. We must therefore reconsider how to identify the weak.

In the final section of my chapter, I shall argue that the characterization of the weak as lacking πίστις should cause us to consider whether the argument

28. It is likely that the communities in Rome would recognize who is in view. See Robert Jewett, *Romans: A Commentary* (Minneapolis: Fortress, 2007), 834n24: "If the Roman churches were not able to see the links between Paul's gnomic references and their situation, the argument would be ineffective."

29. Colin G. Kruse, *Paul's Letter to the Romans*, Pillar New Testament Commentary (Grand Rapids: Eerdmans, 2012), 510.

30. Kruse, *Romans*, 511. Further, he suggests that "weak faith [is] based on an inadequate understanding of the gospel" (514).

31. Nanos, *Mystery of Romans*, 88, states with regard to the commentary tradition that "almost all appear to agree [that] 'Weak' is a pejorative term [representing the Weak's] failure to realize the full measure of their freedom in Christ from the practices of the Law." See also his summary of commentators who exemplify "Luther's trap," where the Jewish practices of the weak are judged, despite Paul's injunction in Rom 14:13 (92–94).

32. See Nanos, *Mystery of Romans*, 108–15, for the argument that nonbelieving Jews are in view.

The Relationship of Faith and Law Observance in Paul

regarding gentile inclusion, as suggested by the purpose of the scriptural catena, is in view. It is clear that the label "weak in faith" is being used to describe the group that has certain apparently Jewish behaviors, but neither their behavior nor the designation explicitly identifies the ethnicity of these believers. My focus here will not be the semantic meaning of the word that is the topic of this volume but rather on how we should interpret the prepositional phrase οὐκ ἐκ πίστεως in which we find the noun. I shall draw heavily on an article by Douglas Campbell that forms the hidden substructure of much of his work on the apocalyptic Paul.[33] Although ethnicity is typically understood as the interpretative key for understanding the situation in Rom 14:1–15:13, I shall argue that the weak should be primarily characterized by something other than their ethnicity.

Πίστις AS A CHARACTERIZATION OF THE TWO GROUPS

After the semantic unit's point of departure in Rom 14:1 that identifies one group as "weak in faith," there are three other references to πίστις in Rom 14:1–15:13.[34] In 14:22 the strong are characterized by their possession of πίστις: σὺ πίστιν [ἣν] ἔχεις κατὰ σεαυτὸν ἔχε ἐνώπιον τοῦ θεοῦ.[35] The other group is then brought into focus in v. 23. A lack of πίστις, with the noun occurring in a negated prepositional phrase, functions as the grounds for the condemnation of the group that is weak, if they were to eat: ὁ δὲ διακρινόμενος ἐὰν φάγῃ κατακέκριται, ὅτι οὐκ ἐκ πίστεως. This is immediately followed by a more general statement, albeit with reference to the same group: πᾶν δὲ ὃ οὐκ ἐκ πίστεως ἁμαρτία ἐστίν. With the same group characterized negatively in relation to πίστις in 14:1 and 14:23, it is plausible that these two negated prepositional phrases, οὐκ ἐκ πίστεως, should play a larger role in the discussion of what it means for the group to be introduced as ὁ ἀσθενῶν τῇ πίστει.[36]

---

33. Douglas A. Campbell, "The Meaning of ΠΙΣΤΙΣ and ΝΟΜΟΣ in Paul: A Linguistic and Structural Perspective," *JBL* 111.1 (1992): 91–103. The importance of this article to Campbell's work is rarely noticed, but when he seeks to clarify his reading of Romans, he frequently draws on this argument by turning to Gal 2:15–16 and the relationship between οὐκ ἐξ ἔργων νόμου and ἐκ πίστεως Χριστοῦ, arguing that these represent two contemporaneous states rather than one past state that is foundational for the other present state. See, for example, Douglas A. Campbell, "An Attempt to Be Understood: A Response to the Concerns of Matlock and Macaskill with *The Deliverance of God*," *JSNT* 34.2 (2011): 162–208.

34. The precise role of the dative here is not important for our argument. Paul also speaks about τὰ ἀσθενήματα τῶν ἀδυνάτων in Rom 15:1.

35. See, inter alia, Moo, *Romans*, 878.

36. Where parallels are drawn between 14:1 and 14:23, the assumption is that the meaning of the noun πίστις in both derives from the use of the verb πιστεύω in v. 2 of that chapter (Moo, *Romans*, 852–53).

Douglas Campbell establishes that ἐκ πίστεως and διὰ πίστεως function in paradigmatic relationship: "In terms of their primary meaning they seem to be saying essentially the same thing when they occur."[37] He also notes that νόμος occurs in a series of prepositional phrases (preceded by ἐκ, διά, and ὑπό), which all share the same paradigmatic relationship.[38] Drawing on Gal 2:16, Rom 3:27–28, and Phil 3:9 in particular, he argues that prepositional phrases involving πίστις and νόμος are often deployed in opposition to each other, which leads him to conclude that "their meaning may be in large measure relational."[39] This "antithetical relationship" has consequences for the understanding of each prepositional phrase, since it suggests that each phrase derives its meaning not just from its propositional content but from this structure of relations.[40] When Campbell's focus moves to the interpretation of the prepositional phrases where Paul speaks about works and the law he argues that these "may have little positive substance of their own. They probably refer instead primarily to the idea of a state which is not by means of πίστις Χριστοῦ."[41] As a result, we have two possible states that are being described in the conflict letters of Galatians, Romans, and Philippians.[42] Irrespective of how exactly we conceptualize these two states, there is one state that is in faith and one that is under the law. In the context of preaching regarding a law-observant gospel from his opponents, Paul speaks about the life of a believer in the eschatological age as being ἐκ πίστεως (cf. Rom 3:26) or διὰ πίστεως (cf. Phil 3:9). This state that depends on a Pauline understanding of the gospel is also οὐκ ἐξ ἔργων νόμου (cf. Gal 2:16) and χωρὶς νόμου (cf. Rom 7:8). This is contrasted with a contemporaneous state in the eschatological age of those who have taken on the law-observant gospel of Paul's opponents: they are living ἐκ νόμου (cf. Phil 3:9),

---

37. Campbell, "Meaning," 96. Campbell uses this insight into the paradigmatic relationship between ἐκ πίστεως and διὰ πίστεως in order to bring more data into the πίστις Χριστοῦ debate (99–100). Having established that ἐκ πίστεως is the "dominant phrase," he identifies Hab 2:4 as the "fundamental linguistic template from which the other phrases, and the structure as a whole, are derived" (101).

38. Campbell, "Meaning," 97.

39. Campbell, "Meaning," 98.

40. Campbell, "Meaning," 98. See his discussion of de Saussure on p. 91.

41. Campbell, "Meaning," 102.

42. The terms also occur outside these three letters, but Campbell, *Deliverance*, 769, argues that it is in these three letters that they occur within this matrix of meaning. If he is correct about this matrix of relations in Romans (as well as Galatians and Philippians), then we must ask whether it is present in Rom 14 too. Campbell makes the distinction between being of Christ and of Adam in Rom 14:23—as he does with Rom 7—but I am yet to be persuaded that one should not note the presence of opposition in Rom 14 (cf. Campbell, *Deliverance*, 832).

The Relationship of Faith and Law Observance in Paul

διὰ νόμου (cf. Rom 3:20), or ὑπὸ νόμον (cf. Rom 6:14). This raises the possibility that this same state is being described as οὐκ ἐκ πίστεως in Rom 14:23.

Rather than ὑπὸ νόμον describing what it means to be ethnically Jewish, on certain occasions it represents one possibility of what it means for an ethnically gentile believer to live in the eschatological age. Campbell's account of the two states that are depicted by this matrix of terminology coheres with the presence of apparently Jewish practices in Rom 14 and suggests that the intra-Jewish dispute concerning the inclusion of the gentiles might be in view. According to the opponents of Paul's gospel, gentiles should live ἐκ νόμου, διὰ νόμου, and even ὑπὸ νόμον. Such a life, according to Paul, is οὐκ ἐκ πίστεως. The "pejorative connotation" of the term ὁ ἀσθενῶν τῇ πίστει is because it is Paul himself who names the group, which is in line with the way he characterizes his opponents.[43]

Conclusion

It has been my intention to demonstrate that the two ways in which Paul characterizes the weak in Rom 14—through their practices and through the language of a lack of πίστις—should not necessarily be put together in such a way to indicate that Paul has a group characterized by Jewish ethnicity in view. The language of a lack of πίστις means that our interpretation of the Jewish practices of Rom 14 should be reoriented away from those who are Jewish. The fact that the weak act οὐκ ἐκ πίστεως instead indicates that Paul has in mind the argument concerning gentile inclusion in the worshiping community, which is confirmed by the Jewish practices that this group enact. The Jewish practices in Rom 14 are not therefore a sinful relic of a past life, since it is not a dispute concerning those who had been ethnically Jewish that is in view. Rather, the argument concerns the inclusion of gentiles in the eschatological age. The weak would principally be ethnic gentiles in Rome, who might have taken the unusual step to become Jewish through the act of circumcision, although this group would include some ethnic Jews who teach such things too.[44] The strong would be distinguished from the weak by their following of Paul's gospel.[45] Again, some ethnic Jews might be included among

---

43. Moo, *Romans*, 852.

44. On the possibility of gentile conversion see Matthew Thiessen, *Contesting Conversion: Genealogy, Circumcision, and Identity in Ancient Judaism and Christianity* (Oxford: Oxford University Press, 2011).

45. The fact that these communities follow Paul's gospel does not mean that there is uniformity between them, as we can see by looking at the tenor of most of Paul's letters to his own congregations! They are the strong only in comparison to the weak.

69

DAVID J. JOHNSTON

them—we can think of Prisca and Aquila—but this group would principally be ethnic gentiles. Both groups would therefore be believers in the messiah, and neither should be characterized by Jewish ethnicity. In fact, ethnicity is not the defining characteristic of either group.

It is Paul's own gospel that we find in the eschatological vision of Rom 15:9–12. The scriptural catena would thus represent a barbed comment on the situation in Rome. It is gentiles as gentiles who should form part of the worshiping community. This reading is suggested by Rom 15:7–9. "Welcome one another," says Paul, "just as the messiah also welcomed you for the glory of God" (καθὼς καὶ ὁ Χριστὸς προσελάβετο ὑμᾶς εἰς δόξαν τοῦ θεοῦ). In the explanatory clause that follows, it is the gentiles that glorify God (εἰς . . . τὰ δὲ ἔθνη ὑπὲρ ἐλέους δοξάσαι τὸν θεόν), which is confirmed (καθὼς γέγραπται) by the scriptural catena that proclaims gentile worship of the Jewish God. The close correlation between the purpose for which the messiah welcomed the two groups in Rome (i.e., for the glory of God) and the purpose of his becoming a servant of the circumcision (i.e., in order that the gentiles might glorify God) suggests that the strong and the weak should both be identified with the gentiles in the scriptural catena. The strong primarily represent Paul's own "eschatological gentiles," and the weak represent the gentiles who are "weak in faith," having decided to live ἐκ νόμου rather than ἐκ πίστεως. Sharing the same ethnicity, they differ in terms of their understanding of the inclusion of gentiles in the eschatological age.

WORKS CITED

Brown, Raymond E. "Further Reflections on the Origins of the Church of Rome." Pages 98–115 in *The Conversation Continues: Studies in Paul and John in Honor of J. Louis Martyn.* Edited by Robert T. Fortna and Beverly Roberts Gaventa. Nashville: Abingdon, 1990.

———. "Not Jewish Christianity and Gentile Christianity but Types of Jewish/Gentile Christianity." *Catholic Biblical Quarterly* 45 (1983): 74–79.

Brown, Raymond E., and John P. Meier. *Antioch and Rome: New Testament Cradles of Catholic Christianity.* London: Chapman, 1983.

Byrne, Brendan. *Romans.* Sacra Pagina. Collegeville, MN: Liturgical, 2007.

Campbell, Douglas A. "An Attempt to Be Understood: A Response to the Concerns of Matlock and Macaskill with *The Deliverance of God.*" *JSNT* 34.2 (2011): 162–208.

———. *The Deliverance of God: An Apocalyptic Rereading of Justification in Paul.* Grand Rapids: Eerdmans, 2009.

———. *Framing Paul: An Epistolary Biography.* Grand Rapids: Eerdmans, 2014.

The Relationship of Faith and Law Observance in Paul

———. "The Meaning of ΠΙΣΤΙΣ and ΝΟΜΟΣ in Paul: A Linguistic and Structural Perspective." *JBL* 111.1 (1992): 91–103.

Fredriksen, Paula. "How Later Contexts Affect Pauline Content, or: Retrospect Is the Mother of Anachronism." Pages 17–51 in *Jews and Christians in the First and Second Centuries: How to Write Their History*. Edited by Peter J. Tomson and Joshua Schwartz. Leiden: Brill, 2014.

———. "Judaism, the Circumcision of Gentiles, and Apocalyptic Hope: Another Look at Galatians 1 and 2." *Journal of Theological Studies* 42.2 (1991): 532–64.

———. "Judaizing the Nations: The Ritual Demands of Paul's Gospel." *NTS* 56 (2010): 232–52.

———. *Paul: The Pagans' Apostle*. New Haven: Yale University Press, 2017.

———. "The Question of Worship: Gods, Pagans, and the Redemption of Israel." Pages 175–202 in *Paul within Judaism: Restoring the First-Century Context to the Apostle*. Edited by Mark D. Nanos and Magnus Zetterholm. Minneapolis: Fortress, 2015.

———. "Why Should a 'Law-Free' Mission Mean a 'Law-Free' Apostle?" *JBL* 134.3 (2015): 637–50.

Hafemann, Scott J. "The Redemption of Israel for the Sake of the Nations." Pages 206–13 in *Introduction to Messianic Judaism: Its Ecclesial Context and Biblical Foundations*. Edited by David Rudolph and Joel Willitts. Grand Rapids: Zondervan, 2013.

Jewett, Robert. *Romans: A Commentary*. Minneapolis: Fortress, 2007.

Kruse, Colin G. *Paul's Letter to the Romans*. Pillar New Testament Commentary. Grand Rapids: Eerdmans, 2012.

Kujanpää, Katja. *The Rhetorical Functions of Scriptural Quotations in Romans: Paul's Argument by Quotations*. Leiden: Brill, 2019.

Lampe, Peter. *From Paul to Valentinus: Christians at Rome in the First Two Centuries*. Edited by Marshall D. Johnson. Translated by Michael Steinhauser. Philadelphia: Fortress, 2003.

Longenecker, Richard N. *The Epistle to the Romans*. New International Greek Testament Commentary. Grand Rapids: Eerdmans, 2016.

———. *Introducing Romans: Critical Issues in Paul's Most Famous Letter*. Grand Rapids: Eerdmans, 2011.

Martyn, J. Louis. "A Law-Observant Mission to Gentiles: The Background of Galatians." *SJT* 38 (1985): 307–24.

McDonald, Denys N. "'Ex-Pagan Pagans'? Paul, Philo, and Gentile Ethnic Reconfiguration." *JSNT* 45.1 (2022): 1–28.

Minear, Paul S. *The Obedience of Faith: The Purposes of Paul in the Epistle to the Romans*. London: SCM, 1971.

Moo, Douglas. *The Epistle to the Romans*. 2nd ed. New International Commentary on the New Testament. Grand Rapids: Eerdmans, 2018.

Nanos, Mark D. *The Mystery of Romans: The Jewish Context of Paul's Letter*. Minneapolis: Fortress, 1996.

Sanders, E. P. *Paul, the Law, and the Jewish People*. Philadelphia: Fortress, 1983.

Schreiner, Thomas R. *Romans*. Baker Exegetical Commentary on the New Testament. Grand Rapids: Baker Academic, 1998.

Thiessen, Matthew. *Contesting Conversion: Genealogy, Circumcision, and Identity in Ancient Judaism and Christianity*. Oxford: Oxford University Press, 2011.

Watson, Francis. *Paul, Judaism, and the Gentiles: A Sociological Approach*. Cambridge: Cambridge University Press, 1986.

Witherington, Ben, III. *Paul's Letter to the Romans: A Socio-Rhetorical Commentary*. Grand Rapids: Eerdmans, 2004.

5

Augustine on Faith

Trust, Acceptance, Credence, and Belief

TERESA MORGAN

The centrality of the concept of "faith" to Christians predates our earliest records. It probably originates in Aramaic, but we first encounter it as Greek πίστις and its cognates πιστεύειν, πιστός, and so on. The center of gravity and most common meanings of πίστις in Greek (to take the noun as an example) are relational trust, trustworthiness, and faithfulness, but it has a wide range of meaning, including good faith, confidence, belief, pledge, argument, proof, guarantee, commercial credit, and a legal trust or trusteeship. In the earliest Christian texts, it usually refers to trust or faithfulness; less often, to belief or the idea of entrustedness. Christian Latin speakers and writers translated πίστις with *fides* (which has a very close, though not identical, range of meanings), πιστός with *fidelis*, and πιστεύειν usually with its nearest equivalent, *credere*.[1]

---

1. On the range of meanings of the πίστις and *fides* lexica and the origins of Christian usage, see Teresa Morgan, *Roman Faith and Christian Faith:* Pistis *and* Fides *in the Early Roman Empire and Early Churches* (Oxford: Oxford University Press, 2015), 5–10, and 234–41. In pre-Christian Greek, belief that something is the case (propositional belief) is commonly expressed in the language of thinking or knowing (e.g., νομίζειν, δοκεῖν, φρονεῖν) rather than with πιστεύειν, but in Latin *credere* often means "to believe." The English phrase "to believe in" is slightly misleading in this context; it appears to refer to belief but, since it invokes relationship and self-commitment, is closest to the "trust" register of πιστεύειν/*credere*. Eugene TeSelle, proposes that *fides* sometimes

---

I am grateful to the Leverhulme Foundation for support of the project of which this essay is part, and to Lewis Ayres for comments on an earlier draft.

Between the first and fifth centuries the concept of πίστις/*fides*, along with its equivalents in other languages around the Roman Empire, became steadily more complex, encompassing confidence, hope, conviction, knowledge, prayer, worship, a collection of teachings, and even something like "the faith" in the sense of the cult as a whole. One of the most striking developments of this period is the increasing importance of belief—both belief as an attitude and the right content of belief—as an aspect of πίστις/*fides*. Belief came to the fore in disputes between Christian groups, for instance about the nature(s) of Christ or the status of new revelations after the Christ event, in arguments between Christians and mainstream philosophers, and where Christians made use of philosophy, especially Platonism, as a tool for explicating Christian teaching. Very early Christians, like most Greek and Latin speakers, talked about belief using the language of thinking and knowing rather than πίστις/*fides*, but under the influence of Platonism πίστις/*fides* was increasingly used to refer to belief.[2]

The creation of the Nicene Creed in 325 was a milestone in the evolution of Christian faith. In structure, the creed broadly follows earlier baptismal formulae, and each article begins πιστεύομεν εἰς/*credimus in* "we put our trust in." Since at baptism people commit themselves and their future lives and hopes to God, the use of πιστεύειν/*credere* in early baptismal formulae is primarily relational, an affirmation of trust and future faithfulness, but such affirmations also contain propositional content (e.g., that God is Father and Christ is God's Son), so belief is also implicated in them.[3] The Nicene Creed, however, was designed to define the content of "the faith" in the sense of Christian teaching and acted as a standard of orthodoxy, so it encouraged Christians to think of belief, specifically right belief, as central to πίστις/*fides*.

By the time Augustine converted to Christianity in 386, both the attitude of belief and the importance of believing the right things were well established as central to Christian faith. Augustine testifies to their importance in *On the Trinity*

---

has a stronger meaning than *credere* perhaps intuiting the range of possible meanings of *credere*. See his *"Fides,"* in *Augustinus-Lexikon*, ed. Cornelius Mayer (Basel: Schwabe, 2002), 2:1334.

2. I am indebted to an unpublished essay by Mark Edwards showing that Plato and Platonists tended to use πιστεύειν, unusually, to refer to unwarranted and unreliable trust or belief in things of this world, which is always inferior to knowledge.

3. Belief by itself is not enough for baptizands, since, for example, polytheists can believe that many divinities exist and have certain qualities without worshiping them, while Jews can believe that Abraham ascended to heaven or identify Enoch with the angel Metatron without worshiping them. To worship God and affirm Christ as Lord, baptizands need to believe certain things and to commit themselves to God in an act that is described as πιστεύειν in what must be its relational, "trust" sense.

Augustine on Faith

(13.2.5), where he describes faith as twofold: *fides quae* (usually translated "the faith which is believed," the content of doctrine), and *fides qua* (usually translated "the faith by which it is believed," what takes place in the mind and heart of a believer). This definition has become highly influential in Western Christianity, so it is worth noting that it is more than a little problematic. It minimizes the relationality of πίστις/*fides*, that is, the ideas of trust and faithfulness that were its essence for the earliest Christians and were still important in the fourth century. It ignores the common uses of ἡ πίστις/*fides* to mean Christian teaching or Christianity as a whole. It does, however, provide a convenient starting point for this essay, which is confined to one half of it. I will explore how Augustine understands the attitude of *fides*, and whether, or in what sense, belief is as central to it as the reception of *On the Trinity* in Western Christianity would suggest.[4]

English translators of Augustine tend to render *fides* as either "faith" or "belief" without explaining what the translator understands by the term. Discussions of belief in Augustine's writings, moreover, rarely give much attention to what attitude is really in play.[5] Modern writing on belief in moral philosophy and epistemology, however, explores belief and related concepts with great sensitiv-

---

4. Normatively, for early Christians as for other ancient Greek and Latin speakers, attitudes and related practices (such as the attitude and act of trust) go together (this is one source of the Christian insistence that faith must be expressed in works), but our focus here, given the restrains of space, will be on attitudes rather than expressions of πίστις/*fides*.

5. Modern interest in Augustine's understanding of *fides/credere* focuses on the relationship between faith and reason. It is well recognized that, for Augustine, faith is intrinsically rational as a faculty and activity of the human mind, which was created by God. Moreover, we act appropriately on faith all the time (e.g., when we treat our parents as our parents, even though we cannot know they are our parents), although, to act appropriately, faith must also act with a will to humility and love, not with arrogance or self-sufficiency. The bibliography is vast, but see e.g., Olivier du Roy, *L'intelligence de la foi en la trinité selon Saint Augustin* (Paris: Études Augustiniennes, 1966); Frederick Van Fleteren, "Authority and Reason, Faith and Understanding in the Thought of St. Augustine," *AugStud* 4 (1973): 33n1, T. J. van Baven, "De la raison à la foi: La conversion d'Augustin," *Augustiniana* 36 (1986): 5–27; TeSelle, "*Credere*," in Mayer, *Augustinus-Lexikon*, 2:122–24; Carol Harrison, *Rethinking Augustine's Early Theology: An Argument for Continuity* (Oxford: Oxford University Press, 2006), 37–70; John Peter Kenney, "Faith and Reason," in *The Cambridge Companion to Augustine*, ed. David Vincent Meconi and Eleonore Stump (Cambridge: Cambridge University Press, 2014), 275–91; Jean-Pierre Fortin, "Critical Theology, Committed Philosophy: Discovering Anew the Faith-Reason Dynamics with Origen of Alexandria and Augustine of Hippo," *Philosophy and Theology* 27 (2015): 25–54; Mark J. Boone, "Augustine and William James on the Rationality of Faith," *Heythrop Journal* 61 (2020): 648–59. Boone is unusual in recognizing the significant role of trust in faith as does Bielby, below, n. 23, though he focuses on Augustine's trust in authority and teaching rather than persons.

ity, distinguishing, for instance, strong or outright belief, where one thinks that something is true and is disposed to rely on it; weak belief or credence, where one thinks that something is more likely than not to be true and may act on it on that basis; assumption, where one presupposes that something is the case; acceptance, where a person comes to terms with what is real or factual, whether or not they like it; assent, where one accepts a proposition intellectually without necessarily holding either an intuition, belief, or proof that it is so (and which is close to one understanding of fideism); and propositional trust, where one is willing to entrust something to a proposition that cannot be known to be true. In addition, a growing group of "pistologists" is interested in the extent to which faith (Christian or secular) may not require "outright belief" or belief alone but instead (or additionally) involves weak belief, acceptance, reliance, hope, imaginative assent, credence, "beliefless assuming," loyalty, faithfulness, self-entrustment, or propositional or relational trust.[6]

What follows takes its cue, on the one hand, from the range of pre-Augustinian Christian understandings of πίστις and *fides*, and, on the other hand, from the range of modern philosophical understandings of belief and other, particularly propositional forms of faith, to consider the nature and role of belief and other concepts in Augustine's treatment of *fides*.[7] What is involved for Augustine when he talks about *fides qua*—belief, trust, one or more other attitudes, or a combination of attitudes?[8] I will argue that although Augustine is keenly interested in the propositional aspect of faith and shows some interest in different kinds of propositional *fides/credere*, he sees relational trust as equally important in the

---

6. See Timothy Williamson, "Knowledge, Credence, and the Strength of Belief," in *Expansive Epistemology: Norms, Actions, and the Social World*, ed. Amy Flowerree and Baron Reed (London: Routledge, forthcoming) on strength of belief and the discussion of Teresa Morgan, *The New Testament and the Theology of Trust: 'This Rich Trust'* (Oxford: Oxford University Press, 2022), 15–16 on alternatives to belief in faith. Timothy Eklund, "The Cognitive Aspect of Christian Faith and Non-doxastic Propositional Attitudes," *Neue Zeitschrift für systematische Theologie und Religionsphilosophie* 60 (2018): 386–405 discusses the main lines of the argument that faith need not involve belief, but rightly concludes that Christian faith requires belief content and so belief.

7. By "propositional forms of faith," I mean belief, credence, assumption, acceptance, assent, and trust *that* something is the case. These are all also forms of cognition, but I avoid talking about cognitive forms of faith because relational trust also has a cognitive dimension, since one can hold an attitude of trust separately from acting with trust.

8. The "rule of faith" is not discussed here, since it concerns the content of faith, but note the observation of Lewis Ayres, "Augustine on the Rule of Faith: Rhetoric, Christology, and the Foundation of Christian Thinking," *AugStud* 36 (2005): 36–37 that one function of the rule is to make possible ascent to the divine mystery, which suggests that it acts in part as a tool of the attitude of πίστις/*fides*.

divine-human relationship. In this, he is more traditional than other Platonist Christians whom he admires and also more in line with the range of thinking about faith in the fourth century than is often recognized. One reason for this may be that his understanding of faith owes a good deal to reflection on his own lived experience of coming to faith.

PHILO, CLEMENT OF ALEXANDRIA, AND ORIGEN ON Πίστις/*FIDES*

Discussion of the nature of πίστις or *fides* in contexts in which the truth or trustworthiness of a person, proposition, or piece of testimony cannot be known already by Augustine's day had a long history within early Judaism and Christianity, not least among Jewish and Christian Platonists. Philo uses πίστις language in the sense of "evidence" or "proof" for any cognitive state and also in the sense of relational trust in God.[9] Trust in God may be based on an assumption that tradition is trustworthy, on proven scriptural evidence that God has been trustworthy in the past (such as prophecies that have been fulfilled), or on propositional trust or hope for the future.[10] It acts as the foundational relationship with God within which a human being can begin to travel toward knowledge of the divine.[11]

Clement of Alexandria builds on his reading of Philo and his own Platonism to develop a multistage account of the relationship between πίστις and reason in the divine-human relationship. Both are gifts from God, which must also be actively exercised by the faithful (*Strom.* 1.7.38; 2.4.48).[12] Πίστις can begin as the kind of trust or assumption that people and things are trustworthy or believable, which most people practice every day (1.6.27; 2.9.45; 2.12.55).[13] At a higher level, it is outright belief in something (such as the Word of God as encountered in the gospels) that is self-evident to reason (2.3.13; 2.11.48–49; 5.1.5–6). This kind of πίστις makes possible further reasoned thought and inquiry, and, by building on belief with reason, the faithful can begin to understand and know God and to judge the truth of claims about God (2.2; 2.4.14–15; 2.9–12; 5.1). This leads to a yet another level of

---

9. See e.g., *Fug.* 136; *Abr.* 141; *Spec.* 4.176; *Virt.* 46 for πίστις as evidence or proof. See *Fug.* 152; *Mut.* 182, 201 for πίστις as trust in God.

10. See *Her.* 96, *Migr.* 43–44. As a Jew by birth, Philo takes for granted that God exists and that there is abundant evidence of God's past faithfulness and trustworthiness to God's people.

11. Morgan, *Roman Faith*, 152–54.

12. See Salvatore R. C. Lilla, *Clement of Alexandria: A Study in Christian Platonism and Gnosticism* (Oxford: Oxford University Press, 1971), section 3; Eric Osborn, "Arguments for Faith in Clement of Alexandria," *VC* 48 (1994): 1–24.

13. For Clement, faith is always a free choice (e.g., *Strom.* 2.2.9; 2.4.12).

πίστις: that which one has in the truth of something that has been demonstrated by reason. This level of πίστις, which is something more than outright belief, is very close, if not identical to, γνῶσις, knowledge of God (2.22.126; 7.10.55).

For both Philo and Clement, the goal of the faithful Jew or Christian is knowledge of God, but both also take a positive view of πίστις as relational trust in God, assumption, and belief short of knowledge. In his apologetic book *Against Celsus*, Origen, another Platonist whom Augustine admires and who seeks knowledge of God, treats πίστις in a slightly different way. Πίστις can be trust in the divine (*Cels.* 1.20–21; 2.3–4), but Origen (who takes a harder line than Philo and perhaps even Clement) thinks that trust is essentially for the uneducated who cannot aspire to knowledge of God (6.13).[14] It can also refer to outright belief based on reason (1.4–5), on the demonstrable reliability of the Scriptures (5.3), or on the fact that Christianity's claims have been proved right by their consequences (1.6, 55). In addition, Origen is conscious of the limits of what Christianity can prove, so he also characterizes πίστις as a rational risk. Just as when we go to sea, get married, or plant our fields, we believe and trust that the enterprise will turn out well based on a combination of past experience and calculated risk (1.11, cf. 1.31; 3.39), so also we trust in God in the same way. This is rational because risk-based trust is rational (1.11); there is always a gap between what we can infer from evidence and the uncertain future, and trust bridges that gap.[15]

During his years as a Manichee, Augustine sought knowledge of God through reason rather than through *fides*. As a Christian, however, he comes to a view of *fides/credere* that is not only more affirmative than that of the Manichaeans and most Platonists but is also arguably more capacious than that of Origen or Clement.

THE VARIETIES OF PROPOSITIONAL ATTITUDES

Augustine is not as concerned as Clement of Alexandria, or even Philo, about demonstrating the role of *fides/credere* at multiple stages in the progress of the Christian toward knowledge of God. He does, however, sometimes seem to distinguish between different propositional attitudes of *fides*. In one passage of *On Order*, an early essay dated to 386 about divine providence and the problem of

---

14. Gunnar af Hällström, *Fides Simpliciorum according to Origen of Alexandria* (Helsinki: Societas Scientiarum Fennica, 1984), 20–42.

15. The idea that trust is a rational risk is now commonplace in trust theory, but it is highly unusual among ancient writings (though cf. Arnobius, *Adv. nat.* 2.8).

Augustine on Faith

evil, Augustine considers the nature of reason (2.11.30). On one level, all human beings have reason, though few are capable of using reason as a guide to knowledge of God (2.11.30–31). On a basic level, even the senses can detect reason. The eye instinctively takes pleasure in something that is beautiful in the sense of being well fashioned and well proportioned according to reason. The ear takes pleasure in rationally ordered harmonies. The sense of taste recognizes when a potion prepared by a doctor is reasonably sweet or bitter (2.11.32–33). When we recognize and take pleasure in things in this way, our senses are not reasoning about what is reasonable or attempting to decide whether their impression of it is true or likely, but they are rather responding directly to a stimulus. A modern epistemologist might say that they are assenting to the reasonableness of what they are encountering.

A passage from Augustine's *On Order* offers what may be another example of assent. It is worth quoting in full:

> Let us suppose that two travelers are journeying to the same place; that one of them is very credulous [*nimis credulus*], and that the other has resolved to believe nobody [*nulli credere*]. When they arrive at a crossroad, the credulous man says to a shepherd or a rustic of some kind, who happens to be there: "Hey, my good man, which is the right road to that place?" He receives this answer: "If you travel by this road, you will not go astray." Then he says to his companion, "This man is telling the truth: let us go this way." The latter smiles, and very facetiously ridicules him for having assented so readily [*tam cito assensum*]. Then, while one proceeds on his journey, the other stands still at the crossroad until his prolonged delay begins to occasion him embarrassment. Now, behold! From another branch of the highway a neatly dressed and urbane man on horseback comes into view; and our man rejoices because this stranger is approaching. He greets the new arrival, informs him of his purpose, and makes inquiry about the road. Esteeming this man more highly than the shepherd, and wishing to win his favor, he tells him of the reason of his delay. But the horseman happened to be one of those who are commonly called *Samardaci*; and the rascal spontaneously followed his usual practice: "Go this way," he said, "for I am now coming from that place." He deceived his inquirer, and went away. But how could that inquirer be deceived? "I do not," he says, "accept that information as something true: I accept it as truth-like. And since it is neither fitting nor profitable to be here idle, I shall take that road." Meanwhile the other traveler has already been refreshed at the place for which they had set out, although he had erred by giving assent when he so readily believed that the words of the shepherd were true. But this one is now wandering around a forest of some

kind, although he has avoided error by following the probable. In fact, he has not yet found anyone who even knows the place to which he had purposed to go. (3.15.42 [Kavanagh])

This story is told to criticize a view, held by early imperial New Academics, that it is appropriate to act on the probability that something is true (i.e., to give it credence), even though one may be wrong. Augustine's elaborate scenario, however, reveals much more than just his objection to this view. The first traveler thinks that the rustic he has questioned is telling him the truth. He seems to have no particular reason for this view, since there is no sign that he knows the rustic. Nor is the rustic described in such a way as to suggest that he is especially likely to be telling the truth. To say, therefore, that the traveler has come to an outright belief that the man is telling the truth, or even that he has decided that what he says is plausible and gives it credence, seems to exaggerate his reasoning process. It seems more likely that he is simply assenting to what the man says in the absence of obvious grounds for something stronger. The second traveler clearly gives credence to what he is told by the urbane horseman. He knows that he cannot be sure the man is telling the truth, but he decides that what he has been told is credible and worth taking a risk on. As it turns out, the first traveler is right to believe the rustic, suggesting that, for Augustine, assent has a role to play in the operation of reason and the search for truth.

Augustine takes a high view of authority, especially that of the Scriptures and the church's teaching, and often says that we can take on authority things of which we cannot know the truth. In *On the Teacher* (11.36), for example, he affirms that we can *accipere* and *credere* stories that we have been told, such as that of the three youths in the fiery furnace (Dan 3:1–30). As in its usage in the response of the first traveler to the rustic, the verb *accipere* here implies the giving of assent rather than credence or belief, since the truth of the story cannot be proven, but Augustine recognizes assent as a valid starting point for the seeker after divine truth.[16]

In *On the Advantage of Believing*—written in the hope of converting his friend Honoratus from Manichaeism to Christianity—Augustine aims to show Honoratus (1.2) that Manichees are wrong to claim that *fides* is imposed on Christians in lieu of reason. It is, however, reasonable and appropriate for people who are not ready "to gaze on that truth which is seen by a pure mind" to "follow" (*sequi*) the

---

16. Though given that it is part of the Scriptures, other parts of which Augustine thinks have been proven true by later events, this story may also be heard as credible by association. The use of *accipere* may point us in that direction in itself but not necessarily so, since although it usually means "accept" without any necessary implication of debate or reasoning, the verb can also mean "interpret" with the aid of reason.

Augustine on Faith

authority of the catholic faith (in the sense of both the church and its teachings) and, by *credere*, to be strengthened and prepared for the God who illuminates humanity. This is a subtle and productively broad characterization of the early stages of Christian *fides*. Augustine does not present *fides* as a risk or as unreasoning. He affirms the catholic faith as something that unilluminated people might, on the basis of their everyday cognitive capacities, think worth following.[17] He does not suggest, though, that their thinking amounts to outright belief, based on reasons, that the Scriptures are true, or even that it amounts to credence based on thinking that they are likely to be true. As in the case in *On the Teacher*, the propositional "following" of the faithful looks more like assent to something not yet proven or even not yet understood.

In other passages, however, Augustine clearly thinks that the faithful can exercise something stronger than either assent or credence. Near the end of *On the Advantage of Believing*, he lists several other bases for *fides* (17.35). Past prophecies have been fulfilled; miracles have been performed; the apostles have undertaken great journeys to bring people to God; the martyrs have been so strengthened by their faith that they were able to die for God; the saints have lived exemplary lives; the catholic church has been acknowledged by the whole human race. All these attest to the help that God has given to humanity, which has been "so profitable and fruitful" for it.[18] The fulfillment of prophecy (according to Christian interpretations of the Jewish Scriptures) had long been regarded by Christians as proof of the truth of the church's teaching and hence its outright believability. Earlier writers had also argued that the apostles, martyrs, and saints could not have lived and died as they did, if what they put their faith in had not been true, while miracles, if not faked, are generally treated as reliable indicators of supernatural or divine power.[19] All these are therefore well-established arguments for believing

---

17. Augustine also thinks (and argues at length in *On Christian Teaching*) that the Scriptures can be read using ordinary, though educated, human reason, and that we do not need to inquire into the nature of everything, as early Greek philosophers did, in order to have an adequate faith (3.9). See Mark Boespflug, "Is Augustinian Faith Rational?," *Religious Studies* 52 (2016): 63–79, who rightly observes that Augustine has good reasons within everyday rationality for believing Christian testimony (i.e., traditional teaching).

18. According to *Ver. rel.* 25.46, God's will for humanity is brought to human attention through history, and in general, history (past or future) is more a matter of *credere* than *intellegere*. At 25.47 Augustine suggests that miracles work by raising human consciousness from temporal to eternal realities.

19. It was well recognized in the ancient world that miracles could be faked. Interestingly, the genuineness of the miracles of Jesus and his followers is almost never disputed, though the source of their power occasionally is (e.g., Matt 12:24 // Mark 3:22; Mark 9:34 // Luke 11:15). At *Ver. rel.* 25.47, however, Augustine says that miracles no longer occur now that the catholic

outright that the church's teaching is true, and they furnish the type of evidence or proof that people tend to think is good enough for more than assent or credence in everyday life. There is no real doubt that some sort of outright belief that disposes the believer to embrace and rely on it is what Augustine is commending here.

On Faith in the Unseen makes a similar point using an example from daily life. Comparing *fides* toward God with *fides* between friends, Augustine observes that you cannot see into your friend's heart, so you cannot be certain that he is not planning to deceive you. But you *credere* in him because you have tried his worth in bad times, and he has stood by you. You might take your friend's track record as a basis to assent to his *fides* or as a reason to think it likely that he will prove believable or trustworthy in the future. But as in the previous example, Augustine points to more than this. By taking past behavior as evidence of stable character, we regularly come to outright beliefs about friends who have been tested by time and circumstances, such that we are disposed to rely on them for the future, and the same is true in our relationship with God.

In these passages Augustine does not, as Clement might have done, suggest that, or how, the faithful might progress from *fides* in the sense of assent to *fides* in the sense of credence or outright belief. He does, however, indicate that assent and belief, at least, are both acceptable starting points for understanding (although the example of the two travelers indicates that he is less keen on credence). It may be that some of the faithful are capable of progressing from assent to belief, but Augustine also seems to recognize that some people (notably his mother, Monnica; see e.g., *Conf.* 9.10.24) can attain sanctity through assent to (or, as we will see, trust in) authority alone.[20] It may therefore be nearer to the mark to see Augustine as recognizing that faith encompasses more than one propositional attitude and that faithful people can appropriately exercise propositional faith in different ways according to their capacities.[21]

COMPLICATING THE PROPOSITIONAL

In none of these writings, however, is faith, for Augustine, a propositional attitude alone. Let us return to the two travelers. The first, as we saw, can be seen

---

church has spread throughout the world to ensure that the faithful do not continue to look for visible signs of God's power.

20. Cf. *Beat.* 2.10; *Ord.* 1.2.32; 2.1.1; *Lib.* 2.5.

21. Their capacities could, on this view, include differences in education and differences in intellectual ability but probably not differences in moral capacity, since elsewhere Augustine clearly thinks that all the faithful are capable of doing good.

as assenting to the directions of the rustic. The second is a more sophisticated thinker, who gives credence to the urbane horseman's directions on the basis that the man seems credible and that he must choose one road or the other. But Augustine also tells us that the second traveler admires the urbane horseman and rejoices to see him, so he is emotionally invested in the interaction. And he wants the man to take a favorable view of him before he gives advice. According to a classic definition of relational trust, he wants to be able to hold "confident positive expectations regarding another's conduct," on the basis that the man is both well informed and well disposed toward him.[22] As it turns out, however, the urbane man is deliberately untrustworthy and so is his testimony. Although Augustine does not discuss here whether emotion and trust are problematic in themselves or only when they are directed at the wrong objects, the role of both in relation to propositional attitudes will recur in his writings.

In *On the Advantage of Believing*, we saw how Augustine sought to show Honoratus that it is reasonable for people who are not ready to "gaze on . . . truth" to "follow" (*sequi*) the authority of the catholic faith. *Sequi* is an interesting choice of word, since one can follow a teaching or tradition but also a person, and both traditions and persons can have authority. Augustine allows readers to infer that the authority of the catholic faith inheres both in its teachings and in those who transmit it, and later he affirms this reading by describing catholic teaching as having flowed down to the faithful from Christ, through the apostles (8.20). Both kinds of authority can bring people to *credere*, so *credere* here encompasses both a propositional attitude to authority and relational trust in it.[23]

Credere, Augustine insists (9.22), is nothing to do with *credulitas*, which is indeed unreasoning. What is more, if it is wrong to *credere* anything (10.23), then it is wrong to *credere* a friend (as he takes it as self-evident we should), and if you do not do that, then your friend is not really your friend, nor are you a friend to them. This is a significant shift of emphasis, because we might believe our friends when they tell us something, and we might also give them credence or assent to something they say without knowing if it is true. But we also trust them, and many people would say that they believe or give credence to their friends *because* they

---

22. Roy J. Lewicki, Daniel J. McAllister, and Robert Bies, "Trust and Distrust: New Relationships and Realities," *Academy of Management Review* 22 (1998): 439.

23. James Bielby, "The Relationship between Faith and Evidence in Saint Augustine," *Sophia* 41 (2002): 25–27, underlines the double role of believing the authority of evidence-based teachings and trusting in the authority of Christ in faith. The dependence of the authority of the content of teaching on persons is discussed by Basil Studer, "History and Faith in Augustine's *De Trinitate*," *AugStud* 28 (1997): 14–17.

trust them.[24] This gives trust a role at the root of other forms of *credere* in human relations. It also hints that *fides* is not only propositional and relational but also emotional. Friendship is, in part, something we feel, so our trust in our friends is, at least, closely related to emotion.[25]

Augustine foresees, however, that Honoratus will still want to know how it can be right to *credere* without knowledge in matters of piety (*religio*). He replies by again underlining the human aspect of *credere* in religious matters (10.23). He claims that it is not wrong to *credere* someone who hands a tradition on to you. Imagine, he says, that you come to someone seeking to receive a tradition. You will want to convince the potential donor that your attitude to what you want to acquire is positive and sincere. Suppose the donor says, "I believe you [*credo tibi*; i.e., I believe that you are sincere and are telling the truth]. Is it not therefore fair that you should believe me [*nonne est aeqius ut etiam tu credas mihi*], since if I hold anything of the truth, I am going to give it to you, and you, by accepting it, are going to get the benefit?"

The donor may want to be able to trust the recipient, but primarily he apparently wants to be able to believe that the recipient is sincere. To believe, however, that the donor is handing on the tradition he wants to receive and as he wants to receive it, the recipient needs to believe that the donor is trustworthy as well as truthful, so trust is involved as well as belief. (It seems likely that belief is involved here rather than assent, for instance, since the recipient seeks what he seeks on the basis that it is truth and is expected to rely on it for some benefit.) The role of trust is underlined further when the donor points out that the recipient is going to get *beneficium* from what he receives. One key aspect of trust, as defined by modern philosophers and psychologists, is that we trust people in the belief (or hope, trust, reliance etc.) that they both can and will do something or give us something that we want or need.[26] This kind of *confidere*, Augustine says (10.24), which involves belief and trust, may not be better in principle than being given proofs about God, but it is very practical because most people are not capable of grasping the arguments that lead the human mind to understanding of the divine.

Augustine returns to the theme of relational *credere* a little later (12.26), arguing that if it is wrong to *credere* something one does not know, then children

---

24. One might also say that one trusts a friend because one believes what they say, which may seem to lead to an infinite regress of trust and belief, but, in fact, trust in a person can end such a regress, unlike trust in the evidence of words and actions, which cannot (Morgan, *New Testament*, 210–11).

25. On whether πίστις/*fides* is understood as an emotion or rather is closely linked with a number of emotions, see Morgan, *Roman Faith*, 117–55.

26. E.g., Russell Hardin, *Trust* (Oxford: Polity, 2006), 16–18.

84

Augustine on Faith

cannot obey their parents and love them in mutual familial piety (*mutua pietate*) without *credere* (e.g., believing, giving credence or assent to the idea, or even trusting propositionally) that they are their parents.[27] Reason, however, cannot tell a child who their parents are. Children *credere* what they do about their father on the authority of their mother, and what they *credere* about their mother on the authority of midwives, nurses, and slaves. Here, trust is even more important than in the previous example, not only because trust is widely taken for granted as one of the fundamental relationships between family members, but also because parentage is, notoriously, something about which mistakes are sometimes made and lies are sometimes told. To believe or give credence to those who tell you who your parents are, or just to assume that they are right, you therefore have to trust them to be well informed, well intentioned, and trustworthy.[28] Here, the propositional attitude in play (it is not clear which one it is) is deeply involved with and even dependent on personal trust. Trust, moreover, is, once again, closely entwined with emotion, this time the emotion of familial love.

In a final passage on why it is reasonable to *credere* the teachings of the catholic church (17.35), Augustine, as we saw above, invokes several other bases for *fides*, including the fulfillment of prophecy, the evidence of miracles, and so on. These arguments were all regarded as strong in Augustine's day, and it comes as no surprise that he includes them. But in the rest of the book, it is notable how much more interested he is in approaching the credibility of the catholic faith by thinking about how tradition is intertwined with the people who practice it and hand it on; how *fides* in that tradition is a matter of trust in people as much as, or even more than, belief or assent is to teaching; and how authority is not simply something possessed and unquestioningly accepted but is rather something expressed and given even as it is received.[29] In this (though Augustine does not make this point), the catholic faith and the faithful person's relationship with it are structurally very like Godself in communication with humanity and humanity's

---

27. No doubt we generally believe that it is true that our parents are our parents, but for everyday purposes it would presumably be enough to assent or give credence to the claim or to trust it propositionally, especially as we are already in the relationship. This distinguishes this example from the previous one, in which we need stronger belief to receive a tradition. Since, however, when Augustine talks about belief, he seems most often to mean outright belief, this may be what Augustine intends in both examples.

28. Morgan, *Roman Faith*, 39–45.

29. *Beat.* 1.4 may subtly distinguish this trust from what, in retrospect, Augustine thinks happened when he became a Manichee. He says that "I persuaded myself that it was better to submit to men who teach rather than those who give orders" (i.e., he submitted to his teachers rather than trusted them).

85

relationship with God. In each case, human beings have to choose to acknowledge either the authority of God or the church and to entrust themselves either to God or the church as well as to believe.

PROPOSITIONAL AND RELATIONAL *FIDES* IN OTHER WRITINGS

Augustine comes back to our relationships with parents and friends in *Confessions* (6.5.7) and *On Faith in the Unseen* (2–4). At *Conf.* 6.5.7 he adds doctors to the list of people we *credere* when they give us advice.[30] If we did not *credere*, he observes, we would never act; the point of both belief and trust is to act on them and to commit oneself to something or someone. This passage follows Augustine's reminiscence that, before his conversion, he wanted to be as certain about things he could not see as he was certain that seven plus three equals ten (6.10.6). He could, he says, have been healed by *credere*, which would have purified his mind's eye and directed it toward God's truth. But just as a person who has had a bad experience of a doctor is reluctant to entrust himself (*se committere*) to a good one, so it was with his soul. Undoubtedly Augustine comes to believe that certain things are true about God, and this contributes to his conversion. But he emphasizes that it is when he shifts from thinking of assent to divine truth as assent to things like mathematical proofs to thinking of it as more like *fides* toward a person that the way is opened for him to *credere* in the Lord, and it is when he allows God to touch his heart "with a most gentle and merciful hand" that he begins to *credere*. It is to relational trust, as much as anything else, that he owes his conversion.

Elsewhere in *Confessions* (10.5.7) Augustine speaks of the faithfulness of God, reminding his listeners that neither trust nor belief is the first move in the divine-human relationship. Jewish and Christian Scripture and tradition speak of the πίστις of God toward God's people, and they take for granted that God's trustworthiness and faithfulness are the starting point for humanity's πίστις/*fides* toward God.[31] Augustine only rarely affirms God's *fides* or *fidelitas*, preferring to speak of God's grace, care, or love.[32] We can assume, however, that he follows scrip-

---

30. Outright belief, rather than assent or credence, is probably involved here, since the patient believes in the doctor's knowledge and expertise with a view to committing him or herself (*se committere*) to the doctor's care. Augustine often refers to God as divine physician; see e.g., *Ver. rel.* 24.45; *Ord.* 1.8.23–24; *Solil.* 1.2.4, 13, 23.

31. E.g., LXX of Deut 7:9; 32:4; Ps 144(145):13; Rom 3:3; 2 Cor 1:18; 1 Thess 5:24.

32. Though he does refer to the "documents of God worthy of trust" (e.g., *Trin.* 14.15.21) written by the prophets, which implies the trustworthiness of Godself as well as that of the prophets and the writings.

Augustine on Faith

tural precedent in taking for granted that God is also *fidelis* to humanity, and that humanity's *fides* is not only a quality of human beings restlessly searching for something they do not know but also a response to God's primary trustworthiness and faithfulness to them.

At *Fid.* 1.2–2.3, as we saw above, Augustine adds to his characterization of relationships with friends by saying that people *credere* in their friends, even though they cannot see into their hearts, because they have proved steadfast in bad times. Experience is not knowledge of another person's heart, but it is a good proxy and makes it reasonable to entrust yourself to her or him (*te committeres*) when you are in danger.[33] We may even say of this kind of friendship that we have such *fides* that even though we cannot really see the truth of our friendship, we judge that, and behave as if, we can. Insofar as *fides* toward one's friends is an analogue of *fides* toward God, this image adds something to the analogies in *On the Advantage of Believing* and *Confessions*. Our personal trust and willingness to believe that our friend wills our good, combined with our experience of our friend's behavior through time, brings us to a certainty that, though it is not sight of the truth hidden in our friend's heart, is a good proxy for it in this life. Similarly, trust in God, the church, and the faithful, combined with willingness to believe in teaching and tradition and experience of history, may bring us to a certainty that is not a direct vision of God but is a good proxy for it in this life. Trust and belief combine and, through time, strengthen and justify each other.

Augustine's interest in the relationship between the elements of *fides* and *credere* is also detectable in a number of passages about Jesus Christ in his earthly life as the incarnate Wisdom or Word of God. In *On the Teacher*, Augustine argues that signs and words in themselves cannot show people realities in such a way that they can know them (11.36). We cannot even recognize a word until we know what it signifies, because it has no meaning except as a sign of something else.[34] We can, however, *accipere* and *credere* things we are told, such as the story of the three young men in the fiery furnace (11.37), even though we know we cannot know the truth of them.

When we do understand something, it is not because of the external sound of the words, but because the truth is in us. The truth that is in us is Christ (11.38), who is the power and wisdom of God and "lives in the inner man" (cf. Eph 3:14–17). Christ is the light that shines on visible objects and shows them to us according

---

33. Belief here is again likely to be outright belief, since it acts as a proxy for knowledge.

34. The argument is set out by Luis H. Mackey, "The Mediator Mediated: Faith and Reason in Augustine's '*De Magistro*,'" *Franciscan Studies* 42 (1982): 135–55, though he focuses on the propositional aspect of faith in signs rather than its relational aspect of trust in Christ (142–45).

to our ability to see them. Presumably, receiving Christ into oneself occurs primarily when one commits oneself to Christ at baptism, or when one receives the Holy Spirit (at baptism or at another time), so it is *fides* above all in the relational sense that makes possible illumination from within and turns *credere* into understanding.[35] In this passage, Augustine's use of *accipere* with *credere* suggests that he is thinking of human beings' starting point as assent rather than outright belief, perhaps because he envisages the *fides* of most people before their reception of Christ as inchoate if not naive. Once people have put their trust in the exalted Christ, however, Christ illuminates them from within and turns *fides* into understanding.

In book 4 of *On the Trinity*, this idea is developed further. Human beings, weighed down by the dirt of their sins, have been incapable of grasping eternal realities (4.18.24). They can, moreover, only be purified and adapted to eternal things by temporal means. The beginning of this process is *fides* in temporal things (*fides temporalibus*). *Fides* here could be either propositional or relational, but both are likely to be involved, since Augustine has just referred to human beings' relationship with temporal things both as relational love and as an activity (whether belief, credence, or assent) of the *mens rationalis*. What need to change are both human beings' understanding and their attachment. *Fides* purifies us in order that we may eventually come to sight and truth.[36] In order for this to happen, however, Truth itself, coeternal with the Father, came and took on our mortality, "so that he might capture our *fides* and through it draw us to his truth."[37] The idea that Christ personally captures the *fides* of (other) human beings has a strong resonance of relational trust. At the same time, the idea that through his action *fides* comes to see the truth has a resonance of propositional assent or belief. Here, as he often does, Augustine neither specifies nor makes as clear as modern philosophers would want to do whether it is assent or belief that he has in mind. However, the fact that he is talking about a relationship between Christ and those whose *fides* he captures allows us to speculate that he could have both in mind. Some of the faithful, say, might only be capable of assent, others might be able to move from assent to outright belief, and still others might be capable of belief from the beginning. By not defining propositional *fides* tightly, Augustine leaves open the possibility that people may arrive at truth via more than one

---

35. Ayres, "Augustine on the Rule of Faith," 152–55 points out that in the gospels, Christ also points *fides* away from himself in his earthly life toward contemplation of the divine and union with it.

36. At which point, for Augustine, we will no longer need faith; see below, p. 90.

37. A similar idea is expressed at *Ver. rel.* 24.45.

propositional attitude. Whatever the propositional attitude of those who come to faith, however, the point of this image—and the point of the incarnation—for Augustine is again that both the propositional and the relational are necessarily involved. By being human with humanity and encouraging humanity, as Augustine says, to follow him to where he has ascended—where we will be able to contemplate truth—Christ exploits humanity's capacity for both relational and propositional *fides*. In doing so, Christ brings human beings to God not only in their intellect but also, as Augustine repeatedly emphasizes throughout his writings, in their whole trusting, loving, and working person.[38]

FIDEISM, FAILURE, AND OTHER ASPECTS OF FAITH

Perfect *fides qua*, says Augustine in a sermon on Luke 18 (*Serm.* 115.1), is scarcely to be found on this earth. Everyone's faith can be increased, and everyone must guard against failure. Augustine shares this view with virtually all early Christian writers, who often use Jesus's disciples as an example of imperfect human faith that, by growth, eventually triumphs over adversity and evil.[39] For Augustine, faith is strengthened especially by prayer (65.1; 115.1) and practice (216.6).[40] For many early Christian writers, although their main concern is not usually to distinguish which aspects of faith are at stake, the biblical passages that they make use of, and the contexts in which they write, nevertheless suggest that they often have in mind both relational trust (when, for instance, the faithful are encouraged to follow the disciples in imitating Jesus's πίστις toward God) and belief (when, for instance, they are encouraged to imitate the disciples' response to the risen Christ).

In another respect, however, Augustine probably moves away from earlier Christian understandings of divine-human πίστις/*fides*. Though it is not certain, there is some reason to think that for Paul and his followers, for instance, πίστις was not only a means by which people could come into their right relationship with God but was also constitutive of that relationship in eternal life. Πίστις is one of a cluster of attitudes and practices that describe the relationship of those

---

38. Cf. e.g., *Serm.* 144.2, which notes that personal *credere* in Christ is not the same as believing things about Christ, which even devils do. See also *Serm.* 29.6 on John. *Enchir.* 31.117 borrows from the relational language of Matt 7:7 // Luke 11:9 to describe faith with love as asking so that it may be given what it does not have, and knocking so that the door may be opened to it.

39. E.g., Origen, *Comm. Matt.* 11.5 (cf. Augustine, *Serm.* 75.4); Cyril of Alexandria, *Comm. in Luc. hom.* 113 (on Luke 17:5); John Chrysostom, *Hom. Gen.* 65.19.

40. On Augustine's treatment of perseverance see Katharina Greschat, *"Perseverantia,"* in Mayer, *Augustinus-Lexikon,* 4:689–93.

who have been made righteous and live with at least one foot in the new creation, which is a foretaste of life in God's kingdom.[41] Paul's portrait of life in the community of the faithful resonates both with visions of the messianic age and with contemporary gentile visions of golden ages, past or future, in which πίστις/*fides*, alongside justice and peace, is imagined as characterizing social relationships and practices. For Augustine, however, the human attitude of *fides*—whether characterized as trust, belief, assent, or something else—is a stepping stone to higher things. He expects it, together with hope, to fall away when the faithful come to sight of God and truth (e.g., *Trin.* 4.18.24), leaving only knowledge and love.

In *Against the Academics*, with which we began this essay, Augustine defends the possibility of knowledge against New Academic skepticism and, in the scenario we discussed, argues that it is not good enough to exercise one's own reason and be wrong; it is vitally important to be right. Throughout his writings, Augustine passionately defends the truth of what he, Christians in general, or, in his controversialist works, members of the catholic church believe. This, not unreasonably, has suggested to generations of commentators that Augustine understands *fides qua* as outright (true) belief. This essay has argued that he is equally interested in the trust aspect of *fides qua*. We have also noted that, in some passages, his use of *fides* in a propositional sense may be understood as "assent," in the sense in which contemporary epistemologists use it to mean intellectual acceptance of a proposition in the absence of reasoned proof or an intuition of its truth. This understanding of *fides*, however, does not amount to fideism in the modern sense of an attitude of "faith" that is independent of reason or even adversarial to it.[42] For Augustine, it is always right that we exercise our reason as far as we can in the trust, hope, belief, and confidence that when we see God face to face, we will fully know and understand what now we can only, as a starting point, trust in, assent to, believe, and reason about within human limits. It need not surprise us that Augustine is not a fideist. Reason and knowledge are treated somewhat differently by different theologians, especially in the fourth century,

---

41. Teresa Morgan, *Being 'in Christ' in the Letters of Paul: Saved through Christ and in His Hands* (Tübingen: Mohr Siebeck, 2020), 207–8, 210–15. They also include justice, grace, peace, freedom, holiness, truth, and hope.

42. Richard Amesbury, "Fideism," in *The Stanford Encyclopedia of Philosophy*, last revised February 5, 2022, https://plato.stanford.edu/archives/spr2022/entries/fideism/. *Epistle* 119 from Consentius to Augustine suggests that some Christians may have been fideists in something like the modern sense. Augustine in response affirms that it is good and natural to employ reason in the search for truth, even if understanding God is impossible in this life (*Ep.* 120.2, 3–4; cf. *Ord.* 2.5.15, *Acad.* 3.20.43; see also *Ord.* 2.9.26, where *fides* and reliance on authority are not enough to lead one to truth).

Augustine on Faith

but, despite the slurs of Christianity's opponents and some well-known misreadings of Tertullian, Christian writers up to the fifth century are not fideists.

Our main interest in this essay has been how *fides* works in a person who has the capacity for it, rather than whether Augustine changes his mind mid-career as to whether *fides* is voluntary or even whether the capacity for *fides* is a gift from God.[43] It is worth noting, however, that Augustine is consistent in affirming that no one can "call on" Christ (cf. Rom 10:14) or commit to him or "become subject to God" before hearing and accepting the teaching about God and Christ.[44] Even the God-given capacity for *fides* does not operate in the absence of specifically Christian teaching; one cannot come to know God without being shown the way. Nor can one come to know God by any way other than that of Christ.

We noted above that Augustine inherited a tradition of baptism in which baptizands affirm that they πιστεύειν/*credere* in God (in both a relational and a propositional sense) as Father, Son, and Holy Spirit.[45] Throughout his writings, moreover, when Augustine speaks of *fides/credere* toward God, we can take for granted that it is the Triune God that he has in mind. That said, though Augustine sometimes speaks of *fides/credere* specifically toward God the Father or Jesus Christ as Savior, he rarely, if ever, refers to *fides/credere* specifically toward the Holy Spirit.[46] In this, though it may seem surprising to modern readers, Augustine is conventional among his contemporaries and earlier Christians. It is rare for the Holy Spirit to be referred to as an object of faith independently of the Father and the Son. One reason may be that it is rare, in literary or visual contexts, for the Spirit to be anthropomorphized.[47] Another may be that when Augustine speaks of

43. The view of Harrison, *Rethinking Augustine's Early Theology*, 136–39, that this is one of the areas in which Augustine's thought changes less than has usually been assumed is now widely accepted.

44. E.g., *Serm.* 56.1; *Fid. symb.* 10.25 (by *credere* the faithful become subject to God).

45. E.g., at Acts 8.37, in an interpolation first attested by Irenaeus (*Haer.* 3.12.8), the Ethiopian eunuch asks to be baptized by the apostle Philip. Philip replies, "if you πιστεύειν with your whole heart, you may," which could imply trust, belief, or both. But the eunuch then affirms, in different textual variants, either, "I believe that Jesus Christ is the Son of God," or, "I believe in Jesus Christ [who is] the Son of God," articulating both trust and belief (and, in the first variant, foregrounding belief). Other early baptismal formulae, such as that in the reconstructed *Apostolic Tradition* (21.11–18), are phrased to foreground πιστεύειν/*credere* in its meaning of trust and self-commitment, while including in each article matters of belief about God the Father, Jesus Christ the Son, and the Holy Spirit.

46. At the time of writing, I have not found an example.

47. The early Christian writer who most often refers to trusting the Spirit is John Chrysostom, though he does not do so often (e.g., *Hom. Jo.* 26.2; *Hom. Heb.* 19.2; *Ep.* 1.2). Depiction of the Spirit in human form remains rare but do occur in later Christian art (the Rublev Icon is a famous

faith as an attitude and practice, in particular, he most often refers to it in relation to God as creator and source of all being or to Christ as Savior, Son of God, and incarnate Word. In part, this is probably an inheritance from the New Testament Epistles and Gospels, where πίστις is most often πίστις toward Christ as Son of God and Savior, but given the atmosphere of intense debate about the Trinity in which Augustine worked, and his own deep interest in it, it is still striking.

CONCLUSION

Augustine inherited a complex landscape of both Christian and everyday conceptions of *fides*, *credere*, and related terms. He takes a particular interest in the attitude of faith in some of his earlier works, up to around the time of the composition of *On the Trinity*. This is partly because his targets in some of these works are Manichees or pagan philosophers along with their treatment of reason and their negative view of (catholic) Christian faith. It may also be because he finds food for thought in his own relatively recent experience of coming to faith.

Modern philosophers, psychologists, and social scientists alike see trust as a risk, one we take in the belief, hope, and assumption *vel similia* that it will turn out well for us. Origen, as we saw, is unusual among Christian philosophers in recognizing the riskiness of trust. For Augustine, however, trust is no kind of risk, because the goodness, power, and love of God are axiomatic, and no existence outside relationship with God brings knowledge of God or eternal life.

Given his interest in Platonism and admiration of earlier Platonist Christian theologians, we are not surprised to find Augustine interested in the belief aspect of *fides* and (although this has not been the focus of this essay) the relationship between belief, reason, and knowledge.[48] Following the lead of modern epistemologists and pistologists, we have noted that *fides* might encompass more than one form of belief and also a number of other attitudes—such as credence, assumption, acceptance, and assent. We have also proposed that Augustine's interest in the propositional is probably in either assent or outright belief. In most of the passages we have examined, however, Augustine is just as interested in the rela-

---

example); see also Louisa Twining, *Symbols and Emblems of Early and Medieval Art*, new ed. (London: Murray, 1885), pl. 32 fig. 1 with p. 66.

48. Augustine never answers the question of Laurence at the beginning of the *Enchiridion* concerning what lies outside the scope of reason and belongs solely to *fides* (in any sense), but he would surely have said it was the wrong question (e.g., to exercise a God-given faculty, assent to something and test the consequences, or trust and *credere* in God, as in your parents, are all reasonable).

tional dimension of *fides/credere*: "faith" as trust together with trustworthiness and faithfulness. This interest in trust is often revealed in his choice of examples, illustrations, or metaphors of faith. Although it has attracted periodic mentions in the scholarly literature, it has received little discussion. Given Augustine's interest in Platonism, it comes as something of a surprise, and it is particularly striking how much more positive Augustine is about trust than is Origen.[49]

One might wonder at this point whether Augustine's treatment of relational *fides* is distinctively Latin and Western, in a line extending perhaps from Tertullian, Cyprian, or Ambrose. Investigating that side of Augustine's inheritance is beyond the scope of this essay, but, as it happens, I doubt Augustine's treatment of relational *fides* owes a great deal to Cyprian or Ambrose, both of whom have much to say about *fides* as loyalty (by individuals or groups) to the church and church leaders but rather less about individual trust in God. Tertullian does use *fides* fairly frequently to mean individual trust and self-commitment to God, following the earliest Christian usage, but there is little sign in the passages discussed that Augustine is drawing self-consciously on a relational reading of πίστις/*fides* language found in first- or second-century Christian writings. It seems at least as likely that he is drawing on his own experience and perhaps also on his experience as a pastor. If his interest in trust does have partly pastoral roots, it is worth noting that he is well in line with his contemporaries in this respect. Across fourth-century Christian writings, πίστις/*fides* is most often referred to as an attitude when the faithful are being told in letters, sermons, or catechetical lectures to remain faithful (in both attitude and works), to imitate Christ's faithfulness to God, to grow in faith, and not to backslide. We also find similar πίστις/*fides* language on tombstones from this period that celebrated the deceased for having remained faithful to death.[50]

Trust in God, for Augustine, is an appropriate response to God's *fidelitas* to humanity, that is, to God's love and grace expressed above all in the Christ event and to the "most gentle and merciful hand" with which God touches the heart of

---

49. Note the contrast here between Augustine and the Cappadocians, who are much less interested in πίστις in general (especially relational πίστις) than Augustine, and more concerned with knowledge.

50. E.g., for πίστις/*fides* concerning remaining faithful, see Cyprian, *Ep.* 5.1–2; 7.5, 7; 10.1; Athanasius, *Ep. fest.* 10.6; Chromatius, *In Matt.* 18.4.1–2. For πίστις/*fides* concerning growth in faith, see Origen, *Cant.* 3.5; *Comm. Matt.* 11.5; Augustine, *Serm.* 65.1. For πίστις/*fides* concerning faith and works, see Leo, *Serm.* 38.5; Jerome, *Comm. Gal.* 2.3.11; Gregory of Nyssa, *Hom. Eccl.* 8; Augustine, *Serm.* 90.4. For πίστις/*fides* regarding the imitation of Christ, see Pol. *Phil.* 10.1; Clement of Alexandria, *Strom.* 4.151.1; Gregory of Nyssa, *Or. cat.* 24; Pelagius, *Ep. ad Claudiam* 19. For tombstones with πίστις/*fides* language, see, e.g., *ICUR* 4.9558; *CIG* 9620.

the struggling non-Christian. It remains an appropriate part of the response of the faithful to God until the time (in this life or another) when the faithful person can see God face to face. Trust is an equally appropriate response to Christ, who comes into the world to "capture our *fides*," and by receiving whom the faithful receive the Wisdom of God and begin to understand Truth. Trust is part of the attitude of the faithful when they affirm that they *credere* in the three persons of the Trinity at baptism and regularly thereafter. It is part of the attitude of the faithful toward the church, tradition, and orthodox teaching, all three of which are embodied by leaders and exemplars of "the faith" and passed on by them to the next generation. Even Augustine's thinking about institutions and institutional authority is colored by his sense of the importance of relational trust.

We have noted that whether trust is an emotion in Greek or Roman thinking is debated, and Augustine is no more explicit about this than other ancient authors. When, however, he talks about *fides* as an aspect of friendship or family love, or when he tells his congregation that, as faithful people, they should, like David, dance for joy in the Lord (*Enarrat. Ps.* 32.3–4), he leaves it open to readers to understand *fides* as having an emotional dimension. An awareness of its emotional aspect may even have contributed something to his interest in relational *fides*, given his deep interest in love and in other emotions that either help or hinder the faithful in their relationship with God and their search for understanding.[51]

Discussion of Augustine's treatment of *fides qua* has tended to form part of discussions about his view of reason and knowledge and his debt to philosophy. It is equally part of his vivid sense of the personal relationship between God and the faithful and between the incarnate and exalted Christ and the faithful, and his understanding of how Christ brings people to their right relationship with God. As such, it is also closely related to his thinking about love and other emotions, prayer, worship, and ethical living. When he talks about *fides/credere*, Augustine is as much the explorer and pastor as the philosopher, using his own experience of coming to faith to develop his understanding, fostering trust and faithfulness in his congregations not least because it is an attitude and practice that all the faithful can share.

We observed at the beginning of this essay that trust, trustworthiness, and faithfulness are the dominant meanings of πίστις language in the earliest Christian writings. We cannot be sure why trust so quickly became so fundamental

---

51. Taking Augustine's positive language (e.g., *affectus, motus, affectio*) as emotional, alongside terms for emotion such as *passio, libido,* and *perturbatio,* which are often negatively marked. See the discussions of Anastasia Scrutton, "Emotion in Augustine of Hippo and Thomas Aquinas: A Way Forward for the Im/possibility Debate?," *International Journal of Systematic Theology* 7 (2005): 170–74; Catherine Conybeare, *The Irrational Augustine* (Oxford: Oxford University Press, 2006), 56–57, 70–71.

Augustine on Faith

to Christian thinking, but we can, in conclusion, make a few observations about the way it is used and why it is significant. In writings from the first century to Augustine's day, trust in God and Christ leads to healing, new life, and new hope, and it forges new and saving relationships and communities. In all these respects, early Christian understandings of trust strikingly pre-echo the understanding of modern philosophers, psychologists, and sociologists. The creation and maintenance of trust are widely recognized in contemporary scholarship as means of reintegrating ex-offenders into society; of restoring survivors of trauma to functional relationships and enabling them to look forward to a different future; of enabling everyone to make and maintain good relationships and to live in stable social groups.[52] Some psychologists emphasize that, even more fundamentally, without being able to trust and feel that one is trustworthy and trusted, people cannot develop a functional sense of self, let alone self-in relationship.[53] Without trust, modern scholarship argues from multiple perspectives, we cannot fully live as individuals or in relationships. From their very different perspectives, early Christians, including Augustine, would fully have agreed.

Works Cited

Amesbury, Richard. "Fideism." *The Stanford Encyclopedia of Philosophy*. Last revised February 5, 2022. https://plato.stanford.edu/archives/spr2022/entries/fideism/.

Armstrong, Ruth. "Trusting the Untrustworthy: The Theology, Practice and Implications of Faith-Based Volunteers' Work with Ex-Prisoners." *Studies in Christian Ethics* 27 (2014): 299–317.

Augustine. *Answer to Skeptics: A Translation of St Augustine's Contra Academicos*. Translated by Denis J. Kavanagh. New York: Cosmopolitan Science and Art Service, 1943.

---

52. E.g., Richard E. Serling, "Reclamation through Trust: A Program for Ex-Offenders," *Christian Century* (December 6, 2000): 1263–64, Ruth Armstrong, "Trusting the Untrustworthy: The Theology, Practice and Implications of Faith-Based Volunteers' Work with Ex-Prisoners," *Studies in Christian Ethics* 27 (2014): 299–317; Eric Y. Tenkorang, Adobea Y. Owusu, and Gubhinder Kundhi, "Help-Seeking Behavior of Female Victims of Intimate Partner Violence in Ghana: The Role of Trust and Perceived Risk of Injury," *Journal of Family Violence* 33 (2018): 341–53; "Learning to Trust Others," Help for Adult Victims Of Child Abuse, https://www.havoca.org/survivors/trust/trust-others/ (restoring survivors). See also Morgan, *Roman Faith*, 15–20 (surveying sociological approaches).

53. Especially Doris Brothers, *Falling Backwards: An Exploration of Trust and Self-Experience* (New York: Norton, 1995), 5–33, with a review of scholarship.

Ayres, Lewis. *Augustine and the Trinity*. Cambridge: Cambridge University Press, 2010.

———. "Augustine on the Rule of Faith: Rhetoric, Christology, and the Foundation of Christian Thinking." *AugStud* 36 (2005): 33–49.

Bavel, T. J. van. "De la raison à la foi: la conversion d'Augustin." *Augustiniana* 36 (1986): 5–27.

Bielby, James. "The Relationship between Faith and Evidence in Saint Augustine." *Sophia* 41 (2002): 19–32.

Boespflug, Mark. "Is Augustinian Faith Rational?" *Religious Studies* 52 (2016): 63–79.

Boone, Mark J. "Augustine and William James on the Rationality of Faith." *Heythrop Journal* 61 (2020): 648–59.

Brothers, Doris. *Falling Backwards: An Exploration of Trust and Self-Experience*. New York: Norton, 1995.

Conybeare, Catherine. *The Irrational Augustine*. Oxford: Oxford University Press, 2006.

Eklund, Timothy. "The Cognitive Aspect of Christian Faith and Non-doxastic Propositional Attitudes." *Neue Zeitschrift für systematische Theologie und Religionsphilosophie* 60 (2018): 386–405.

Fortin, Jean-Pierre. "Critical Theology, Committed Philosophy: Discovering Anew the Faith-Reason Dynamics with Origen of Alexandria and Augustine of Hippo." *Philosophy and Theology* 27 (2015): 25–54.

Greschat, Katharina. "*Perseverantia*." Pages 689–93 in vol. 4 of *Augustinus-Lexikon*. Edited by Cornelius Mayer. Basel: Schwabe, 2014.

Hällström, Gunnar af. *Fides Simpliciorum According to Origen of Alexandria*. Helsinki: Societas Scientiarum Fennica, 1984.

Hardin, Russell. *Trust*. Oxford: Polity, 2006.

Harrison, Carol. *Rethinking Augustine's Early Theology: An Argument for Continuity*. Oxford: Oxford University Press, 2006.

Kenney, John Peter. "Faith and Reason." Pages 275–91 in *The Cambridge Companion to Augustine*. Edited by David Vincent Meconi and Eleonore Stump. 2nd ed. Cambridge: Cambridge University Press, 2014.

Lewicki, Roy J., Daniel J. McAllister, and Robert Bies. "Trust and Distrust: New Relationships and Realities." *Academy of Management Review* 22 (1998): 438–58.

Lilla, Salvatore R. C. *Clement of Alexandria: A Study in Christian Platonism and Gnosticism*. Oxford: Oxford University Press, 1971.

Mackey, Louis H. "The Mediator Mediated: Faith and Reason in Augustine's '*De Magistro*.'" *Franciscan Studies* 42 (1982): 135–55.

Morgan, Teresa. *Being 'in Christ' in the Letters of Paul: Saved through Christ and in His Hands*. Tübingen: Mohr Siebeck, 2020.

———. *The New Testament and the Theology of Trust: 'This Rich Trust.'* Oxford: Oxford University Press, 2022.

―――. *Roman Faith and Christian Faith: Pistis and Fides in the Early Roman Empire and Early Churches.* Oxford: Oxford University Press, 2015.

Osborn, Eric. "Arguments for Faith in Clement of Alexandria." *VC* 48 (1994): 1–24.

Roy, Olivier du. *L'intelligence de la foi en la trinité selon Saint Augustin.* Paris: Études Augustiniennes, 1966.

Scrutton, Anastasia. "Emotion in Augustine of Hippo and Thomas Aquinas: A Way Forward for the Im/possibility Debate?" *International Journal of Systematic Theology* 7 (2005): 169–77.

Serling, Richard E. "Reclamation through Trust: A Program for Ex-Offenders." *Christian Century* (December 6, 2000): 1263–64.

Studer, Basil. "History and Faith in Augustine's *De Trinitate*." *AugStud* 28 (1997): 7–50.

Tenkorang, Eric Y., Adobea Y. Owusu, and Gubhinder Kundhi. "Help-Seeking Behavior of Female Victims of Intimate Partner Violence in Ghana: The Role of Trust and Perceived Risk of Injury." *Journal of Family Violence* 33 (2018): 341–53.

TeSelle, Eugene. "*Credere*." Pages 119–31 in vol. 2 of *Augustinus-Lexikon.* Edited by Cornelius Mayer. Basel: Schwabe, 1996.

―――. "*Fides*." Pages 1334–40 in vol. 2 of *Augustinus-Lexikon.* Edited by Cornelius Mayer. Basel: Schwabe, 1996.

Twining, Louisa. *Symbols and Emblems of Early and Mediaeval Art.* New ed. London: Murray, 1885.

Van Fleteren, Frederick. "Authority and Reason, Faith and Understanding in the Thought of St. Augustine." *AugStud* 4 (1973): 33–71.

Williamson, Timothy. "Knowledge, Credence, and the Strength of Belief." In *Expansive Epistemology: Norms, Actions, and the Social World.* Edited by Amy Flowerree and Baron Reed. London: Routledge, forthcoming.

6

The Point of Belief(s)

Ritual, Explanation, and the Demonstration of the Divine

THOMAS HARRISON

What is the *point* of belief? As I near—painfully—the end of a decades-long project on the nature of religious belief, this is not just a despairing rhetorical question. Nor is it a reference to the long-running question of the applicability of the term "belief" to antiquity, a suggestion that "belief" has no point in the context of ancient religion.[1] Instead, this chapter asks the question of what function (if any) belief may serve. While this question might seem jarringly reductionist, I explore it here for two reasons. First, this question is worth exploring because— whether implicitly or explicitly—we *have* tended to ascribe uses or purposes to belief. Second, even naive questions may generate rewarding results. I approach the question predominantly on the basis of a particular dataset: the evidence for ancient Greek religious beliefs. In what follows, however, I draw also from examples from more modern contexts (including instances of nonreligious belief) and so am making tentative claims for the character of religious belief more widely.

BELIEFS AS SUPPORTING RITUAL

One point of belief, first, might be to justify or support the performance of ritual or, more widely, to guide action. There has been a long-standing and understand-

---

1. For a summary of the issues, see H. S. Versnel, *Coping with the Gods: Wayward Readings in Greek Theology* (Leiden: Brill, 2011), appendix 4.

The Point of Belief(s)

able reluctance within scholarship on antiquity to see ritual practice as (necessarily) preceded by belief, a reluctance related to the elision of "belief" as a category more widely. This was expressed, for example, by Robertson Smith in his *Lectures on the Religion of the Semites*:

> Religion in primitive times was not a system of belief with practical applications; it was a body of fixed traditional practices, to which every member of society conformed as a matter of course. Men would not be men if they agreed to do certain things without having a reason for their action; but in ancient religion the reason was not first formulated as a doctrine and then expressed in practice, but conversely, practice preceded doctrinal theory.[2]

No one, I think, will imagine that one could hope realistically to map a ritual action neatly to a corresponding supporting belief (or that this would constitute a satisfying explanation of ritual).[3] However, ritual performance might nevertheless be "grounded in a *set of* beliefs."[4] This becomes easier to digest, moreover, if we conceive of beliefs not only as "creedal"—a list of discrete propositions to which a worshiper is, in some sense, expected to subscribe—but also as being broader in character. One might think, for example, of higher-order beliefs supported by others: about belief in the efficacy of ritual, how reward is given for a consistent pattern of pious action, or whether one's dedications should be proportional to one's wealth.

Alongside the danger that rituals and beliefs are seen as crudely keyed to one another, there is an additional hazard: that "belief" is envisaged exclusively in relation to ritual. One outcome of the debate within the study of Greek religion on the applicability of the term "belief" has been the acknowledgment that *of course* there is such a thing as belief; we always knew that. In the words of Robert Parker, for example, "Yet surely even a ritual is performed in the belief that there was some purpose in doing it."[5] A religious act can be defined, for Parker, as a group of worshipers approaching a god "via a set of traditional procedures, acting on the basis (or at least 'as if' on the basis of) certain beliefs."[6] This minimal concession of a role for belief is problematic, however. First, it can underestimate the complexity—hinted at a moment ago—of ideas about ritual performance: the complexity,

2. William Robertson Smith, *Lectures on the Religion of the Semites* (London: Black, 1894), 20.

3. See Robert Parker's cautions on instrumental views of ritual in *Polytheism and Society at Athens* (Oxford: Oxford University Press, 2005), 157–58.

4. Frederick G. Naerebout, *Attractive Performances: Ancient Greek Dance; Three Preliminary Studies* (Amsterdam: Gieben, 1997), 329.

5. Robert Parker, *On Greek Religion* (Ithaca: Cornell University Press, 2011), 2.

6. Robert Parker, *Athenian Religion: A History* (Oxford: Oxford University Press, 1996), 1.

that is, of the grounding of ritual in belief. (Instead, in Parker's first formulation, "the belief that there was some purpose in doing it" is merely inferred from the ritual act itself). Second, this approach fails adequately to acknowledge the large number of religious beliefs that have no necessary relationship with ritual action: beliefs about the unknowability of the divine, or about what an image of the god *is*, to give just two examples.

Or at least, we might qualify, no *direct* relationship with ritual action. Here it may be useful to step aside to look at the relationship between beliefs and action more widely. The proposition that beliefs necessarily guide action is a long-standing one, implicit, for example, in Wittgenstein's analogy of belief to a picture that regulates our actions.[7] To believe, according to one definition, in a proposition *p* means "entertaining *p* and being disposed to act appropriately to *p*'s being true."[8] A similar understanding is reflected in Rodney Needham's classic discussion of belief, a text frequently cited to support the objections to the use of the term in cultural contexts other than our own. Needham expressed scorn for beliefs that "need have no expression in action"—for example, "beliefs about the inscrutable purposes of God, or about conjectured beings on other planets."[9]

A fundamental difficulty here, however, is the tendency to see beliefs as atomized propositions rather than in relation to one another. To return to the context of Greek religion, there are ample instances of religious beliefs that may not result in a single related action but which are capable of being *activated*, if external circumstances align in the right way. So, for example, the belief in the possibility of omens (i.e., that chance occurrences are, in some sense, divine signs) is awakened if, for example, someone sneezes at a significant moment of decision, prompting an act of sacrifice (Xenophon, *Anab.* 3.2.1–13). The belief in the possibility of divine retribution for certain crimes may lead you to avoid getting on a boat with a notorious oath breaker. The belief in the unknowability of the divine—equivalent to Needham's "inscrutable purposes of god"—again has no direct corollary in action, let alone in ritual action. It is arguable, however, that it is fundamental to ritual action in a more general sense. It is because you know that the nature of the gods

---

7. Ludwig Wittgenstein, *Lectures and Conversations on Aesthetics, Psychology and Religious Belief: Compiled from Notes Taken by Yorick Smythies, Rush Rhees and James Taylor*, ed. Cyril Barrett (Oxford: Blackwell, 1966), 53–54, 56: "A belief is like a picture (of the Last Judgement), constantly in the believers' mind, 'admonishing' them: 'It will show, not by reasoning or by appeal to ordinary grounds for belief, but rather by regulating for all in his life. This is a very much stronger fact—foregoing pleasures, always appealing to this picture.'"

8. R. B. Braithwaite, "The Nature of Believing," *Proceedings of the Aristotelian Society* 33 (1933): 132–33; cf. Stuart Hampshire, *Thought and Action* (London: Chatto & Windus, 1959), 159.

9. Rodney Needham, *Belief, Language, and Experience* (Oxford: Blackwell, 1972), 100.

The Point of Belief(s)

is unknowable—that Aphrodite could just as easily be represented as a hyper-real superhuman or as a conical lump of basalt rock—that you get on with worshiping the gods "as if" you are certain. Unknowability is "priced in."

Finally, it is important not to imagine that the relationship between beliefs and actions is unidirectional, that is, that it leads only from beliefs to actions. The playwright Arthur Miller observed that the number of standing ovations on Broadway increased with ticket prices: "To confirm to themselves that they had a good time, they applaud wildly."[10] The famous study by Leon Festinger and others of a Midwestern US doomsday cult gives another striking example.[11] Like the nineteenth-century "Millerites," who stopped sowing or taking in crops, individuals made concrete demonstrations of their commitment. One member of the group, Kitty, is recorded as saying: "I have to believe the flood is coming on the 21st . . . I've spent nearly all my money. I quit my job, I quit comptometer school, and my apartment costs me $100 a month. I have to believe." This may be an extreme manifestation, a kind of burning of one's psychological boats, rather than an act in an ongoing pattern of the reinforcement of belief. Such extreme exhibitions of confidence—or even the manic applause of Broadway audiences—might even seem to suggest a "belief that was not sure of itself" and encourage us not to take statements about beliefs at face value.[12] At the same time, however, it is arguable that the expression of belief *always* contains a germ of doubt, a "recognized element of uncertainty."[13] It is also likely that the mechanisms revealed here may be operative in more ev-

10. Jon Elster, *Explaining Social Behavior: More Nuts and Bolts for the Social Sciences* (Cambridge: Cambridge University Press, 2007), 17.

11. Leon Festinger, Henry W. Riecken, and Stanley Schachter, *When Prophecy Fails: A Social and Psychological Study of a Modern Group That Predicted the Destruction of the World* (Minneapolis: Pinter & Martin, 1956), 130; cf. 107 for the distressed choice of another participant, Edna. For a reinterpretation of Festinger et al.'s project, suggesting social causes in place of psychological motivations, see Tim Jenkins, *Of Flying Saucers and Social Scientists: A Re-Reading of "When Prophecy Fails" and of Cognitive Dissonance* (Basingstoke: Palgrave Macmillan, 2013).

12. Elster, *Explaining Social Behavior*, 70, in the context of the medieval belief in scrofula (and the eagerness of the king's court to seek out evidence of healings).

13. And not merely in the sense of Braithwaite, "Nature of Believing," 129, that belief or disbelief in a proposition imply the opposite stance toward the contradictory proposition. Quotation from Needham, *Belief, Language and Experience*, 90, citing Kant: "The expression of belief is, from the objective point of view, an expression of modesty, and yet at the same time, from the subjective point of view, an expression of the firmness of our confidence." Cf. J. Pouillon, "Remarks on the Verb 'to Believe,'" in *Between Belief and Transgression: Structuralist Essays in Religion, History and Myth*, ed. M. Izard and P. Smith, trans. J. Leavitt (Chicago: University of Chicago Press, 1979), 1; see also 6: "The Christian must simultaneously assume both his affirmation and the challenge to it, a challenge that belief is, nonetheless, supposed to make impossible on its own level."

eryday circumstances. "Acting as if we believe something promotes belief itself," to paraphrase Festinger.[14] Groups hold together more securely when involvement brings with it significant sacrifice.[15] It is reasonable to suppose, then, that the more the Greek worshiper invests (in financial terms) in religious dedications, the more they are likely to invest psychologically in the outcome of those dedications.

Belief as Explanation

A second use for religious belief is what we might term the "explanatory" function. This can be given very different emphases, and it can quickly be seen that this explanatory function is one that can be ascribed to religion in general (and, for example, the symbolic meanings of ritual) and not only to "belief." In the Greek context, for example, John Gould states that religion is "both a framework of explanation for human experience and a system of responses to all that is wayward, uncanny and a threat to the perception of order in that experience."[16] An explanatory function is also fundamental to Versnel's focus on cognitive dissonance: it is because of the Greeks' capacity to embrace various, inconsistent models of explanation (simultaneously or in swift alternation) that Greek religion served as so effective a means of "coping with the gods" (in the title of his *magnum opus*) and with all the vicissitudes of human life.[17] Whereas Versnel's examples are predominantly concerned with universal human experiences—he adduces a powerful example from his own experience of a young girl's death from drowning in Greece[18]—Gould's notion of

14. Festinger, as paraphrased by Todd Tremlin, *Minds and Gods: The Cognitive Foundations of Religion* (New York: Oxford University Press, 2006), 131.

15. Robin Dunbar, Louise Barrett, and John Lycett, *Evolutionary Psychology* (London: Red Globe, 2007), 174; Richard Sosis and Candace Alcorta, "Signalling, Solidarity and the Sacred: Evolution of Religious Behaviour," *Evolutionary Anthropology* 12 (2003): 264–74.

16. John Gould, "On Making Sense of Greek Religion," in *Greek Religion and Society*, ed. P. E. Easterling and J. V. Muir (Cambridge: Cambridge University Press), 5.

17. Versnel, *Coping with the Gods*.

18. Versnel, *Coping with the Gods*, 218–19: "During a holiday in Greece I discussed a young girl's death by drowning with the owner of the local tavern who like me had witnessed the event. I asked her if there was a 'theological' explanation for this terrible tragedy. In an avalanche of words she explained that this was a *punishment* by God, that it was the *will* of God, that it *was written* (γραμμένον ειναι), that those *whom* God *loves* die young. What can we do? (Τί να κάνομε;). The baffling thing was that these different explanations—multiple, different and *in my view* partly discordant—were presented not as discursive alternatives open for discussion or rational choice, but in an asyndetic chain of assertions. When, later, I recounted the whole event to Greek friends who had read their classics and asked what the difference might be between

The Point of Belief(s)

religion is more concerned with the dark forces of myth. Both, however, conceive of the role of religion as mitigating. In other studies, the "explanatory" function perhaps has a more proactive, can-do tone. In the account of Esther Eidinow (a risk consultant before she returned to ancient history), the consultation of oracles or use of magic were strategies for mitigating and controlling risk.[19]

The approach of looking to Greek religious beliefs as an effective explanatory framework is one that I have found highly attractive. When, for example, I set out to try to make sense of the religious beliefs reflected in one ancient text (in this case, Herodotus's *Histories*), the kind of approach adopted by Gould offered what seemed like a track through the forest. How can you explain, for example, a terrible misfortune? To summarize brutally, it can either be interpreted as an instance of divine retribution or as the (divinely motivated) instability of human fortune. Whether the one or the other interpretative choice is made depends on context. Did the misfortune happen to your child or to your enemy? Was the the victim of such misfortune notorious for their crimes or were they as white as snow? It depends, in other words, on some tacit "scripts."

This is an approach that still, to my mind, has merit as a way of making sense of relevant Greek texts. And yet, there are also some grounds for concern that the picture that it generates may be a partial one. First, this impression of religion as a form of explanation is given disproportionate emphasis because we take our vantage points at the end of our literary narratives. The end of the story is the point at which the divine role is made manifest, and the story's loose ends are all neatly tied up. In the case of oracle stories, for example, it becomes clear—from lots of small matches between the outcome of the story and the original oracular text—that one interpretation and only that interpretation could ever possibly have been correct. Most famously, in the course of the Persian Wars it becomes clear from the outcome of the battle of Salamis that the oracle telling the Athenians to take refuge within their wooden walls indeed signified taking to their ships (Herodotus, *Hist.* 7.140–144). Simply, it worked out. What, however, if we try to imagine ourselves in the middle of the narrative? The wooden wall oracle is a rare instance in which we hear about alternative interpretations in detail: there were some Athenians who thought that the wooden walls were a thicket

---

'it is the will of God' and 'it is written,' they first explained to me that το γραμμένον actually is an abbreviation of τῆς μοίρας γραμμένον, 'the writing of fate'—which I knew—, and next that there *is* no difference—which I did not." See, however, the critique of Anthony Ellis, "Proverbs in Herodotus' Dialogue between Solon and Croesus (1.30–33): Methodology and 'Making Sense' in the Study of Greek Religion," *Bulletin of the Institute of Classical Studies* 58 (2015): 100.

19. Esther Eidinow, *Oracles, Curses and Risk among the Ancient Greeks* (Oxford: Oxford University Press, 2007).

around the Athenian acropolis. Although Herodotus's account of the debate on the meaning of the oracle carries you energetically toward the "right" outcome, it is clear that the debate was not a foregone conclusion.

If you are in the midst of that debate then, the focus on a pair of oracular texts may certainly provide a kind of framework for your decision-making, but the belief in the efficacy of divination, of the god's ability to communicate, doesn't so much provide answers as much as it gives shape to the mental torture. Moreover, the happy outcome was not happy for everyone. Those that took an opposite view of the meaning of the oracle held out for their interpretation (Herodotus, *Hist.* 8.51–53). When the Persians took the city of Athens, while most of the Athenians had taken to their ships, the Persians found a small group holed up on the acropolis. These few Athenians,

> stewards of the sacred precinct and poor people, . . . defended themselves against the assault by fencing the acropolis with doors and logs. They had not withdrawn to Salamis not only because of poverty but also because they thought they had discovered the meaning of the oracle the Pythia had given, namely that the wooden wall would be impregnable. They believed that according to the oracle this, not the ships, was the refuge.[20]

The Persians fired flaming arrows at the Athenians' barricade. When the barricade began to fail, still they continued to defend themselves "although they had come to the utmost danger." They refused peace terms and started rolling boulders down onto the Persians. Only when the Persians actually breached their defenses did the Athenians either throw themselves off the cliffs or take refuge in the shrine. They are, in short, in the position of Kitty in Festinger's *When Prophecy Fails.* She and her fellow "seekers" are last seen waiting on a ramp for a spaceship to take them away from imminent catastrophe. When it fails to arrive, they either melt away in a shame-faced fashion or find reasons why they had miscalculated their timings. Those who held out on the acropolis had no such luxury.

In reality then, not everything gets tied up with ribbons at the end of the story. There are winners and losers, and the losers are not always the people that you expect or would prefer. (A large proportion of Greek religious thought attempts to address that reality.) If, on the other hand, we look not to the end of the story but to its heart, we see a very different picture: one of the individual or group beset on all sides by potential omens, anticipating divine retribution and feeling anxious about their record of piety. We can get some flavor of this from the intensified

20. *Herodotus*, trans. A. D. Godley (London: Heinemann, 1930).

The Point of Belief(s)

circumstances of the narrator of Xenophon's *Anabasis* and his account of the ten thousand Greek mercenaries making their return from the heart of the Persian Empire. We can perceive this in the predicament of the Athenians trapped in Sicily in Thucydides's account (in particular, from Nicias's restrained hope for relief in *P.W.* 7.77). We can observe this in the pleas of Sappho for relief from anxiety (frag. 1). Indeed, the long-standing drive to distance Greek religion from "Christianizing assumptions" has perhaps led to our underestimating the emotive force of such moments. At the same time, however, we may wonder whether one reason why we have tended to give such a positive emphasis to the explanatory function of Greek religion is that we are tacitly concerned to find ways in which it may have satisfied the ancient worshiper—to find some way to answer the old line that pre-Christian religions in their worldly focus were inadequate, making the rise of Christianity inevitable.

Belief, then, not only generates the solution to crisis for those that come through, but it also frequently generates (or gives shape to) the crisis itself. To return to cognitive dissonance, if human beings are driven to reduce dissonance, we also have a parallel inclination to *produce* it—to believe what we fear.[21] We can believe (in an example often given by cognitivists) that the rustling leaves we hear in the dark are some human (or nonhuman) agent coming to get us. We can believe—or at least worry—that a misfortune we have suffered is the result of retribution for a past crime or for a failure of ritual observance.

Of course, even these types of beliefs might still prove useful. In the case of rustling leaves, if we follow the cognitivists, our detection of agency behind the noise helps us in our basic need to avoid predators (so-called hyperactive agency detection) and keeps us safe. In the case of divine retribution, one could make the more general claim that the belief in divine retribution reinforces social norms of behavior. In individual cases, it is easy to imagine, however, that our reactions might prove counter to one's interests. You might take a balanced view, rationalizing away your own everyday impieties. (There wouldn't be "sacred laws" against littering in sacred streams if people did not do it all the time.) Or you might end up like Theophrastus's superstitious man seeing omens in everything.

Beliefs can, in fact, straightforwardly serve as traps.[22] To use a nonreligious example, during the Boer War the British were so concerned with the question

---

21. Elster, *Explaining Social Behavior*, 55. And wishful thinking as well as other beliefs shaped by one's interests may be as likely to be counterproductive as beneficial. As Jon Elster writes in *Sour Grapes: Studies in the Subversion of Rationality* (Cambridge: Cambridge University Press, 1983), 156: "If out of wishful thinking I form a belief that I am about to be promoted, my subsequent display of unwarranted self-confidence may destroy whatever chance of promotion I had."

22. Elster, *Explaining Social Behavior*, 211: "A rational agent may find himself in a belief trap

whether or not certain acts of war were "cricket" that their soldiers were given "no training in the 'cowardly' art of building defensive positions or head cover."[23] (As a result, a lot of people died unnecessarily from bombardments.) Are there analogues to this in Greek religious experience? Greek military divination is usually envisaged as being molded to pragmatic concerns. If you do not receive the answer you desire (i.e., good omens that show that you should join battle), you keep trying until you do. Clearly also, the effect of divination in raising morale is critical; this is an instance where conviction in a course of action leads to a successful outcome, regardless of whether that conviction is well grounded. At the same time, there *must have been* numerous instances in which divination obstructed good decision-making, otherwise Xenophon would not have recommended that the good commander should pick up enough knowledge of how to examine entrails that he could keep a check on his seers.[24]

Another type of belief that is strikingly double edged in its effect—and here I am talking about a pattern of belief rather than a theme—is the phenomenon of "sour grapes," that is, the belief that you do not want what you cannot have. On the one hand, this is a classic form of dissonance reduction that can lend the believer "momentary relief from frustration and unhappiness."[25] On the other hand, it can also have the effect of reconciling us to situations that are simply unjust; it could benefit tyrannical rulers by encouraging the ruled to come to terms with the "necessity of the social order that oppresses them."[26] The manifold ways in which religious beliefs serve to reinforce divisions of class and status are significantly underexplored.

So, to tie together the strands of the second of my two sections, the idea of beliefs as explanatory is only fine up to a point. First, it tidies up religious experience too neatly. But, second, perhaps it renders religious experience epiphenomenal: beliefs shape as well as explaining or reflecting experience. And they intersect with and confound a variety of real-life interests. "Ideas and beliefs drift," as Tanya Luhrmann has put it, "in a complex interdependency of concept and experience."[27]

---

that leaves him stuck with a false belief, namely, if the believed costs of testing the belief are too high." Here Elster is developing the example of female genital mutilation.

23. Norman F. Dixon, *On the Psychology of Military Incompetence* (London: Futura, 1976), 54–55, cited by Elster, *Alchemies of the Mind: Rationality and the Emotions* (Cambridge: Cambridge University Press, 1999), 148.

24. Cf. Thucydides's comments in *P.W.* 7.50 on Nicias suggesting a right degree of engagement with divination.

25. Elster, *Sour Grapes*, 163–65. Cf. p. 143: "There is no reason to suppose that beliefs shaped by a social position tend to serve the interests of the persons in that position."

26. Elster, *Sour Grapes*, 116, 145, citing Paul Veyne, *Le Pain et le cirque* (Paris: Seuil, 1976), 554, 696.

27. T. M. Luhrmann, *Persuasions of the Witch's Craft: Ritual Magic in Contemporary England* (Cambridge: Harvard University Press, 1989), 353.

The Point of Belief(s)

SECTION IN SEARCH OF A HEADING

This third and final section is by far the briefest. It is also the hardest to identify a heading for. Beliefs about divine intervention in the world can, as we have seen in the case of divine retribution, support just-world beliefs (an area of thought that never really settled in the Greek context). They can reinforce norms of behavior. Frequently, however, such instances of divine intervention have a much more general moral, mainly, that the gods can intervene, that they are there.

One of the healing cures (the so-called *iamata*) from the Temple of Asclepius at Epidaurus, for example, concerns a slave who accidentally breaks his master's favorite cup.[28] "Not even Asclepius in Epidaurus would be able to make that cup whole," a passerby observes. What happens next is predictable: the god, implicitly, can accomplish any impossible task. (If the clay pot serves as an analogy for the human body, as has been suggested, this miracle represents the god's potential to heal more generally.[29]) The same conclusion is expressed as an explicit moral in fragment 122 of Archilochus: "Now that Zeus has established night out of noonday, hiding away the light of the shining sun [i.e., through an eclipse, that some have dated to 648 BCE] nothing is to be unexpected or sworn impossible or marveled at [χρημάτων ἄελπτον οὐδέν ἐστιν οὐδ᾽ ἀπώμοτον | οὐδὲ θαυμάσιον]; from now on everything will be believable and expected by men [ἐκ δὲ τοῦ κἀι πιστὰ πάντα κἀπίελπτα γίνέται | ἀνδράσιν]."

This is not the full picture, however. As the cognitive literature tells us, some miracle stories do better than others. Those that do not violate too many expectations but do so in memorable ways are more likely to survive and prosper.[30] Miracle stories need also to be rare; in Andrew Lang's phrase, there is an "economy of miracles."[31] And we can also track the ways in which such stories are generated

---

28. Lynn R. LiDonnici, *The Epidaurian Miracle Inscriptions: Text, Translation, Commentary* (Atlanta: Scholars, 1995), A10. The Epidaurian *iamata* then express a range of more specific morals: One should carry out a promised act of propitiation (C4; cf. B2); One should be careful what one wishes for (or, more precisely, what one *fails* to wish for, A2); The size of an ideal dedication is in proportion to one's capacity to make dedications (A8: the boy who only has a handful of dice still goes away cured).

29. Jessica Hughes, *Votive Body Parts in Greek and Roman Religion* (Cambridge: Cambridge University Press, 2017), 57–58; cf. Fred S. Naiden, "*Hiketai* and *Theôroi* at Epidauros," in *Pilgrimage in Graeco-Roman and Early Christian Antiquity: Seeing the Gods*, ed. Jaś Elsner and Ian Rutherford (Oxford: Oxford University Press, 2005), 86.

30. Todd Tremlin, *Minds and Gods: The Cognitive Foundations of Religion* (New York: Oxford University Press, 2006).

31. Andrew Lang, *Literary Criticism, History, Biography*, vol. 2 of *The Selected Works of Andrew Lang*, ed. Andrew Teverson, Alexandra Warwick, and Leigh Wilson (Edinburgh: Edinburgh University Press, 2015), 29.

over time. Jon Elster has written of the human tendency to "stop up the chinks" in an account of a rumor to avoid our individually being at odds with a collective response, citing Montaigne for "what may have been the first analysis of the micromechanism of rumour transmission":

> The distance is greater from nothing to the minutest thing than it is from the minutest thing to the biggest. Now when the first people who drank their fill from the original oddity come to spread their tale abroad, they can tell by the opposition which they arouse what it is that others find it difficult to accept; they then stop up the chinks with some false piece of oakum. . . . At first the individual error creates the public one; then, in its turn, the public error creates the individual one. And so it passes from hand to hand, the whole fabric is padded out and reshaped, so that the most far-off witness is better informed about it than the closest one, and the last to be told more convinced than the first. It is a natural progression. For whoever believes anything reckons that it is a work of charity to convince someone else of it; and to do this he is not afraid to add, out of his own invention, whatever his story needs to overcome the resistance.[32]

We can see much of this dynamic at work in the Greek context also in the concern to generate proofs of an instance of divine intervention, such as specific details or corroborating witnesses. The accounts of the healing cures at Epidaurus, for example, include details of the names and the cities of the individuals cured. They make mention of crowds of witnesses standing around the scene. And they frequently conclude with the individuals' dedications to Delphi—such as a cup or a huge boulder[33]—so providing suggestive evidence that the stories themselves may have grown organically out of the dedications to serve as explanations.[34]

Perhaps most interestingly, the Epidaurian *iamata* also include what we might think of as embedded skeptics: Ambrosia from Athens, who ridiculed the cures as unlikely and impossible (ἀπίθανα καὶ ἀδύνατα; A4); Kaphisias who, after laughing at Asclepius's cures, was trampled by his own horse (B16); and the man who mocked the inscriptions and decried the cures until he himself had need of the god's attention and was thereafter called (by the god) "Apistos" or "Disbeliever" (A3).[35]

---

32. Elster, *Explaining Social Behavior*, 382–83. Elster introduces other explanations in addition, such as the fear of cowardice; see also p. 381 for the counterproductive effects of denials of rumors.

33. LiDonnici, *Epidaurian Miracle Inscriptions*, A10, A15.

34. For this pattern in ancient historical sources, Emilio Gabba, "True History and False History in Classical Antiquity," *Journal of Roman History* 71 (1981): 50–62.

35. All citations from LiDonnici, *Epidaurian Miracle Inscriptions*. For A3, see also P. J. Rhodes

The Point of Belief(s)

(Conversely, in A9 we are also presented with the story of a man whose faith in the possibility of a cure was laughed at as plain simplemindedness [εὐηθίαν].) The role of these embedded skeptics—whether they are third-party observers or the figures acted upon—is, of course, to be confounded by the course of events and so to underline the power of the god. It is a striking aspect of the *iamata*, moreover, that ultimately the god does not punish the doubter too severely—only forcing them to pay for a silver pig, for example, or transferring tattoos onto them[36]—but rather realigns the individual into a believer.[37] The moral of the story of the simpleminded believer is similarly that his seemingly naive stance—that his eye could be healed, though his eye socket was completely empty—is, in fact, affirmed. The message is all but made explicit: believe and your belief will be vindicated.[38]

How to headline this section then? The point of beliefs here is simply to sustain themselves; they exist to exist. They contain within themselves the means to reproduce themselves. When I think of Greek religious belief as a whole, because I am focused on charting the relationships between propositional beliefs, the image that I find myself reaching for is often of a building. Like some Gothic cathedral, I think of them together as forming a magnificent work of the imagination. Looking at the whole picture in a snapshot, this may be appropriate, but it misses the dynamic nature of these beliefs, the way in which they are all activated in constantly shifting contexts. Perhaps a more apposite analogy might be drawn from our recent history. The virus too exists to propagate itself; it is endlessly resilient, and—as we all now know—it mutates.[39]

Works Cited

Braithwaite, R. B. "The Nature of Believing." *Proceedings of the Aristotelian Society* 33 (1933): 129–46.

Dixon, Norman F. *On the Psychology of Military Incompetence*. London: Futura, 1976.

Dunbar, Robin, Louise Barrett, and John Lycett. *Evolutionary Psychology*. London: Red Globe, 2007.

---

and Robin Osborne, *Greek Historical Inscriptions 404–323 BC* (Oxford: Oxford University Press, 2003), no. 102.

36. LiDonnici, *Epidaurian Miracle Inscriptions*, A4, A7.

37. Cf., for a more extreme punishment, LiDonnici, *Epidaurian Miracle Inscriptions*, B16.

38. Cf. LiDonnici, *Epidaurian Miracle Inscriptions*, A10.

39. I am undoubtedly influenced here by Sperber's adoption of "epidemiology." See Dan Sperber, "Anthropology and Psychology: Towards an Epidemiology of Representations," *Man* 20.1 (1985): 73–89.

Eidinow, Esther. *Oracles, Curses and Risk among the Ancient Greeks.* Oxford: Oxford University Press, 2007.

Ellis, Anthony. "Proverbs in Herodotus' Dialogue between Solon and Croesus (1.30–33): Methodology and 'Making Sense' in the Study of Greek Religion." *Bulletin of the Institute of Classical Studies* 58 (2015): 83–106.

Elster, Jon. *Alchemies of the Mind: Rationality and the Emotions.* Cambridge: Cambridge University Press, 1999.

———. *Explaining Social Behavior: More Nuts and Bolts for the Social Sciences.* Cambridge: Cambridge University Press, 2007.

———. *Sour Grapes: Studies in the Subversion of Rationality.* Cambridge: Cambridge University Press, 1983.

Festinger, Leon, Henry W. Riecken, and Stanley Schachter. *When Prophecy Fails: A Social and Psychological Study of a Modern Group That Predicted the Destruction of the World.* Minneapolis: Pinter & Martin, 1956.

Gabba, Emilio. "True History and False History in Classical Antiquity." *Journal of Roman History* 71 (1981): 50–62.

Gould, John. "On Making Sense of Greek Religion." Pages 1–33 in *Greek Religion and Society.* Edited by P. E. Easterling and J. V. Muir. Cambridge: Cambridge University Press, 1985.

Hampshire, Stuart. *Thought and Action.* London: Chatto & Windus, 1959.

Hughes, Jessica. *Votive Body Parts in Greek and Roman Religion.* Cambridge: Cambridge University Press, 2017.

Jenkins, Tim. *Of Flying Saucers and Social Scientists: A Re-Reading of "When Prophecy Fails" and of Cognitive Dissonance.* Basingstoke: Palgrave Macmillan, 2013.

Lang, Andrew. *Literary Criticism, History, Biography.* Vol. 2 of *The Selected Works of Andrew Lang.* Edited by Andrew Teverson, Alexandra Warwick, and Leigh Wilson. Edinburgh: Edinburgh University Press, 2015.

LiDonnici, Lynn R. *The Epidaurian Miracle Inscriptions. Text, Translation, Commentary.* Atlanta: Scholars Press, 1995.

Luhrmann, T. M. *Persuasions of the Witch's Craft: Ritual Magic in Contemporary England.* Cambridge: Harvard University Press, 1989.

Naerebout, Frederick G. *Attractive Performances: Ancient Greek Dance; Three Preliminary Studies.* Amsterdam: Gieben, 1997.

Naiden, Fred S. "*Hiketai* and *Theôroi* at Epidauros." Pages 73–95 in *Pilgrimage in Graeco-Roman and Early Christian Antiquity: Seeing the Gods.* Edited by Jaś Elsner and Ian Rutherford. Oxford: Oxford University Press, 2005.

Needham, Rodney. *Belief, Language and Experience.* Oxford: Blackwell, 1972.

Parker, Robert. *Athenian Religion: A History.* Oxford: Oxford University Press, 1996.

———. *On Greek Religion.* Ithaca: Cornell University Press, 2011.

The Point of Belief(s)

————. *Polytheism and Society at Athens.* Oxford: Oxford University Press, 2005.

Pouillon, J. "Remarks on the Verb 'to Believe.'" Pages 1–8 in *Between Belief and Transgression: Structuralist Essays in Religion, History and Myth.* Edited by M. Izard and P. Smith. Translated by J. Leavitt. Chicago: University of Chicago Press, 1979.

Rhodes, P. J., and Robin Osborne. *Greek Historical Inscriptions 404–323 BC.* Oxford: Oxford University Press, 2003.

Robertson Smith, William. *Lectures on the Religion of the Semites.* London: Black, 1894.

Sosis, Richard, and Candace Alcorta. "Signalling, Solidarity and the Sacred: Evolution of Religious Behaviour." *Evolutionary Anthropology* 12 (2003): 264–74.

Tremlin, Todd. *Minds and Gods: The Cognitive Foundations of Religion.* New York: Oxford University Press, 2006.

Versnel, Henk S. *Coping with the Gods: Wayward Readings in Greek Theology.* Leiden: Brill, 2011.

Veyne, Paul. *Le Pain et le cirque.* Paris: Seuil, 1976.

Wittgenstein, Ludwig. *Lectures and Conversations on Aesthetics, Psychology and Religious Belief: Compiled from Notes Taken by Yorick Smythies, Rush Rhees and James Taylor.* Edited by Cyril Barrett. Oxford: Blackwell, 1966.

7

From Bar Rakib to Cyrus

What Do Royal Portrayals of Divinity Have to Do with Belief?

THEODORE J. LEWIS

How we conceptualize ideas about (belief in) God says a lot about us. How we portray God (and other gods) is a window into our thoughts—cultural, sociological, political, and theological. The same holds true for the ancients and their ideas about and portrayals of God and other gods.

Consider how people interpret the opening of the book of Ezra that presents the following words from the lips of the Persian king Cyrus: "Yahweh, the God of Heaven, has given me all the kingdoms of the earth and has charged me with building him a temple in Jerusalem, which is in Judah" (Ezra 1:2).[1] A simplistic reading of the king's announcement could easily lead devout people (both Jewish and Christian) using their sacred texts to make a conclusion about belief—that the Persian Cyrus was in some way a believer in Yahweh, the Judean god, who "roused his spirit" (הֵעִיר . . . אֶת-רוּחַ; Ezra 1:1) and sent him on a personal mission to rebuild his temple in Jerusalem. Despite the fact that historically, according to Albert de Jong, we "know next to nothing" of Cyrus's religious beliefs, speculation could ensue, positing either the king's personal conversion from his own worship (perhaps of the god Ahura Mazda) to Yahwism or a syncretistic belief blending his native Persian religious traditions with those of Yehud.[2]

---

1. All translations are my own.

2. Quote from Albert de Jong, "The Religion of the Achaemenid Rulers," in *A Companion to the Achaemenid Persian Empire*, ed. Bruno Jacobs and Robert Rollinger (Hoboken: Wiley-

From Bar Rakib to Cyrus

Second Isaiah's famous Cyrus passages (Isa 41:2–4; 44:28; 45:1–7, 13; 46:10–11; 48:14–15) could be added to the picture, as Yahweh strikingly designates Cyrus (note, *not* a Davidide) as his hand-selected messiah (מָשִׁיחַ; Isa 45:1) to accomplish his restoration goals. Second Isaiah adds a complication with regard to any notion of Cyrus's personal beliefs: Yahweh twice states that he is using Cyrus "though you [Cyrus] do not know/have not known me" (לֹא יְדַעְתָּנִי; Isa 45:4–5). In Joseph Blenkinsopp's opinion, "it seems unlikely that the author anticipated the conversion of Cyrus to the Jewish faith."[3] Similarly, Erich S. Grüen writes: "There is little likelihood in fact that the king proclaimed to all the Persian realm that he owed his position to the Jewish deity, a posture that few would have taken seriously and fewer still would have reckoned as acceptable."[4] In contrast, Josephus portrays Cyrus as actually reading and being inspired by the book of Isaiah.[5] Carl F. Keil writes "with a high degree of [historical] probability" that Cyrus "must have been acquainted with this God [Yahweh], have conceived a high respect for Him, and have honored Him as the God of heaven. It was not possible that he should arrive at such a resolution by faith in Ahuramazdâ, but only by means of facts which had inspired him with reverence for [Yahweh] the God of Israel."[6] Blending a fuller

---

Blackwell, 2021), 1204. Regarding Cyrus's religious background, Joseph Blenkinsopp writes: "It has not yet been established beyond doubt that Cyrus worshipped as a Zoroastrian." Joseph Blenkinsopp, *Ezra-Nehemiah* (Philadelphia: Westminster, 1988), 75. See too Blenkinsopp, *Isaiah 40–55*, Anchor Bible Commentary (New York: Doubleday, 2002), 250. For more detailed examinations of Achaemenid religious practices and pantheon, see the treatments of Albert de Jong ("The Religion of the Achaemenid Rulers"), Wouter F. M. Henkelman ("The Heartland Pantheon" and "Practice of Worship in the Achaemenid Heartland"), Manfred Hutter ("Religions in the Empire") and Josef Wiesehöfer ("The Achaemenid Empire: Realm of Tyranny or Founder of Human Rights?") in Jacobs and Rollinger, *Companion to the Achaemenid Persian Empire*.

3. Blenkinsopp, *Isaiah 40–55*, 249. Bob Becking also writes that Cyrus's recognition of Yahweh "is not a sign of a Persian conversion to Yahwism." See Bob Becking, *Ezra-Nehemiah* (Leuven: Peeters, 2018), 28.

4. Erich S. Gruen, "Jewish Perspectives on Persia," in Jacobs and Rollinger, *Companion to the Achaemenid Persian Empire*, 1462.

5. Josephus, *Ant.* 11.1–7. This has been noted by many, including, most recently, Gruen, "Jewish Perspectives on Persia," 1462.

6. Carl F. Keil, "The Books of Ezra, Nehemiah, and Esther," in Carl F. Keil and Franz Delitzsch, *Biblical Commentary on the Old Testament* (Grand Rapids: Eerdmans, 1986), 23–24. Keil also uses Daniel's elevated position with Darius to conclude: "We are perfectly justified in adopting the opinion that Cyrus had been acquainted with the God of the Jews, and with the prophecies of Isaiah concerning Coresh, by Daniel.... [The] essential contents [of the edict of Cyrus] are ... faithfully reproduced; there are not sufficient grounds even for the view that the God who had inspired Cyrus with this resolution was in the royal edict designated only as the God of heaven, and not expressly called Jahve."

pantheon into his devotion, F. Charles Fensham argues that "the Lord [Yahweh] could have been acknowledged by Cyrus as being one of the many gods who assisted him in becoming a world monarch."[7]

Obviously, we could strip away any historical notion of Cyrus's belief in Yahweh by easily noting that these texts are what biblical authors are theologically projecting onto the good king. Yehudite theologians could have easily imagined that if Yahweh was controlling all of history, then of course whatever Cyrus did would be refracted through a Yahwistic lens. There's nothing wrong, they might have said, with presenting the king's actions via a fictitious conversion story or noting that a sovereign Yahweh could use whomever Yahweh chooses (even a non-Davidide pagan) to accomplish the divine will. In both scenarios, one could say that Cyrus's own belief has nothing to do with it. We are dealing with theological presentations and projections of Yahwistic belief onto the Persian king. It's certainly not a *historical* commentary on the king's personal beliefs. In the words of Erich Gruen, it is simply "a Jewish literary construct. For them, Cyrus' successes were best explained and most readily embraced as making him the agent of the Lord."[8] Manfred Hutter looks particularly to Yahweh's epithet "the God of Heaven" in Ezra 1:2 (cf. Neh 1:5; 2 Chr 36:23) as exhibiting "traces of influences of Zoroastrian religious thought." Situating this influence within the dynamics of Yehud, he writes of "a politically inspired religious change fostered by Jewish theologians," one where "this 'new' title possibly results from efforts to express some similarity between Yahweh (as 'god of heaven') and Auramazda's heavenly features. But the new title also had the advantage of giving the 'national god' Yahweh universal aspects which were well suited to Jehud's (political) position within an international empire, and the 'god of heaven' could also build an excellent common bond between all Jews living dispersed in different parts of this empire."[9] In contrast, Bob Becking notes how the epithet "the God of Heaven . . . does not appear in Achaemenid or Avestan texts," and thus we should look to the Persian period worshipers of "Yahô, the God of Heaven" at Elephantine as well as preexilic biblical texts (Gen 24:7; Ps 136:26) for better background material.[10]

There is a third option, and one that is often found among biblical scholars interested in a comparative historical perspective. If we are not talking about a personal belief on the part of the good king or a literary projection of belief

---

7. F. Charles Fensham, *The Books of Ezra and Nehemiah*, New International Commentary on the Old Testament (Grand Rapids: Eerdmans, 1982), 44.

8. Gruen, "Jewish Perspectives on Persia," 1462.

9. Hutter, "Religions in the Empire," 1298.

10. Becking, *Ezra-Nehemiah*, in Jacobs and Rollinger, *Companion to the Achaemenid Persian Empire*, 27–28.

From Bar Rakib to Cyrus

(i.e., theologizing), then perhaps we have here a pragmatic situation, whereby the Persian king was said to have appropriated the belief system of a local population for his own political means. In short, it is skilled propaganda. Here scholars regularly turn to the Cyrus Cylinder's comments on the restoration of the cult of Marduk in Babylon together with details from the Chronicle of Nabonidus.[11] Cyrus describes at great length how his military victories were due to the providence of the Babylonian god Marduk whom he calls "my lord" (*bēlīya*). These victories

---

11. E.g. Blenkinsopp, *Ezra-Nehemiah*, 75: "[Cyrus's] attribution of his success to YHVH and the consequent need to restore his cult are historically plausible as a political adaptation of the language and ideology of the Cyrus cylinder, which credits the Babylonian imperial deity Marduk with his success." Writing on whether Cyrus "would have attributed his victories to this [Judean] God [Yahweh]" and also using the Cyrus Cylinder for support, Williamson notes that "it was consistent Achaemenid policy . . . to use the title of the god or gods recognized by the local population." See Hugh G. M. Williamson, *Ezra, Nehemiah*, WBC 16 (Waco, TX: Word, 1985), 11–12.

According to R. J. van der Spek's broader contextualization, "Cyrus' propaganda and policy [were] highly traditional with Babylonian as well as Assyrian precedents." With regard to divinity, van der Spek notes the presence of foreign gods as cursing agents (and, we might add, as witnesses) in treaties to show how rulers would pragmatically embrace another nation's gods. In his words, "a polytheist can easily accept other gods than his own . . . it is easy to multiply the number of kings who take the existence of such [foreign] gods seriously. . . . Recognition of foreign gods is, in short, completely normal in the polytheistic mind frame." Van der Spek goes on to highlight how "the kings themselves clearly *believed* that there were religious reasons for their policies. . . . In a polytheistic worldview, *all* gods, the ones of the foreign nations included, can send prosperity and calamities. It is possible to use one's own gods to intimidate foreign deities, but one can also try to become friendly with them. When, for example, one builds a temple for a foreign god, and one makes his nation pray on your behalf, the god may return the favor. It is at least worth trying." For the quotes cited here, see R. J. van der Spek, "Cyrus the Great, Exiles, and Foreign Gods: A Comparison of Assyrian and Persian Policies on Subject Nations," in *Extraction and Control: Studies in Honor of Matthew W. Stolper*, ed. Michael Kozuh et al. (Chicago: Oriental Institute of the University of Chicago, 2014), 239–40, 247, 255. Van der Spek's treatment includes a splendid collection of and interaction with the secondary literature.

It is beyond the scope of the present treatment to cite the voluminous literature on the Cyrus Cylinder and the Chronicle of Nabonidus. For the primary text of the former, see Irving L. Finkel, ed., *The Cyrus Cylinder: The King of Persia's Proclamation from Ancient Babylon* (London: I. B. Tauris, 2013); and van der Spek, "Cyrus the Great, Exiles, and Foreign Gods," 261–63. For the relevant section in the Chronicle of Nabonidus, see Jean-Jacques Glassner, *Mesopotamian Chronicles* (Atlanta: Society of Biblical Literature, 2004), 236–39.

The question of the history and ideology of Ezra-Nehemiah is also beyond the scope of the present treatment. See Sara Japhet, "Periodization between History and Ideology II: Chronology and Ideology in Ezra-Nehemiah," in *Judah and the Judeans in the Persian Period*, ed. Oded Lipschits and Manfred Oeming (Winona Lake: Eisenbrauns, 2006), 491–508; and Lester L. Grabbe, "The 'Persian Documents' in the Book of Ezra: Are They Authentic?," in Lipschits and Oeming, *Judeans in the Persian Period*, 531–70.

included a peaceful overtaking of Marduk's own city of Babylon, where the inhabitants rejoiced over Cyrus's kingship. Using his own words (cf. Ezra 1:2), Cyrus proclaims how he daily attended to the worship of Marduk, the great lord, who in turn rejoiced over Cyrus's good deeds and poured out his gracious blessing on the king.

This historical option leads me to the subject of my paper. To gain another perspective, it switches gears to examine a case study of the political portrayal of divinity coming from the early history of the Arameans, where we have a large dataset, both textual and iconographic. Using larger datasets will reveal that the historical situation regarding royal portrayals of divinity is far more complicated than any scenarios that we might envision. Two results will be offered to help address the topic: (1) Portrayals of divinity are incredibly complex, as they are culturally and sociologically contingent, and with regard to royal portrayals they are politically oriented; and (2) The data belie simplistic and reductionist notions of a king's "belief" in any particular god.

King Bar Rakib: A Case Study

The present paper is part of a larger project exploring the political dimensions of the Sam'alian King Bar Rakib (r. ca. 733–713/711 BCE). For those readers interested in intersections with biblical chronology, during the famous Syro-Ephraimite War (cf. Isa 7), the Judean King Ahaz (r. ca. 737–727 BCE) seeks the help of Tiglath-Pileser III, who appears throughout Bar Rakib's inscriptions.[12] In particular, Bar Rakib's father, Panamuwa II, died fighting for Tiglath-Pileser III in his battle against Damascus (2 Kgs 16:9; *KAI* 215, ll. 16–19). After the war, Ahaz travels to meet Tiglath-Pileser III in Damascus. Ahaz then dismantles established

---

12. The three Bar Rakib inscriptions (abbreviated as BR1, BR2, and BR3 hereforth) have been published as *KAI* 216, 217, and 218 respectively. Other editions of these inscriptions can be found in Josef Tropper, *Die Inschriften von Zincirli: Neue Edition und vergleichende Grammatik des phönizischen, sam'alischen und aramäischen Textkorpus* (Münster: Ugarit-Verlag, 1993); John C. L. Gibson, *Aramaic Inscriptions Including Inscriptions in the Dialect of Zenjirli*, vol. 2 of *Textbook of Syrian Semitic Inscriptions* (Oxford: Clarendon, 1975); Dirk Schwiderski, *Die alt- und reichsaramäischen Inschriften*, vol. 2 (Berlin: de Gruyter, 2004); Alessandra Gilibert, *Syro-Hittite Monumental Art and the Archaeology of Performance: The Stone Reliefs at Carchemish and Zincirli in the Earlier First Millennium BCE* (Berlin: de Gruyter, 2011). These inscriptions are cataloged in these volumes as follows:

BR1/*KAI* 216 = Tropper B1 // Gibson 2:15 // Schwiderski BarRak:1 // Gilibert Zincirli 74
BR2/*KAI* 217 = Tropper B2 // Gibson 2:16 // Schwiderski BarRak:8 // Gilibert Zincirli 75
BR3/*KAI* 218 = Tropper B3 // Gibson 2:17 // Schwiderski BarRak:2 // Gilibert Zincirli 66

Judean cultic paraphernalia in favor of Aramean (likely Assyrianized) versions (2 Kgs 16:10–18).

In two earlier studies, I've explored the earliest and latest stages of Bar Rakib's remarkable reign. The first study examined *KAI* 215 in order to focus on a most precarious beginning (see fig. 7.1 on p. 117).[13] Bar Rakib was forced to act quickly and strategically to secure his place on the throne when his father Panamuwa II unexpectedly died on the Damascus battlefield fighting on behalf of Tiglath-Pileser III. The Neo-Assyrian hegemon, in acts of unparalleled benevolence, transported the body of Panamuwa II to Assyria for burial and acted as a surrogate in providing funerary rites. As benevolent as this was for a vassal king, it robbed Bar Rakib of the opportunity to stage a state funeral for his father, a political event filled with symbolism that could have helped him legitimate his ascendancy to the throne. Moreover, without a burial site, Bar Rakib was seemingly robbed of the privilege and symbolism of carrying out his filial mortuary duties closely tied to dynastic succession. Bar Rakib's response was astute. He recognized that Tiglath-Pileser III's funerary rites need *not* rob him of his own ritual performance. He may not have his father's

Fig. 7.1. The statue of King Panamuwa II erected by his son Bar Rakib containing an inscription written in Sam'alian Aramaic (KAI 215). Photo courtesy of the Oriental Institute of the University of Chicago. Illustration reconstructing Panamuwa II's upper torso and head by Karen Reczuch, used by permission.

13. See Theodore J. Lewis, "Bar-Rakib's Legitimation and the Problem of a Missing Corpse: The End of the Panamuwa Inscription in Light of the Katumuwa Inscription," *ARAM Periodical* 3.2 (2019): 349–74.

corpse to bury, yet he could set up a stele—engraved with his father's image and name—in which his father's disembodied essence (*nabš*) could reside and receive cult. As we clearly see in the Katumuwa Stele (see fig. 7.3 on p. 124), local belief (of Anatolian influence) held that his father's *nabš*-essence could indeed reside apart from his father's body. Moreover, as with the Katumuwa Stele, the stele of Panamuwa II can be the location of *ongoing* funerary cult. As regular offerings are prescribed in the Katumuwa Stele, so too Bar Rakib could demonstrate his loyalty to his father by offering ongoing funerary cult—and in Sam'al in full view of his local constituency.

Seth Sanders asserts that "mortuary feeding [is bonded] to kingship." A "successor must invoke and feed [his ancestor and the god(s)] if he wishes to keep the throne."[14] Having astutely demonstrated his filial role, Bar Rakib ends his memorial inscription for his father by invoking the gods:

(22) *wzkr . znh . h' . p' . hdd . w'l .* ⌐ *wr* ⌐*kb*⌐ *'l* ⌐ *. b*⌐ *l* ⌐ *. byt . wšmš . wkl . 'lhy . y'dy* [. *yrqw. wty. br. pnmw*] [*wytn rkb'l ḥn*] (23) *y . qdm . 'lhy . wqdm . 'nš .*

(22) The (stele) constitutes a *dikr* memorial.[15] Thus may Hadad, El, Rakib-El, the lord of the dynastic house, and Shamsh, and all the gods of Yảdiya [have favor upon me, the son of Panamuwa (II)]. [And may Rakib-El show favor] to (23) me before the gods and before men.[16]

In short, what we have in *KAI* 215 is Bar Rakib's use of ritual performance to curry favor with the gods (especially the dynastic god Rakib-El) and his local constituency in order to legitimize his new reign in its infancy. "The King is dead; Long live the King!"

The second study probed the rest of Bar Rakib's reign and how he found political success for two decades despite having to address multiple audiences.[17] Bar Rakib was the last ruler of ancient Yảdiya/Sam'al, a polity marked for

14. Seth Sanders, "The Appetites of the Dead: West Semitic Linguistic and Ritual Aspects of the Katumuwa Stele," *BASOR* 369 (2013): 48.

15. For the significance of *zkr* invocations for the cult of the dead, see Lewis, "Bar-Rakib's Legitimation," 371.

16. The two restorations are based respectively on *KAI* 214, line 13 and BR3/*KAI* 217, lines 7–9. For those favoring such restorations, see Lewis, "Bar-Rakib's Legitimation," 371n59.

17. See Theodore J. Lewis, "Kings, Peoples and Their Gods: Bar Rakib's Political Portrayal of Divinity," in *"A Community of Peoples": Studies on Society and Politics in the Bible and Ancient Near East in Honor of Daniel E. Fleming* (Leiden: Brill, 2022), 212–52.

its hybridity as it blended Anatolian and West Semitic cultural traditions while at the same time navigating the power dynamics of the Neo-Assyrian Empire. Employing a variety of media (orthostats, inscriptions, seals) combining textual and visual narratives, Bar Rakib shaped the perceptions of his local constituents and external powers. In particular, he used a persuasive language of divinity for political purposes. Textually, he describes how the gods were actively engaged in every aspect of royal life: installing the king on the throne; preserving an ongoing dynasty from internal and external threats; rebuilding a shattered economy; building a magnificent palace; administering with justice; securing favor with local constituencies and foreign powers; and banqueting, both in this life and in the hereafter. As for intended audiences, Bar Rakib's royal inscriptions were restricted to a small but prestigious class of local and Neo-Assyrian scribes along with the educated officials (including kings, viziers, and ambassadors) who possessed the ability to read his Sam'alian Aramaic (*KAI* 215) and Old Aramaic (*KAI* 216–221) inscriptions. Astutely, Bar Rakib learned of the power of visual narratives from his Sam'alian predecessors (esp. King Kulamuwa in *KAI* 24 and his great-grandfather Panamuwa I in *KAI* 214), as they could reach an even larger audience. The physical location of his orthostats was the palace complex, where the majority of viewers would be elite officials and visiting dignitaries, though open reception and ceremonial spaces could entertain groups from Yådiya at large. Certain legal and economic functions could also bring members of the society at large into royal space.[18]

Bar Rakib's Presentation of Divinity: Numerical Diversity

When entering into a dialogue with biblical religion and ancient Israelite religion on matters of divinity, one is immediately forced to address numerical questions of divine singularity, divine plurality, and pantheon reduction. These questions are posed to literary traditions (especially the Hebrew Bible) as well as to material culture (cf. standing stones marking divinity that can be singular or multiple).[19]

18. Space does not allow for a more detailed discussion including interactions with a plethora of secondary literature. Readers are directed to the detailed analyses of Alessandra Gilibert, Virginia R. Herrmann, Herbert Niehr, Marina Pucci, and K. Lawson Younger Jr. For bibliographies see Lewis, "Bar-Rakib's Legitimation"; and Lewis, "Kings, Peoples and Their Gods."

19. I address the differences between biblical religion, literary religion, and Israelite religion (including material culture) with respect to divine representation in Theodore J. Lewis, *The Origin and Character of God: Ancient Israelite Religion through the Lens of Divinity* (New York:

THEODORE J. LEWIS

Combining Bar Rakib's iconographic portrayals with his textual narratives reveals remarkable diversity with regard to quantity, ranging from henotheistic singularity (Rakib-El; Hadad; Ba'al Harran) to duality (Rakib-El together with Shamsh) to varying fivefold clusters of divinity (Hadad, El, Rakib-El, Shamsh and all the gods of Yådiya in *KAI* 215; Hadad, Rakib-El, Shamsh, Sin/Śahr, Rašap in BR1/*KAI* 216; Rakib-El, Shamsh, Rakib-El, El, Hadad in *KAI* 217).[20]

Bar Rakib's Presentation of Divinity: Visual Restrictions

When looking at divine images throughout the ancient Near East, scholars organize the data into four primary categories of representation: anthropomorphic, theriomorphic, symbolic, and aniconic. The ancients were creative in employing many differing modes of divine representation. In contrast, Bar Rakib's visual representations always use symbols to represent divinity and show a slight preference toward an astralization of divinity (winged sun disk, lunar symbol, encircled star). This preference also contrasts elsewhere at Zincirli, where we have many anthropomorphic images, such as the anthropomorphic Hadad Inscription of Bar Rakib's great-grandfather Panamuwa I (fig. 7.2 on p. 121); the many anthropomorphic figures found at the Southern City Gate and the Outer Citadel Gate (D); the seven silver anthropomorphic "encircled Ishtar" pendants; the bronze fan/crescent shaped object (perhaps of a chariot pole) with a nude "mistress of animals"; and the naked female on a horse frontlet. Bar Rakib's only concession to anthropomorphism is the two-faced janiform symbol in BR2/*KAI* 217 (see fig. 7.9 on p. 133). Due to their ubiquity in the ancient Near East—including elsewhere at Zincirli[21]—it is also surprising that theriomorphic representations of divinity are also nonexistent in Bar

---

Oxford University Press, 2023). An illustrated synthesis can be found in Lewis, "From Standing Stones to Sacred Emptiness: Textual and Visual Portrayals of Israel's God," Paper presented at the American Society of Overseas Research (ASOR) Webinar, July 2021, https://www.asor.org/news/2021/07/lewis-webinar-yahweh/.

20. For textual and visual documentation of these varying numerical groupings, see Lewis, "Kings, Peoples and Their Gods."

21. Elsewhere at Zincirli we have the attendant lion on which the "encircled Ishtar" rides; the lions associated with the (divine?) ancestor Gabbar; the numerous theriomorphic images (especially portal lions and hunting scenes) of the Southern City Gate, the Outer Citadel Gate, the Lion's Pit and Gate Q; and again the "mistress of animals." For the latter, see Izak Cornelius, "In Search of the Goddesses of Zincirli (Sam'al)," *ZDPV* 128 (2012): 19–20, fig. 3.

From Bar Rakib to Cyrus

Rakib's portrayal of divinity, apart from the bull horns on the helmet, which serve as symbols for the god Hadad that could be some type of a concession to a theriomorphic heritage.

BAR RAKIB'S PRESENTATION OF DIVINITY: GENDERED RESTRICTIONS

Bar Rakib is also restrictive when we consider gendered divinity. Following his predecessors (e.g., Kulamuwa, Panamuwa I, and Panamuwa II), Bar Rakib is male-centric. Apart from two possible visuals in BR1/*KAI* 216—the double-circled five-pointed star, if it represents Ishtar and not Rašap (but see below), and the rosette with the sun disk[22]—Bar Rakib references only male divinities in his visuals and his textual representations. Had the king wanted explicitly to invoke Ishtar, he could have used her dominant six- or eight-pointed star. Note how his personal seal does not contain the rosette within its sun disk. All of this is surprising since we know definitively of the cult of Ishtar, Kubaba, and the "mistress of animals" elsewhere at the site.[23] Goddesses must have been included in Bar Rakib's generic references to the "gods" or "all the gods" or "the gods of Yàdiya." And perhaps Bar Rakib wore an "encircled Ishtar" medallion around his neck.[24] Yet, the explicit data we have to work with is that of a male-gendered portrayal of divinity.

Fig. 7.2. A colossal statue of the god Hadad erected by King Panamuwa I containing an inscription written in Sam'alian Aramaic (*KAI* 214). Photo courtesy of Virginia Herrmann.

22. According to Tallay Ornan, the rosette with the sun disk could be "alluding to a female deity" (i.e., Ishtar). Tallay Ornan, *The Triumph of the Symbol: Pictorial Representation of Deities in Mesopotamia and the Biblical Image Ban* (Fribourg: Academic Press Fribourg, 2005), 152.

23. See Izak Cornelius, "In Search of the Goddesses of Zincirli."

24. For an illustrated discussion of the double-circled five-pointed star and the seven "encircled Ishtar" medallions found at Zincirli, see Lewis, "Kings, Peoples and Their Gods," 220–27.

THEODORE J. LEWIS

Bar Rakib's Presentation of Divinity: Local (Sam'alian) and Familial Attentiveness

The University of St Andrews interdisciplinary conference that occasioned this essay interrogated the concept of "belief" in the ancient world. The data left behind by King Bar Rakib provide windows into the political, social, and cultural dimensions of "belief," which adds balance to those who might restrict belief as having to do with one's personal or theological preferences. This is not to say that our good king did not have a personal connection with divinity, especially Rakib-El, the god of his family's dynasty who is a constant in all of Bar Rakib's portrayals of divinity apart from one (see BR3/*KAI* 218 below). Notably, the deity Rakib-El is not known outside of our royal inscriptions from Yȧdiya/Sam'al. All signs point to Rakib-El's being a local god who had an enduring legacy as "the Lord of the dynastic house" (*bʿl byt*) for more than 120 years from King Kulamuwa, whose reign started around 840 BCE, until the end of Bar Rakib's reign around 713/711 BCE.[25] This conscious and consistent royal promulgation of a local Sam'alian god is expressed visually using a distinctive symbol (the yoke bar) that is also, remarkably, unattested elsewhere.

In addition to the local god Rakib-El, our Sam'alian inscriptions also highlight devotion to "the (local) gods of Yȧdiya" (*ʾlhy yʾdy*; *KAI* 215, line 22) and to ancestral gods. Familial language is used in the Hadad Inscription, where an oath is pronounced in conjunction with the lifting of one's hands to "the god of his father" (*ʾlh ʾbh*; *KAI* 214, line 29). The language here is ambiguous, referring either to one's deified ancestor or to the patron god of one's ancestor. Recent studies on family religion underscore the powerful kinship ties of divinity.[26] Bar Rakib uses similar language yet with a plural referent: "the gods of the house of my father" (*ʾlhy byt ʾby*) occurring after his likely mention of Rakib-El (BR2/*KAI* 217, line 3).[27] Bar Rakib does not articulate the corporate gods' names, assuming perhaps that they were well known (cf. the standard five in *KAI* 214 noted below) or that his audience would easily see here a reference to the local "gods of Yȧdiya" noted above.

25. Textually, Rakib-El is attested in *KAI* 24, line 16; 25, lines 4, 6; 214, lines 2–3, 11, 18; 215, line 22; 216, line 5.

26. For introductions to the many works on family religion, see Rainer Albertz and Rüdiger Schmitt, *Family and Household Religion in Ancient Israel and the Levant* (Winona Lake, IN: Eisenbrauns, 2012); John Bodel and Saul M. Olyan, eds., *Household and Family Religion in Antiquity* (Oxford: Blackwell, 2008); and Lewis, *Origin and Character of God*, 473–94.

27. The reconstructed reading of [*rkbʾl*] in BR2/*KAI* 217, line 3 is advocated by many scholars.

From Bar Rakib to Cyrus

In this light, one is tempted to use the catchphrase "all politics is local." And yet with Bar Rakib, as we will see, his multiple portrayals of divinity are far more nuanced and sophisticated, evincing a thoughtful political agenda that addressed various internal audiences as well as external audiences. The remarkable diversity of his presentations goes even beyond the quantity mentioned above. First, let us consider portrayals of divinity aimed at his hybrid local audience.

Bar Rakib's Presentation of Divinity: Ethnocultural Considerations

As noted above, the Syro-Hittite city we are discussing was culturally hybrid as evidenced on many fronts, including the various names for the locale used by its inhabitants. Local Aramaic speakers likely referred to the polity as Bīt-Gabbāri ("the house of Gabbar") that they identified with the West Semitic Gabbar, the eponymous "heroic" (*gabbār*) founder of the dynasty, who reigned ca. 920/900–880 BCE.[28] A second indigenous name, Yảdiya, has a long history of debate, with K. Lawson Younger concluding that "it seems likely that Y'dy was the Luwian derived name for the city-state."[29] Luwian is a sister language of Hittite that one finds elsewhere in the Neo-Hittite polities of Cilicia, Karkamish, Tel Ahmar, Maras, Malatya, Commagene, Amuq, Aleppo, Hama, and Tabal that were located in regions formerly ruled by the Hittite Empire.[30] The name Yảdiya regularly occurs in Sam'alian Aramaic on the two primary inscriptions found at the site (*KAI* 214, lines 1, 9, 21, 25; *KAI* 215, lines 1–2, 5, 7–8, 12). The late ninth-century BCE Phoenician Kulamuwa Inscription also found at Zincirli refers to the polity as Yảdiya. The only occurrence of the toponym Yảdi[ya] in Old Aramaic is in the Sefire Inscription (*KAI* 222 B9). Third, we find the name Sam'al, which is the preferred name in Akkadian sources as well as in Old Aramaic sources that reflect Neo-Assyrian influence (Zakkur *KAI* 202 A7; BR1/*KAI* 216, lines 2–3, 17; BR2/*KAI* 217, line 1).[31]

---

28. A colossal 2.5 m high basalt statue of a bearded man located outside Building J at Zincirli may very well be a representation of the (divine?) ancestor Gabbar. See Gilibert, *Syro-Hittite Monumental Art*, 76–79, 211, fig. Zincirli 63.

29. K. Lawson Younger Jr., *A Political History of the Arameans: From Their Origins to the End of Their Polities* (Atlanta: SBL Press, 2016), 383–84.

30. For a convenient collection of these texts, see Annick Payne, *Iron Age Hieroglyphic Luwian Inscriptions* (Atlanta: SBL Press, 2012).

31. Younger, *Political History*, 379.

Fig. 7.3. An eighth-century BCE mortuary stele from Zincirli depicting Katumuwa, an elite servant of Panamuwa II. Photo courtesy of the Neubauer Expedition to Zincirli of the University of Chicago.

The cultural hybridity of the city is also seen through the names of its ruler, which attest to Luwian names (Kulamuwa, Qarali, Panamuwa I, Panamuwa II; cf. the elite official Katumuwa) residing alongside West Semitic names (Gabbār, Ḥayyāʾ, Šåīl, Barṣūr, Bar Rakib). As for artistic expression, K. Lawson Younger's political history of the Arameans at Yådiya notes how "the art and pantheon of Samʾal exhibit numerous Luwian links" with an array of Luwian divine portrayals at the Outer Citadel Gate (D) including Kubaba, Tarḫunza, Ḫebat, and Karḫuha.[32] Textually, note how the high official Katumuwa—who worked within Panamuwa II's (Bar Rakib's father) administration—inscribes three (possibly four) Luwian deities on his mortuary stela: Hadad Qarpatalli, *ngd/r ṣwd/rn*, Hadad of the Vineyards, and Kubaba (spelled curiously with a final *w*).[33]

---

32. Younger, *Political History*, 394. See too the detailed treatment by Younger, "Gods at the Gates: A Study of the Identification of the Deities Represented at the Gates of Ancient Samʾal (Zincirli) with Possible Historical Implications," *ARAM Periodical* 31.2 (2019): 317–48.

33. On Hadad Qarpatalli, see Ilya Yakubovich, "The West Semitic God El in Anatolian Hieroglyphic Transmission," in *Pax Hethitica: Studies on the Hittites and Their Neighbours in Honour of Itamar Singer*, ed. Y. Cohen, A. Gilan, and J. L. Miller (Wiesbaden: Harrassowitz, 2010), 396; Virginia R. Herrmann, "Cosmopolitan Politics in the Neo-Assyrian Empire: Local Elite Identity at Zincirli-Samʾal," *Semitica* 60 (2018): 515; Dennis Pardee, "The KTMW Inscription," in *Supplements*, vol. 4 of *The Context of Scripture*, ed. K. Lawson Younger Jr. (Leiden: Brill, 2017), 95n6; Sanders,

From Bar Rakib to Cyrus

At nearby Ördekburnu (20 km south-southwest of Zincirli), we have a royal mortuary stele written in Sam'alian Aramaic that also reveals a divine hybridity, twice mentioning the Luwian goddess Kubaba alongside the double mention of Rakib-El, whose yoke bar image is visible at the top of the now damaged stele (fig. 7.4 on p. 126).[34] The writer, a royal woman whose Luwian name is partially

---

"Appetites of the Dead," 44–45. See too Younger, "The Ördekburnu and Katumuwa Stelae: Some Reflections on Two *Grabdenkmäler*," *BASOR* 384 (2020): 10–11, where Younger expresses reservations on this issue.

Several scholars posit that Hadad of the Vineyards is the local equivalent of "Tarhunza of the Vineyards." See, for example, Dennis Pardee "A New Aramaic Inscription from Zincirli," *BASOR* 356 (2009): 62; Younger, "Gods at the Gates," 321; Younger, "Ördekburnu and Katumuwa Stelae," 11.

The nature of the god *ngd/r ṣwd/rn* is complicated due to epigraphically ambiguous readings of either *d* or *r*. See Pardee "New Aramaic Inscription," 54–56. Several scholars see a reference to a local (West Semitic) deity: "he who is in charge of provisions" (*ngd ṣwd/rn*). See Pardee "New Aramaic Inscription," 61; Sanders, "Appetites of the Dead," 45. In contrast, Fales and Grassi translate "l'Ufficiale (?) della cacce" (*ngd ṣwdn*) with Runtiya/Runzas in mind. See Frederick Mario Fales and Giulia Francesca Grassi, *L'aramaico antico: Storia, grammatica, testi commentate* (Udine: Forum, 2016), 205, 208; cf. Younger, "Gods at the Gates," 332–33. See too Émilia Masson, "La stèle mortuaire de Kuttamuwa [Zincirli]: Comment l'appréhender," *Semitica et Classica* 3 (2010): 52–53, who sees a reference to Nikarawas/Nikaruhas of hunters (reading *ngr ṣwdn*), but see the reservations by Younger, "Ördekburnu and Katumuwa Stelae," 11.

On Kubaba, especially in hieroglyphic Luwian texts of the first millennium BCE, see Manfred Hutter, "Kubaba in the Hittite Empire and the Consequences for Her Expansion to Western Anatolia," in *Hittitology Today: Studies on Hittite and Neo-Hittite Anatolia in Honor of Emmanuel Laroche's 100th Birthday*, ed. Alice Mouton (Istanbul: Institut français d'études anatoliennes, 2014), 116–17.

34. The Ördekburnu inscription has had a lengthy history of resisting decipherment until the new collation by André Lemaire and Benjamin Sass, "The Mortuary Stele with Sam'alian Inscription from Ördekburnu near Zincirli," *BASOR* 369 (2013): 57–136. As for the divine symbols, Lemaire and Sass are confident that we have three symbols, and "originally perhaps five or more" (74). Their tentative reconstruction sees a centered yoke bar with two circular "flanking symbols" that "portray celestial bodies." Younger ("Ördekburnu and Katumuwa Stelae," 2; *Political History*, 411 and 412n128) also sees two "disk-shaped" symbols flanking a centered yoke bar. Yadin had previously reconstructed four divine symbols: a crescent moon disk, the yoke bar, a horned helmet, and overhead remnants of a winged disk. See Yigael Yadin, "Symbols of Deities at Zinjirli, Carthage and Hazor," in *Near Eastern Archaeology in the Twentieth Century*, ed. James A. Sanders (Garden City, NY: Doubleday, 1970), 201 (fig. 7). Lemaire and Sass ("Mortuary Stele," 74) reject the horned helmet outright as being "very uncertain," as they are unable to see the crescent on the circular disk. While they admit the possibility of a winged disk above the yoke bar "in theory," they nevertheless state that "there is no trace supporting this." More recently, Baruch Brandl has proposed an entirely different interpretation with four divine symbols at the top of the stele—a partial winged disk imposed over a janiform head, a yoke bar, and a horned helmet. See Baruch Brandl, "Rakib'il and 'Kubaba of Aram' at Ördekburnu and Zincirli and New Observations on Kubaba at Zincirli, Carchemish and Ugarit,"

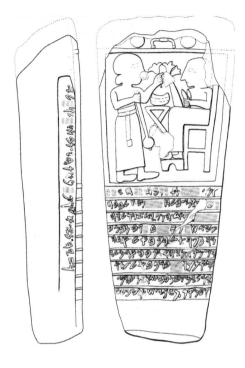

Fig. 7.4. The Sam'alian Ördekburnu royal mortuary stele as analyzed by Lemaire and Sass, "Morturary Stele," fig. 2 on p. 60, and drawn by Rodica Penchas and Yulia Gottlieb. Photo courtesy of the American Schools of Oriental Research, André Lemaire, and Benjamin Sass.

preserved (Piya-), refers to Rakib-El personally as "my god" (*rkb'l 'lhy*) and, curiously, to "Kubaba of Aram," perhaps referring to the goddess's cult at Arpad.[35]

Turning our attention to Bar Rakib, we find a fascinating case study in ethnocultural interactions at Zincirli especially when viewed through a political lens. Bar Rakib shows a clear preference for "Aramean" over Luwian.[36] His Aramean

---

in *Alphabets, Texts and Artifacts in the Ancient Near East: Studies Presented to Benjamin Sass*, ed. I. Finkelstein, C. Robin, and T. Römer (Paris: Van Dieren, 2016), 47–61. Unfortunately, the years of wear do not allow any firm conclusion other than the solid presence of the yoke bar and perhaps the bottom of the sun disk.

35. See Younger, "Ördekburnu and Katumuwa Stelae," 5–7, and his critique of Brandl, who understands the two prominent anthropomorphic figures to depict not a mortuary scene (the consensus) but rather the two deities, Rakib-El standing on the left before a seated Aramean Kubaba of Aram.

36. "Aramean" is intentionally placed in quotation marks in acknowledgment of the need to interrogate any notion of "Aramean ethnicity" especially in material imagery, as highlighted by recent studies such as those of Tamur and Cornelius. It makes more sense to focus on identity construction with a focus on how a particular individual can use linguistic markers and distinguishing scripts to adopt various identities to serve one's purpose. See Erhan Tamur, "Style, Ethnicity and the Archaeology of the Aramaeans: The Problem of Ethnic Markers in the Art

name contrasts with the Luwian names of Kulamuwa, his great-grandfather Panamuwa I, and his father Panamuwa II and is in concert with his Semitic named predecessors, including his grandfather Barṣūr and the earliest Semitic rulers of his city (Ḥayyā', Šảīl), especially Gabbār, the founder of the Iron Age kingdom of Sam'al, itself a Semitic toponym. The royal orthostats that he erects for his father and himself are all written in either Sam'alian Aramaic/Sam'alian or Old Aramaic, never Luwian.[37] The three languages and scripts used at Sam'al to celebrate the local and dynastic god Rakib-El are Northwest Semitic (Phoenician, Sam'alian Aramaic/Sam'alian, and Old Aramaic) and employ a linear alphabet in contrast to the hieroglyphic writing system of Luwian. In addition to Rakib-El, four of the named deities (Hadad, El, Śahr, Rašap) in his Sam'alian (*KAI* 215) and Old Aramaic inscriptions (*KAI* 216, 217, 218) are Aramean in contrast to the textual and visual Luwian portrayals at Zincirli mentioned above. These four deities can broadly be called "Aramean" in that they are not only Sam'alian but also occur in other Old Aramaic inscriptions such as those at Tel Fakhariyah (Hadad), Sefire (El), Tel Dan (Hadad), Nerab I and II (Śahr), Zakkur (Śahr), and the Bukan Inscription (Hadad).

Fig. 7.5. A gold signet ring with black and white onyx containing Bar Rakib's name written in cursive hieroglyphic Luwian. Image from von Luschan, *Die Kleinfunde von Sendschirli*, pl. 45l.

---

of the Syro-Anatolian Region in the Iron Age," *Forum Kritische Archäologie* 6 (2017): 1–72; Izak Cornelius, "The Material Imagery of the Sam'al (Zincirli) Monuments and 'Aramaean Identity,'" *Die Welt des Orients* 49.2 (2019): 183–205.

37. Linguistically, we need to carefully distinguish Samàlian Aramaic from Old Aramaic and appreciate how Bar Rakib intentionally changed from writing the former at the beginning of his reign (*KAI* 215) to the latter as his reign progressed (*KAI* 216, 217, 218). The significance of this will be addressed below.

While most scholars refer to the Hadad Inscription (*KAI* 214) and the Panamuwa Inscription (*KAI* 215) as Sam'alian Aramaic, Pat-El and Wilson-Wright argue that Sam'alian is a separate, independent branch of Northwest Semitic. See Na'ama Pat-El and Aren Wilson-Wright, "The Subgrouping of Samalian: Arguments in Favor of an Independent Branch," *Maarav* 23.2 (2019): 371–87.

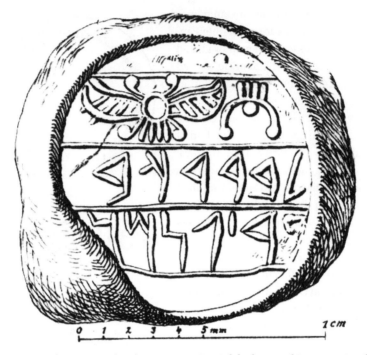

Fig. 7.6. A seal impression (BR7) mentioning "Bar Rakib, the son of Panamuwa" and two divine symbols. From von Luschan, *Die Kleinfunde von Sendschirli*, 73–74, plate 38b (S 3706) with description on p. 159.

Yet we should be careful not to be too restrictive extrapolating from these royal monumental displays. Bar Rakib never fails in his self-identification (on his orthostats, seal impression, and three silver ingots) to proclaim that he is the son of the Luwian named Panamuwa II.[38] Though the inscriptions on his orthostats use a linear alphabet, they are carved (not incised) in bas-relief likely inspired by hieroglyphic Luwian raised script (cf. too Kulamuwa's ductus). Bar Rakib possessed an expensive signet (fig. 7.5 on p. 127) with his name engraved in cursive hieroglyphic Luwian (*pa + ra/i-ki-pa-sa*). The ring is of the highest quality (a heavy gold ring

---

38. Though our sample size of these orthostats is small, it splendidly depicts three different social contexts: a royal building program (BR1); administration involving a scribe (BR3); and banqueting (BR2; Gilibert, *Syro-Hittite Monumental Art*, Zincirli 69). Gilibert's Zincirli 69 is based on the reconstruction of Joachim Voos, "Zu einigen späthethitischen Reliefs aus den Beständen des Vorderasiatischen Museums Berlin," *Altorientalische Forschungen* 12 (1985): 65–86.

with black and white onyx), lending prestige to its owner. This ring could represent a purely antiquarian object of status. Much more likely it was used by an astute monarch, who recognized that many of his constituents (again cf. Katumuwa) and neighboring communities held vibrant Luwian cultural traditions. One can imagine Bar Rakib using this conspicuous ring for all sorts of transactional purposes involving numerous individuals with a Luwian heritage.[39] For his Semitic constituents, Bar Rakib owned another seal (BR7; see fig. 7.6 on p. 128), this one containing the divine symbols of Rakib-El (the yoke bar) and Shamsh (a winged disk) together with his name ("Bar Rakib, the son of Panamuwa").[40] The small size of a seal forced its owner toward minimalist self-presentation and pragmatically driven pantheon reduction. Rakib-El's presence as the dynastic god was a certainty. Bar Rakib also chose Shamsh, likely due to his role as the guarantor of justice.[41] Compare this to how royal seals were used for a variety of political (e.g., treaties) and economic functions.

BAR RAKIB'S PRESENTATION OF DIVINITY: CONSERVATISM AND INNOVATION WITH REGARD TO INHERITED TRADITIONS

Bar Rakib was politically astute and diplomatically savvy. This is revealed in the ways in which he was both conservative and innovative when it came to portraying divinity. Both of these aspects are on display in the visual portrayal of divinity on the dolerite orthostat known as BR1/*KAI* 216 where Bar Rakib stands before five divine symbols. This fivefold cluster of symbols must be understood in relation to a fourfold cluster of divinity presented by his predecessor King Kulamuwa, who reigned a hundred years earlier from 840 to 815/810 BCE. Space does not allow for a full articulation of the many ways in which Bar Rakib consciously framed his building programs (including the erection of multiple orthostats) in conver-

---

39. Schloen and Fink astutely posit that "Barrakib, no doubt following the practice of his predecessors, possessed a Luwian signet ring in a nod to the prestigious Hittite tradition (and perhaps for use in correspondence with Luwian rulers)." See J. David Schloen and Amir S. Fink, "New Excavations at Zincirli Höyük in Turkey (Ancient Sam'al) and the Discovery of an Inscribed Mortuary Stele," *BASOR* 356 (2009): 10.

40. BR7 = Schwiderski BarRak:7 // Nahman Avigad and Benjamin Sass, *Corpus of West Semitic Stamp Seals* (Jerusalem: The Israel Academy of Sciences and Humanities, 1997), 280, #750.

41. Herbert Niehr, "Questions of Text and Image in Ancient Sam'al (Zincirli)," in *Text and Image: Proceedings of the 61e Rencontre Assyriologique Internationale, Geneva and Bern, 22–26 June 2015*, ed. Pascal Attinger, Antoine Cavigneaux, Catherine Mittermayer, and Mirko Novàk (Leuven: Peeters, 2018), 312–13.

Fig. 7.7. An orthostat of Bar Rakib portraying the king in Assyrian dress together with five symbols of divinity (BR1) and a lengthy inscription written in Old Aramaic in a raised script (*KAI* 216). Photo courtesy of Mark Ahsmann.

sation with Kulamuwa.[42] Bar Rakib explicitly brags about expanding "the house of Kulamuwa" (*byt klmw*) (*KAI* 216, lines 12–20) by which he means the palatial complex located in the northwestern half of the citadel.[43] For our present purposes, consider how the hundred-year-old orthostat of Kulamuwa (*KAI* 24) was

---

42. See especially Gilibert, *Syro-Hittite Monumental Art*, 87–88; Marina Pucci, *Functional Analysis of Space in Syro-Hittite Architecture* (Oxford: Archaeopress, 2008), 78.

43. Specifically, Herrmann writes that Bar Rakib "added to the old *bit-hilani* palaces of Kulamuwa's day (Buildings J and K with courtyard M) a new courtyard surrounded by porticoes and two new palaces, Hilanis III and IV." See Herrmann, "Cosmopolitan Politics," 508.

From Bar Rakib to Cyrus

Fig. 7.8. A ninth-century BCE orthostat of Kulamuwa found at Zincirli. The king wears Assyrian attire and showcases four divine symbols with their Aramean/Assyrian divinity hybridity. The accompanying inscription is written in Phoenician and in raised script (*KAI* 24). Photo courtesy of Gryffindor.

still standing at the time, and with it an ongoing communicative presence showing allegiance to four deities represented by the following symbols: a horned cap (Hadad), a yoke bar (Rakib-El), a winged sun disk (Shamsh), and a lunar symbol (either the Neo-Assyrian Sin or the local Aramean Śahr; see fig. 7.8 on p. 131). Bar Rakib stands within this royal heritage and shows respect with his portrayal of divinity that includes the same four gods via the same four symbols and in the same order, except for one dramatic innovation: the addition of a rare unprecedented double-circled five-pointed star, highlighting (seemingly) Rašap.[44] Just as Bar Rakib expanded Kulamuwa's royal palace—in his words "making (the physical and dynastic) house better [*hyṭbth*]"—so too he expands his divine portrayal with a fivefold cluster that was surely also "made better" in his eyes.

It's likely that Bar Rakib found inspiration for a fivefold cluster of divinity (and with the potential addition of Rašap) by again working within his inherited traditions, especially those of his great-grandfather, Panamuwa I (r. ca. 790–750 BCE). Panamuwa I's orthostat (*KAI* 214; see fig. 7.2 on p. 121) was also still standing for all to see (decades old at the time) and with it a textual, fivefold cluster of divinity. Though *KAI* 214 overall is very Hadad-centric (indeed, the colossal orthostat is of Hadad), Panamuwa I also singles out the god Rašap for supporting him (*wqm 'my ršp*; *KAI* 214, line 3). These two gods work in concert within a fivefold group of deities mentioned repeatedly in the text in a nearly fixed order (there is minor variation as to the placement of the god Rašap/'Arqû-Rašap):

KAI 214, line 2a	Hadad, El, Rašap, Rakib-El and Šamš
KAI 214, lines 2b–3a	Hadad, El, Rakib-El Šamš and Rašap
KAI 214, line 11	Hadad, El, Rakib-El, Šamš, 'Arqû-Rašap
KAI 214, lines 18b–19a	Hadad, El, Rakib-El, Šamš, [Rašap]

Turning to another of Bar Rakib's orthostats (*KAI* 215; see fig. 7.1 on p. 117) brings yet another example of his conservatism mixed with innovation. Bar Rakib erected this orthostat of Panamuwa II (r. ca. 743–733 BCE), his recently deceased father, at the very beginning of his reign with the dual goals of memorializing his father and legitimating his claim to the dynastic throne (see above). In the closing lines of the inscription, he writes: "May Hadad, El, Rakib-El, the lord of the dynastic house, Shamsh, and all the gods of Yàdiya [have favor upon me, Bar Rakib, the son of Panamuwa II]" (*KAI* 215, line 22). In this instance, he again has a fivefold cluster of divinity, and yet he strategically breaks with his great-grandfather's cluster. Bar Rakib omits the god Rašap altogether (he could have used a sixfold list) in favor of listing "all the gods of Yàdiya" whom he praised at the outset of the inscription (*KAI* 215, line 2). It seems that he is intentionally focusing on his local constituency as he seeks to claim the throne. Another look at BR1/*KAI* 216 (see fig. 7.7 on p. 130) reveals that while Bar Rakib was framing his portrayal in conversation with the ancient king Kulamuwa, he chose to do this in ways the broke with the tradition

---

44. For my argument favoring Rašap, see Lewis, "Kings, Peoples and Their Gods," 220–27.

of his great-grandfather Panamuwa I. Bar Rakib's visual narrative in BR1/*KAI* 216 is fivefold, but he breaks with family tradition in adding a lunar symbol referencing a moon god Sin/Śahr (like Kulumuwa) in place of his great-grandfather's El. What we have here on these two orthostats (*KAI* 215 and BR1/*KAI* 216) is a balancing act that shows a respect for long-standing traditions along with a pragmatism focused on his local constituency.

A third Bar Rakib orthostat depicting a banquet scene (BR2/*KAI* 217) has yet another fivefold visual cluster and, as we've come to expect, it too breaks with tradition, this time in two respects (fig. 7.9 on p. 133). It underscores the prominence of and allegiance to the dynastic god Rakib-El by adding in a second slightly variant yoke bar symbol. Strikingly, Bar Rakib also adds a unique double-human faced symbol—with the two faces facing in opposite directions—that is regularly referred to anachronistically as a "Janus" symbol known from Roman religion. While some scholars have suggested a Mesopotamian candidate for this two-headed symbol (e.g., Usmu/Isimud, a lesser deity who functioned as a minister of Enki/Ea), the consensus of scholars is to see El here due to the four occurrences of his name in Panamuwa I's inscription (*KAI* 214) mentioned above.[45]

Fig. 7.9. A fragment depicting Bar Rakib in a banquet context together with five divine symbols (BR2) and an inscription written in Old Aramaic (*KAI* 217) and carved in raised script. Relief from the citadel of Sam'al (Zincirli) in Turkey, ca. 730 BCE; Pergamon Museum, Berlin. Photo courtesy of Richard Mortel.

---

45. Additional support may be found in Philo of Byblos, though admittedly this material is notoriously difficult. See Lewis, *Origin and Character of God*, 87, 255–56. Philo of Byblos mentions that the god Taautos (Egyptian Thoth) "invented as royal emblems for Kronos [El] four eyes, on the front and in the rear, <two awake>, and two closed restfully.... This a symbol, since Kronos [El] was watchful even when in repose."

THEODORE J. LEWIS

There must have been some relevance for using this unique symbol within the hybrid audience at Sam'al, yet our lack of data allows us little ability to probe further. What is certain though is that it is highly innovative and we suspect that astute Bar Rakib knew exactly what he was doing.

BAR RAKIB'S PRESENTATION OF DIVINITY: PLAYING TO IMPERIAL POWER

Bar Rakib's diplomatic intentionality is seen in the textual narratives of BR1/ *KAI* 216 and BR2/*KAI* 217. At the outset of the former, Bar Rakib self identifies as "the servant of Tiglath-Pileser III" and proclaims that he "runs at the (chariot) wheel" of the king, just as his recently killed father had done on the king's military campaign. Using customary Mesopotamian royal rhetoric, Bar Rakib praises Tiglath-Pileser III with the epithet "the lord of the four quarters of the earth." In the same breath, he then highlights both the dynastic god Rakib-El and the Neo-Assyrian monarch Tiglath-Pileser III for "causing him to sit on the throne of his father" based on generational *ṣidq* "right conduct/loyalty/political fidelity" (*bṣdq 'by wbṣdqy hwšbny mr'y rkb'l wmr'y tgltplysr 'l krs' 'by*; *KAI* 216, lines 4b–7a). In contrast to the five divine symbols in the visual narrative, Bar Rakib's textual portrayal of divinity in *KAI* 216 is remarkable for its minimalism. The only individual deity mentioned is the dynastic god Rakib-El, whom Bar Rakib refers to as "my lord" (*mari'ī rkb'l*; *KAI* 216, line 5). Astutely, the vassal Bar Rakib accentuates the agency of Tiglath-Pileser III, whom he also calls "my lord" (*mari'ī tgltplysr*). Bar Rakib writes similarly in BR2/*KAI* 217 by combining god and king, yet he takes his royal praise one step further. Here he refers to Tiglath-Pileser III as "lord" or "my lord" seemingly five times (three occurrences are likely reconstructions) with no use of the title "lord" for Rakib-El. Whereas a visual audience can be broader, as noted above texts are targeted at an educated audience, specifically here Neo-Assyrian scribes and ambassadors who would have carried this content back to Tiglath-Pileser III. Indeed, imperial representatives are specifically mentioned in *KAI* 217, line 4 (*'bdy byt [mr'y mlk 'šwr]*).

This brings us to Bar Rakib's most stunning diplomatic move: the erection of an imposing orthostat (BR3/*KAI* 218) with the enthroned monarch sitting on an Assyrian-style throne receiving a scribe (sometimes referred to as a "state secretary") with writing tools (fig. 7.10 on p. 135). Unlike his other orthostats, here the visual and textual narratives offer a unified representation of divinity celebrating a single deity. Surprisingly, the deity in focus is not Bar Rakib's dynastic god Rakib-El (a constant in *all* his other inscriptions) but rather the moon god,

134

Fig. 7.10. An orthostat of an enthroned Bar Rakib that is administrative in nature (note the presence of a scribe before the king) and focuses on the moon god, here specifically called Ba'al Harran. Photo courtesy of Gary Todd.

here specifically called Ba'al Harran (*b'lḥrn*), whom he tellingly refers to as "my lord" (*mari'ī*). Rather than employing a simple crescent moon disk as he had done previously (on BR1/*KAI* 216), here he uses an elaborate moon disk situated on a pole with two hanging tassels on each side. Space does not allow us to discuss the international fame of the moon god of Harran in northern Mesopotamia and his "highly visible role in the ideological architecture of Assyrian imperialism in the West."[46] Suffice it to say, Bar Rakib is intentionally and boldly making an ideolog-

46. Steven W. Holloway, *Aššur Is King! Aššur Is King!: Religion in the Exercise of Power in the Neo-Assyrian Empire* (Leiden: Brill, 2002), 417. Additional secondary literature can be found in Lewis, "Kings, Peoples and Their Gods."

ical proclamation that his allegiance is not to the local moon god associated with Yảdiya (the Aramean god Śahr) but rather to the moon god of Harran with all of its Neo-Assyrian connections.[47]

There are additional indicators of Bar Rakib's pro-Assyrian positioning. Whereas he used his local Sam'alian Aramaic dialect at the beginning of his reign (*KAI* 215), he abandoned it in favor of Old Aramaic in his later inscriptions (*KAI* 216, 217), as this would align with the language used for early Neo-Assyrian westward expansion.[48] A pro-Assyrian ideology is also behind Bar Rakib's nomenclature, where he turns from previously referring to his city as Yảdiya, a local preference dating back over a hundred years to Kulamuwa (*KAI* 24, line 2), to consistently using the toponym Sam'al preferred in Akkadian sources.

Royal Portrayals of Divinity: What Do They Have to Do with "Belief"?

What can we glean from our case study of Bar Rakib's portrayal of divinity with regard to a monarch's "belief" in a particular god or gods? By using both textual and visual data, we are able to conclude that royal presentations of divinity are highly complex and can be tied, at least with regard to Bar Rakib, to a consummate politician who is trying to cover all his bases, both locally and abroad. Bar Rakib's diverse portrayal of divinity reveals a monarch's finessing of multiple religious narratives to satisfy the complex demands of his various audiences. Overall, Bar Rakib presents a fluid portrayal of divinity that changes depending on his audience. Though he shows a strong allegiance to Rakib-El, the dynastic deity, he is not wedded solely to this deity if the pragmatics of a situation demand otherwise. He is respectful of inherited traditions, though at the same time he can break quite dramatically from these traditions.

---

47. Niehr perceptively notes how, apart from our inscription, "the moon-god of Harran is never mentioned" in the entire corpus of inscriptions from Zincirli, currently twenty-three in number. See Niehr, "Questions of Text and Image," 314.

48. For the distinctions between these two dialects with regard to the Bar Rakib inscriptions, see Lewis, "Kings, Peoples and Their Gods," 237. Niehr astutely notes how "Bar-Rakib chose Old Aramaic in order to open up a way to both inner Syria and also towards the Assyrians on whom he depended." See Herbert Niehr, "The Power of Language: Language Situation and Language Policy in Sam'al," in *In Search for Aram and Israel: Politics, Culture, and Identity*, ed. Omer Sergi, Manfred Oeming, and Izaak J. de Hulster (Tübingen: Mohr Siebeck, 2016), 327.

From Bar Rakib to Cyrus

METHODOLOGICAL CONSIDERATIONS: TURNING BACK TO CYRUS

Royal portrayals of divinity can be quite entangled. Providential language regarding divinity may lead interpreters to project the personal nature of divinity onto a monarch's belief system, especially when a ruler writes in relational (though often stereotypical) terms about how a particular god came to his assistance. Yet royal portrayals are politically, culturally, and sociologically contingent. We have seen with Bar Rakib that varying data from differing media belie simplistic and reductionist notions of his "belief" in any particular god. Why would we think that the situation would be any different for Cyrus? With Bar Rakib, we have the benefit of having a lot of data within a narrow time span (ca. 730–727 BCE), within controlled space (the Hilani IV palace complex), and within narrow geographic parameters and polities (the Sam'alian administration of Zincirli in northern Syria). In contrast, compare the paltry data for Cyrus that led Albert de Jong to conclude that we "know next to nothing" of Cyrus's religious beliefs.[49] Stripping away the literary portrayal in the book of Ezra leaves an extremely minimal dataset. With regard to Yehud of the Persian period, we do not have Cyrus's own textual narrative, like we have with the Cyrus Cylinder. We do not have his use of visual propagandistic narratives aimed at a variety of audiences. Surely Cyrus must have used a variety of media to legitimize his reign. Had we these larger datasets at our disposal, we would likely conclude that the historical situation regarding Cyrus's royal portrayal of divinity is far more complicated than our simplistic scenarios. In short, without more data, any historical conclusion about Cyrus is premature. We must remain agnostic.

What the case study with Bar Rakib has taught us is that we should imagine what it would be like to have a fuller data set that would allow us to formulate a host of questions for any ancient Near Eastern ruler, Cyrus or otherwise. What media are being used to portray divinity? Visual and textual narratives have diverse functions and audiences, and they also reflect different kinds of literacies. What audiences (internal and external) are being addressed, and what are their cultural make-ups, especially for hybrid audiences? What legacy of divinity has been handed down from royal predecessors, and how is a given monarch positioning himself in dialogue with inherited traditions (i.e., degrees of conservatism versus innovation)? Are a variety of portrayals being used to present divinity in different ways for different audiences for political gain? What visual or numerical restrictions are in play and for what reasons? Does the ruler project a gendered view of divinity and, if so, why? As with so many questions regarding antiquity, we

---

49. De Jong, "Religion of the Achaemenid Rulers," in Jacobs and Rollinger, *Companion to the Achaemenid Persian Empire*, 1204.

face the limitation of having a *very small* dataset with which to work. This dataset shrinks further when what we have is someone else's (for Cyrus, the author of the book of Ezra) literary portrayal rather than a ruler's own inscriptions. We stand at such a cultural and historical distance that we need to be more agnostic with our conclusions.

Works Cited

Albertz, Rainer, and Rüdiger Schmitt. *Family and Household Religion in Ancient Israel and the Levant*. Winona Lake, IN: Eisenbrauns, 2012.

Avigad, Nahman, and Benjamin Sass. *Corpus of West Semitic Stamp Seals*. Jerusalem: The Israel Academy of Sciences and Humanities, 1997.

Becking, Bob. *Ezra-Nehemiah*. Leuven: Peeters, 2018.

Blenkinsopp, Joseph. *Ezra-Nehemiah*. Philadelphia: Westminster, 1988.

———. *Isaiah 40–55*. Anchor Bible Commentary. New York: Doubleday, 2002.

Bodel, John, and Saul M. Olyan, eds. *Household and Family Religion in Antiquity*. Oxford: Blackwell, 2008.

Brandl, Baruch. "Rakib'il and 'Kubaba of Aram' at Ördekburnu and Zincirli and New Observations on Kubaba at Zincirli, Carchemish and Ugarit." Pages 47–61 in *Texts and Artifacts in the Ancient Near East: Studies Presented to Benjamin Sass*. Edited by Israel Finkelstein, Christian Robin, and Thomas Römer. Paris: Van Dieren, 2016.

Cornelius, Izak. "In Search of the Goddesses of Zincirli (Sam'al)." *ZDPV* 128 (2012): 15–25.

———. "The Material Imagery of the Sam'al (Zincirli) Monuments and 'Aramaean Identity.'" *Die Welt des Orients* 49.2 (2019): 183–205.

Fales, Frederick Mario, and Giulia Francesca Grassi. *L'aramaico antico: Storia, grammatica, testi commentate*. Udine: Forum, 2016.

Fensham, F. Charles. *The Books of Ezra and Nehemiah*. New International Commentary on the Old Testament. Grand Rapids: Eerdmans, 1982.

Finkel, Irving L., ed. *The Cyrus Cylinder: The King of Persia's Proclamation from Ancient Babylon*. London: I. B. Tauris, 2013.

Gibson, John C. L. *Aramaic Inscriptions Including Inscriptions in the Dialect of Zenjirli*. Vol. 2 of *Textbook of Syrian Semitic Inscriptions*. Oxford: Clarendon, 1975.

Gilibert, Alessandra. *Syro-Hittite Monumental Art and the Archaeology of Performance: The Stone Reliefs at Carchemish and Zincirli in the Earlier First Millennium BCE*. Berlin: de Gruyter, 2011.

Glassner, Jean-Jacques. *Mesopotamian Chronicles*. Atlanta: SBL Press, 2004.

Grabbe, Lester L. "The 'Persian Documents' in the Book of Ezra: Are They Authentic?" Pages 531–70 in *Judah and the Judeans in the Persian Period*. Edited by Oded Lipschits and Manfred Oeming. Winona Lake, IN: Eisenbrauns, 2006.

Gruen, Erich S. "Jewish Perspectives on Persia." Pages 1461–78 in *Companion to the Achaemenid Persian Empire*. Edited by Bruno Jacobs and Robert Rollinger. Hoboken: Wiley-Blackwell, 2021.

Herrmann, Virginia R. "Cosmopolitan Politics in the Neo-Assyrian Empire: Local Elite Identity at Zincirli-Sam'al." *Semitica* 60 (2018): 493–535.

Holloway, Steven W. *Aššur Is King! Aššur Is King!: Religion in the Exercise of Power in the Neo-Assyrian Empire*. Leiden/Boston: Brill, 2002.

Hutter, Manfred. "Kubaba in the Hittite Empire and the Consequences for Her Expansion to Western Anatolia." Pages 113–22 in *Hittitology Today: Studies on Hittite and Neo-Hittite Anatolia in Honor of Emmanuel Laroche's 100th Birthday*. Edited by Alice Mouton. Istanbul: Institut français d'études anatoliennes, 2014.

———. "Religions in the Empire." Pages 1285–302 in *A Companion to the Achaemenid Persian Empire*. Edited by Bruno Jacobs and Robert Rollinger. Hoboken: Wiley-Blackwell, 2021.

Jacobs, Bruno and Robert Rollinger, eds., *A Companion to the Achaemenid Persian Empire*. Hoboken: Wiley-Blackwell, 2021.

Japhet, Sara. "Periodization between History and Ideology II: Chronology and Ideology in Ezra-Nehemiah." Pages 491–508 in *Judah and the Judeans in the Persian Period*. Edited by Oded Lipschits and Manfred Oeming. Winona Lake, IN: Eisenbrauns, 2006.

Jong, Albert de. "The Religion of the Achaemenid Rulers." Pages 1199–209 in *A Companion to the Achaemenid Persian Empire*. Edited by Bruno Jacobs and Robert Rollinger. Hoboken: Wiley-Blackwell, 2021.

Keil, Carl F., and Franz Delitzsch. *Biblical Commentary on the Old Testament*. Grand Rapids: Eerdmans, 1986.

Kuhrt, Amélie. "The Cyrus Cylinder and Achaemenid Imperial Policy." *JSOT* 25 (1983): 83–97.

Lemaire, André, and Benjamin Sass. "The Mortuary Stele with Sam'alian Inscription from Ördekburnu near Zincirli." *BASOR* 369 (2013): 57–136.

Lewis, Theodore J. "Bar-Rakib's Legitimation and the Problem of a Missing Corpse: The End of the Panamuwa Inscription in Light of the Katumuwa Inscription." *ARAM Periodical* 31.2 (2019): 349–74.

———. "From Standing Stones to Sacred Emptiness: Textual and Visual Portrayals of Israel's God." Paper presented at the American Society of Overseas Research (ASOR) Webinar, July 2021. https://www.asor.org/news/2021/07/lewis-webinar-yahweh/.

—. "Kings, Peoples and Their Gods: Bar Rakib's Political Portrayal of Divinity." Pages 212–52 in *"A Community of Peoples": Studies on Society and Politics in the Bible and Ancient Near East in Honor of Daniel E. Fleming*. Edited by Mahri Leonard-Fleckman, Lauren Monroe, and Michael Stahl. Leiden: Brill, 2022.

—. *The Origin and Character of God: Ancient Israelite Religion through the Lens of Divinity*. New York: Oxford University Press, 2023.

Luschan, Felix von. *Die Kleinfunde von Sendschirli*. Ausgrabungen in Sendschirli 5. Mitteilungen aus den Orientalischen Sammlungen 15. Berlin: de Gruyter, 1943.

Masson, Émilia. "La stèle mortuaire de Kuttamuwa (Zincirli): Comment l'appréhender." *Semitica et Classica* 3 (2010): 47–58.

Niehr, Herbert. "The Power of Language: Language Situation and Language Policy in Sam'al." Pages 305–32 in *Search for Aram and Israel: Politics, Culture, and Identity*. Edited by Omer Sergi, Manfred Oeming, and Izaak J. de Hulster. Tübingen: Mohr Siebeck, 2016.

—. "Questions of Text and Image in Ancient Sam'al (Zincirli)." Pages 309–19 in *Text and Image: Proceedings of the 61e Rencontre Assyriologique Internationale, Geneva and Bern, 22–26 June 2015*. Edited by Pascal Attinger, Antoine Cavigneaux, Catherine Mittermayer, and Mirko Novàk. Leuven: Peeters, 2018.

Ornan, Tallay. *The Triumph of the Symbol: Pictorial Representation of Deities in Mesopotamia and the Biblical Image Ban*. Fribourg: Academic Press, 2005.

Pardee, Dennis. "The KTMW Inscription." Pages 95–96 in *Supplements*. Vol. 4 of *The Context of Scripture 4*. Edited by K. Lawson Younger Jr. Leiden: Brill, 2017.

—. "A New Aramaic Inscription from Zincirli." *BASOR* 356 (2009): 51–71.

Pat-El, Na'ama, and Aren Wilson-Wright. "The Subgrouping of Samalian: Arguments in Favor of an Independent Branch." *Maarav* 23.2 (2019): 371–87.

Payne, Annick. *Iron Age Hieroglyphic Luwian Inscriptions*. Atlanta: SBL Press, 2012.

Pucci, Marina. *Functional Analysis of Space in Syro-Hittite Architecture*. Oxford: Archaeopress, 2008.

Sanders, Seth L. "The Appetites of the Dead: West Semitic Linguistic and Ritual Aspects of the Katumuwa Stele." *BASOR* 369 (2013): 35–55.

Schloen, J. David, and Amir S. Fink. "New Excavations at Zincirli Höyük in Turkey (Ancient Sam'al) and the Discovery of an Inscribed Mortuary Stele." *BASOR* 356 (2009): 1–13.

Schwiderski, Dirk. *Die alt- und reichsaramäischen Inschriften*. Vol. 2. Berlin: de Gruyter, 2004.

Spek, R. J. van der. "Cyrus the Great, Exiles, and Foreign Gods: A Comparison of Assyrian and Persian Policies on Subject Nations." Pages 233–64 in *Extraction and Control: Studies in Honor of Matthew W. Stolper*. Edited by Michael Kozuh,

Wouter Henkelman, Charles Ellwood Jones, and Christopher Woods. Chicago: Oriental Institute of the University of Chicago, 2014.

Tamur, Erhan. "Style, Ethnicity and the Archaeology of the Aramaeans: The Problem of Ethnic Markers in the Art of the Syro-Anatolian Region in the Iron Age." *Forum Kritische Archäologie* 6 (2017): 1–72.

Tropper, Josef. *Die Inschriften von Zincirli: Neue Edition und vergleichende Grammatik des phönizischen, sam'alischen und aramäischen Textkorpus.* Münster: Ugarit-Verlag, 1993.

Voos, Joachim. "Zu einigen späthethitischen Reliefs aus den Beständen des Vorderasiatischen Museums Berlin." *Altorientalische Forschungen* 12 (1985): 65–86.

Williamson, Hugh G. M. *Ezra, Nehemiah.* WBC 16. Waco, TX: Word, 1985

Yadin, Yigael. "Symbols of Deities at Zinjirli, Carthage and Hazor." Pages 199–231 in *Near Eastern Archaeology in the Twentieth Century.* Edited by James A. Sanders. Garden City, NY: Doubleday, 1970.

Yakubovich, Ilya. "The West Semitic God El in Anatolian Hieroglyphic Transmission." Pages 385–98 in *Pax Hethitica: Studies on the Hittites and Their Neighbours in Honour of Itamar Singer.* Edited by Y. Cohen, A. Gilan, and J. L. Mille. Wiesbaden: Harrassowitz, 2010.

Younger, K. Lawson, Jr. "Gods at the Gates: A Study of the Identification of the Deities Represented at the Gates of Ancient Sam'al (Zincirli) with Possible Historical Implications." *ARAM Periodical* 31.2 (2019): 317–48.

———. "The Ördekburnu and Katumuwa Stelae: Some Reflections on Two Grabdenkmäler." *BASOR* 384 (2020): 1–19.

———. *A Political History of the Arameans: From Their Origins to the End of Their Polities.* Atlanta: SBL Press, 2016.

8

Bad Blood?

Varying Attitudes on Human Sacrifice in Archaic Greek Art

MICHAEL ANTHONY FOWLER

Greek authors from the classical period on suggest that human sacrifice was a bygone practice confined to remote history, or that it was condemned in the present as an unthinkably barbaric inversion of civilizational norms.[1] Among the first extant ancient sources to criticize human sacrifice is Plato's *Republic* (391b). Therein, Socrates denies that Achilles ever slaughtered twelve highborn Trojan youths over

[1]. The literary evidence has been the subject of several articles and monographs. See inter alia Friedrich Schwenn, *Die Menschenopfer bei den Griechen und Römern* (Giessen: Töpelmann, 1915), 20–139; Angelo Brelich, "Symbol of a Symbol," in *Myths and Symbols: Studies in Honor of Mircea Eliade*, ed. Joseph M. Kitagawa and Charles H. Long (Chicago: University of Chicago Press, 1969), 195–207; Albert Henrichs, "Human Sacrifice in Greek Religion: Three Case Studies," in *Le sacrifice dans l'Antiquité*, ed. Jean Rudhardt and Olivier Reverdin (Vandœuvres-Geneva: Fondation Hardt, 1981), 195–242; Dennis Hughes, *Human Sacrifice in Ancient Greece* (London: Routledge, 1991), esp. 49–138; Pierre Bonnechere, *Sacrifice humain en Grèce ancienne* (Athens: Centre international d'étude de la religion grecque antique, 1994), which is the most exhaustive; and Jan Bremmer, "Myth and Ritual in Greek Human Sacrifice: Lykaon, Polyxena, and the Case of the Rhodian Criminal," in *The Strange World of Human Sacrifice*, ed. Jan Bremmer (Leuven: Peeters, 2006), 65–78.

Composing this contribution to the St Andrews Biblical Studies Symposium "Aspects of Belief in West Asia and the Mediterranean Basin (1000 BCE–100 CE)" furnished a valuable opportunity to reflect and expand upon a topic that I treated previously in my unpublished doctoral thesis, Michael Anthony Fowler, "Human Sacrifice in Greek Antiquity: Between Myth, Image, and Reality" (PhD diss., Columbia University, 2019).

the pyre of Patroklos—a deed relayed by no less an authority than Homer's *Iliad* (23.175–177). The philosopher's denial is predicated upon his belief that Achilles's noble lineage and character were inconsistent with the performance of such an outrage against gods and men. Earlier literary sources do not offer such clear moral judgments, nor do they betray any doubt over or disbelief in the historical reality of human sacrifices, including those commemorated in the traditional stories that today we classify as "myth."[2]

The extant corpus of Greek literature abounds in accounts of human sacrifice. These accounts derive almost exclusively from well-known myths. The rare "historical" case of Themistokles's slaughter of three noble Persian prisoners prior to the battle of Salamis in 480 BCE (Plutarch, *Them.* 13.2–5 citing Phanias of Eresos) lacks any contemporary witness and seems rather to be a fiction inspired by its author's individual biases and objectives.[3] Indeed, Themistokles's alleged act exhibits striking parallels with the mythic sacrifice of Iphigenia at Aulis. The study of human sacrifice from a textual perspective is, therefore, essentially an examination of mythic accounts and their reception or use in different authors' works. However, in surviving texts of the preclassical period (that is, before 480 BCE), we find no evaluation of the plausibility, truth, or morality of any instance of human sacrifice.

All the same, a critical consciousness regarding the credibility of myth and its sources is voiced early on in Greek literary history in the proem of Hesiod's *Theogony* (late eighth or early seventh century BCE).[4] So, the seeming lack of preclassical evaluations of human sacrifice does not rule out the possibility that varying attitudes and beliefs on the topic may have already existed. In this essay, I suggest that just such a critical consciousness about human sacrifice can be recovered for the preclassical period, if we redirect our attention to a small yet remarkable group of Archaic-era artworks.

In spite of the rich mythic repertoire available to them, Greek artists produced scenes of human sacrifice rather infrequently and drew upon an extremely re-

---

2. While some scholars have interpreted the words κακὰ δὲ φρεσὶ μήδετο ἔργα (Homer, *Il.* 23.176) as a Homeric rebuke of Achilles's actions, this is highly unlikely in view of the epic's overall compositional features; in fact, the line may even be a later interpolation. On the latter point see Hughes, *Human Sacrifice*, 53–54 (with references).

3. For a sensitive analysis of the Themistoklean human sacrifice, see Henrichs, "Human Sacrifice in Greek Religion," 208–24.

4. On the embeddedness of criticism in Greek (literary) engagements with myth, see Vinciane Pirenne-Delforge, "Under Which Conditions Did the Greeks 'Believe' in Their Myths? The Religious Criteria of Adherence," in *Antike Mythen: Medien, Transformationen, und Konstruktionen; Festschrift für Fritz Graf*, ed. Ueli Dill and Christine Walde (Berlin: de Gruyter, 2009), 38–54 (with further references).

stricted range of subjects. Across the entire history of Greek art, there are fewer than fifty human sacrificial images, and almost all of them feature the maidens Polyxena or Iphigeneia as the victim. In the Archaic period (700–480 BCE), which shall be our focus, painters and sculptors were almost exclusively interested in the sacrificial fate of the Trojan princess Polyxena.[5]

As I shall argue, in Archaic representations of the sacrifice of Polyxena the viewer may detect a diversity of attitudes or positions on the practice of human sacrifice ranging from acceptance to repudiation. On this point, it is worth observing that the material record evinces a parallel dynamic: Archaeological evidence for the practice of human sacrifice among Greek communities is exceedingly rare and may therefore indicate the general avoidance, if not rejection, of its practice (and certainly the absence of a custom thereof). Nevertheless, there is isolated evidence of ritualized killings in elite funerary contexts even as late as the third quarter of the sixth century BCE at a few Archaic-era tumular monuments in the Milesian colony of Istros on the west coast of the Black Sea.[6] The existence of archaeological evidence contemporary with our Archaic images is one ready indication that funerary human sacrifices were not universally condemned by

---

5. Although the circumstances of Polyxena's death varied in Greek myth, sacrifice was among the earliest versions and soon predominated in the literary accounts, as attested by fragmentary choral lyric attributed to three different Archaic-era poets: Arktinos (*Ilioupersis*), Stesichoros (*Ilioupersis*), and Leches (*Little Iliad*), if in the latter work Achilles's apparition instructed Neoptolemos to make the sacrifice. The antiquity of this myth is further corroborated by the visual evidence to be discussed below. For a detailed discussion of the textual evidence associated with the poems of the Trojan Cycle, see Martin L. West, *The Epic Cycle: A Commentary on the Lost Troy Epics* (Oxford: Oxford University Press, 2013). While certainly an early tradition, our extant contemporary evidence is less informative about the reasons for the sacrifice of Polyxena. Scholars have looked to later texts and images for elucidation, finding in them romantic and marital themes. Of the Greek and Roman authors who treated the subject of Polyxena's sacrifice, Seneca in his tragedy *Trojans* made this connection most explicit and developed. See Charles Fontinoy, "Le sacrifice nuptial de Polyxène," *L'Antiquité Classique* 19 (1950): 383–96. As for Iphigeneia's sacrifice, the first secure image, painted on a white-ground lekythos by Douris (Palermo, Museo Archeologico Regionale 1886), does not appear until the opening decades of the fifth century.

6. Consult Michael Anthony Fowler, "Of Human Sacrifice and Barbarity: A Case Study of the Late Archaic Tumulus XVII at Istros," *História: Questões & Debates* 69.1 (2021): 81–120 (with bibliography). Of additional relevance is the ritually executed man, whose remains were found alongside cremation Pyre A in the Orthi Petra Cemetery at Eleutherna (Crete; ca. 700 BCE). The principal publication of this find is Nicholas Chr. Stampolidis, *"Reprisals": Contribution to the Study of Customs of the Geometric-Archaic Period* (Rethymno: University of Crete, 1996), esp. 25–91. Istros and Eleutherna are discussed in greater length in Fowler, "Human Sacrifice in Greek Antiquity," 177–205 and 230–68.

144

Bad Blood?

Greeks of the preclassical era. Furthermore, in the case of the sacrifices at Istros the available evidence suggests that a group of local elite incorporated human sacrifices into their funerals in direct emulation of heroic burials commemorated in myth (namely, Patroklos and Achilles).[7] Myths involving human sacrifice are thus a common source of inspiration for the artist and the elite practitioner.

The phrase that comprises the title of this essay, *bad blood*, has a twofold sense. On the one hand, it refers to the underlying issue of belief, and specifically visual articulations thereof, as well as to the specific thesis that is advanced herein. This first sense is idiomatic and indicative: Polyxena's sacrifice was a matter of *bad blood*, since it was believed to placate the wrathful and aggrieved ghost of Achilles, who denied the Greeks safe passage home until he was granted the spoils due to him (cf. Euripides, *Hec.* 35–44; Quintus Smyrnaeus, *Post.* 14.324–338). On the other hand, the phrase *bad blood* in a more literal sense is interrogative. To wit, did Archaic Greeks believe the ritual shedding of Polyxena's blood to be bad per se? While the preclassical literary record is bereft of explicit answers, the small yet rich group of Archaic representations of Polyxena's sacrifice attests to a range of beliefs and attitudes on the matter of human sacrifice.

Whereas Greeks generally held a historicist view of their myths, seeing them as real events from the past that continued to impact contemporary life, myths also maintained their force through their ability to be adapted to suit new circumstances, functions, or ends. Myths were fundamental to the formation of collective identities, providing etiologies for peoples, places, things, cults, and rituals. To the mythic era belonged the glorious race of heroes, stories of whose great deeds (and misdeeds!) played a significant role in the education of youth, as they offered enduring models of conduct and character. Recall that elites at Istros performed funerary rituals of heroic proportions, including human sacrifices, as a means to elevate the status of their dead.

A related meeting of mythic past and present obtained in the realm of art. When artists undertook to visualize scenes from myth—by far the most common source of subject matter in Greek art—they created temporal "amalgams."[8] Even as artists drew their subjects from the stuff of legends, in their representations they modeled the elements of their stories after the *realia* of the contemporary world. In addition to draping their scenes in more modern garb, the choice of mythic subject could be determined by its thematic or conceptual relevance to the intended context of use or display. The Greeks' recourse to the same myths

---

7. See Fowler, "Of Human Sacrifice and Barbarity," esp. 109–12.

8. Jocelyn Penny Small, *The Parallel Worlds of Classical Art and Text* (Cambridge: Cambridge University Press, 2003), 35–36.

in their art over several centuries is a credit not only to the adaptability of their myths but also to the enduring relevance of their content to the life and times of their varying audiences. Or, as Ken Dowden writes, "the whole of Greek Mythology may be viewed as an enormous text in dialogue with that other text, the world in which we live."[9]

The iconographic evidence should be included in studies of Greek human sacrifice, since it is not only through literal "texts" that Greek ideas about this ritual and mythic instances thereof may be apprehended. Indeed, as Jean-Pierre Vernant stated in his preface to the groundbreaking project *A City of Images*, the visual language of Greek art is distinct; it "has its particular aims, its norms and requirements, its own means of expression and communication."[10] Images were not merely illustrative handmaidens to literary accounts. Through their work, artists composed their own "texts," their own retellings or versions of the myth by (de)emphasizing, manipulating, or combining the various elements of the narrative in different, at times even novel, ways.

Studying representations of human sacrifice in Greek art presents, then, an opportunity not only to learn the particular "grammar" and semiotics of the images but also to examine the ways in which the images complement, contradict, or offer alternatives to the mythic accounts and judgments—aesthetic as well as moral—that are preserved in the literary sources. Indeed, as we shall see, the iconographic record of the Archaic period offers a unique glimpse into the various attitudes that Greeks might have had on the subject of human sacrifice.

Visualizing Archaic Greek Attitudes on Human Sacrifice

The most famous Greek visual representation of Polyxena's sacrifice appears on the shoulder of an Attic black-figure neck amphora of the Tyrrhenian Group attributed to the Timiades Painter (fig. 8.1 on p. 147).[11] The scene centers on the tumulus of Achilles, around which we find seven Greek warriors, three of whom

---

9. Ken Dowden, *The Uses of Greek Mythology: Approaching the Ancient World* (London: Routledge, 1992), 53.

10. Jean-Pierre Vernant, preface to *A City of Images: Iconography and Society in Ancient Greece*, ed. Claude Bérard et al., trans. Deborah Lyons (Princeton: Princeton University Press, 1989), 7.

11. London, British Museum 1897,0727.2 = *LIMC*, s.v. "Polyxène," 7:433 (no. 26 with pl. 347). See esp. Ioannis Mylonopoulos, "Gory Details? The Iconography of Human Sacrifice in Greek Art," in *Sacrifices humains: Perspectives croisées et représentations*, ed. Pierre Bonnechere and Renaud Gagné (Liège: Presses universitaires de Liège, 2013), 74–76; and Jean-Louis Durand and

Fig. 8.1. Timiades Painter (attributed), Side A of an Attic black-figure amphora of the Tyrrhenian Group, ca. 560 BCE, ceramic, 38 cm (h), said to come from Italy, London, British Museum. Photo © The Trustees of the British Museum.

steady the maiden victim while a fourth, Achilles's son Neoptolemos, delivers the mortal blow. A painted label identifies each character.[12] The noble victim is

---

François Lissarrague, "Mourir à l'autel: Remarques sur l'imagerie du 'sacrifice humain' dans la céramique attique," *Archiv für Religionsgeschichte* 1 (1999): 91–92.

12. Richard Neer, "'A Tomb Both Great and Blameless': Marriage and Murder on a Sarcophagus from the Hellespont," *Res: Anthropology and Aesthetics* 61/62 (2012): 100, states that the names of the Greeks "don't make much sense," contending that two of the men bearing Polyxena, presumably Amphilochos and Antiphates, have Trojan names. While it is indeed difficult to explain the choice of these names on the basis of the textual accounts of the sacrifice

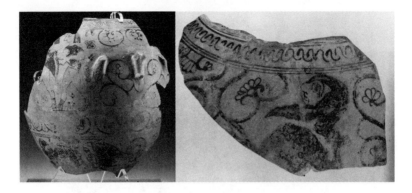

Figs. 8.2a–2b. Painter of the New York Nessos Amphora (attributed), Sides A and B of a fragmentary Middle Protoattic krater, ca. 650–630 BCE, ceramic, 52 cm (max h), unknown provenance. Photos courtesy of the Antikenmuseum and Sammlung Ludwig.

emphasized through her horizontal position and the considerable elongation of her body. That she goes to the altar unwillingly is betrayed by the men's tight grip on her body and her carriage to the altar. Although the attitude of the maiden toward her own fate would become a critical element of fifth-century dramas, one exploited for its emotional, ethical, and political potential, the willingness of the victim was not necessary to the correct performance or efficacy of this rite.[13]

---

that come down to us, there is nevertheless literary evidence for Greek men with such names. Henry B. Walters, "On Some Black-Figured Vases Recently Acquired by the British Museum," *JHS* 18 (1898): 285n4, had already referenced a seer named Amphilochos, who stayed behind with Kalchas after the Greeks quit Troy (Quintus Smyrnaeus, *Post.* 14.396), and an Antiphates, who was among the warriors inside the Trojan Horse (Tryphiodoros, *Sack of Troy* 180; John Tzetzes, *Posthomerica* 648). Walters also suggests as an additional possibility that the name Antilochos might have been intended where Amphilochos was written and would fit well in a scene that already includes his father, Nestor. We shall return to Nestor shortly.

13. For the varying uses of virgin sacrifice on the Athenian stage, see, for example, Nicole Loraux, *Tragic Ways of Killing a Woman*, trans. Anthony Forster (Cambridge: Harvard University Press, 1987), 31–48; relatedly, Anthony Mangieri, *Virgin Sacrifice in Classical Art: Women, Agency, and the Trojan War* (New York: Routledge, 2018), 141–60, considers how ancient viewers would have experienced visual images of maiden sacrifice with respect to the female victim's volition or resistance. While the victim's agency was certainly of great interest to artists and playwrights, it is equally true that the integrity of the sacrifice was not dependent upon the victim's consent or cooperation. On this point, see Fred S. Naiden, "The Fallacy of the Willing Victim," *JHS* 127 (2007): 61–73; and Stella Georgoudi, "L'occultation de la violence' dans le sacrifice grec: Données

Bad Blood?

This visual schema, in which a recalcitrant Polyxena is carried horizontally, emerges in the earliest unambiguous representation of the myth found on a late Middle Protoattic krater (650–630 BCE) by the painter of the New York Nessos Amphora (figs. 2a–2b on p. 148).[14] However, the vase's fragmentary condition frustrates any determination of the precise narrative moment painted upon it. The striding legs of the male captors suggest that Polyxena is actively moving toward the tomb, in a manner akin to the sacrifice as depicted in a narrative pastiche of the fall of Troy on a late Middle Corinthian pyxis (ca. 570 BCE).[15] Of particular note in the representation on the pyxis is the rendering of the maiden's dramatically flailing arms, which heightens the viewer's appreciation of her desperation.

In addition to the physical violence at its core, the Timiades Painter's vase includes three figures who play more passive roles. We shall focus on two of them: the aged king Nestor Pylios and Achilles's elder mentor Phoinix, who are respectively positioned at the left and right margins of the scene. The men adopt an identical pose: standing in profile to the right with the left leg slightly advanced, the right arm bent at a right angle with the hand closed into a fist at waist height, and the left hand steadying a spear vertically. Apart from the provision of labels, the men are differentiated by the details of their dress and hair. Phoinix is also provided with a folding chair. This furnishing punctuates the compositional space, creating a visual break that is compounded by Phoinix's averted gaze. Unlike Nestor, Phoinix either does not wish to countenance the gruesome act before him, or something outside the narrative core of the image

---

anciennes, discours modernes," in *La cuisine et l'autel: Les sacrifices en questions dans les sociétés de la Méditerranée ancienne*, ed. Stella Georgoudi, Renée Koch Piettre, and Francis Schmidt (Turnhout: Brepols, 2005), esp. 131–34.

14. Private collection, formerly on loan to the Museum of Fine Arts, Boston 6.67; most recently loaned to Basel, Antikenmuseum und Sammlung Ludwig = *LIMC*, s.v. "Iphigeneia," 5:709 (no. 2). First published in Emily Vermeule and Suzanne Chapman, "A Protoattic Human Sacrifice?" *American Journal of Archaeology* 75.3 (1971): 285–93 with pls. 69–71, whence the sacrificial reading originates (on p. 291). The thirteen extant fragments come from the back and front sides of the vase and join together to make up only about one quarter of the original vessel, ranging from the rim to just above the foot or stand (287n8).

15. The vessel entered the collection of the State Hermitage Museum (B.2397) in 1908 as a gift of the Egyptologist Vassily S. Golenischev. For the first full publication of the pyxis, see Anastasia G. Bukina, "*Ilioupersis* on a Corinthian Black-Figured Pyxis in the State Hermitage Museum," *Antike Kunst* 53 (2010): 3–11. The pyxis's dating is suggested by the style of the painting as well as the compressed, globular, handleless form of the vase. Prior to my dissertation, this image had not been included in any synthetic study on the iconography of human sacrifice in Greek art.

has attracted his attention.[16] Commentators favor the former explanation for this compositional asymmetry.[17]

I would like to signal here two other features of the vase that corroborate the notion that Achilles's teacher, Phoinix, has indeed turned away in horror or disgust. The first is the use of added white paint. Every figure in the scene who participates physically or visually in the sacrifice, including the maiden herself, has some part of their body or clothing painted white. In contrast, Phoinix bears no such pigment. The white accents, therefore, seem to be a technical means to visually unify the sacrificial group and distinguish its members from Phoinix. In so doing, the painter creates two distinct parties to the sacrifice with whom the implied viewer of the vase could associate.

16. Although we will pursue the former interpretation in what follows, to my eye Nestor's centrifugal position also serves to direct the viewer's attention to the opposite side of the vase. There, one encounters on the shoulder a subject evidently favored by the Timiades Painter throughout his career, and one with a cheerful, homoerotic tenor markedly distinct from the bloody, somber spectacle of the maiden's exsanguination over the hero's tomb. There, a cadre of four nude male komasts, one bearded and three beardless, dances in a strikingly "playful, uninhibited manner" positioned between two larger-than-life roosters. For a discussion of the heightened realism and variance of poses in komastic scenes on Tyrrhenian vases, whence the above characterization of the dancing comes, see Tyler Jo Smith, *Komast Dancers in Archaic Greek Art* (Oxford: Oxford University Press, 2010), 59–70, 317 with pl. 14B. Smith observes that the wreaths held by two of the young men may indicate a ritual or festive atmosphere of the dance (p. 70). For the frequency of komastic scenes in the iconographic repertoire of the Timiades Painter, see Jeroen Kluiver, "Early 'Tyrrhenian': The Prometheus Painter, Timiades Painter, Goltyr Painter," *Bulletin Antieke Beschaving* 70 (1995): 85.

17. When the narrative action is centripetal, spectator figures typically occupy the margins of the scene and orient their gaze toward the center. The infrequent exceptions to this "rule" therefore require specific explanations. On the asymmetrical spectators on the Timiades Painter's vase see Michael J. Anderson, *The Fall of Troy in Early Greek Poetry and Art* (Oxford: Clarendon, 1997), 231; Gerda Schwarz, "Der Tod und das Mädchen: Frühe Polyxena-Bilder," *Mitteilungen des Deutschen Archäologischen Instituts, Athenische Abteilung* 116 (2001): 37; Mylonopoulos, "Gory Details?," 75. In a recent review article, Stella Georgoudi, "Le sacrifice humain en tous ses états," *Kernos* 28 (2015): 259, questions Mylonopoulos's "psychologizing" reading but does not offer an alternative explanation for the particular manner in which Phoinix is rendered. While Georgoudi's interpretative caveat is generally worth bearing in mind when interpreting ancient Greek body language, there are two further components of the vase's decoration that I believe validate and strengthen the reading that Anderson, Schwarz, and Mylonopoulos offer with respect to this particular composition. I discuss these two aspects below. Furthermore, the Timiades Painter's vase is not unique in its incorporation of divergent figures, as I shall demonstrate shortly. For a concise presentation of the analytical promise and interpretive limitations of studying body language in ancient Greek and Roman art, see Odette Touchefeu-Meynier and François Lissarrague, introduction to *L'expression du corps: Gestes, attitudes, regards dans l'iconographie antique*, ed. Lydie Bodiou, Dominique Frère, and Véronique Mehl (Rennes: Presses universitaires de Rennes, 2006), 17–22.

Bad Blood?

The second detail is situated in one of the vase's smaller "subsidiary" friezes of animals, mythical creatures, and floral motifs (see fig. 8.1 on p. 147).[18] While these friezes may be characterized aptly as Corinthianizing elements consciously employed by Tyrrhenian-style workshops to appeal to the tastes of their target market(s),[19] in this instance the Timiades Painter shows ingenuity in their use. Two sirens flanking the central palmette-and-lotus motif, located directly below and in axial alignment with Achilles's tomb, abandon their purely ornamental function. Despite their conventional rendering in profile and heraldic positioning, the sirens direct their attention *above* rather than ahead of or behind themselves, as is typical in animal friezes. This is most obviously demonstrated by the siren on the right, who raises her head to gaze upon Polyxena's hemorrhaging throat. The siren's counterpart on the left also observes the gore, albeit more subtly by only raising her eyes. Whereas the expression on the leftmost siren's face is generally impassive, the tightening of the other siren's eyes and the lowering of her inner brows might convey an emotional response.[20] However, it is difficult to determine whether the siren's possible expression is one of contempt, approbation, or simply focused interest, since the details of her mouth are not well preserved.

It is also worth considering whether the sirens, who are but one of the myriad chimeras that populate the sea of the epic imagination, represent the perilousness of marine voyages and the inclemency of the sea.[21] If so, we could argue that the painter was integrating "secondary" figures into the principal narrative in a

18. A high-resolution image of the vase is also available through the British Museum's website: https://www.britishmuseum.org/collection/object/G_1897-0727-2.

19. Alexandra Alexandridou, "Early Sixth-Century Directional Trade: The Evidence of Attic Early Black-Figured Pottery," in *The Contexts of Painted Pottery in the Ancient Mediterranean World (Seventh-Fourth Centuries BCE)*, ed. Dimitris Paleothodoros (Oxford: Archaeopress, 2012), 11, 15.

20. While Greek art is generally characterized as less emotionally expressive before the Hellenistic period, emotions are not absent in Archaic and classical art. The degree of emotional expressivity depends on a variety of factors, such as the intended use context of the artwork and the identity of the subjects depicted. In addition, emotion may be denoted through culturally conditioned postures and gestures instead of facial expressions. In the case of the facial expressions, they may be subtle (so-called microexpressions, as perhaps with our abovementioned sirens). The study of emotions in pre-Hellenistic art thus rewards close looking. On this topic, see Ioannis Mylonopoulos, "Emotions in Greek Art," in *A World of Emotions: Ancient Greece, 700 B.C.–200 A.D.*, ed. Angelos Chaniotis, Nikolaos Kaltsas, and Ioannis Mylonopoulos (New York: Alexander S. Onassis Public Benefit Foundation, 2017), 72–85, esp. 78–80.

21. For a brief discussion of the relationship between sirens and the dangers of the sea, see Bruno d'Agostino, "I pericoli del mare: Spunti per una grammatica dell'immaginario visuale," in *Modi e funzioni del racconto mitico nella ceramica greca, italiota ed etrusca dal VI al IV secolo a.C.: Atti del Convegno Internazionale Raito di Vietri sul Mare, Auditorium di Villa Guariglia 29/31 maggio 1994* (Salerno: Edizioni 10/17, 1995), 201–13 (with conference discussion on 264–66).

manner akin to the hybrid sea monsters that float beneath the human sacrifice on the aforementioned Protoattic krater (see fig. 8.2a on p. 148).[22] While it is difficult to date the origins of the myth of Achilles's angry apparition, if it was already circulating in the Archaic period, then the sirens on the Timiades Painter's vase may have served as visual analogs for the unfavorable marine conditions that Polyxena's sacrifice was meant to ameliorate. Homeric epic informs us, moreover, that the hero's tumulus was erected upon a promontory for passing sailors to see (Homer, *Il.* 7.84–90; 23.245–248, *Od.* 24.80–84). We will return to this aspect of *bad blood* momentarily.

The rendering of the sirens appears to implicate them in the mythic episode. Whatever the reading of their facial expressions, they serve not only as additional witnesses to the sacrifice but also show individualized reactions to it. Indeed, the fact that the action unfolding above them is so interesting or extraordinary that it would disrupt the sirens' decorative function makes Phoinix's inattentiveness to the sacrifice all the more conspicuous. This aspect of the painter's composition lends support to Ioannis Mylonopoulos's suggestion that "the structure of the scene expresses the acceptance and rejection of the human sacrifice within one composition."[23] Phoinix is well outnumbered by those who countenance the human sacrifice and might therefore be seen to represent an unpopular attitude toward the ritual.[24] Yet, I wonder whether the legitimacy of the majority's action is not undermined by the interest of the sirens. Demons of death, the sirens may be present in their Homeric guise either as malevolent entities who delight in the bloody spectacle or in their funereal aspect as sympathetic attendants of the dying princess.[25]

The marginal pairing of Nestor and Phoinix relates to a category of spectators on Athenian vase paintings of the Archaic period that Mark D. Stansbury-O'Donnell has termed "interested."[26] Nestor and Phoinix are directly associated

22. Vermeule and Chapman, "Protoattic Human Sacrifice," esp. 292–93. Schwarz, "Der Tod und das Mädchen," 47–49, attempts to relate them to the myth of Polyxena's sacrifice (rather than Iphigeneia, as in the former article).

23. Mylonopoulos, "Gory Details?," 75.

24. Note here the second "assenting" spectator to the right of Nestor (Diomedes).

25. For the iconography of sirens in Archaic and classical Greek art and their associations with death and the underworld, see Despoina Tsiafakis, "'ΠΕΛΩΡΑ': Fabulous Creatures and/ or Demons of Death?" in *The Centaur's Smile: The Human Animal in Early Greek Art*, ed. J. Michael Padgett (New Haven: Yale University Press, 2004), esp. 74–78, 97–98. The funereal, mourning aspect of the siren is evidenced as early as the sixth century as sculptural decoration on tomb markers.

26. Mark D. Stansbury-O'Donnell, *Vase Painting, Gender, and Social Identity in Archaic Athens* (Cambridge: Cambridge University Press, 2006), 16, 23. The study is limited, however, to Stansbury-O'Donnell's narratively distanced classes of "detached" and "pure" spectators, since

Bad Blood?

with the scene's narrative core (the sacrificial act) and serve to allude to actions or ideas (conflicting counsel) that exist outside the immediate context of the scene. But both men exhibit a limited degree of involvement in the sacrificial proceedings as well as an inability to modify their outcome. As stationary, spear-bearing, older adult men with spatially consolidated poses, Nestor and Phoinix likewise embody Stansbury-O'Donnell's "inert" mood.[27] Such figures, when anonymous, are considered by Stansbury-O'Donnell to function as models for the ideal Athenian male citizen, who strictly regulated his body, especially as concerns any emphatic expression of emotion—even when witnessing a rousing scene.[28] In the case of mythic scenes, generic male spectators very frequently exhibit "reactive" moods, using restrained gestures that attest to the exemplary quality of the deeds before them. In the case of Nestor and Phoinix, their responses are less active. It is only the opposing orientations of their bodies with respect to the sacrificial scene that suggest variance in their interests and attitudes.

But were mythical deeds invariably invoked as *positive* exempla? Or could certain acts—even those committed by gods and heroes—be regarded with disapproval or ambivalence?[29] The Timiades Painter accommodates two diametrically opposed viewpoints. While one viewpoint evidently meets with the majority's consent, neither Nestor nor Phoinix is portrayed in a way that undermines the

---

the author is ultimately interested in understanding how such generic characters may represent certain identity groups and the social ideals and expectations associated with them. Being named, mythical characters, Nestor and Phoinix do not belong to this category; but as adult men visually demarcated only by their labels, they may be compared to the author's findings with respect to this general identity group. It may be objected that Phoinix is not technically a spectator, since he does not actually watch the sacrifice unfold. I would argue, however, that this configuration resulted from the deliberate disruption of the compositional convention of symmetry, and that this disruption marks Phoinix as an inverse of Nestor, that is, as a negation of visual participation in the human sacrifice. This negation cannot exist without reference to the convention of spectators arranged in mirror positions at the opposite edges of the scene.

27. Stansbury-O'Donnell, *Vase Painting*, 23–24.

28. Stansbury-O'Donnell, *Vase Painting*, 136. Cf. Timothy J. McNiven, "Behaving Like an Other: Telltale Gestures in Athenian Vase Painting," in *Not the Classical Ideal: Athens and the Construction of the Other in Greek Art*, ed. Beth Cohen (Leiden: Brill, 2000), 71–96.

29. Here I am reminded of an especially germane aside in Mylonopoulos, "Emotions in Greek Art," 85n41, as concerns the emotionally evocative—if not itself emotional—nature of Archaic and classical images: "One can only imagine the ancient reactions to the brutal scene on a hydria [attributed to the Leagros Group (510–500 BCE); British Museum B326] that shows Achilles throwing Troilos' head at Trojan warriors." How would one have understood the perpetration of such outrageous violence by the *best* among the Achaians? On the ambivalent, norm-defying conduct of heroes, see Tonio Hölscher, *Krieg und Kunst im antiken Griechenland und Rom: Heldentum, Identität, Herrschaft, Ideologie* (Berlin: de Gruyter, 2019), 58–80.

validity of their respective positions. That is, both spectators embody self-control, as befits their roles either as wise, heroic counselors or as models of ideal male conduct. The men's disagreement is visualized, but the rehearsal or evaluation of their discursive exchange devolves to the users and viewers of the vase.[30]

The Timiades Painter's composition is neither unique nor the first in the representation of diverse perspectives on human sacrifice. Turning to the opposite side of the aforementioned Protoattic krater (see fig. 8.2b on p. 148), we encounter an isolated man set within a dense forest of palmette motifs. That he should be interpreted in connection with the sacrificial scene is suggested by his posture: While the man, whose torso is rendered frontally, seems to lean away from the sacrificial scene, he turns his head back to glance at it over his right shoulder. He bends his left arm and raises his hand toward his head to form a gesture with the thumb extended out from the palm, while the other fingers are gathered together and slightly bent. The man's right arm is also bent but lowered, with the forearm extending away from the body.

What does this body language denote? The notion that the solitary man is represented as turning away sharply, perhaps in "revulsion" or to "express startled concern," was initially proposed by Emily Vermeule and Suzanne Chapman and, in my view, has rightly enjoyed near unanimous scholarly approval.[31] However, his identity as the diviner Kalchas is less persuasive in consideration of the mythological scene with which he is associated.[32] In my view, he should be identified as Phoinix.[33] The man's beard would suit his more advanced age by comparison to

---

30. In the context of this short essay, I cannot enter into a discussion of the specific contexts wherein a vase like this might have been used and seen. The Timiades Painter's amphora, like the overwhelming majority of his workshop's output, was evidently destined for Italy and most probably an Etruscan client. Indeed, we lack information about the provenience of this and many other Greek vase paintings. And even when the final depositional context is known, this context does not exclude the possibility that the object had earlier stages of use. The amphora may well have ended its "life" as a gift or offering in a sanctuary or, more likely, a tomb; but it could also have been previously used for other ends. Here, I limit myself to observing that the foreign context of discovery opens up still more discursive possibilities concerning the evaluation of the ritual of human sacrifice. For an excellent recent monograph on the Etruscan reception of Greek pottery (in their functional and iconographic dimensions), see now Sheramy D. Bundrick, *Athens, Etruria, and the Many Lives of Greek Figured Pottery* (Madison: University of Wisconsin Press, 2019).

31. Vermeule and Chapman, "Protoattic Human Sacrifice," 288.

32. That is, the sacrificial victim is Polyxena and not Iphigeneia, as was initially proposed in Vermeule and Chapman, "Protoattic Human Sacrifice."

33. I therefore disagree with A. John N. W. Prag, *The Oresteia: Iconographic and Narrative Tradition* (Warminster: Aris & Phillips, 1985), 64, who asserts that the turning figure "would have no place in the Sacrifice of Polyxena."

Bad Blood?

Fig. 8.3a. Albertinum Group (attributed), fragmentary headboard of a Klazomenian sarcophagus, 500–480 BCE, ceramic, 78 cm x 20.5 cm x 40 cm, unknown provenance. Photo courtesy of the Rijksmuseum. *Fig. 8.3b.* Watercolor drawing of the Klazomenian sarcophagus. Drawing © Robert M. Cook, published in Cook, *Clazomenian Sarcophagi*, pl. 48.3.

his Achaian compatriots, while his spatial detachment and body language would communicate his exception to the performance of the sacrifice—a salient element reprised by the Timiades Painter.[34]

In another representation on a fragmentary Klazomenian sarcophagus dating to the first quarter of the fifth century (figs. 8.3a–3b on p. 155), Neoptolemos

---

34. The two representations of Phoinix exhibit vastly different degrees of emotional expressivity. But we must keep in mind that as much as one hundred years separates the production of these two vases, and that the sixth century saw the development of new iconographic conventions concerning the expression of emotion.

steps from the right onto the lower of two steps upon which his father's tumulus is erected and tows Polyxena along by the wrist.[35] The tumulus, which is positioned in the center of the headboard, is balanced on its left side by a roughly symmetrical configuration of warriors, whose leading figure also strides upon the lower step of the tomb.[36] The striding figure opposite Neoptolemos raises and bends his left arm in a gesture that is difficult to read, especially since the hand is missing. In his analysis of this scene, Friedrich von Duhn interprets the gesture as communicating the warrior's empathy for the victim and his inner tension about his participation in the sacrifice.[37] Whatever response the warrior's gesture was meant to convey, we can safely assume that it contributed to the discursive quality of the scene. If the gesture was reproachful or conflicted rather than hortatory, it perhaps also offered a critique of the act—akin to the minority figure of Phoinix on the Timiades Painter's vase and, according to my view, the emphatically twisting figure on the opposite side of the Middle Protoattic krater.

It is worth noting that the representation of Nestor and Phoinix as opposing parties resurfaces roughly 150 years later on an unparalleled Apulian volute krater attributed to the Dareios Painter.[38] The complex composition centers on Achilles's sacrifice of a group of captive Trojan youths alongside Patroklos's funerary pyre—the very event whose historicity had, by then, been contested in Plato's *Republic*. Whereas the Timiades Painter employed antipodal positioning and divergent gazes to indicate Nestor and Phoinix's disagreement, the Dareios Painter collapses the spatial divide and its attendant silence. The sage warriors

---

35. Leiden, Rijksmuseum I 1896-12.1a = *LIMC*, s.v. "Polyxène," 7:433 (no. 21 with pl. 347). See Friedrich von Duhn, "Zur Deutung des klazomenischen Sarkophags in Leiden," *Jahrbuch des Deutschen Archäologischen Instituts* 28 (1913): 272–73; Robert M. Cook, *Clazomenian Sarcophagi* (Mainz: von Zabern, 1981), 36, cat. G8 (Albertinum Group) with pl. 48.3.

36. Symmetric or heraldic arrangements are a standard feature of Klazomenian sarcophagi; the presence of a single female figure is therefore all the more indicative of a specific mythic reference. See Cook, *Clazomenian Sarcophagi*, 114.

37. Von Duhn, "Zur Deutung," 273: "um seine Teilnahme und innere Erregung auszudrücken."

38. Naples, Museo Archeological Nazionale H 3254 (81393) = *LIMC*, s.v. "Achilleus," 1:118 (no. 487). See inter alia Adolf Furtwängler and Karl Reichold, *Griechische Vasenmalerei*, vol. 2 (Munich: Bruckmann, 1909), 156–60 with pl. 89; Jean-Marc Moret, *L'Ilioupersis dans la céramique italiote: Les mythes et leur expression figurée au IVe siècle* (Rome: Institut suisse de Rome, 1975), 214–15; Arthur D. Trendall and Alexander Cambitoglou, *The Red-Figured Vases of Apulia*, vol. 2 (Oxford: Clarendon, 1982), 495n39; Claude Pouzadoux, "Les funérailles de Patrocle ou la mise en image des indices de la gloire," in *Iconografía ibérica, iconografía itálica: Propuestas de interpretación y lectura. Roma 11–13, nov. 1993, Coloquio Internacional*, ed. Ricardo Olmos Romera and Juan Antonio Santos Velasco (Madrid: Universidad Autómoma de Madrid, 1997), 137–52; Mylonopoulos, "Gory Details?," 65–67.

Figs. 8.4a–4b. Anonymous, one long side and one short side of the so-called Polyxena Sarcophagus, 510–500 BCE, Proconnesian marble, 280 cm x 80 cm, from Gümüsçay (northwest Turkey), Kizöldün tumulus. Photos courtesy of the Troy Museum.

now convene in a common space (likely a tent) and engage in direct discursive exchange. The plaintive state of the standing man, whom I identify as Phoinix, is expressed through the slight but telling movements of his face and upraised hand.

His brows slant upward toward the bridge of the nose and his eyelids droop; unlike his interlocutor, his forehead is marked with furrows. The furrowing of the brow is a detail observed only on the faces of the most emotionally agitated figures in the composition: Achilles and his Trojan victims. The corners of Phoinix's mouth are downturned to form a frown. As for his hand, a comparison with Hermes or the young man's statue on the reverse side of the vase's body evinces the painter's use of varying forms of eloquent gestures in distinct contexts, each of which was linked to a different sort of verbal address. Arthur Trendall and Alexander Cambitoglou, who likewise identify the gesticulating man as Phoinix, keenly recognized "the raising of one hand with two fingers slightly parted and pointing upwards" as "the admonitory conversational gesture."[39] Therefore, a distinct and rather attractive possibility is that Phoinix and Nestor are debating Achilles's enraged actions, which unfold "below" them: the human sacrifices and the desecration of Hektor's corpse.[40]

Due to the complexity of the object, I shall make but two brief comments on one final Archaic-era work: the Polyxena Sarcophagus (510–500 BCE; figs. 8.4a–4b on p. 157).[41] First, behind the sacrificing figure of Neoptolemos, on the other side of Achilles's tumulus, stands a tripod. As the emblem par excellence of Apollo, the tripod could conjure the presence of the very god responsible for Achilles's demise. At the same time, tripods functioned as highly prized symbols of victory and aristocratic excellence.[42] What is more, the tripod functions as a pendant to Polyxena herself. Like the tripod, the maiden's cascading blood is an offering to the hero, albeit one that is much more precious on account of its comparative rarity.[43] The tripod will make a brief reappearance, at least one decade later, on a black-figure Haimonian lekythos.[44] While the lekythos bears a markedly differ-

39. Trendall and Cambitoglou, *Red-Figured Vases of Apulia*, 492.

40. Such would be well suited to the vase painter's compositional focus on Achilles and his wrath. In this respect, I agree with Furtwängler and Reichold, *Griechische Vasenmalerei*, 159, who assert that the topic of Phoinix and Nestor's discussion is Achilles's acts of reprisal.

41. Çanakkale, Museum of Troy E.7670 = *LIMC* suppl., s.v. "Polyxène," 431 (add. 5, with pl. 207). The bibliography on the sarcophagus is vast and ever growing; see Nurten Sevinç, "A New Sarcophagus of Polyxena from the Salvage Excavations at Gümüşçay," *Studia Troica* 6 (1996): 251–64; Mylonopoulos, "Gory Details?," 76–78; Neer, "'Tomb Both Great and Blameless,'" 98–115; and C. Brian Rose, *The Archaeology of Greek and Roman Troy* (Cambridge: Cambridge University Press, 2014), esp. 72–103.

42. For a recent, archaeologically informed study of the tripod and its diverse range of localized uses and meanings, see Nassos Papalexandrou, "Boiotian Tripods: The Tenacity of a Panhellenic Symbol in a Regional Context," *Hesperia* 77.2 (2008): 251–82.

43. Cf. Rose, *Archaeology of Greek and Roman Troy*, 86–87.

44. Paris, Musée du Louvre CA 1743 = *LIMC*, s.v. "Polyxène," 7:434 (no. 36); Mangieri, *Virgin Sacrifice*, 75–76.

Bad Blood?

ent visualization of the sacrifice itself, the polyvalent significance of the tripod remains in play.[45] These images suggest that already in the Archaic era, Polyxena is counted among Achilles's share of the spoils, which predates the earliest textual attestation of this idea by at least a century.

Second, the Polyxena Sarcophagus constitutes an important transitional moment in the maiden's iconographic history. While it repeats the Timiades Painter's interest in imagining the violence of Polyxena's death in graphic detail, the dedication of so great a proportion of the compositional space to Trojan mourners (including Polyxena's disconsolate mother on one of its short sides! [see fig. 8.4b on p. 157]) and the literal marginalization of Achilles's tumulus, heralds a significant shift in how Greek artists treat the story. The focus shifts increasingly to the experience of the victimized parties, especially during the fraught moments before the sacrificial bloodshed.[46] The protesting figure of Phoinix is replaced with a complementary and hitherto unexplored *Trojan* perspective, thereby expanding the range of possible responses to the sacrifice.[47]

CONCLUSION

A consideration of the repertoire of Archaic Greek representations of Polyxena's sacrifice indicates that the tradition of Achilles's *bad blood* may well be traced back to the preclassical era. The analogous relationship between Polyxena and

45. At the turn of the fifth century BCE, Polyxena begins to walk toward her place of sacrifice rather than being carried—a feature that we already encountered on the fragmentary Klazomenian sarcophagus. The Haimonian lekythos is additionally distinct for its transformation of the sacrifice into an unceremonious graveside slaughter (yet Neoptolemos still observes the ritual norm of wounding the sacrificial victim's neck).

46. See (1) an Attic black-figure hydria by the Leagros Group (510–500 BCE), Berlin Antikensammlung F1902 = *LIMC*, s.v. "Polyxène," 7:433 (no. 22 with pl. 347); (2) an Attic black-figure lekythos attributed to the Acheloos Painter (ca. 510 BCE), Metropolitan Museum of Art, Callimanopoulos Collection, L1983.71.4; and (3) a fragmentary Attic red-figure kylix by Makron (490–480 BCE), Louvre G153 = *LIMC*, s.v. "Polyxène," 7:433 (no. 24). See Durand and Lissarrague, "Mourir à l'autel," 97–98; Mangieri, *Virgin Sacrifice*, 67; Mylonopoulos, "Gory Details?," 79.

47. The inclusion of an audience of extended family is more characteristic of representations of Iphigeneia's sacrifice, the earliest secure instance of which is dated to around 490 BCE. The presence of Trojans at the sacrifice of Polyxena may have been repeated on at least one further vase produced in Italy, in an Etruscan workshop likely with heavy influence taken from Attic products: a black-figure neck amphora of (Etrusco-)Campanian style (ca. 470 BCE), British Museum B70 = *LIMC*, s.v. "Polyxène," 7:434 (no. 37). See Franca Parise Badoni, *Ceramica campana a figure nere* (Florence: Sansoni, 1968), 60n5. The subject of this scene is not certain (it may also be Iphigeneia who, contrary to the Archaic Greek manner, was shown being carried over the altar in later, Hellenistic-era Etruscan images of her sacrifice).

the tripod on the Polyxena Sarcophagus and the Haimonian lekythos point up the status of the maiden as war booty to be awarded to Achilles. Relatedly, the inclusion of marine monsters on the Protoattic krater and Tyrrhenian amphora could suggest that her sacrifice was intended to palliate the dead hero's wrath, thereby placating the sea and enabling the Greeks to sail home—in short, an exceptional sacrifice meant to restore order to the cosmos.

As to whether Polyxena's sacrifice was, ethically or religiously speaking, *bad blood*, in Archaic Greek art the answer was evidently plural. As with the opposing figures of Nestor and Phoinix, it depended on one's perspective. In advancing this position, I do not mean to suggest that the two opposing views were equally popular, or that there were not intermediate positions, such as the possibly conflicted warrior on the headboard of the Klazomenian sarcophagus. And, of course, we must also consider the diversity of perspectives adopted by those who would have seen and used these mythological representations. We cannot exclude the possibility that at least some Archaic viewers would have regarded the sacrifice of Polyxena as good to think *and* to do, especially when we observe the rare yet compelling evidence of ritualized killings of human beings preserved in the archaeological record, which dates to as late as third quarter of the sixth century BCE.[48] Indeed, the latest of this evidence is roughly contemporary with the production of the famous Tyrrhenian amphora by the Timiades Painter, with which we began. Albeit mythological in nature, the sacrifice of Polyxena—the subject of all the Archaic images we considered herein—likewise transpired in an aristocratic funerary context. Far from being universally regarded as obsolete, outrageous, false, or otherwise settled, in Archaic Greece human sacrifice—or at the very least those instances with a funereal inflection—remained *in contention*.

Works Cited

Alexandridou, Alexandra. "Early Sixth-Century Directional Trade: The Evidence of Attic Early Black-Figured Pottery." Pages 5–20 in *The Contexts of Painted Pottery in the Ancient Mediterranean World (Seventh-Fourth Centuries BCE)*. Edited by Dimitris Paleothodoros. Oxford: Archaeopress, 2012.

Anderson, Michael J. *The Fall of Troy in Early Greek Poetry and Art*. Oxford: Clarendon, 1997.

Bonnechere, Pierre. *Sacrifice humain en Grèce ancienne*. Athens: Centre international d'étude de la religion grecque antique, 1994.

48. Fowler, "Of Human Sacrifice."

Brelich, Angelo. "Symbol of a Symbol." Pages 195–207 in *Myths and Symbols: Studies in Honor of Mircea Eliade*. Edited by Joseph M. Kitagawa and Charles H. Long. Chicago: University of Chicago Press, 1969.

Bremmer, Jan. "Myth and Ritual in Greek Human Sacrifice: Lykaon, Polyxena, and the Case of the Rhodian Criminal." Pages 65–78 in *The Strange World of Human Sacrifice*. Edited by Jan Bremmer. Leuven: Peeters, 2006.

Bukina, Anastasia G. "*Ilioupersis* on a Corinthian Black-Figured Pyxis in the State Hermitage Museum." *Antike Kunst* 53 (2010): 3–11.

Bundrick, Sheramy D. *Athens, Etruria, and the Many Lives of Greek Figured Pottery*. Madison: University of Wisconsin Press, 2019.

Cook, Robert M. *Clazomenian Sarcophagi*. Mainz: von Zabern, 1981.

d'Agostino, Bruno. "I pericoli del mare: Spunti per una grammatica dell'immaginario visuale." Pages 201–13, 264–66 in *Modi e funzioni del racconto mitico nella ceramica greca, italiota ed etrusca dal VI al IV secolo a.C.: Atti del Convegno Internazionale Raito di Vietri sul Mare, Auditorium di Villa Guariglia 29/31 maggio 1994*. Salerno: Edizioni 10/17, 1995.

Dowden, Ken. *The Uses of Greek Mythology: Approaching the Ancient World*. London: Routledge, 1992.

Duhn, Friedrich von. "Zur Deutung des klazomenischen Sarkophags in Leiden." *Jahrbuch des Deutschen Archäologischen Instituts* 28 (1913): 272–73.

Durand, Jean-Louis, and François Lissarrague. "Mourir à l'autel: Remarques sur l'imagerie du 'sacrifice humain' dans la céramique attique." *Archiv für Religionsgeschichte* 1 (1999): 83–106.

Fontinoy, Charles. "Le sacrifice nuptial de Polyxène." *L'Antiquité Classique* 19 (1950): 383–96.

Fowler, Michael Anthony. "Human Sacrifice in Greek Antiquity: Between Myth, Image, and Reality." PhD diss., Columbia University, 2019.

———. "Of Human Sacrifice and Barbarity: A Case Study of the Late Archaic Tumulus XVII at Istros." *História: Questões & Debates* 69.1 (2021): 81–120.

Furtwängler, Adolf, and Karl Reichold. *Griechische Vasenmalerei*. Vol. 2. Munich: Bruckmann, 1909.

Georgoudi, Stella. "Le sacrifice humain en tous ses états." *Kernos* 28 (2015): 255–73.

———. "L'occultation de la violence' dans le sacrifice grec: Données anciennes, discours modernes." Pages 115–47 in *La cuisine et l'autel: Les sacrifices en questions dans les societés de la Méditerranée ancienne*. Edited by Stella Georgoudi, Renée Koch Piettre, and Francis Schmidt. Turnhout: Brepols, 2005.

Henrichs, Albert. "Human Sacrifice in Greek Religion: Three Case Studies." Pages 195–242 in *Le sacrifice dans l'Antiquité*. Edited by Jean Rudhardt and Olivier Reverdin. Vandœuvres-Geneva: Fondation Hardt, 1981.

Hölscher, Tonio. *Krieg und Kunst im antiken Griechenland und Rom: Heldentum, Identität, Herrschaft, Ideologie.* Berlin: de Gruyter, 2019.

Hughes, Dennis. *Human Sacrifice in Ancient Greece.* London: Routledge, 1991.

Kluiver, Jeroen. "Early 'Tyrrhenian': The Prometheus Painter, Timiades Painter, Goltyr Painter." *Bulletin Antieke Beschaving* 70 (1995): 55–104.

Loraux, Nicole. *Tragic Ways of Killing a Woman.* Translated by Anthony Forster. Cambridge: Harvard University Press, 1987.

Mangieri, Anthony. *Virgin Sacrifice in Classical Art: Women, Agency, and the Trojan War.* New York, Routledge, 2018.

McNiven, Timothy J. "Behaving Like an Other: Telltale Gestures in Athenian Vase Painting." Pages 71–96 in *Not the Classical Ideal: Athens and the Construction of the Other in Greek Art.* Edited by Beth Cohen. Leiden: Brill, 2000.

Moret, Jean-Marc. *L'Iloupersis dans la céramique italiote: Les mythes et leur expression figurée au IVe siècle.* Rome: Institut suisse de Rome, 1975.

Mylonopoulos, Ioannis. "Emotions in Greek Art." Pages 72–85 in *A World of Emotions: Ancient Greece, 700 B.C.–200 A.D.* Edited by Angelos Chaniotis, Nikolaos Kaltsas, and Ioannis Mylonopoulos. New York: Alexander S. Onassis Public Benefit Foundation, 2017.

———. "Gory Details? The Iconography of Human Sacrifice in Greek Art." Pages 61–85 in *Sacrifices humains: Perspectives croisées et représentations.* Edited by Pierre Bonnechere and Renaud Gagné. Liège: Presses universitaires de Liège, 2013.

Naiden, Fred S. "The Fallacy of the Willing Victim." *JHS* 127 (2007): 61–73.

Neer, Richard. "'A Tomb Both Great and Blameless': Marriage and Murder on a Sarcophagus from the Hellespont." *Res: Anthropology and Aesthetics* 61/62 (2012): 98–115.

Papalexandrou, Nassos. "Boiotian Tripods: The Tenacity of a Panhellenic Symbol in a Regional Context." *Hesperia* 77.2 (2008): 251–82.

Parise Badoni, Franca. *Ceramica campana a figure nere.* Florence: Sansoni, 1968.

Pirenne-Delforge, Vinciane. "Under Which Conditions Did the Greeks 'Believe' in Their Myths? The Religion Case of Adherence." Pages 38–54 in *Antike Mythen: Medien, Tranformationen, und Konstruktionen; Festschrift für Fritz Graf.* Edited by Ueli Dill and Christine Walde. Berlin: de Gruyter, 2009.

Pouzadoux, Claude. "Les funérailles de Patrocle ou la mise en image des indices de la gloire." Pages 137–52 in *Iconografía ibérica, iconografía itálica: Propuestas de interpretación y lectura. Roma 11–13, nov. 1993, Coloquio Internacional.* Edited by Ricardo Olmos Romera and Juan Antonio Santos Velasco. Madrid: Universidad Autómona de Madrid, 1997.

Prag, A. John N. W. *The Oresteia: Iconographic and Narrative Tradition.* Warminster: Aris & Phillips, 1985.

Rose, C. Brian. *The Archaeology of Greek and Roman Troy*. Cambridge: Cambridge University Press, 2014.

Schwarz, Gerda. "Der Tod und das Mädchen: Frühe Polyxena-Bilder." *Mitteilungen des Deutschen Archäologischen Instituts, Athenische Abteilung* 116 (2001): 35–50.

Schwenn, Friedrich. *Die Menschenopfer bei den Griechen und Römern*. Geissen: Töpelmann, 1915.

Sevinç, Nurten. "A New Sarcophagus of Polyxena from the Salvage Excavations at Gümüşçay." *Studia Troica* 6 (1996): 251–64.

Small, Jocelyn Penny. *The Parallel Worlds of Classical Art and Text*. Cambridge: Cambridge University Press, 2003.

Smith, Tyler Jo. *Komast Dancers in Archaic Greek Art*. Oxford Monographs on Classical Archaeology. Oxford: Oxford University Press, 2010.

Stampolidis, Nicholas Chr. *"Reprisals": Contribution to the Study of Customs of the Geometric-Archaic Period*. Rethymno: University of Crete, 1996.

Stansbury-O'Donnell, Mark D. *Vase Painting, Gender, and Social Identity in Archaic Athens*. Cambridge: Cambridge University Press, 2006.

Touchefeu-Meynier, Odette, and François Lissarrague. Introduction to *L'expression du corps: Gestes, attitudes, regards dans l'iconographie antique*. Edited by Lydie Bodiou, Dominique Frère, and Véronique Mehl. Rennes: Presses universitaires de Rennes, 2006.

Trendall, Arthur D., and Alexander Cambitoglou. *The Red-Figured Vases of Apulia*. Vol. 2. Oxford: Clarendon, 1982.

Tsiafakis, Despoina. "'ΠΕΛΩΡΑ': Fabulous Creatures and/or Demons of Death?" Pages 73–104 in *The Centaur's Smile: The Human Animal in Early Greek Art*. Edited by J. Michael Padgett. New Haven: Yale University Press, 2004.

Vermeule, Emily, and Suzanne Chapman. "A Protoattic Human Sacrifice?" *American Journal of Archaeology* 75.3 (1971): 285–93.

Vernant, Jean-Pierre. Preface to *A City of Images: Iconography and Society in Ancient Greece*. Edited by Claude Bérard, Christiane Bron, Jean-Louis Durand, Françoise Frontisi-Ducroux, François Lissarrague, Alain Schnapp, and Jean-Pierre Vernant. Translated by Deborah Lyons. Princeton: Princeton University Press, 1989.

Walters, Henry B. "On Some Black-Figured Vases Recently Acquired by the British Museum." *JHS* 18 (1898): 282–88.

West, Martin L. *The Epic Cycle: A Commentary on the Lost Troy Epics*. Oxford: Oxford University Press, 2013.

9

"God Is Our King"

How Beliefs Surrounding the Ptolemaic Monarchy Influenced the Depiction of God in the LXX Pentateuch on a Lexical Level

CAMILLA RECALCATI

This chapter analyzes translation choices made within the LXX version of the Pentateuch regarding the depiction of God. It suggests that beliefs about Ptolemaic kingship informed the translation process. Thus, the main goal is to explore some lexical features that convey matters of faith relevant to the LXX that have been influenced by the Ptolemaic administration and its ideology concerning the divinization and cult of the Hellenistic king.[1] Thanks to an analysis of some lexical traits of the LXX, it seems that kingship and power-related images created in Ptolemaic times slowly shifted in their meaning, with features that were usually attributed to the Hellenistic sovereign slowly entering into much of the common imagery and vocabulary, such that they came to be used in the Greek translation of the Torah as epithets of God.[2]

---

1. A countertendency will also be presented.
2. Κύριος will not be treated here, as it would deserve extended explanation and analysis.

I would like to dedicate this paper to the memory of my grandmother, Patrizia Ottaviani, to whom I promised to devote my first doctoral paper when she passed away in November 2020.

"God Is Our King"

GOD AS RULER: KINGSHIP-ORIENTED BELIEFS AND THE EPITHETS OF GOD

As this contribution aims at showing how the terminology surrounding the Ptolemaic kings in Hellenistic Egypt influenced some of the translation of attributes of God in the LXX, it situates itself along the line of beliefs in translation. That is to say, by analyzing the way in which God is represented in the LXX, possibly due to an influence of the kingship-related vocabulary, this study highlights how the possibility to convey slightly different beliefs is possible through translation. Moreover, this chapter aims at shedding light on the fact that the highly syncretic environment of Alexandria of Egypt, where the translation of the LXX took place, shaped part of the beliefs expressed in these Jewish writings. In a cultural and religious milieu where many cults were merged, it is not a surprise that the earthly king (the Ptolemaic sovereign) and the heavenly one (God) would become associated with one another on a linguistic level, thanks to the translational choices featured in the LXX.

Although the focus will be on how the portrayal of God in the language of the LXX, a short example of how beliefs and depictions regarding the Jewish deity were interchangeable with those regarding the Hellenistic kings should also be brought forward. One starts to notice a tendency to represent sovereigns in a way not necessarily linked to their royal power in the Letter of Aristeas (second century BCE), a pseudepigraphic document that narrates the origins of the translation of the Torah into Greek. The Letter of Aristeas tends to celebrate the Lagid ruler Ptolemy II Philadelphus, who promotes the initiative of the Greek translation. In the Letter of Aristeas, Ptolemy II is presented not only as a Hellenistic king but also as a Jewish savant whose role model is the Jewish God.[3] Thus, an accurate reading of the Letter of Aristeas suggests that the document is proof that within the Jewish community, there was a sort of conceptual overlap between the divine and royal domain concerning the heavenly king God and the earthly Ptolemaic king.[4] Additionally, even the Ptolemies, starting with Ptolemy II Philadelphus,

---

3. Anna Passoni-Dell'Acqua, "Lessico giuridico e vocabolario teologico: colpe e ira divina nel Pentateuco dei LXX," in *Sophia–Paideia: Sapienza e educazione (Sir 1,27). Miscellanea di studi in onore del prof. Don Mario Cimosa*, ed. G. Bonney and R.Vincent (Rome: LAS, 2012), 177–78; Timothy H. Lim, "The Idealization of Ptolemaic Kingship in the Legend of the Origins of the Septuagint," in *Times of Transition: Judea in the Early Hellenistic Period*, ed. S. Honigman, C. Nihan, and O. Lipschits (Winona Lake, IN: Eisenbrauns, 2021), 232.

4. The Ptolemaic period is usually dated from the defeat of Persians in Egypt by Alexander the Great in 332 BCE until the death of Cleopatra VII in 30 BCE. After the death of Alexander

165

developed their own cults that merged the divine realm with the domain of the Hellenistic sovereign.[5]

As an indirect consequence, a similar tendency is detectable in the LXX.[6] Indeed, some lexical choices in the Greek Pentateuch seem to be influenced by the epithets used for the Lagid sovereigns. Some of epithets of God used in the LXX appear to be inspired by the Lagid royal titles of the time. Therefore, one could presume that the translators of the LXX were influenced in their choices of the epithets used for God by the beliefs and cults that surrounded Hellenistic kings in their day. In doing so, the translators attribute some feature of the temporal ruler to God, who was perceived both in the LXX and the MT as the absolute sovereign of the Jewish people.

The combination of the beliefs surrounding the Ptolemaic king and those about the God of Israel was partly induced by the fact that the LXX translators saw some similarities between the God of the Pentateuch and the Lagid sovereigns. The reason is easily understandable. In the Pentateuch, Yhwh's actions toward Yhwh's people are described like those of a king, which would have made the association rather simple for later Jewish translators. Already in the MT, God gives orders to the people, guides them, gives them divine laws (i.e., commandments), exhibiting characteristics typically associated with sovereigns and kings.[7]

Because of this juxtaposition of imagery, it is mostly in the political lexicon that the kingship of the Lagids influenced the depiction of the God of Israel in the

---

the Great (323 BCE), one of his generals, Ptolemy, gained the right to administer Egypt. He then became the first Ptolemaic king (ca. 305 BCE), taking the name Ptolemy I Soter and starting the Ptolemaic dynasty. See Eric G. Turner, "Ptolemaic Egypt," in *The Hellenistic World*, ed. F. W. Walbank, A. E. Astin, M. W. Frederiksen, and R. M. Ogilvie, vol. 7.1 of *The Cambridge Ancient History* (Cambridge: Cambridge University Press, 1984), 118–74.

5. Regarding the cult of the Hellenistic sovereign, it should be remembered that the praxis of naming eponymous priests was established by Ptolemy II Philadelphus. Additionally, the Canopus decree (238 BCE; see *OGIS* 56), which honors Ptolemy III Euergetes and his wife Berenice, is a testimony to the cult of the Benefactor Gods. See Stefan Pfeiffer, "The God Serapis, His Cult and the Beginnings of the Ruler Cult in Ptolemaic Egypt," in *Ptolemy II Philadephus and His Word*, ed. P. McKechnie and P. Guillaume (Leiden: Brill, 2008), 398–400.

6. Classically, the term Septuagint (LXX) refers to the first Greek translation of the Torah that took place in Alexandria under the reign of Ptolemy II Philadelphus (309–246 BCE). By extension, the term is used to refer to the first Greek translations of all the other books of the Hebrew Bible as well along with the Apocrypha. See Natalio Fernández Marcos, *The Septuagint in Context: Introduction to the Greek Version of the Bible* (Leiden: Brill, 2000).

7. As examples: in Exod 3:10 God sends Moses off to the Pharaoh as God's messenger, as a king would do with an envoy to another king; the entirety of Exod 19 could be read as a king giving laws to his people; in the first chapter of Numbers, God gives specific demographic ordinances much like a king orders a census.

LXX. Therefore, a lexical analysis of how the translators of the LXX represented the Jewish God in Greek must survey their adaptation of Hellenistic royal titles for God. Although it should be stated that such titles are not abounding—especially in the Pentateuch—some of the divine epithets that appear therein do appear to derive from the vocabulary of Ptolemaic kingship.

The Language of Kingship: Δεσπότης and Δυνάστης in the Septuagint

In the following paragraph, the epithets of δεσπότης "master, lord," and δυνάστης, "master, ruler" will be analyzed. Because these two terms were used in reference to the Ptolemies, they might have influenced the LXX translators to use them as epithets referring to God. Although these two aulic titles for God are not used extensively in the Greek version of the Pentateuch, when these titles are used they offer good insight into the combination of king-oriented beliefs with the representation of God.

Remarkably, it should be said that the word δεσπότης was used in Greek already in classical times. We find occurrences of the word with the meaning of "master" already in the writings of Herodotus, Aeschylus, Plato and many others.[8] Additionally, the term is used as an epithet of gods by Euripides and Xenophon.[9]

The term underwent a significant shift in meaning under the Lagids, acquiring greater prominence during this period. It gained a new status, with cognate words being employed to refer to the Hellenistic absolute sovereign, as is well documented in the official records of the sovereigns. Many inscriptions attest to the use of these terms as epithets for the Ptolemaic rulers. The term δεσπότης is used, for example, in an inscription alongside the term βασιλεύς "king" to refer to the Ptolemaic king and his wife.[10] Concerning the use of δεσπότης, the participle of the connected verb δεσποτέω (or δεσπόζω) "to be lord or master" is found referring to the Ptolemies in a particularly relevant inscription that is dated from the reign of Ptolemy III Euergetes.[11]

The epithet δεσπότης is only found in the LXX Pentateuch in Gen 15:2 and 15:8. Unexpectedly, in both verses the word is used as a translation of the Hebrew

---

8. The word δεσποτεία is found in Plato, *Leg.* 698a already with the political sense of despotism (see also *Leg.* 757a). See Gerhard Thür, "Despoteia," in *Brill's New Pauly, Encyclopaedia of the Ancient World*, ed. Manfred Landfester, Hubert Cancik, and Helmuth Schneider (Leiden: Brill, 2002–2010). See also Aeschylus, *Pers.* 169; Herodotus, *Hist.* 1.91.

9. Euripides, *Hipp.* 88; Xenophon, *Anab.* 3.2.13.

10. See *SB* 3:6155.

11. *OGIS* 1:56a.

periphrasis אֲדֹנָי יְהוִה "Lord Yhwh." Nevertheless, between the two Greek verses a slight difference can be found. In Gen 15:2, only the vocative δέσποτα is used to translate אֲדֹנָי יְהוִה, while in Gen 15:8 אֲדֹנָי יְהוִה is glossed as δέσποτα κύριε "master Lord." In the latter case, the Greek translation seems to render more precisely the two lexical items the Hebrew contains, since the usual translational equivalent found in the LXX for אֲדֹנָי is κύριος.[12] Importantly, the use of δέσποτα (κύριε) is not the standard rendering of the Hebrew periphrasis אדני יהוה in the LXX. Typically, the Hebrew locution is glossed with the reduplication of the vocative κύριε.[13] The epithet δεσπότης finds itself attributed to God only in these two occurrences across the whole LXX Pentateuch.

As noted above, the two occurrences of the epithet δεσπότης in reference to God in the LXX Pentateuch occur only in Gen 15. However, if we observe the number of occurrences of the root δεσποτ- in the LXX, we find that the number increases especially in those books of the LXX that were translated into Greek at a later date (underlined in the table) as well as in those books originally composed in Greek (mostly around the first century BCE) found in the LXX (in bold in the table).[14]

Δεσποτ- REFERRING TO GOD

Pentateuch	Historical books	Sapiential books	Prophets
2 occurrences	*7 occurrences*	*9 occurrences*	*12 occurrences*
Gen 15:2	Jdt 5:20	Prov 29:25	Jonah 4:3
Gen 15:8	Jdt 9:12	Sir 23:1	Isa 1:24
	Tob 8:17	Sir 34:1	Isa 3:1
	2 Macc 15:22	Sir 36:1	Isa 10:33[15]

12. For a treatment of divine epithets and their translation in the Bible, see Martin Rösel, "The Reading and Translation of the Divine Name in the Masoretic Tradition and the Greek Pentateuch," *JSOT* 31 (2007): 411–28; Rösel, "The Septuagint: Translating and Adapting the Torah to the 3rd Century BCE," in Honigman, Nihan, and Lipschits, *Times of Transition*, 257.

13. Additionally, the same identical Hebrew periphrasis is present only two more times in the text of the Pentateuch (Deut 3:24; 9:26), where it is translated in Greek with a redoubling of the vocative κύριε.

14. As a general tendency, the epithet seems to recur more in its attribution to God by Jewish-Greek writers; see J. B. Fischer, "The Term ΔΕΣΠΟΤΗΣ in Josephus," *Jewish Quarterly Review* 49.2 (1958): 132–38.

15. It should be noticed that the verses of Isaiah where we find the root are probably of a later translation. For a better insight on LXX Isaiah and its relationship to its *Vorlage*, see Ronald Troxel, *LXX-Isaiah as Translation and Interpretation: The Strategies of the Translator of the Septuagint of Isaiah* (Leiden: Brill, 2008), 73–85.

Pentateuch	Historical books	Sapiential books	Prophets
	2 Macc 5:20	Job 5:8	Jer 1:6
	2 Macc 6:14	Wis 6:7	Jer 4:10
	3 Macc 2:2	Wis 8:3	Jer 15:11
		Wis 11:26	Dan 3:37
		Wis 18:11	Dan 9:8
			Dan 9:15
			Dan 9:16
			Dan 9:19

In addition to δεσπότης, it is plausible that Ptolemaic terminology influenced the use of the epithet δυνάστης in the LXX. Δυνάστης is attributed to God only in Gen 49:24 LXX. Much like δεσπότης, the term δυνάστης was connected to absolute rulership in Hellenistic Egypt. The absolute power of the sovereign was also designated with the related term δυναστεία "power, domination," which appears more frequently than δυνάστης in the LXX. One example is found in Exod 6:6 with the same meaning as, in the passage, the term connotes the power of Egypt over the sons of Israel, that is absolute as Israelites are slaves in Egypt.[16]

Once more, for better clarity, a table of the development of the root δυνασ- throughout the LXX will be offered. The same pattern of occurrences is detectable for the usage of δυνάστης as a divine epithet, as δεσπότης. The term is extensively used in books translated later in time and in those that have been written in Greek.

As done before for δεσπότης, a table summing the uses of δυνάστης used for God is presented.

Δυναστ- REFERRING TO GOD

Pentateuch	Historical Books	Sapiential Books	Prophets
1 occurrence	*10 occurrences*	*3 occurrences*	*No occurrences*
Gen 49:24	2 Macc 3:24	Job 13:15	
	2 Macc 12:15	Sir 46:5	
	2 Macc 12:28	Sir 46:1	
	2 Macc 15:3		

16. Even though Exod 6:6 shows clearly the meaning of δυναστεία as an absolute power, it should be noticed that it is in contrast with the context of Gen 49:24, which is part of the blessing of Jacob on his sons. Both verses are connected to the history of the people of Israel in Egypt, however, there is a substantial theological difference in Gen 49:24: the δυναστεία of God, expressed through the epithet δυνάστης, knows no limits, while in Exod 6:6 the absolute power of Egypt on the Israelites will know its end thanks to the absolute power of God.

Pentateuch	Historical Books	Sapiential Books	Prophets
	2 Macc 15:4		
	2 Macc 15:23		
	2 Macc 15:29		
	3 Macc 2:3		
	3 Macc 5:51		
	3 Macc 6:39		

The LXX Pentateuch shows few instances in which the epithet is used, while it is abundantly present in books translated later in time. The increasing frequency of such epithets in later books could be looked at as a good argument for its use to be influenced by king-oriented beliefs in the Pentateuch. As the term was less strongly connected to the sovereignty—or the translators get more acquainted with its use—the term became less connoted toward the earthly kingship and as such could be applied even to the heavenly ruler—God. In the Greek translation of the Pentateuch there seems to be a tendency of avoiding—in most cases—epithets associated with the Lagids. However, as later LXX translations of Hebrew texts and texts composed in Greek show, the avoidance of aulic titles such as δεσπότης and δυνάστης is progressively abandoned. The tolerance for such titles in later texts is due to the acquaintance of translators to kingship-related features. Thus, from the comparison between the Pentateuch and the other LXX books it emerges that kinship-oriented beliefs—symbolized using an epithet—influenced the depiction of God as the absolute ruler of God's people progressively. At the same time, it can also be stated, that in the Pentateuch the tendency of depicting God as a Hellenistic ruler finds his first few occurrences, before being used more extensively with time.

A Countertendency: From Ptolemy Εὐεργέτης to the Absence of God's Εὐεργετεῖν

Among the frequently used titles for the Lagids, one must also consider the aulic title of εὐεργέτης "benefactor." Indeed, Ptolemy III officially selected εὐεργέτης as his regal title.[17] Although the term εὐεργέτης was broadly used even before the assumption of the title by Ptolemy III, it is surprising that such a well-spread and widely used term is completely absent from the LXX. If the verb εὐεργετέω "to do good, show kindness," is to be intended as the action of caring and having a beneficial effect for one's people, it cannot be denied that this notion is central for the

17. See *OGIS* 1:56A; *SB* 1:4624.

depiction of God in the Bible.[18] This concept is expressed in the MT by the root יטב "to do good," which is used to present God as the greatest benefactor. So, even though the presence of the Greek verb or epithet would be more than fitting in the LXX Pentateuch, εὐεργέτης and any other word etymologically linked to it are completely absent from it.[19] Instead, the LXX translates יטב with εὖ ποιέω "to do good" (e.g., Gen 32:10, 13; Exod 1:20; Num 10:29, 32). Within the LXX Pentateuch, another verb ἀγαθοποιέω "to do good" is also used as the equivalent of יטב. However, ἀγαθοποιέω has its first attestation in the LXX and only in a later time becomes increasingly used. This verb can be considered as neologism introduced by the Jewish translators, as there is no evidence in contemporary extrabiblical documentary evidence of a similar use of ἀγαθοποιέω. Moreover, it is worth noticing that only in Symmachus is the root יטב translated as one would expect with εὐεργετέω.

Two reasons could explain why the translators of the LXX Pentateuch avoided any word connected to the lexical domain of εὐεργετέω. The first one is lexical: the translators probably wanted to mimic the Hebrew syntax and maintain a certain level of coherence in order to have a faithful and literal rendering of the text. Thus, if the adjective טוב "good" is mostly translated with ἀγαθός, it is then logical that the translators would coin a verb derived from the adjective when dealing with the Hebrew verbal form of the root. On the other hand, the translators simplified their Greek version of the Hebrew text by using a much more generic verb ποιέω "to do," in connection with the particle εὖ "well" in rendering the verb יטב.

The second possible reason is the one that connects beliefs to translation techniques and etymological choices.[20] It is plausible that the LXX's translators deliberately avoided using any word connected to the lexical field of εὐεργέτης that was too obviously linked to the Hellenistic sovereigns, since this word was the title of Ptolemy III. In other words, the translators decided to search for another lexical family that did not have direct conceptual connections with the Lagid dynasty. They did this so as not to mix the cultic practices that developed around the sovereign family with biblical religion and monotheistic beliefs.[21] As opposed to the previous case presented, here the biblical translators adopt a detectable

18. The clearest instance in this sense is found in Num 10:32.

19. See Anna Passoni-Dell'Acqua, "Euergetes," *Aegyptus* 56 (1976): 184–91. In Hebrew there is no such thing as a compound name, so the corresponding form for what should have been εὐεργέτης is the causative form of the root יטב / טוב conveying the idea of "doing good."

20. See about theologically and ideologically motivated translations Emanuel Tov, *The Greek and Hebrew Bible: Collected Essays on the Septuagint* (Leiden: Brill, 2014), 257–69. The whole chapter is centered on this kind of phenomenon and similar ones.

21. On this regard, Ptolemy II Philadelphus was officially the one who started the worshiping process among the Ptolemies when he deified his parents as gods of the new Ptolemaic

171

lexical strategy that avoids mixing the beliefs associated with the Ptolemies with those expressed by the Hebrew text.

However, the contradiction between the use of δεσπότης and δυνάστης and the avoidance of εὐεργέτης is only apparent. On the one hand, the latter term had starker connotations, as it was the official epithet of one of the Ptolemy rulers. On the other hand, δεσπότης and δυνάστης were more generic titles used for all rulers with no distinction; using one or the other did not evoke a specific sovereign but rather referred to royalty more in general. Seen as such, the avoidance of the epithet εὐεργέτης for God and of the verb εὐεργετέω can still be accounted for as being derived from the influence of king-oriented beliefs on the translation of the LXX, an influence that generated a countertendency.

A DEVELOPMENT OF REGAL FEATURES: GOD AS A JUDGE

As previously stated, in Hellenistic Egypt the Ptolemies were the absolute rulers, and as such the ultimate decisional power in juridical matters was also accorded to them. For instance, the Lagid sovereign was the only one who could promulgate a decree of amnesty.[22] Cognitively, the Jewish translators of the LXX could have drawn a parallel between the biblical depiction of God and the reality in which they lived. God in the Pentateuch forgives sins and punishes the people, just as the Ptolemies did in Hellenistic times, and this simple mental association could have influenced the translators' choices. Additionally, thanks to a lexical analysis it can be noticed that several Ptolemaic juridical terms have influenced lexical features in the LXX that concern the theology of forgiveness and punishment surrounding the figure of God.[23] As a result of this influence, in the realm of guilt, fault, and sin the mercifulness of God came to be depicted as the power of the remission of penalties and debts that was exercised in Hellenistic times exclusively by the Lagid sovereign.

An analysis of the verb ἀφαιρέω, usually rendered as "to take away," which is often chosen by the LXX to describe God's remission of human faults, can help explain this phenomenon.[24] This Greek verb was used in Ptolemaic times in the de-

---

Kingdom, and when in 272/271 BCE, he associated his cult and that of his sister Arsinoe as θεοὶ ἀδέλφοι to that of Alexander the Great.

22. H. S. Smith, "A Note on Amnesty," *Journal of Egyptian Archaeology* (1968): 209–14.

23. E.g., Passoni-Dell'Acqua, "Lessico giuridico e vocabolario teologico," 219–35.

24. See Anna Passoni-Dell'Acqua, "Sin and Forgiveness," in *Die Sprache der Septuaginta / The Language of the Septuagint*, ed. Eberhard Bons and Jan Joosten (Gütersloh: Gütersloher, 2016), 336–37. Once again, according to a tendency previously shown, the verb ἀφαιρέω appears increasingly frequent in books translated in a later period, but it can already be found in the LXX Pentateuch.

crees of amnesty that could only be issued by the king. We find the verb used in two decrees preserved on papyrus: P.Tebt.1 5.3 (decree of amnesty signed by Ptolemy the VIII) and P.Tebt.3 1.739.43–45. Because of its meaning of forgiving or lifting a crime from someone, the verb ἀφαιρέω is typical of legal documents concerning crimes, Hellenistic Ptolemaic amnesties, or exemption from tax payment.[25] In that way, it deviates slightly from its classical Greek range of meanings.[26] Similarly, in Exod 34:7 and Num 14:18 ἀφαιρέω has a meaning connected to absolute remission. Additionally, the way in which the term is used in both passages might lead to interpreting the verb as a divine epithet.[27] In fact, the present active participle present ἀφαιρῶν that translates the Hebrew active participle נֹשֵׂא can also be read as an epithet-like attribute of God that refers to God's forgiveness. In both passages, God is said to be ἀφαιρῶν ἀνομίας καὶ ἀδικίας καὶ ἁμαρτίας "forgiving lawlessness, un-rightfulness, and sins." The terms ἀνομία, ἀδικία, and ἁμαρτία that are here the object of God's remission in Ptolemaic times were all used as legal terms for different crimes.[28]

Through this example, we understand how the royal imagery of power linked to the Lagids' court influenced the depiction of God and God's actions in the LXX Pentateuch, consequently influencing some beliefs and theological connotations. In the LXX Pentateuch, God is depicted somewhat like the Ptolemaic king through the choice of words describing his forgiveness and the sins of the people. The image of God as the ultimate judge, the only one who has the power of remission—already present in the MT—is thus strengthened by the connection to Ptolemaic power and the feature of the Hellenistic king as the supreme judge.

FROM GOD'S WRATH TO THE PEOPLE'S FAULT: NUMBERS 1:53

Regarding belief-related lexical items in the LXX connected to the realm of forgiveness and sins, one curious case is that in Num 1:53.[29] In the verse, we do not

---

25. See e.g., P.Cair.Zen 3.59322.

26. See LSJ, s.v. "ἀφαιρέω."

27. The verb ἀφίημι is also found in its imperative aorist form that has an interesting shift in meaning that comes closer to that of ἀφαιρέω in Exod 32:32 and Num 14:19, where the action of forgiving is still referred to God.

28. See: Passoni-Dell'Acqua, "Lessico giuridico e vocabolario teologico," 225.

29. The text of Num 1:53 reads as follows:

וְהַלְוִיִּם יַחֲנוּ סָבִיב לְמִשְׁכַּן הָעֵדֻת וְלֹא־יִהְיֶה קֶצֶף עַל־עֲדַת בְּנֵי יִשְׂרָאֵל וְשָׁמְרוּ הַלְוִיִּם אֶת־מִשְׁמֶרֶת מִשְׁכַּן הָעֵדוּת

οἱ δὲ Λευῖται παρεμβαλέτωσαν ἐναντίον κυρίου κύκλῳ τῆς σκηνῆς τοῦ μαρτυρίου καὶ οὐκ ἔσται ἁμάρτημα ἐν υἱοῖς Ισραηλ καὶ φυλάξουσιν οἱ Λευῖται αὐτοὶ τὴν φυλακὴν τῆς σκηνῆς τοῦ μαρτυρίου.

find the usual translational equivalent θυμός "wrath," for the Hebrew word קֶצֶף "wrath."[30] Instead, the translator chose the term ἁμάρτημα "fault."[31]

It is worth noticing that the shift from the term of the MT to the one chosen by the LXX translator has some more implications. In the MT, wrath belongs to God.[32] Even though Yhwh is not directly mentioned in Num 1:53, scholars agree that קֶצֶף is to be attributed to God.[33] Furthermore, in this passage the word קֶצֶף has no specification, but it is quite clear that it refers to God. This is seen even in other passages in which the LXX translation seems to be more coherent with its Hebrew counterpart. In fact, as Num 1:48 reveals, God is the one giving instructions to Moses. However, by reading the translation presented in the LXX, a problem emerges. The phrase καὶ οὐκ ἔσται ἁμάρτημα ἐν υἱοῖς Ισραηλ seems to exclude any agency coming from God, as the word ἁμάρτημα seems to be more logically attributed to the "sons of Israel." Additionally, another feature of the MT is missing in the LXX as well, as the LXX lacks the specification עַל־עֲדַת בְּנֵי יִשְׂרָאֵל by presenting only ἐν υἱοῖς Ισραηλ. The differences in the passage cannot be attributed to different *Vorlagen* or an erroneous interpretation on the behalf of the Greek translator. Rather, it seems this represents a wilful change that conveys a slightly different belief within the text of the LXX.[34] The first thing to notice is that in the LXX there is a change of agent from the MT.[35] The word ἁμάρτημα cannot refer to God, as God is essentially with no fault, so the word must refer to the Levites. The Greek translation apparently attempts to shift a belief from the wrath of God to the fault of the Levites, which provokes God's wrath. Moreover, the term ἁμάρτημα—as seen in Exod 34:7 and Num 14:18—in the Ptolemaic legal terminology was used to designate legally a crime.[36]

---

30. Out of the four occurrences of קֶצֶף in the Pentateuch, the term is translated twice with θυμός and once with the passive form of the verb ὀργίζω. According to the other translation of the term in the other books, the occurrence of Num 1:53 seems odd.

31. Wevers and Quast signal in the *apparatus criticus* of their edition of Numbers that codices 52 and 318 present the variant ἁμαρτία. See John William Wevers and Udo Quast, eds., *Numeri*, Septuaginta: Vetus Testamentum Graecum 3 (Göttingen: Vandenhoeck & Ruprecht, 1982), 61. One should pay attention to the fact that there is little to no questioning concerning the *Vorlage* of the LXX of this passage that seems to be matching the MT.

32. E.g., Num 16:22; Deut 1:34; 9:7–8 and so on.

33. See the treatment of קֶצֶף in *DCH* 7:283–84.

34. Speaking of theological variant could perhaps be too risky, but this passage could certainly offer some insights on the matter.

35. Nonetheless, this does not seem the case of the LXX translators wanting to overpass a theological difficulty.

36. Although late, the term is found in in P.Oxy. 8.1119 that consists of a petition to authorities for an exemption of payment.

"God Is Our King"

Furthermore, the wrath of God in the LXX Pentateuch is presented as the manifestation of God's royal authority, exactly as it was associated with the Hellenistic sovereign's power in all those passages where the term קֶצֶף is translated with θυμός or ὀργή. So, it appears as if in Num 1:53 the Greek translator portrays God as a Hellenistic king that acts and exercises his power over his people, whose fault is associated with an offense.

Conclusion

From the instances presented, it seems that the royal courtly environment of Alexandria where the translation of the LXX took place influenced some lexical features of the LXX regarding the depiction of God. Kingship-oriented beliefs affected the translational choices of the LXX's Pentateuch. Aulic titles and epithets attributed to the Ptolemaic kings entered the LXX vocabulary. However, they did so progressively. We find only a sporadic start in the Pentateuch, as seen in the emblematic case of δεσπότης and δυνάστης, while the epithets become more frequent in later Greek translation. However, even a countertendency is visible. As the total avoidance of the root of εὐεργετέω and εὐεργέτης shows, the Jewish translators' did not want to mix specific king-oriented beliefs with their God-oriented ones in the Bible.

Legal terms in use under the Ptolemies played a role in influencing the depiction of God, as they were adapted in the LXX to describe divine actions such as the remission of sin and fault. In such a manner, the translator associated some of the kingship-oriented beliefs with the portrayal of God in the Septuagint and, at times, made the translator shift from straight adherence to their *Vorlage* to adding new connotations, as seen with Num 1:53.

To conclude, it should be stated that connecting lexical features of the LXX to the cults and the imagery that surrounded the Ptolemies in Hellenistic Alexandria poses some difficulties and challenges. Even though an aimed lexical analysis can outline some features, as witnessed in this chapter a deeper, more extensive investigation on such matters is necessary.

Works Cited

Fernández Marcos, Natalio. *The Septuagint in Context: Introduction to the Greek Version of the Bible.* Leiden: Brill, 2000.

Fischer, J. B. "The Term ΔΕΣΠΟΤΗΣ in Josephus." *Jewish Quarterly Review* 49.2 (1958): 132–38.

Lim, Timothy H. "The Idealization of Ptolemaic Kingship in the Legend of the Origins of the Septuagint." Pages 231–39 in *Times of Transition: Judea in the Early Hellenistic Period*. Edited by Sylvie Honigman, Christophe Nihan, and Oded Lipschits. Winona Lake, IN: Eisenbrauns, 2021.

Passoni-Dell'Acqua, Anna. "Euergetes." *Aegyptus* 56 (1976): 184–91.

———. "Il Pentateuco dei LXX testimone di istituzioni di età tolemaica." *Annali di Scienze religiose* 4 (1999): 171–200.

———. "Lessico giuridico e vocabolario teologico: colpe e ira divina nel Pentateuco dei LXX." Pages 219–35 *Sophia-Paideia. Sapienza e educazione (Sir 1,27). Miscellanea di studi in onore del prof. Don Mario Cimosa*. Edited by Gillian Bonney and Rafael Vincent. Roma: Las, 2012.

———. "Sin and Forgiveness." Pages 335–39 in *Die Sprache der Septuaginta / The Language of the Septuagint*. Edited by Eberhard Bons and Jan Joosten. Gütersloh: Gütersloher, 2016.

Pfeiffer, Stefan. "The God Serapis, His Cult and the Beginnings of the Ruler Cult in Ptolemaic Egypt." Pages 397–413 in *Ptolemy II Philadephus and His Word*. Edited by Paul R. McKechnie and Philippe Guillaume. Leiden: Brill, 2008.

Rösel, Martin. "The Reading and Translation of the Divine Name in the Masoretic Tradition and the Greek Pentateuch." *JSOT* 31(2007): 411–28.

———. "The Septuagint: Translating and Adapting the Torah to the 3rd Century BCE." Pages 253–62 in *Times of Transition: Judea in the Early Hellenistic Period*. Edited by Sylvie Honigman, Christophe Nihan, and Oded Lipschits. Winona Lake, IN: Eisenbrauns, 2021.

Smith, H. S. "A Note on Amnesty." *Journal of Egyptian Archaeology* (1968): 209–14.

Thür, Gerhard. "Despoteia." Pages 2002–10 in *Brill's New Pauly, Encyclopaedia of the Ancient World*. Edited by Manfred Landfester, Hubert Cancik, and Helmuth Schneider. Leiden: Brill, 2002–2010.

Tov, Emanuel. *The Greek and Hebrew Bible: Collected Essays on the Septuagint*. Leiden: Brill, 2014.

Troxel, Ronald L. *LXX-Isaiah as Translation and Interpretation: The Strategies of the Translator of the Septuagint of Isaiah*. Leiden: Brill, 2008.

Turner, E. G. "Ptolemaic Egypt." Pages 118–74 in *The Hellenistic World*. Edited by F. W. Walbank, A. E. Astin, M. W. Frederiksen, and R. M. Ogilvie. Vol. 7.1 of *The Cambridge Ancient History*. Cambridge: Cambridge University Press, 1984.

Wevers, John William, and Udo Quast, eds. *Numeri*. Septuaginta: Vetus Testamentum Graecum 3. Göttingen: Vandenhoeck & Ruprecht, 1982.

10

Is Belief (or Is It Faith?) an Ancient Israelite Notion?

Thinking and/as Seeing, Seeing and/as Thinking . . . and Believing

BRENT A. STRAWN

Many people get nervous when it comes to the topic of *belief*, even when the people in question happen to be *religious* people. Two contrasting but representative statements regarding contemporary Judaism are instructive. The first belongs to Rabbi Mickey Rosen who, in a 2014 article published in the *New York Times*, is quoted as saying "belief . . . is not a Jewish notion."[1] The second opinion comes from the noted Jewish scholar Michael Wyschogrod, who wrote the following: "I am . . . a theological Jew. . . . Theology has a philosophical side to it but its point of departure and ultimate validation are scripture and history. And this enterprise is not at all foreign to Judaism."[2] The statements are clearly at odds, but it is

---

1. Gary Cutting, "Is Belief a Jewish Notion?," *New York Times*, March 30, 2014, http://opin ionator.blogs.nytimes.com/2014/03/30/is-belief-a-jewish-notion/?_php=true&_type=blogs&hp &rref=opinion&_r=0.

2. Michael Wyschogrod, "The Impact of Dialogue with Christianity on My Self-Understanding as a Jew," in *Die Hebräische Bibel und ihre zweifache Nachgeschichte: Festschrift für Rolf Rendtorff zum 65. Geburtstag*, ed. Erhard Blum, Christian Macholz, and Ekkehard W. Stegemann (Neukirchen-Vluyn: Neukirchener, 1990), 728–29.

I am grateful to the editors for their assistance and patience. I also register my gratitude to those who attended and presented at the St Andrews symposium. I benefited greatly from the discussion, critique, and encouragement I received at that time, especially from Christopher Porter. J. Gerald Janzen proved, as ever, a fascinating interlocutor about this paper and the topics it touches on. I owe him my thanks.

also clear that they are not exactly opposite: Rabbi Rosen speaks of *belief*, while Professor Wyschogrod speaks of *theology*, including its *philosophical side*. And yet, these two concepts—*belief* (and its synonyms) and *theology* (and its synonyms)—are often lumped together, whether as identical or otherwise, and in turn are often connected and/or contrasted with still other things, perhaps above all *faith* and *practice*, whether these latter terms are seen as friendly congeners or stark antonyms.[3]

It is the correlation (or noncorrelation) of these various concepts, but preeminently of *faith* and *belief*, that is the subject of the present essay. From the start, it is obvious that much hangs on matters of definition. What exactly is *belief*, especially (for present purposes) in the ancient world as reflected in the Hebrew Bible and known from ancient Israelite religion? Is *belief* the right word at all within those contexts or is an entirely different term in order (à la Rabbi Rosen on contemporary Judaism)? How does *theology* with its *philosophical* aspect ("not at all foreign" to Judaism according to Wyschogrod) fit in, if it does? Is *theology* the equivalent of *belief* and/or (also a part of) *faith*?

These are large questions—too large for any one essay—but I hope to begin to approach them by attempting three distinct, but interrelated things in what follows:

1. first, by offering some preliminary definition(s) of *belief* and/or/versus *faith* in the Hebrew Bible and, consequently or correlatively, in ancient Israelite religion (see "Defining Belief (or Is It Faith?) in the Hebrew Bible" below);

2. next, by discussing the role of cognition in said "belief/faith" (see "The Place of Cognition: Theological Belief/Faith?" below); and

3. finally, by considering the practice of sight as a locus of and for "belief/faith" (see "Seeing and/as Believing: The Visual as a Locus for and of Belief/Faith" below)—"seeing," as the old adage goes, "is believing," despite the facts that the author of Hebrews remarked that belief/faith (there πίστις) is "the evidence of things *not* seen" (Heb 11:1 KJV), and the world's most famous rabbi once uttered a blessing on those who have *not* seen but who have nevertheless still believed (πιστεύσαντες; John 20:29).

3. Sometimes the matter thins down to a contest between *theology* versus *religion*. For discussion of that dichotomy and resistance to it, see Brent A. Strawn, "The History of Israelite Religion," in *The Cambridge Companion to the Hebrew Bible/Old Testament*, ed. Stephen B. Chapman and Marvin A. Sweeney (Cambridge: Cambridge University Press, 2016), 86–107, esp. 98–101; and Christine Helmer, "Theology and the Study of Religion: A Relationship," in *The Cambridge Companion to Religious Studies*, ed. Robert A. Orsi (Cambridge: Cambridge University Press, 2012), 230–54.

Is Belief (or Is It Faith?) an Ancient Israelite Notion?

To be sure, each of these three tasks is ambitious on its own—each of them too large for any one essay—but something is gained by treating them in the aggregate, at least in provisional fashion.

DEFINING BELIEF (OR IS IT FAITH?) IN THE HEBREW BIBLE

The first task, which in truth is quite complex, gives the false impression of being relatively straightforward given the existence of several extended treatments of biblical terms for *belief* . . . or, rather, is it biblical terms for *faith*? Once again, the terminological (and definitional) conundrum presents itself as signaled above by the formulation "*belief* and/or/versus *faith*," which was then collapsed into the compound "belief/faith." Which is it? Are there two distinct things here or just one, albeit one with two closely related sides? Not far into the first task of this essay and things have already become very complicated very quickly. Indeed, the larger definitional question appears to be at something of an impasse.

This impasse was suggested already in the opposition of belief and faith reflected in Rabbi Rosen's comment. According to him, the "notion" of belief is alien to Judaism, which must be understood as marked not by it but by something else—faith perhaps (if the two terms are not, in fact, synonymous) or practice or perhaps yet something(s) else. Rabbi Rosen's position, regardless, is hardly novel. It is evident, for example, in Martin Buber's *Two Types of Faith*, or in Wilfred Cantwell Smith's *Faith and Belief*, or, more compactly, in Jon D. Levenson's seminal essay, "Why Jews Are Not Interested in Biblical Theology."[4] These works are not entirely of a piece, of course, but the general gist is that *belief* is a cognitive category (perhaps even systematic in some way) that is to be identified especially with Christianity (particularly Protestant Christianity) and its heavily noetic bent that is likely due to Greek philosophical influence.[5] Within this perspective, *belief*

---

4. Martin Buber, *Two Types of Faith*, trans. Norman P. Goldhawk (New York: Syracuse University Press, 2003); Wilfred Cantwell Smith, *Faith and Belief* (Princeton: Princeton University Press, 1979); see also Smith, *Believing: An Historical Perspective* (Charlottesville: University of Virginia Press, 1977; repr., Oxford: Oneworld, 1998); and Jon D. Levenson, *The Hebrew Bible, the Old Testament, and Historical Criticism: Jews and Christians in Biblical Studies* (Louisville: Westminster John Knox, 1993), 33–61.

5. Buber, *Two Types*, 11. See the discussion in R. W. L. Moberly, "Knowing God and Knowing about God: Martin Buber's *Two Types of Faith* Revisited," *SJT* 65 (2012): 402–20, esp. 406n10, for a critique of Buber's "clear-cut contrast" between Jewish and Greek modes of thought. Moberly himself notes the "long history within Christian theology" of a dyad not unlike the one posited by Buber: *fides qua creditur* (the *act* of believing) and *fides quae creditur* (the *content* of believing). But, "instead of two modes of faith, as in the Augustinian shorthand, Buber presents

can be equated, as Buber himself does, with the Pauline πίστις ὅτι "belief *that*" something is the case. That can be contrasted, as Buber himself does, with the Hebrew term אֱמוּנָה, usually translated as "faith" or "trust," which is a different beast altogether.[6] An example of this difference may be captured in the Epistle of James, which notes that even the demons *believe* (πιστεύουσιν) that God is one (2:19) but then immediately indicates that such belief (perhaps equivalent to knowledge?) is deficient. The demons, certainly, are not "trusting" or putting their "faith" in God, whatever the latter might mean. And so, again, for Buber, אֱמוּנָה is to be associated with Judaism and πίστις with Christianity (no offense to the Jewishness of St. James!) and thus, voila, we have two types of faith, which are captured nicely by Rabbi Rosen's remark that belief is most certainly *not* a Jewish notion but, presumably, is such a thing for Christians.[7]

But then along comes Professor Wyschogrod, "a theological Jew" by his own account, and his testimony to otherwise. Is he some sort of anomaly? That seems unlikely for a number of reasons, which presents us, again, with an impasse: Rosen and company versus Wyschogrod and company.[8] Be that as it may, the opposition

---

two types of faith which are deeply different one from the other" (403–4). Buber's position—especially the reification of belief (read: theological reflection?)—is simply not necessary in Moberly's view. As one kind of alternative, see Davis Hankins, "'Much Madness Is Divinest Sense': The Economic Consequences of Yahweh's Parasocial Identity," *The Bible and Critical Theory* 14 (2018): 17–41, who shows how Yhwh worship was "creatively engaged" with a host of social realities. For another connection between understanding(s) of God and various ethical practices, see Robert L. Brawley, "Generating Ethics from God's Character in Mark," in *Character Ethics and the New Testament: Moral Dimensions of Scripture*, ed. Robert L. Brawley (Louisville: Westminster John Knox, 2007), 57–74.

6. See the previous note and also Jack B. Scott, "אָמַן," *TWOT* 1:51–53, who states that, in the *hiphil*, √אמן "basically means 'to cause to be certain, sure' or 'to be certain about,' 'to be assured.' In this sense, the word in the Hiphil conjugation *is* the biblical word for 'to believe' and shows that biblical faith is *an assurance, a certainty*, in contrast with modern conceptions of faith as something possible, hopefully true, but not certain" (51; emphases added). James Barr made a similar point earlier in *The Semantics of Biblical Language* (Oxford: Oxford University Press, 1961), 175: "*He'emin* does not mean and never did mean 'be faithful, show faithfulness'; it means 'trust, believe.'" Barr says much the same later and traces the specific form "*he'emin* 'trust, believe'" to "internal certainty of the mind" (187; cf. 173, 201).

7. Buber, *Two Types*, 7, 173. For James and the place of "propositional belief" (!) in that epistle (especially in the context of dispute), see Teresa Morgan, *Roman Faith and Christian Faith: Pistis and Fides in the Early Roman Empire and Early Church* (Oxford: Oxford University Press, 2015), 346.

8. Note the impressive listing of dogmatic beliefs collated in Menachem Kellner, *Dogma in Medieval Jewish Thought: From Maimonides to Abravanel* (Oxford: Oxford University Press, 1986), esp. 200–207, and the notable lack of schisms, sects, and charges of heresy within medieval Judaism. That said, Kellner inclines toward the view that a new emphasis on belief *about* God

Is Belief (or Is It Faith?) an Ancient Israelite Notion?

of belief versus faith can be approached from another, somewhat more oblique angle—from within Christianity itself, the guilty suspect in the case of "(overly) cognitive belief." Mention might be made of Christian communions that stress "deeds, not creeds" (itself a sort of creed).[9] As another example, it might be noted that even the use of the verbs *credo* or πιστεύω in the creeds is less a statement of cognitive assent than a *speech act* that promises something, expressing and thereby enacting a *habitus*.[10]

As one might imagine, the problems surrounding the definition of belief/faith becomes even more complex when recourse is made to the pertinent biblical materials. R. W. L. Moberly, for example, has mounted a compelling critique of Buber's two types of faith, observing (inter alia) that "there is probably nothing ... in Buber's account of *Emunah* with which a Christian is likely to disagree."[11]

---

is the achievement of Maimonides, whose "enunciation of the principles of Judaism marks a turning point in the history of Jewish thought, emphasizing as it does the adoption of a mode of thought which understands faith primarily in propositional as opposed to attitudinal terms" (207–8; similarly 213). In this regard, Kellner's work seems aligned with Buber's and Rabbi Rosen's opinions. See more popularly, Menachem Kellner, *Must a Jew Believe Anything?* 2nd ed. (Oxford: Littman Library of Jewish Civilization, 2006). At the same time, Kellner's work shows that "theological Jews" are found long before Wyschogrod. See the two previous notes on √אמן (*hiphil*) in the Hebrew Bible and πίστις in James, and further below for arguments that dispute Kellner's (and others') position that the nature of biblical faith is absent of dogmatic content. Yet another example, perhaps split like Kellner, may be found in the essays "Jewish Theology" and "Faith" in Abraham Joshua Heschel, *Moral Grandeur and Spiritual Audacity: Essays*, ed. Susannah Heschel (New York: Farrar, Straus & Giroux, 1996), 154–63 and 328–39, respectively. The former speaks of systems, principles, and fundamental statements about God (viz., "*God is in search of [hu]man[ity]*" [158] or "*God is the meaning beyond the mystery*" [163]); the latter distinguishes "faith as the act of believing ... from creed as the content, as that in which we believe" and speaks of faith "as little rational as love of beauty or motherly affection" (335). For the connections between rationality and affect, see "The Place of Cognition: Theological Belief/ Faith?" below.

9. See Jaroslav Pelikan, *Credo: Historical and Theological Guide to Creeds and Confessions of Faith in the Christian Tradition* (New Haven: Yale University Press, 2003), 278–305. Note Nicholas Lash, *The Beginning and the End of 'Religion'* (Cambridge: Cambridge University Press, 1996), 132–49, which addresses a not unrelated matter: that point in time when certain theologians "lost interest" in theology. Cf., in a different vein, Tom Greggs, *Theology against Religion: Constructive Dialogues with Bonhoeffer and Barth* (London: T&T Clark, 2011).

10. See, e.g., Nicholas Lash, *Believing Three Ways in One God: A Reading of the Apostles' Creed* (Notre Dame: University of Notre Dame Press, 1993), 17–19.

11. Moberly, "Knowing God," 405, see 410n25, for Hans Urs van Balthasar's critique of Buber's antithesis of אֱמוּנָה and πίστις. Note also Moberly's earlier formulation: "The difference [between the OT and NT on the language of belief/faith], however, is perhaps more one of terminology than of basic outlook." See Moberly, "אמן," *NIDOTTE* 1:427–33, citation from 427.

Buber has thus overstated the Jewish versus Christian distinction on this matter and in more than one way. So, on the one hand, there are Pauline texts that speak of "faith working through love" (πίστις δι' ἀγάπης ἐνεργουμένη; Gal 5:6 NRSV) and the larger New Testament notion of being "in Christ" (ἐν Χριστῷ)—both of which Buber leaves unaddressed.[12] On the other hand, Buber seems to have underestimated the belief content of faith (אֱמוּנָה) in the Old Testament proper. Moberly demonstrates the latter point by exploring the idiom "to know that" (יָדַע + כִּי) in the Hebrew Bible.[13] Moberly's conclusions (pages cited in-text) may be briefly summarized as follows:

- First, there are instances of "believing that" with √ידע that seem semantically equivalent to the sense of √אמן insofar as the idiom *to know Yhwh* "is regularly linked with integrity of lifestyle (e.g., 1 Sam 2:12, Jer 22:16) and at least once with steadfast perseverance (Dan 11:32)" (p. 411).
- Second, there are many instances of the "recognition formula" or "demonstration oracle," especially in Ezekiel, the point of which "seems to be the desire for an existential realization . . . of the reality of YHWH who is speaking through the prophet" (pp. 411–12).[14]
- Third, כִּי + יָדַע in Deuteronomy "is based on the particularities of YHWH's engagement with Israel in both deed and word. The appeal is not to theological abstractions. The implication is that without the particularities there would be no acknowledgement" (p. 412). The content of this acknowledgment is that *Yhwh is God*, which involves "a recognition of the uniqueness and su-

---

He proceeds to delineate a difference between √אמן (*hiphil*) + -לְ and √אמן (*hiphil*) + -בְּ with the former involving "accepting what someone says as true" and the latter including a sense "of acting in response to what is heard with trust or obedience" (431), but he also admits that this "is not an absolute distinction" (432).

12. Moberly, "Knowing God," 406n11. Moberly points out that David Flusser's parsing of the issues in his afterword to Buber's book is likely superior (407n16) and also notes an apologetic tendency in *Two Types of Faith* that makes it "impossible to come away from Buber's book without the sense that Christian faith, as he depicts it, is not only different from, but inferior to, its Jewish counterpart" (407–8n17). The concept of participation ("in Christ") is now a large topic. See, e.g., Teresa Morgan, *Being 'in Christ' in the Letters of Paul: Saved through Christ and in His Hands* (Tübingen: Mohr Siebeck, 2020); and Ben C. Blackwell, *Christosis: Engaging Paul's Soteriology with His Patristic Interpreters* (Grand Rapids: Eerdmans, 2016).

13. Buber leaves this phrase undiscussed with the same true for Smith's *Faith and Belief*. See Moberly, "Knowing God," 411 and n. 29.

14. The seminal study on the recognition formula remains Walther Zimmerli, *I Am Yahweh*, trans. Douglas W. Scott (Atlanta: Knox, 1982).

Is Belief (or Is It Faith?) an Ancient Israelite Notion?

premacy of YHWH" (p. 412, cf. 416).[15] According to Moberly, "the force of this acknowledgement is as much existential as it is intellectual," because, while other, theological rivals exist, the "urge" is "that these alternatives should be thrust aside and that only one way should be recognized as the way ahead" (p. 413). To know that Yhwh is God, therefore, is "a recognition that is *both intellectual and existential*" (p. 414, emphasis added) and, one might add, also *ethical* in the sense that individuals come to know something "that is the case about God," which leads them to alter "*how they think* and *what they do* accordingly" (p. 414, emphasis added).

To sum up, there exists, already in the Hebrew Bible itself, a knowledge *about* God that has cognitive content (roughly equivalent to πίστις in Buber's view) and that is also existential (roughly equivalent to אֱמוּנָה in Buber's view). There is, therefore, something of a "formal similarity" between כִּי + יָדַע and πιστεύω ὅτι, at least in some passages of the Old Testament.[16] Put differently, "'knowing that' and 'believing that' alike depict a state of epistemic assurance, related to a particular kind of orientation of human life towards God."[17]

Even if Buber is incorrect in some ways (whether large or small), there is no doubt something quite right about his underlying concern—namely, the desire "to resist a widespread tendency since the Enlightenment to reduce religious

15. See also pp. 417–18 on how the recognized content—namely, that Yhwh is the true God—"is certainly much less developed than the creedal affirmations which have typically characterized Christianity and which might arguably be Buber's real target." Perhaps. Then again, the identification of the true God is, arguably, the main force of a great many of the Christian creeds. For an extensive collection, see Jaroslav Pelikan and Valerie Hotchkiss, eds., *Creeds and Confessions of Faith in the Christian Tradition*, 3 vols. (New Haven: Yale University Press, 2003); as well as Pelikan, *Credo*, esp. 43–53 on "faith defined."

16. Moberly, "Knowing God," 417; and further 419. See now also Morgan, *Roman Faith*, which suggests that Buber's construction of Pauline belief is also not accurate. Morgan consistently equates πίστις and *fides* (i.e., as "*pistis/fides*") and traces the use of these terms alongside "thinking/knowing" language (75), noting that Paul thinks of πίστις as "dominantly an exercise of trust which involves heart, mind, and action . . . [and that] like all trust . . . is intimately connected with belief, on which it depends and which depends on it. That certain things are true . . . is integral to Paul's preaching, and he undoubtedly wants those to whom he preaches to believe them" (261). "Propositional belief," she continues, "is always implicit in trust relationships" and "comes to the fore in the letter of James" (346). Πίστις/*fides* is also related to "a substantial and at times complex interiority" which "takes its seat variously in the mind, heart, or soul, and encompasses thought, emotion, and ethical goodness or rightness . . . interiority, relationality, and action are inseparable wherever *pistis/fides* operates" (472). One of Morgan's major conclusions, therefore, is that "trust and propositional belief are *everywhere entwined*" (508, emphasis added).

17. Moberly, "Knowing God," 419.

183

faith to propositional belief."[18] That, surely, is a worthy resistance to mount. Yet even here, it isn't difficult to find lurking in various nooks and crannies of the discussion rather old and hackneyed issues like primitivism (i.e., early is best) or developmentalism (i.e., later is better). Whatever the case, the surface issue in these definitional discussions is manifestly cognition versus something else: something more basic, perhaps, or more fundamentally affective and emotional, that is, "existential" to use Moberly's term. Buber and others' perspective is a decidedly "non-cognitivist account of knowing God."[19] The problem, of course, is that, as Moberly has demonstrated, כִּי + יָדַע "shows no unease with affirmation of cognitive content in relation to YHWH, and so is at odds with any strongly non-cognitivist account."[20] Hence, in the end Moberly deems Buber's formulation to be marked by a certain "carelessness," which has, in turn, "helped give rise to other careless accounts in which existential religious commitment is polarised in a facile way over against intellectual formulations."[21] At this point, the *et alios* of "Buber et al.'s perspective" come in for similar critique. On the basis of the biblical data, a far better approach would seem to be "the refusal to play these ['knowing God' and 'knowing about God'] off against each other." There is, instead, a "complementarity" between the two that should be recognized. Even if "there is less overt credal content" in the Old Testament than in later Christian theology, that "does not mean that there is no credal content at all."[22] Put differently, while (biblical) knowledge of God is not to be reduced to or seen as coterminous with cognitive content (whether propositional or some other kind; Buber's point), it also simply cannot be separated from all that (Moberly's point). In this way, belief involves faith, and faith involves belief. It seems best, then, to see them not as distinct and unrelated but as profoundly interconnected: "belief/faith."

The Place of Cognition: Theological Belief/Faith?

With the first task of this essay temporarily (but most certainly not finally) complete, we are well along the way toward addressing the second task. Belief and faith must not be opposed improperly or excessively. There may well be a type of

18. Moberly, "Knowing God," 409.

19. Moberly, "Knowing God," 418.

20. See again Barr, *Semantics of Biblical Language*, 187; and Morgan, *Roman Faith*, 508—both cited above. For the fundamental role belief plays in our knowledge of the world and reality, see Nils J. Nilsson, *Understanding Beliefs* (Cambridge: MIT Press, 2014).

21. Moberly, "Knowing God," 418.

22. Moberly, "Knowing God," 419.

Is Belief (or Is It Faith?) an Ancient Israelite Notion?

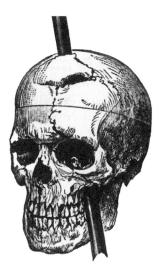

Fig. 10.1. Phineas Gage. *Left*, skull. Originally from John M. Harlow, "Recover from the Passage of an Iron Bar through the Head," *Bulletin of the Massachusetts Medical Society* (1869). *Right*, photograph of Gage. From the Gage family of Texas photo collection.

faith that is less content oriented, and a kind of belief that is more heavily content oriented, but in either scenario belief and faith are definitely *not* nonoverlapping, entirely discrete sets: there seems to be plenty of "belief" in the Old Testament in addition to "faith" and vice versa—hence "belief/faith." Whether this conclusion from "Defining Belief (or Is It Faith?) in the Hebrew Bible" above would convince Rabbi Rosen is unclear. Regardless, it remains true that √ידע and √אמן are not to be identified entirely with one another, treated as if they were *completely* overlapping and coterminous sets. Instead, the "complementarity" Moberly speaks of is a helpful *via media* and a reminder that a hard and fast division between belief and faith, with never the twain meeting, must be vigorously resisted. At this point, Professor Wyschogrod's self-description as a "theological Jew" returns in force, especially since, by his own account, he is aware of theology's "philosophical side." But, while we are well down the road on the second task of this essay, it remains to be addressed head on: what, exactly, is the place of cognition in belief/faith, particularly in the ancient contexts of the Hebrew Bible and ancient Israelite religion?

Once more we face a very complicated issue that cannot be resolved here. Even so, two observations should be made, one more recent and one truly ancient.

First, a modern observation: Neuroscience has demonstrated the close relationship between emotion and cognition in the brain, such that it is impossible to extricate fully the two from one another. Patient zero, as it were, was a man named Phineas Gage (1823–1860), a railroad construction worker who inadvertently blasted an iron rod through his head, destroying much of the front left lobe of his brain, but who survived for twelve years after this horrible accident (see fig. 10.1 on p. 185). Gage was, of course, never the same; in fact, some of his friends designated him as "no longer Gage."[23] Cognitive scientists like Antonio Damasio have demonstrated that Gage's injury and subsequent behavior demonstrate the profound interrelationship of emotion and thinking within the architecture of the brain. Any attempt to separate these from each other is to commit what Damasio calls "Descartes' error": the false imposition of a mind/body dualism.[24] Instead, to cite the title of another one of his books, Damasio argues for "the feeling of what happens," including when "what happens" is *thinking*.[25] Whatever one may call it, this first observation is simply that human beings apparently do not and cannot think without also feeling at the same time. Conversely, neither do individuals feel without thinking in some capacity. Put in the categories that are in focus in the present essay, one might say, comparably, that "faith" or "trust" (אֱמוּנָה and congeners) does not happen without cognition and some cognitive content; neither does "belief" or "cognition" (√ידע, πίστις, and so forth) happen without affective (approximating Moberly's "existential") elements.[26] This is not to accuse Buber and others of Descartes's error per se, though it is possible that at least some of those who draw overly precise or unduly "careless" distinctions between belief and faith may well be; these latter would belong to the "the other careless accounts" category that Moberly worries about.[27] For readers who might be worrying about something else—namely, the application of modern cognitive science research

23. See John Martyn Harlow, "Recovery from the Passage of an Iron Bar through the Head," *Publications of the Massachusetts Medical Society* 2 (1868): 340.

24. Antonio Damasio, *Descartes' Error: Emotion, Reason, and the Human Brain* (New York: Quill, 2000).

25. Antonio Damasio, *The Feeling of What Happens: Body and Emotion in the Making of Consciousness* (San Diego: Harcourt, 1999). Note also, most recently, Damasio, *Feeling and Knowing: Making Minds Conscious* (New York: Pantheon, 2021).

26. To be sure, the cognitive element, especially at certain affectual levels, may be implicit (autonomic) rather than explicit (reflective)—thinking fast as opposed to thinking slow. For this distinction, see Daniel Kahneman, *Thinking, Fast and Slow* (New York: Farrar, Straus & Giroux, 2011).

27. Moberly, "Knowing God," 418.

to ancient cultures and peoples—the recent work by Brett Maiden should suffice as reassurance that the application is a legitimate and worthwhile one.[28] One of the facts Maiden depends upon is that the human brain has undergone no major architectural changes for at least the last 35,000 years.[29] So, while this first, cognitive observation depends on modern research, it has profound ramifications for antiquity.

The second observation comes from the study of ancient Egypt. In his seminal work, *Egyptian Solar Religion in the New Kingdom*, Jan Assmann begins by rehearsing the faith and belief dichotomy (see "Defining Belief (or Is It Faith?) in the Hebrew Bible" above), with belief belonging to the realm of theology properly so called. Theology, Assmann notes pro forma, is typically thought to belong to those religions "that are primarily concerned with the conception of god, i.e. monotheistic religions"; indeed, the word *theology* has often been reserved for the Christian religion alone "as the only religion that worships God as 'logos.'"[30] Assmann himself deems such restrictive use unnecessary—it is "extreme" in his terms—because *theology* "is also used in the broader sense of a logically and argumentatively organized knowledge and discourse on the divine." That kind

---

28. Brett E. Maiden, *Cognitive Science and Ancient Israelite Religion: New Perspectives on Texts, Artifacts, and Culture* (Cambridge: Cambridge University Press, 2020). See also Daniel O. McClellan, *Yhwh's Divine Images: A Cognitive Approach* (Atlanta: SBL Press, 2022); and, earlier, Peter Westh, "Illuminator of the Wide Earth; Unbribable Judge; Strong Weapon of the Gods: Intuitive Ontology and Divine Epithets in Assyro-Babylonian Religious Texts," in *Past Minds: Studies in Cognitive Historiography*, ed. Luther H. Martin and Jesper Sørensen (London: Equinox, 2011), 45–61. Mention might also be made of Michael Carasik, *Theologies of the Mind in Biblical Israel* (New York: Lang, 2006). I am fully aware of debates over ancient emotion as captured, for example, in the essays collected in Sara Kipfer, ed., *Visualizing Emotions in the Ancient Near East* (Fribourg: Academic Press; Göttingen: Vandenhoeck & Ruprecht, 2017). I will say here only that I am not convinced by those who argue that access to ancient affect states simply cannot be had. *Visualizing Emotions* includes essays that confidently find expression of animal emotion in the ancient record but then fail, for no obvious or compelling reason, to draw similar conclusions for the human animal. For other recent treatments on emotion and affect, see F. Scott Spencer, ed., *Mixed Feelings and Vexed Passions: Exploring Emotions in Biblical Literature* (Atanta: SBL Press, 2017); Fiona C. Black and Jennifer L. Koosed, eds., *Reading with Feeling: Affect Theory and the Bible* (Atlanta: SBL Press, 2019); Shih-Wei Hus and Jaume Llop Raduà, eds., *The Expression of Emotions in Ancient Egypt and Mesopotamia* (Leiden: Brill, 2021); and Karen Sonik and Ulrike Steinert, eds., *The Routledge Handbook of Emotions in the Ancient Near East* (New York: Routledge, 2023).

29. See, inter alia, Simon Neubauer, Jean-Jacques Hublin, and Philipp Gunz, "The Evolution of Modern Human Brain Shape," *Science Advances* 4.1 (2018): 1–8.

30. Jan Assmann, *Egyptian Solar Religion in the New Kingdom: Re, Amun and the Crisis of Polytheism*, trans. Anthony Alcock (London: Kegan Paul, 1995), xi.

of knowledge and discourse need not be restricted to Christianity. Still further, one need not presume that this broader definition of theology is limited to what Assmann calls "secondary religions" (those that "shift from ritual practice to semantics, to verbal expression and communication") because "as improbable and implausible as this fact might appear: there are many hundreds of ancient Egyptian texts . . . that expound a 'discourse on the divine' which, as far as terminological differentiation and conceptual complexity is concerned, has no equivalent in the Old Testament."[31] That is to say that Egyptian theological discourse is *more developed* than the (later) Old Testament materials. Assmann deems this type of divine discourse a highly literate phenomenon, worthy perhaps of the name *theography* rather than *theology*.[32] But he also thinks it "would be a reductionist fallacy to explain the emergence and unfolding of the Theological Discourse by the rise of literacy alone. Literacy here is a necessary but not a sufficient condition."[33] Equally important, therefore, is the facilitating environment that gave rise to this type of theological reflection. According to Assmann, it was "a fundamental 'crisis of polytheism'" that produced this type of discourse in ancient Egypt.[34]

So far, then, this second observation is simply to note that such a thing as *theology* existed in ancient Egypt in no small measure ("many hundreds of . . . texts") and in no mean form at a time that long antedates the final form of the writings in the Hebrew Bible. Still further, it turns out that Professor Wyschogrod is not the only theological Jew who is aware of the philosophical side of things: Philo of Alexandria comes to mind long before him, but long before Philo—also in Egypt but not of Jewish heritage—there is something Assmann identifies as "Theological Discourse," and of a fairly sophisticated sort (marked by "terminological differentiation and conceptual complexity"). Theology in the sense of cognitive content (often glossed as "belief" and contrasted erroneously with "faith") is, in short, a truly ancient phenomenon.[35]

31. Assmann focuses on "over 500 texts from the New Kingdom that reflect solar and Amun theology" (*Egyptian Solar Religion*, 9; and see 12–15 for seven "standard texts").

32. Assmann, *Egyptian Solar Religion*, xi–xii.

33. Assmann, *Egyptian Solar Religion*, xii. Assmann's use of capital letters in "Theological Discourse" is noteworthy (see also the next note).

34. Assmann, *Egyptian Solar Religion*, xii: "The crisis of polytheism is primarily concerned with the conception of god, with questions of unity and plurality that are pushed—long before the rise of monotheistic religions in the proper sense—to the extremes of radical and revolutionary monotheism. It would again be a reductionist fallacy to see in this conflict nothing but the expression of political and economical tensions. The *intellectual dimension* of this conflict is revealed by the texts and the Theological Discourse they expound" (emphasis added).

35. An even earlier repository that reflects profound theological struggle with the nature of the gods might be found in the corpus of Sumerian *balaĝ* litanies of the second (and first) mil-

Is Belief (or Is It Faith?) an Ancient Israelite Notion?

To cite Assmann again, he is at pains to explain "to an English speaking audience an undertaking that, for whatever reasons, appears somewhat less extravagant in the German context, where the term 'theology' has been in use among Egyptologists since the days of Richard Lepsius [1810–1884]."[36] Assmann is thus offering something of an *apologia* for why it is perfectly fine to use the word *theology* when it comes to ancient Egypt.[37] To be sure, some Egyptologists may prefer the term *philosophy*—as in James P. Allen's *Genesis in Egypt: The Philosophy of Egyptian Creation Accounts*[38]—with the same applying to some biblical scholars, early or late.[39] But, per Wyschogrod, theology is not without a philosophical side and remains by far the better term for the ancient world, because there, as in "theo-logy" etymologically defined, the place of the god(s) is inescapable in a

---

lennium, though the kind of theological work that Assmann is pointing to is found even earlier. See Sebastian Fink, "Metaphors for the Unrecognizability of God in Balaĝs and Xenophanes," in *Mesopotamia in the Ancient World: Impact, Continuities, Parallels; Proceedings of the Seventh Symposium of the Melammu Project Held in Obergurgl, Austria, November 4–8, 2013*, ed. Robert Rollinger and Erik van Dongen (Münster: Ugarit-Verlag, 2015), 231–43, esp. 234–35: "Already in the 3rd millennium BCE scribes tried to interpret and understand the divine by etymologizing and interpreting divine names." For a collection of these texts, see Mark E. Cohen, *The Canonical Lamentations of Ancient Mesopotamia*, 2 vols. (Potomac, MD: Capital Decisions Limited, 1988). An insightful, even moving account of *Ludlul bēl nēmeqi*'s theology may be found in William L. Moran, "The Babylonian Job," in *The Most Magic Word*, ed. Ronald S. Hendel (Washington, DC: Catholic Biblical Association, 2002), 182–200.

36. Assmann, *Egyptian Solar Religion*, xii.

37. Note also Vincent Arieh Tobin, *Theological Principles of Egyptian Religion* (New York: Lang, 1989), whose conclusions are somewhat skeptical, but who does speak of "Egyptian religion as an all-embracing and all-encompassing *system and method* of perception and articulation. . . . Religion was in effect the *articulation of existential being* . . . a matter of experience, or perhaps . . . better . . . a means of experiencing the universe as an *ordered cosmos*" (196, emphases added). On the matter of theological ethics in ancient Egypt, see Maulana Karenga, *Maat: The Moral Ideal in Ancient Egypt: A Study in Classical African Ethics* (New York: Routledge, 2004), 135–74. On the Assyriological side of things, Mario Liverani is not afraid to use theological terminology in his *Assyria: The Imperial Mission*, trans. Andrea Trameri and Jonathan Valk (Winona Lake, IN: Eisenbrauns, 2017). See further below for the use of *theology* in classics.

38. James P. Allen, *Genesis in Egypt: The Philosophy of Ancient Egyptian Creation Accounts* (New Haven: Yale University Press, 1988); also James P. Allen et al., *Religion and Philosophy in Ancient Egypt* (New Haven: Yale University Press, 1989).

39. E.g., Yoram Hazony, *The Philosophy of Hebrew Scripture* (New York: Cambridge University Press, 2012); Dru Johnson, *Biblical Philosophy: A Hebraic Approach to the Old and New Testaments* (Cambridge: Cambridge University Press, 2021); Johnson, *Biblical Knowing: A Scriptural Epistemology of Error* (Eugene, OR: Cascade, 2013). Cf. also Jaco Gericke, *The Hebrew Bible and Philosophy of Religion* (Atlanta: Society of Biblical Literature, 2012). Beyond the biblical and Egyptological fields, see Marc Van De Mieroop, *Philosophy before the Greeks: The Pursuit of Truth in Ancient Babylonia* (Princeton: Princeton University Press, 2016).

way that is just not true for the term "philo-sophy," especially in its more modern iterations.[40]

Here is where things get interesting with reference to ancient Israel. "Israel," Assmann writes, "in its earlier, prophetic states, is beyond this crisis [of polytheism] and less literate. It is simply unconcerned with questions of the One and the Many that preoccupy the minds of the Egyptian priests, sages and *literati*. . . . The many do not exist [for the prophets]. Radical monotheism means a radical reduction of complexity."[41] And so, "the statement," which is "at first sight so strikingly implausible," namely, "that Egyptian theology (or theography) is in some respect superior to the Biblical one . . . finds a very simple explanation."[42] Egyptian theology is more advanced, that is, at least in some respect(s) according to Assmann, because it is more literate (though that factor is less important) and because (more importantly) it is working through the complicated question of the one and the many. "The uniqueness or oneness of god is the central theological problem of the New Kingdom," according to Assmann.[43]

Yet with all due respect to Assmann, it seems safe to say that a "crisis of monotheism"—especially when that is glossed as having to do with "the conception of god, with questions of unity and plurality"[44]—was at work within ancient Israelite religion as well, even if only belatedly so, and on both the question of the conception of Yhwh's own person as well as Yhwh's place and status among the gods. Such matters are the foci of a massive body of literature within biblical studies, which shows that this crisis (or these crises) also shows up within the pages of the Old Testament.[45] Whether the Old Testament's treatment is somehow less

40. Cf. Brent Nongbri, *Before Religion: A History of a Modern Concept* (New Haven: Yale University Press, 2013); also Carlin A. Barton and Daniel Boyarin, *Imagine No Religion: How Modern Abstractions Hide Ancient Realities* (New York: Fordham University Press, 2016).

41. Assmann, *Egyptian Solar Religion*, xii.

42. Assmann, *Egyptian Solar Religion*, xii.

43. Assmann, *Egyptian Solar Religion*, 2.

44. Assmann, *Egyptian Solar Religion*, xii.

45. To list only a very few important studies, see Walter Brueggemann, *Theology of the Old Testament: Testimony, Dispute, Advocacy* (Minneapolis: Fortress, 1997); Othmar Keel and Christoph Uehlinger, *Gods, Goddesses, and Images of God in Ancient Israel*, trans. Thomas H. Trapp (Minneapolis: Fortress, 1998); Patrick D. Miller, *The Religion of Ancient Israel* (Louisville: Westminster John Knox, 2000); Mark S. Smith, *God in Translation: Deities in Cross-Cultural Discourse in the Biblical World* (Grand Rapids: Eerdmans, 2010); Beate Pongratz-Leisten, ed., *Reconsidering the Concept of Revolutionary Monotheism* (Winona Lake, IN: Eisenbrauns, 2011); Theodore J. Lewis, *The Origin and Character of God: Ancient Israelite Religion through the Lens of Divinity* (Oxford: Oxford University Press, 2020); and Collin Cornell, ed., *Divine Doppelgängers: YHWH's Ancient Look-Alikes* (University Park, PA: Eisenbrauns, 2020).

Is Belief (or Is It Faith?) an Ancient Israelite Notion?

than that of ancient Egypt's (so Assmann) is a judgment that may be debated; it is enough to note that, in the aggregate, the Hebrew Bible, too, reflects extensive attention to the theological problem of the "uniqueness or oneness of god," and it does so in a fairly sophisticated sort of way, one marked by "terminological differentiation and conceptual complexity." If ancient Israel at whatever period was not yet literate enough to engage in such (high) theological reflection *in writing* (a significant caveat), the Hebrew Bible (once again in the aggregate) reflects exactly such a literary deposit. In its final complete form, the Old Testament is, of course, the achievement only of a much later period, but people can think—and at high levels—without writing those thoughts down, and literacy can be parsed in more than one way. Indeed, the existence of something called "visual literacy" leads directly to the third and final task of this essay.[46]

Seeing and/as Believing: The Visual as a Locus for and of Belief/Faith

Thus far, then, I have attempted to show that belief and faith need not and should not be bifurcated—at least not entirely—when it comes to the biblical texts and, presumably, the religious experience and practice that gave rise to them.[47] It is far better to imagine a sliding scale or spectrum of sorts, as long as that image does not suggest distinct and far distant poles, since it seems clear that belief and faith are deeply intertwined and connected, not at all entirely unrelated. The previous section noted that cognitive science will not permit any overly hard and fast division between thinking and feeling, or what people have tended to divide into belief and faith, πίστις and אֱמוּנָה. Still further, and with reference to antiquity, Egyptologists seem perfectly comfortable with a heavily cognitive side (i.e., *belief* in the common understanding) of ancient Egyptian religion, finding it present in numerous Egyptian texts that date to (or antedate) the same general horizon

46. For questions of literacy and visual literacy in ancient Israel, see Ryan P. Bonfiglio, *Reading Images, Seeing Texts: Towards a Visual Hermeneutics for Biblical Studies* (Fribourg: Academic Press; Göttingen: Vandenhoeck & Ruprecht, 2016), 17–63.

47. See Mark S. Smith, "Recent Study of Israelite Religion in Light of the Ugaritic Texts," in *Ugarit at Seventy-Five*, ed. K. Lawson Younger Jr. (Winona Lake, IN: Eisenbrauns, 2007), 1–26, esp. 5: "Out of experience comes literature, and out of religious experience comes religious literature." From a different angle, note Judah Goldin, *Studies in Midrash and Related Literature*, ed. Barry L. Eichler and Jeffrey H. Tigay (Philadelphia: Jewish Publication Society, 1988), 271–81. For yet another (one that distinguishes belief from experience), see Rodney Needham, *Belief, Language, and Experience* (Chicago: University of Chicago Press, 1972).

as the ancient Israelites and the (later) biblical texts they produced. Much later than the New Kingdom materials that Assmann adduces, but still overlapping the biblical period(s), is the field of classics. Here, too, the word *theology* has enjoyed recent renewed interest and use.[48]

To this point, however, the discussion has been somewhat theoretical and at points fully analogical. As a result, it will be helpful to turn to the third task of this essay to consider a particular locus of belief/faith and the role of cognition therein. The focus here is the artistic record, specifically, the study of ancient Near Eastern iconography and the Hebrew Bible. Before examining three examples more closely, it will be helpful to consider the role of cognition in art more broadly, since this ties back nicely to the discussion of neuroscience and Egyptology (see "The Place of Cognition: Theological Belief/Faith?" above).

Rudolf Arnheim, professor of the psychology of art at Harvard University, wrote about "visual thinking" as early as 1969.[49] Visual perception, according to Arnheim, is "a cognitive activity," and that makes "artistic activity . . . a form of reasoning, in which perceiving and thinking are invisibly intertwined."[50] What we see when we look at something is processed cognitively, and what is processed cognitively is, according to Arnheim, processed pictorially. There is, in short, a profound connection between seeing and thinking.[51] The remarkable mechanisms by which the senses understand the environment are all but identical with the operations described by the psychology of thinking. Inversely, there is much evidence that truly productive thinking in whatever area of cognition takes place in the realm of imagery.[52]

---

48. See, e.g., Esther Eidinow, Julia Kindt, and Robin Osborne, eds., *Theologies of Ancient Greek Religion* (Cambridge: Cambridge University Press, 2016); and H. S. Versnel, *Coping with the Gods: Wayward Readings in Greek Theology* (Leiden: Brill, 2011). See also Jonathan Klawans, *Josephus and the Theologies of Ancient Judaism* (Oxford: Oxford University Press, 2012).

49. Rudolf Arnheim, *Visual Thinking* (Berkeley: University of California Press, 1969). For earlier texts, see Albert Hofstadter and Richard Kuhns, eds., *Philosophies of Art and Beauty: Selected Readings in Aesthetics from Plato to Heidegger* (Chicago: University of Chicago Press, 1964).

50. Arnheim, *Visual Thinking*, v.

51. Cf. Rudolf Arnheim, *Art and Visual Perception: A Psychology of the Creative Eye* (Berkeley: University of California, 1974), 3: "All seeing is in the realm of the psychologist, and no one has ever discussed the processes of creating or experiencing art without talking psychology." Cf. the notion of dual coding (the role of both the verbal and the visual) in cognition, for which see Mark Sadoski and Allan Paivio, *Imagery and Text: A Dual Coding Theory of Reading and Writing*, 2nd ed. (New York: Routledge, 2013); and Allan Paivio, *Mental Representations: A Dual Coding Approach* (New York: Oxford University Press, 1986).

52. Arnheim, *Visual Thinking*, v. See further Arnheim, *Art and Visual Perception*; and Arnheim, *Toward a Psychology of Art: Collected Essays* (Berkeley: University of California, 1966).

Is Belief (or Is It Faith?) an Ancient Israelite Notion?

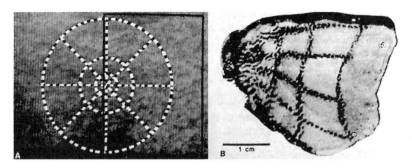

Fig. 10.2. Comparison of an image viewed by a monkey (A, *left*) along with the pattern of brain activation (B, *right*). Tootell et al., "Deoxyglucose Analysis of Retinotopic Organization in Primate Striate Cortex," 902, fig. 1. Used with permission.

Arnheim's now dated work has received more recent support in the research of neuroscientists, who have demonstrated that "seeing an image with the eye and imagining one within the mind's eye are not just phenomenologically analogous experiences but also neurologically overlapping processes."[53] For example, an experiment conducted by Roger Tootell and his colleagues demonstrated that the visual pattern shown to monkeys was neutrally replicated on their brains[54]—it was, that is, actually and physically laid out on

---

More recently, see Manfredo Massironi, *The Psychology of Graphic Images: Seeing, Drawing, Communicating*, trans. Nicolo Bruno (Mahwah, NJ: Erlbaum, 2002); Alberto Argenton, *Art and Expression: Studies in the Psychology of Art*, ed. Ian Verstegen (London: Routledge, 2019); and John Carvalho, *Thinking with Images: An Enactivist Aesthetics* (New York: Routledge, 2019). See also the next note.

53. Justin Walker, *The Power of Images: The Poetics of Violence in Lamentations 2 and Ancient Near Eastern Art* (Leuven: Peeters, 2022), 15. See further, e.g., Steven Pinker, ed., *Visual Cognition* (Cambridge: MIT Press, 1985); and Stephen M. Kosslyn, William L. Thompson, and Giorgio Ganis, *The Case for Mental Imagery* (Oxford: Oxford University Press, 2006). For how cognitive science relates to mental images and imagery, not least during reading, see also Mark Turner, *Reading Minds: The Study of English in the Age of Cognitive Science* (Princeton: Princeton University Press, 1991); Ellen J. Esrock, *The Reader's Eye: Visual Imaging as Reader Response* (Baltimore: Johns Hopkins University Press, 1994); Elaine Scarry, *Dreaming by the Book* (New York: Farrar, Straus & Giroux, 1999); Paul B. Armstrong, *How Literature Plays with the Brain: The Neuroscience of Reading and Art* (Baltimore: Johns Hopkins University Press, 2013); Reuven Tsur, *Poetic Conventions as Cognitive Fossils* (Oxford: Oxford University Press, 2017); and Maryanne Wolf, *Reader, Come Home: The Reading Brain in a Digital World* (New York: Harper, 2018). A fascinating treatment may be found in Peter Mendelsund, *What We See When We Read* (New York: Vintage, 2014).

54. R. B. H. Tootell et al., "Deoxyglucose Analysis of Retinotopic Organization in Primate Striate Cortex," *Science* 218 (1982): 902–4.

their cortices (see fig. 10.2 on p. 193).[55] Other experiments have shown the same, namely, that "the cortex is topographically organized and thus uses the available space in the cortex to render what is seen in a depictive manner."[56] Research like this shows that seeing is part of cognitive function (how could it be otherwise?), and cognitive function depends, at least in part (and maybe no small part), on seeing—hence Arnheim's early (and accurate) postulation. Much more recently than Arnheim and on the basis of far more advanced brain research, the neuroscientist V. S. Ramachandran has gone so far as to posit ten "artistic universals."[57] Even more recently, Ludovico Portuese has connected neuropsychological research in analyzing Mesopotamian art, identifying various "cues" that draw attention to a picture and that also manipulate a viewer's gaze: "amplification, contrast, emotional salience, simplification, symmetry, distribution and central positioning of elements, composition regarding the flow of elements, and significant objects."[58] These cues are apparently transcultural "due to the basic competencies that are hard-wired both in the brain

55. See Kosslyn, Thompson, and Ganis, *The Case for Mental Imagery*, 15.

56. Walker, *Power of Images*, 14, who depends, inter alia, on E. A. DeYoe et al., "Functional Magnetic Resonance Imaging (FMRI) of the Human Brain," *Journal of Neuroscience Methods* 54 (1994): 171–87; S. A. Engel et al., "fMRI of Human Visual Cortex," *Nature* 369 (1994): 525; M. I. Sereno et al., "Borders of Multiple Visual Areas in Humans Revealed by Functional Magnetic Resonance Imaging," *Science* 268 (1995): 889–93; M. K. Hasnain, P. T. Fox, and M. G. Woldorff, "Intersubject Variability of Functional Areas in the Human Visual Cortex," *Human Brain Mapping* 6 (1998): 301–15; D. C. Van Essen et al., "Mapping Visual Cortex in Monkeys and Humans Using Surface-Based Atlases," *Vision Research* 41 (2001): 1359–78; Isabelle Klein et al., "Retinotopic Organization of Visual Mental Images as Revealed by Functional Magnetic Resonance Imaging," *Cognitive Brain Research* 22 (2004): 26–31; S. D. Slotnick et al., "Visual Mental Imagery Induces Retinotopically Organized Activation of Early Visual Areas," *Cerebral Cortex* 15 (2005): 1570–83; Bertrand Thirion et al., "Inverse Retinotopy: Inferring the Visual Content of Images from Brain Activation Patterns," *NeuroImage* 33 (2006): 1104–16; and Grégoire Borst, "Neural Underpinning of Object Mental Imagery, Spatial Imagery, and Motor Imagery," in *The Oxford Handbook of Cognitive Neuroscience*, ed. Kevin N. Ochsner and Stephen Michael Kosslyn (Oxford: Oxford University Press, 2014), 74–87.

57. V. S. Ramachandran, *A Brief Tour of Human Consciousness: From Imposter Poodles to Purple Numbers* (New York: Pi, 2004), 40–59, esp. 44.

58. Ludovico Portuese, "Toward a (Neuro-)Psychology of Art: Cues for Attention in Mesopotamian Art," *Ash-Sharq* 4 (2020): 157–86, esp. 160–79 (quotation from 159). Portuese cites two works by V. S. Ramachandran: Ramachandran and W. Hirstein, "The Science of Art: A Neurological Theory of Aesthetic Experience," *Journal of Consciousness Studies* 6.6–7 (1999): 15–51; and Ramachandran, *The Tell-Tale Brain: A Neuroscientist's Quest for What Makes Us Human* (New York: Norton, 2011). Note also Portuese's monograph *Life at Court: Ideology and Audience in the Late Assyrian Palace* (Münster: Zaphon, 2020), which also discusses aesthetic response.

Is Belief (or Is It Faith?) an Ancient Israelite Notion?

and the human cognitive system."[59] And so, writes Portuese, "in the light of the universality of cues for attention and orientation in what is being observed, sometimes shared by both animals and humans, even across cultures, it seems reasonable to believe that also for Mesopotamian artists and viewers these visual cues possessed the same qualities as today and were similarly conceived and perceived."[60] Given his own set of universals, Ramachandran would no doubt agree. Turning from Ludovico's focus in Mesopotamia to the south and east, it is not hard to imagine that within an image-rich society like Egypt—even in the image-rich Egyptian writing system considered all by itself—a whole lot is happening cognitively. A huge amount of synapses are firing in the creation and reception of the image-infused culture of ancient Egypt.

Of course, not all of the brain function involved in seeing is conscious, but at least some of it is, especially when it comes to art (used) as a language of communication.[61] At this point, however, we need more information than just that provided by fMRI machines and so should turn to the study of visual culture to see how it impinges on matters of religion, including belief/faith.[62] Already

59. Portuese, "Toward a (Neuro-)Psychology of Art," 179.

60. Portuese, "Toward a (Neuro-)Psychology of Art," 179, with important and immediate qualifications, while still holding that "it seems that at least primary perceptions are somehow universal." Portuese admits that his analyses "must be considered as an informed approximation" but also observes that things like emotional impact or original context are constraints that "are not immune to human beings' natural cognitive dispositions" and so "pictures may have [a] life on their own able to universally affect any viewer" (180). He concludes: "I feel justified to assert that Mesopotamian artists consciously used specific cues in images to attract and direct the viewer's attention and orientation" (180). Cf. Lewis, *Origin and Character of God*, 422, on the "pragmatic attention-focusing devices to rivet eyes and actions on the sacred during cultic activity" that are present in aniconic traditions. See also Portuese, "Toward a (Neuro-)Psychology of Art," 159n7, for bottom-up (stimulus driven) and top-down (cognitive/psychological) factors. The latter are in part what allow artistic cues "to affect the viewer even in the absentia of context or explanations" (159). For physiological constraints (and universals) more generally, see Steven Pinker, *The Blank Slate: The Modern Denial of Human Nature* (New York: Penguin, 2002); Pinker discusses the arts on 400–420.

61. See, e.g., Ramachandran, *Brief Tour of Human Consciousness*, 28–32, on the phenomenon of "blindsight." The complex system of seeing coupled with visual processing means that much is happening in terms of fast (intuitive) thinking, regardless of what is or may also be happening in terms of slow (reflective) thinking. More generally, seeing/vision belongs to the context biases that Maiden discusses, a good bit of which may function as "credibility enhancing displays" (CREDs). Here again, cognitive processes are at work, even if these are not all at the level of conscious belief. That said, CREDs seem specifically designed to shore up belief, particularly around more explicit and cognitively costly aspects of religious thought and practice; see Maiden, *Cognitive Science and Ancient Israelite Religion*, 177–210, esp. 206–7.

62. For a recent accessible introduction, see Alexis L. Boylan, *Visual Culture* (Cambridge: MIT

in Arnheim's psychological work "experiencing art is an interplay between the properties of the object and the nature of the observing subject," but visual studies places even more importance on the role of the viewer.[63] This is not to say that issues of artistic production or intention are no longer important, but it is to say that *equally* important are issues of viewer reception and interpretation. So, as Portuese puts it, "This line of investigation overturns the archaeological analysis of objects making its relationship with the observer the primary research."[64] Drawing on W. J. T. Mitchell, Portuese asserts that this kind of approach makes "the relationality of image and beholder the field of investigation" in order "to turn analysis of pictures towards questions of process, affect, and to put in question the spectator position."[65] In Ryan Bonfiglio's apt phrasing, "the meaning of an image . . . [is] a function of both its production *and* its reception, the intentions of the original producers *and* the interpretations of later viewers."[66] If this is the case, then a large number of things are immediately involved: "the whole realm of

---

Press, 2020). For a more popular formulation, see Alexandra Horowitz, *On Looking: A Walker's Guide to the Art of Observation* (New York: Scribner, 2013). A very important treatment remains David Freedberg, *The Power of Images: Studies in the History and Theory of Response* (Chicago: University of Chicago Press, 1989). For a review of visual culture and ancient religion, see Christoph Uehlinger, "Approaches to Visual Culture and Religion: Disciplinary Trajectories, Interdisciplinary Connections and Some Suggestions for Further Progress," *MTSR* 27 (2015): 384–422.

63. Portuese, "Toward a (Neuro-)Psychology of Art," 158.

64. Portuese, "Toward a (Neuro-)Psychology of Art," 158. Cf. Boylan, *Visual Culture*, 29: "If you can see it, if it was made to be seen, then it's visual culture."

65. Portuese, "Toward a (Neuro-)Psychology of Art," 158, citing W. J. T. Mitchell, *What Do Pictures Want? The Lives and Loves of Images* (Chicago: University of Chicago Press, 2015), 49. Cf. Ann C. Tyler, "Shaping Belief: The Role of Audience in Visual Communication," *Design Issues* 9 (1992): 28–29: "The argument of these ads is a display of beliefs and the *role of the audience* within that argument is to experience the beliefs exhibited. . . . The audience is a dynamic participant in the argument." See also Robin M. Jensen, "Visuality," in *The Cambridge Companion to Ancient Mediterranean Religions*, ed. Barbette Stanley Spaeth (Cambridge: Cambridge University Press, 2013), 309–43, esp. 310–13.

66. Bonfiglio, *Reading Images, Seeing Texts*, 244, with reference to David Morgan, *The Sacred Gaze: Religious Visual Culture in Theory and Practice* (Berkeley: University of California Press, 2005), 30. Bonfiglio devotes considerable time to justifying—with all due caution—the application of visual culture studies (a mostly modern-facing discipline) to the ancient world. E.g., he discusses ancient image mutilation, which speaks directly to how ancient viewers responded to images (207–19). Note his important caveat: "Evidence of ancient Israelite visual practices and ways of seeing can only be indirectly inferred from archaeological data, textual materials and/or a broader understanding of the nature, role, and function of images in the ANE world. Therefore, investigations of ancient visual culture are bound to be somewhat speculative in nature, though I should be quick to add, not any more so than studies that focus on ancient *textual* materials" (252).

Is Belief (or Is It Faith?) an Ancient Israelite Notion?

visuality and, with it, the cultural and social dimensions of sight."[67] Put differently, "insofar as religion happens visually" *the practice of viewing* along with *the images themselves* together "constitute the visual medium of belief."[68]

The study of visual culture is yet another vast subject area, one which cannot be adequately dealt with here. It must suffice, to borrow from works by David Morgan, who has written of the visual aspects of religion as *visual piety* and the religious act of viewing as *the sacred gaze*.[69] For his part, Bonfiglio employs the dyad *the visual medium of belief* and *the religious apparatus of sight*.[70] We may illustrate these terms and the larger issue of visuality as a locus of belief/faith by means of three vignettes. Before turning to them, it should be stressed that, given visual studies' attention to *reception* (i.e., observers, viewers), there is a real possibility if not probability that "ancient viewers, at least on occasion, interpreted, responded to, and employed an art object in ways that were not entirely consistent with the intentions of those who originally produced or commissioned it."[71] Said differently: "Knowledge about the production of an image does not rigidly predict

---

67. Bonfiglio, *Reading Images, Seeing Texts*, 228, who goes on to mention "not only a broader expanse of visual objects but also the social, cultural institutional, and intellectual practices that put . . . images to use" (229). "Vision," Bonfiglio writes, "is a culturally shaped habit" (229). In brief, art—ancient no less than modern—participates "in the social and cultural construction of reality" (230), and "seeing is a thoroughly engaged, purposeful, and constructive activity" (240).

68. D. Morgan, *Sacred Gaze*, 6.

69. Defined, respectively, as "the visual formation and practice of religious belief" (David Morgan, *Visual Piety: A History and Theory of Popular Religious Images* [Berkeley: University of Califonria Press, 1998], 1) and "the particular configuration of ideas, attitudes, and customs that informs a religious act of seeing as it occurs within a given cultural and historical setting . . . the manner in which a way of seeing invests an image, a viewer, or an act of viewing with spiritual significance . . . [signaling] that the entire visual field that constitutes seeing is the framework of analysis, not just the image itself" (D. Morgan, *Sacred Gaze*, 3). As Bonfiglio notes, Morgan often uses these and yet still other terms interchangeably, even though they are not exactly identical (*Reading Images, Seeing Texts*, 242n50).

70. See Bonfligio, *Reading Images, Seeing Texts*, 233, 240–42. The former term is that of David Morgan, by which he means the combination of visual practice and the images proper (*Sacred Gaze*, 6). The title of another volume edited by David Morgan is instructive; see *Religion and Material Culture: The Matter of Belief* (London: Routledge, 2010). There, Morgan defines *belief* "in many ways," including dogmatically, affectively, voluntaristically, and practically (7).

71. Bonfiglio, *Reading Images, Seeing Texts*, 230; similarly 240n44: "Later viewers often attribute meanings to images that diverge from what was intended by its original producers." A corollary is that "scholars should not *a priori* assume that different types of images are always utilized in different ways or that certain iconographic themes or subject matter rigidly determine whether an image is 'religious.' In fact, it is often the case that worshipers respond to and deploy a wide variety of visual representations in a very similar fashion" (239).

how viewers process, interact with, or respond to visual materials."[72] As but one example, Lawson Younger has recently posited differing interpretations of the same divine symbol by different viewers at ancient Sam'al (Zincirli).[73] Whatever the case, one of the main takeaways for the purposes of the present essay is that "belief routinely happens not only through what people *say* (i.e., words and creeds)," or through what they *make* (i.e., arts, monuments, buildings) "but also through what they *see*—paintings and photographs, architecture and landscapes, performances and rituals, liturgical garments and illuminated manuscripts. . . . Regardless of their form, these ['visual articulations of faith'] . . . have the capacity to facilitate belief by cultivating religious feelings and sensibilities."[74] This happens in part because "seeing is a means by which viewers, whether consciously or unconsciously, search for what they hope to see or have been trained to look for."[75] The several connections here between visual studies, cognition, and belief/faith should be readily apparent.[76] As Ann Tyler has put it, though this time with equal or greater emphasis on the artistic producer, "The goal of visual communication

---

72. Bonfiglio, *Reading Images, Seeing Texts*, 230. Cf. D. Morgan, *Sacred Gaze*, 30: "The study of visual culture will regard the image as part of a cultural system of production and reception, in which original intention does not eclipse the use to which images are put by those who are not their makers."

73. K. Lawson Younger Jr., "Gods at the Gates: A Study of the Identification of the Deities Represented at the Gates of Ancient Sam'al (Zincirli) with Possible Historical Implications," *ARAM Periodical* 31 (2019): 317–48. This reference is courtesy of Theodore Lewis.

74. Bonfiglio, *Reading Images, Seeing Texts*, 234. See further pp. 236–37 for a typology of image use derived from D. Morgan, *Sacred Gaze*, 55–74. Of particular importance for the present essay are those that "embody forms of communion with the divine" and "influence thought and behavior" (Bonfiglio, *Reading Images, Seeing Texts*, 236–37). Bonfiglio also offers a typology of gazes (243) derived from David Morgan, *The Embodied Eye: Religious Visual Culture and the Social Life of Feeling* (Berkeley: University of California Press, 2012), 70–83, one of which is "the devotional gaze."

75. Bonfiglio, *Reading Images, Seeing Texts*, 241, with reference to D. Morgan, *Embodied Eye*, 68.

76. See further Bonfiglio, *Reading Images, Seeing Texts*, 241, for viewers' predisposition "to see in an image what they already believe." D. Morgan, *Sacred Gaze*, 75, speaks of viewers' imaginative participation in seeing, "contributing what the image itself may not provide but must presuppose if it is to touch the viewer." Morgan uses the term "image covenants" for the tacit agreements "that a viewer observes when viewing an image in order to be engaged by it, in order to believe what the image reveals or says or means or makes one feel—indeed, in order to believe there is something to believe, some legitimate claim to truth to be affirmed" (76). In other words, "image covenants . . . describe the epistemological and moral conditions that shape what viewers expect from an image" (Bonfiglio, *Reading Images, Seeing Texts*, 249). Morgan delineates a number of these image covenants, the most important for present purposes being non-mimetic covenants like "the allegorical covenant" and "the expressivist covenant" (*Sacred Gaze*, 105–12; cf. Bonfiglio, *Reading Images, Seeing*

is to persuade an audience to adopt a new belief. . . . In developing an argument, a designer does not have a choice of referencing beliefs or not referencing beliefs; the choice lies [only] in what beliefs are referenced. In making this choice, existing beliefs will be affected (maintained, rejected, or transformed) and a new belief will be shaped."[77]

Vignette 1: Warner Sallman's Head of Christ

The first vignette draws from David Morgan's work on Warner Sallman's (1892–1968) well-known painting *Head of Christ*, completed in 1941.[78] Morgan solicited letters from devout viewers about this painting, and he discovered a number of fascinating things when he analyzed the responses. One finding was that even though the painting is not labeled, and despite the fact that it bears no known resemblance to the historical Jesus of Nazareth, countless viewers "recognized" Jesus in this and other paintings by Sallman. This recognition was clearly not predicated on external corroboration that the portrait was "realistic" but depended, instead, on discerning "a spiritual essence behind the image, a vision of Jesus learned and cultivated through Sunday School education and popular American Christian visual culture."[79] Bonfiglio summarizes the point nicely: "Through the eyes of faith, these paintings of Jesus become an icon of his spiritual presence despite the fact that they do not constitute a naturalistic portrait. Devout viewers see Jesus *in* or perhaps *beyond* these paintings because they reinforce what the viewers already have been trained to believe."[80] Morgan's study reveals still other intriguing aspects of what "the eyes of faith" saw "in or . . . beyond" this painting. It turns out that Sallman's *Head of Christ* is something of a "spiritual Rorschach blot," because viewers have seen or, perhaps better, *have found*, additional images in the painting (see fig. 10.3 on p. 200).[81] These additional images include (a) a communion chalice, (b) the eucharistic host, (c) a prophet or priest, (d) a cross, (e) three nuns in prayer, (f) an angel in prayer, (g) the Virgin Mary kneeling, (h) a dove, and (i) a serpent.[82] Even more fascinating than the nine (!) additional images

---

Texts, 250). These covenants are not mutually exclusive, and more than one can be operative in a viewer simultaneously.

77. Tyler, "Shaping Belief," 29.

78. Available online at https://www.warnersallman.com/collection/images/head-of-christ/.

79. Bonfiglio, *Reading Images, Seeing Texts*, 246.

80. Bonfiglio, *Reading Images, Seeing Texts*, 246.

81. D. Morgan, *Visual Piety*, 125.

82. These additional images were identified by twenty-two Catholic and Lutheran respondents; see D. Morgan, *Visual Piety*, 126–28; Bonfiglio, *Reading Images, Seeing Texts*, 248 and n. 72.

discovered by the devout is the fact that Sallman explicitly denied consciously including these symbols in *Head of Christ*.[83] The identification of these items by viewers is, therefore, nothing less than proof of "the sacred gaze, a religious way of seeing that has led viewers 'to textualize images, to treat them as the illustration of devotional or theological discourse.'"[84]

Two additional notes about Sallman's *Head of Christ* deserve mention. First, in later public talks that he gave about the painting, Sallmann—apparently influenced by comments from devout viewers—said that while he did not consciously put these additional images into the painting, they nevertheless "appeared as he was drawing."[85] While this phrasing is ambiguous, Bonfiglio is correct in finding here "an interesting case of reverse reception history—that is, the religious ways of seeing of later viewers prompted the author to reassess his own understanding about the original production of the painting!"[86] Second, the respondents who saw additional images in the painting did not see them in exactly the same way. Catholic respondents, for example, identified item (c), the figure on Jesus's left shoulder, as a priest or a monk, while Lutheran viewers said the same figure was a prophet.[87]

Fig. 10.3. Diagram of hidden images in Sallman's *Head of Christ*, by D. Morgan, *Visual Piety*, 128, fig. 42. Used with permission.

---

83. See D. Morgan, *Visual Piety*, 128 and 240n12.

84. Bonfiglio, *Reading Images, Seeing Texts*, 248, citing D. Morgan, *Visual Piety*, 140. Morgan is specifically concerned with textualization based on "the primary language of the Bible" and "the preexisting biblical text," and he deems its presence the result of childhood religious education. One may doubt that "textualize" is entirely the right word, however. See also n. 88 below.

85. D. Morgan, *Visual Piety*, 129.

86. Bonfiglio, *Reading Images, Seeing Texts*, 248n73. Sallman consciously included symbols in other paintings, like the cross found in *The Boy Christ* and *Christ in Gethsemane* (see D. Morgan, *Visual Piety*, 129–30) but these symbols are rather obvious. The additional images in *Head of Christ* thus remain a different matter.

87. See D. Morgan, *Visual Piety*, 131; also Bonfiglio, *Reading Images, Seeing Texts*, 248–49.

Is Belief (or Is It Faith?) an Ancient Israelite Notion?

Although they disagreed on the precise referent, both sets of observers "effectively insert[ed] the painting 'into a mode of discourse built on the primary language of the Bible'" or on their respective religious practices.[88] The different percepts, as well as the underlying cognitive similarity that gave rise to them, means that "what some religious viewers are able to see in the painting is conditioned by what they have come to believe as a result of certain theological traditions. In this way, religious ways of seeing corroborate prior biblical interpretation."[89]

While this vignette about Sallman's *Head of Christ* concerns a piece of modern art, it is nevertheless remarkably illuminating. It takes very little imagination to see (!) the religious ways of viewing (predicated on prior theological knowledge) evident in receptions of Sallman's painting as plausibly operative in the reception of other images as well, including ancient ones. To anticipate the next vignette, it seems possible, therefore, if not quite likely, that "deeply held beliefs and expectations would have led at least some ancient Israelite viewers to look for and even 'recognize' Yahweh in images that were not originally intended to represent the deity."[90] The point to be emphasized, regardless, is that to see an image (religious or otherwise) in a religious way involves cognitive activity even as it already reflects the same.

---

88. Bonfiglio, *Reading Images, Seeing Texts*, 249, citing D. Morgan, *Visual Piety*, 140. My own, further qualifier regarding "respective religious practices" is necessary since the monastic practice of saying the *Confiteor* is not part of the Bible's "primary language." See n. 84 above.

89. Bonfiglio, *Reading Images, Seeing Texts*, 249. Perhaps "biblical" should be placed in brackets as a possible but not exclusive referent of the interpretation in question, which may be more broadly religious or Christian or Lutheran and so forth. See the previous note.

90. Bonfiglio, *Reading Images, Seeing Texts*, 249. I do not mean to beg the question, in the technical sense, by assuming belief informs images that in turn represent belief, though such a feedback loop seems extremely likely. I concur with Bonfiglio in positing preexistent cognitive content within ancient Israelite viewers, some of which may now be codified in the Hebrew Bible. That need not mean that ancient Israelite viewers knew specific biblical texts, though that possibility cannot be strictly ruled out, at least in some cases and with certain later texts and in later periods. Instead of a direct, genetic kind of relationship, the shared information between ancient Israelite "pre-knowledge" and later biblical texts may lie at the level of tradition (cf. Assmann's notion of the icon in *Egyptian Solar Religion*, 38, which can manifest in different media such as language and image), making tradition history, especially in comparative perspective, quite important in establishing plausible relationships. Cf. Bonfiglio, *Reading Images, Seeing Texts*, 308; for tradition history and iconography see further, Michael J. Chan, *The Wealth of Nations: A Tradition-Historical Study* (Tübingen: Mohr Siebeck, 2017). In short, Bonfiglio's suggestion that the image-text relationship should proceed along both directions of the axis is both instructive and evocative. Too often the direction of influence and interpretation has proceeded unilaterally: art (iconography) → text (Bible).

Vignette 2: Kuntillet ʿAjrud

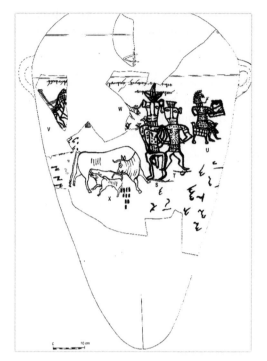

Fig. 10.4. Pithos A, partial. Ze'ev Meshel, ed., *Kuntillet ʿAjrud (Ḥorvat Teman): An Iron Age II Religious Site on the Judah-Sinai Border* (Jerusalem: Israel Exploration Society, 2012), fig. 6.4a.

The well-known images on Pithos A from Kuntillet ʿAjrud (see fig. 10.4) owe their fame in part—or, more accurately, owe their fame almost entirely—to the inscription written above them that mentions "Yhwh of Shomron (Samaria) and his A/asherah" (KAjr 3.1).[91] In point of fact, the inscription is not as straightforward as it might seem, with the various complexities discussed at great length in the secondary literature. Pirhiya Beck, the iconographer tasked with the analysis of the visual remains from the site for the final excavation report, offered what might be considered a "stratigraphic" analysis of Pithos A.[92] In her considered judgment,

---

91. For the main inscriptions, see conveniently Brent A. Strawn and Joel M. LeMon, "Religion in Eighth-Century Judah: The Case of Kuntillet ʿAjrud (and Beyond)," in *Archaeology and History of Eighth-Century Judah*, ed. Zev I. Farber and Jacob L. Wright (Atlanta: Society of Biblical Literature, 2018), 386–88; see also Joel M. LeMon and Brent A. Strawn, "Once More, Yhwh and Company at Kuntillet ʿAjrud," *Maarav* 20 (2013): 86–96. Following the latter (83n2) I use "A/asherah" to signal ongoing uncertainty about whether the referent is a proper (divine) name or a common noun. The final publication of all of the inscriptions recovered from the site is found in Shmuel Aḥituv, Esther Eshel, and Ze'ev Meshel, "The Inscriptions," in *Kuntillet ʿAjrud (Ḥorvat Teman): An Iron Age II Religious Site on the Judah-Sinai Border*, ed. Ze'ev Meshel (Jerusalem: Israel Exploration Society, 2012), 73–142.

92. See Pirhiya Beck, "The Drawings and Decorative Designs," in Meshel, *Kuntillet ʿAjrud*, 143–203, an earlier version of which appeared as Pirhiya Beck, "The Drawings from Ḥorvat Teman (Kuntillet ʿAjrud)," *Tel Aviv* 9 (1982): 3–68; reprinted in Pirhiya Beck, *Imagery and Representation: Studies in the Art and Iconography of Ancient Palestine: Collected Articles* (Tel Aviv: Emery and Claire Yass Publications in Archeology, 2002), 94–170 (citations hereafter come from

Is Belief (or Is It Faith?) an Ancient Israelite Notion?

Fig. 10.5. Stage 1 of Pithos A (partial). LeMon and Strawn, "Yhwh and Company," 107, fig. 9. Reconstructed from Meshel, *Kuntillet ʿAjrud (Ḥorvat Teman)*, fig. 6.5.

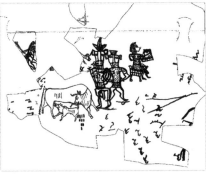

Fig. 10.6. Stage 2 of Pithos A (partial). LeMon and Strawn, "Yhwh and Company," 108, fig. 10. Reconstructed from Meshel, *Kuntillet ʿAjrud (Ḥorvat Teman)*, fig. 6.5.

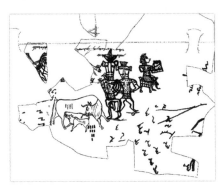

Fig. 10.7. Stage 3 of Pithos A (partial). Meshel, *Kuntillet ʿAjrud (Ḥorvat Teman)*, fig. 6.5.

the inscription and images are *unrelated* because the inscription is secondary (note that at one point the inscription is written directly *across and on top of* one

---

Meshel's volume). The earlier version(s) is not identical to the final version found in Meshel's volume, which contains a few important but largely unmarked changes. See LeMon and Strawn, "Yhwh and Company," 85n7 for discussion.

of the figures' headdresses) and comes from a different hand; indeed, the images themselves are not all contemporaneous.[93] On the basis of her work, a kind of "composition history" of the image-plus-inscription cluster on Pithos A may be posited that involves at least three stages (see figs. 10.5–7 on p. 203).

Even if Beck is correct—and she has convinced some of the best iconographers in the field[94]—one might wonder how far separated in time the different stages and hands (artistic or epigraphic) might be. Kuntillet 'Ajrud is, after all, notable for being "a short-lived, single-stratum, one-period site," dated to the first half of the eighth century, that was occupied only briefly, perhaps for as few as twenty-five years.[95] That is a rather brief period of time compared to the much longer stretches usually imagined in *textual* composition-critical scenarios. So, while it is possible that the different figures on Pithos A and the inscription come from different hands and thus different times (the inscriptional hand has to be later than the one responsible for the larger Bes figure), it is equally possible that the time difference in question might be negligible. It is possible, that is, that the second figure and the inscription might have been added sequentially and almost immediately, not unlike, say, a second scribe correcting the work of a first upon the latter's completion of a column of text.

While it is impossible to know which scenario is correct (and that is no small part of the point to be argued below), the literary analogy of one scribe reviewing and correcting the work of another is intriguing, especially as it relates to the work of Brian Schmidt on Pithos A.[96] Schmidt argues that the pithos is best seen through the lens of redaction criticism, with the inscription itself functioning as "a *conscious textual interpretation* inscribed above the image of the two figures *as a way of interpreting their juxtaposition*."[97] Schmidt's interpretation, which understands the inscription as an intentional caption for the images beneath it, is thus

---

93. Beck, "Drawings and Decorative Designs," 183–84.

94. Most especially Keel and Uehlinger, *Gods, Goddesses, and Images of God*.

95. Ze'ev Meshel, preface to Meshel, *Kuntillet 'Ajrud*, xxi. See also Strawn and LeMon, "Religion in Eighth-Century Judah," 380–81. The timeframe in question is 800–775 BCE according to Keel and Uehlinger, *Gods, Goddesses, and Images of God*, 248. This chronology has been challenged by William Schniedewind, "An Early Iron Age Phrase to Kuntillet 'Ajrud?" in *Le-ma'an Ziony: Essays in Honor of Ziony Zevit*, ed. Frederick E. Greenspahn and Gary A. Rendsburg (Eugene, OR: Cascade, 2017), 134–45, who argues that "the evidence allows for a much longer period of activity . . . ranging from the late 10th through the late 8th century BCE" (144).

96. Brian B. Schmidt, "The Aniconic Tradition: On Reading Images and Viewing Texts," in *The Triumph of Elohim: From Yahwisms to Judaisms*, ed. Diana V. Edelman (Grand Rapids: Eerdmans, 1995), 75–105.

97. LeMon and Strawn, "Yhwh and Company," 103 (emphases added), summarizing Schmidt, "Aniconic Tradition," 97–102. Note also Ziony Zevit, *The Religions of Ancient Israel: A Synthesis*

Is Belief (or Is It Faith?) an Ancient Israelite Notion?

a kind of "final form" reading of the pithos that is not entirely unrelated to the canonical work of Brevard Childs.[98] A visual studies approach could make this same point, however, without the literary analogy and its correlative "baggage," that is, the speculative or at least not yet definitively demonstrated (indeed, perhaps undemonstrable?) stages that preexist and underlie the final textual form. In fact, a visual studies approach could reach Schmidt's conclusion—namely, a connection between the figures and Yhwh (and his A/asherah)—*quite apart from the inscription*. Precious few individuals would have been able to read the inscription, after all.[99] Positing an interpretation of the figures as Yhwh and his A/asherah, that is, need not depend solely on some intentional (i.e., "conscious") interpretation of the (earlier) figures by the (later) hand of the inscription. How would such intent be proven in the first place? Is it even possible to prove intent here? Neither must a connection between the figures and Yhwh and his A/asherah depend on subsequent viewers understanding the inscription and being ineluctably shaped by its putatively definitive identification(s). Instead, viewers of the pithos may well have seen these figures as divine, as Yhwh and companion(s)—consciously, perhaps, but maybe in a more immediate (fast thinking) rather than reflective (slow thinking) fashion—and might have done so *whether they could read the inscription or not* and *quite apart from the intentionality of the artist(s) and scribe(s) who had a hand in what is now on Pithos A*.[100] In light of the visual medium of belief, the religious apparatus of sight, the sacred gaze, visual piety, image covenants, and other key insights from visual studies, it matters very little and perhaps not at all if the figures on Pithos A are identified as the Egyptian god Bes or somehow "Beslike" at the point of original production. In my own judgment, the figures are more Bes-*like* than Bes proper, and I do not think they bear an obvious relationship to Yhwh prima facie (!). The main point, however, is that belated scholarly judgments of whatever sort do not finally settle the matter, *even* if they approximate the view

---

of Parallactic Approaches (London: Continuum, 2001), 386: "The inscriptions can be considered oblique commentaries on the drawings."

98. Brevard S. Childs, *Introduction to the Old Testament as Scripture* (Philadelphia: Fortress, 1979).

99. Much depends here on the nature of the site, of course, as well as the people who lived or passed through it. Yet another factor is if certain words like proper or divine names might have been recognizable (legible, to some degree) by people who were otherwise illiterate.

100. Cf. LeMon and Strawn, "Yhwh and Company," 110: "A visual studies approach to Pithos A that attends to image-reception renders unnecessary any direct association of the image with the inscription. The inscription does not force the viewer into any one interpretation of the image (especially if the viewer cannot read it). Likewise, the image does not force the viewer to any one interpretation of the text. The nexus of the image(s) and the text(s) on Pithos A *can* guide the viewer, but need not do so and certainly not in only one unambiguous direction."

205

of the ancient artist(s). What matters just as much is how the images were (then, and also now are) received, observed, viewed, gazed upon.[101]

The point of this second vignette is that it is not unthinkable—if anything quite the contrary—that ancient Israelites may have recognized their deity or aspects of their deity in a wide range of images, regardless of their original authorial (artistic) intent. "Upon encountering such [imagery], a religious adherent may well have thought (or said), '*That's* YHWH right there' or, at least, 'That's *some aspect* of YHWH.'"[102] There can be no doubt that meaning-making is taking place at each stage(s) of the production of any given artifact (or its layers), especially one designed to communicate something via text and/or image, but the crucial point to be made— one often underestimated by scholars who focus primarily or exclusively on ancient *texts* and *history*—is that there is also meaning-making *in the process of viewing(s)*.[103] When such viewing is religious in nature, then even the mundane can become divine (see further the next vignette below). How much more true when the thing that is (religiously) seen is itself religious in nature! That kind of situation would seem primed to facilitate even deeper acts of religious viewing, acts of seeing that are potentially ripe with even more layers of (religious) meaning and significance.

This second vignette reveals that scholars' prior training, exposure, and, yes, *belief* (in this case, cognitive content about religious topics)—particularly around textual phenomena (KAjr 3.1 but also the biblical text)—are operative in the many attempts to "find" Yhwh in the figures at Kuntillet 'Ajrud.[104] Scholarly identification of the figures from Pithos A with Yhwh and a possible consort named Asherah are thus instances of the sacred gaze, even if a somewhat secularized species of the same. The point, regardless, is that the quest to "find" an image of Yhwh in the archaeological record, whether at Kuntillet 'Ajrud or anywhere else (see further below), is to no small degree a *constructed* phenomenon. Even the most objective scholar pursuing such a goal is, therefore, participating in a kind of image covenant: attending to an image "in order to be engaged by it, in order to believe what the image reveals or says or means."[105] If that is true, then it is clear that the

---

101. Cf. Bonfiglio, *Reading Images, Seeing Texts*, 251: "The oft-debated search for Yahweh's image should not only involve careful archaeological and iconographic analysis but also critical reflection on how image covenants establish the epistemological and moral conditions under which a viewer comes to believe that a given image contains religiously meaningful information."

102. LeMon and Strawn, "Yhwh and Company," 106.

103. LeMon and Strawn, "Yhwh and Company," 110.

104. Cf. Bonfiglio, *Reading Images, Seeing Texts*, 297: "The impulse to see Yahweh in light of the inscription on pithos A is consistent with the theory of the image-text dialectic."

105. Morgan, *Sacred Gaze*, 76.

Is Belief (or Is It Faith?) an Ancient Israelite Notion?

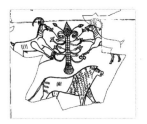

Fig. 10.8. Details from Pithos A. Meshel, *Kuntillet 'Ajrud (Ḥorvat Teman)*, fig. 6.4a.

hermeneutical situation at play is no longer (and never was) solely a matter of *original production* restricted entirely to *back then*. It is also a matter of *reception and viewing*—both *back then* and also *here and now*.

This larger hermeneutical point should help answer a burning question: how would (or could) we know how ancient viewers saw things? This is an entirely legitimate question; to answer it fully would require a monograph (or two).[106] The quest to access ancient viewers and ancient practices of viewing is, obviously, a historical one and therefore depends on the data presently available (both artistic and textual) and the best methods of data assessment.[107] A visual studies approach to these matters is thus patently not *ahistorical*; it is just not reducible solely to matters of origination. Too much goes into the act of seeing—*all* seeing but certainly also religious seeing and/of religious items—a good bit of which is cognitive (both fast and slow), to think that the heat and light lies solely with the artistic or scribal hand that first set ink or other instrument to ostracon, parchment, rock, or wall.

This means, finally, that without a contemporary scholar's particular set of preexisting knowledge and training, or with a different set of knowledge and training,

---

106. The best on the subject to date (and by far) is Bonfiglio, *Reading Images, Seeing Texts*. For comparable poetics in textual and artistic media, see Walker, *Power of Images*. The cognitive research and stability of brain architecture discussed above in "The Place of Cognition: Theological Belief/Faith?" are also obviously pertinent.

107. For a recent and insightful attempt, see Portuese, *Life at Court*. Already in his classic work, *Studies in Iconology: Humanistic Themes in the Art of the Renaissance* (New York: Oxford University Press, 1939; repr., Oxford: Westview, 1972), Erwin Panofsky proposed that iconographical analysis "presupposes a familiarity with specific *themes* or *concepts* as transmitted through literary sources, whether acquired by purposeful reading or by oral tradition" (11). He continues: "While an acquaintance with specific *themes* and *concepts* transmitted through literary sources is indispensable and sufficient material for an *iconographical analysis*, it does not guarantee its correctness." Indeed: "We should be entirely at a loss did we depend on the literary sources alone" (12).

Fig. 10.9. Details from Pithos B. Meshel, *Kuntillet ʿAjrud (Ḥorvat Teman)*, fig. 6.6.

or (regardless of knowledge and training) with attention paid to different part(s) of Pithos A, one could easily imagine a viewer receiving the Kuntillet ʿAjrud images not simply as Yhwh and his A/asherah, but more generally (or instead) as "Yhwh and Company"—maybe Yhwh and his buddy Bes, or Yhwh and his consort Beset (?), but also Yhwh and the animals (including one of his favorites, the lion), Yhwh and the/his (sacred) tree, and Yhwh and (his) worshipers (see figs. 10.8–9 on pp. 207–8).[108]

It pays to remember that this larger host of Yahwistic confreres is abundantly attested in the Old Testament where Yhwh is frequently found amid many other entities: other deities, objects, animals, and human beings.[109] Of course, a viewer of the Kuntillet ʿAjrud images may have just as likely *not* thought of Yhwh at all, especially if the viewer saw the image(s) before the inscription was added, or saw it after the inscription was added but couldn't read it, or saw the inscription and could read it but "recognized" the image(s) as some other entity/deity than Yhwh. To be sure, this range of interpretive conclusions—whether the image(s) were received as Yhwh (or some other) and Company (or some other)—may strike some people as far less exciting than a clear and unambiguous solution to "the case of the missing Yhwh image." *Perhaps* that missing image of Yhwh, at least in the mind of some ancient producer, is indeed found at Kuntillet ʿAjrud, but it seems just as likely that it *may not be*. A visual studies approach is no counsel of despair, however. A visual studies approach is not a case of "anything goes" and so "nothing goes." It is, instead, a broadening of the possibilities: while there may be no one-to-one Yhwh-and-specific-image at Kuntillet ʿAjrud, a visual studies approach opens up a large number of other possibilities for Yhwh *and many images* at Kuntillet ʿAjrud *and far beyond it*. This leads directly to the third and final vignette.

---

108. See LeMon and Strawn, "Yhwh and Company," 113 and n. 112 there. A fuller analysis of Kuntillet ʿAjrud would need to include all of Pithos B as well as the wall paintings (esp. nos. 1, 9, and 11–12) recovered from the site.

109. Cf. Bonfiglio, *Reading Images, Seeing Texts*, 287n208: "one might reasonably suppose that Yahweh's iconography would reflect characteristics known about Israel's God from textual data, such as Yahweh's association with a cherubim throne, lion imagery, solar imagery, wings, archers, and so forth." See also 297: "The search for Yahweh's image would need to reconsider how knowledge of written texts, whether from the inscription on pithos A or from the metaphors and similes used to characterize Yahweh in the Hebrew Bible, might have led viewers to identify Yahweh in images that, on (art) historical grounds, were never meant to depict their deity."

Vignette 3: Yhwh's Cult Image and Seal Art

In this third vignette, the main points from the second vignette are shown to be, mutatis mutandis, applicable to virtually every image that has so far been offered as a possible depiction of Yhwh (not to mention many others that have not yet been proposed as such but very well might). Most of the candidates for the job of "Yhwh's long-lost cult image" are singularly unimpressive or at least uninspiring, if only because they are often highly damaged and/or are devoid of additional data or context that would clarify their interpretation. Still further, none are particularly convincing if the driving forces in making a final determination are production and intention, knowing, that is, with some level of confidence that the image in question was *consciously wrought* as a depiction of Yhwh. Despite all that, if the apparatus of visual piety is considered, then reception and interpretation come into play as equally important driving forces, and the situation changes drastically. Could, therefore, the famous Munich terracotta acquired by J. Jeremias in 1990 on the antiquities market (see fig. 10.10) be a depiction of Yhwh and his consort?[110] What about the Persian period coin inscribed with יהד or יהו (see fig. 10.11 on p. 210)?[111] The answer may be "yes" in both cases: it depends on who saw these images and when and where they saw them, but most importantly on *how they saw them*—and this quite apart from original intention or reference on the part of the artisans responsible.

Fig. 10.10. Munich terracotta; unprovenanced (eighth century BCE?). Jörg Jeremias, "Thron oder Wagen? Eine außergewöhnliche Terrakotte aus der späten Eisenzeit in Juda," in *Biblische Welten: Festschrift für Martin Metzger zu seinem 65. Geburtstag*, ed. Wolfgang Zwickel, OBO 123 (Freiburg: Universitätsverlag/Göttingen: Vandenhoeck & Ruprecht, 1993), 46 Abb. 1.

A more recent, altogether comparable phenomenon is how people have found Jesus or the Blessed Virgin Mary on everything from rocks to pieces of toast. Such is the power of the sacred gaze and visual piety! Rather than searching for one

---

110. See Christoph Uehlinger, "Anthropomorphic Cult Statuary in Iron Age Palestine and the Search for Yahweh's Cult Images," in *The Image and the Book: Iconic Cults, Aniconism, and the Rise of Book Religion in Israel and the Ancient Near East*, ed. Karel van der Toorn (Leuven: Peeters, 1997), 97–155, esp. 149–52.

111. See Izaak J. de Hulster, *Iconographic Exegesis and Third Isaiah* (Tübingen: Mohr Siebeck, 2009), 194–205.

Fig. 10.11. BMC Palestine XIX 29; unprovenanced (likely fourth century; ca. 380–360 BCE?). Izaak J. de Hulster and Brent A. Strawn, "The Power of Images: Isaiah 60, Jerusalem, and Persian Imperial Propaganda," in *Iconographic Exegesis of the Hebrew Bible/Old Testament: An Introduction to Its Method and Practice*, ed. Izaak J. de Hulster, Brent A. Strawn, and Ryan P. Bonfiglio (Göttingen: Vandenhoeck & Ruprecht, 2015), 202, fig. 10.2.

definitive image of Yhwh, therefore, scholars should consider how *any and every divine image* recovered from ancient Israel/Palestine might have been seen and received as a divine image *of Yhwh*. There is, again, no obvious reason why that should not be possible. If someone counters with the existence and content of the Second Commandment, there is the witness of the archaeological record to contend with; *In Israel gab es Bilder* to cite the title of Silvia Schorer's important study.[112] Perhaps the presence of so many images in ancient Israel/Palestine is proof that the Decalogue is late.[113] Or perhaps it means that the second commandment applies only to certain media types.[114] But even if the second commandment is generously dated early and interpreted rather capaciously—even then it speaks only of *making* (√עשׂה) not *viewing* (√חזה, √ראה) images.[115] To be sure, the second commandment goes on to speak of not bowing down to (√חוה, *histhtaphel*) or serving (√עבד) an idol (פֶּסֶל) or form (תְּמוּנָה) of anything in the heavens, on the earth, or in the waters under the earth, but those actions may be

---

112. Silvia Schroer, *In Israel gab es Bilder: Nachrichten von darstellender Kunst im Alten Testament* (Freiburg: Universitätsverlag Freiburg Schweiz, 1987).

113. See, e.g., Christoph Dohmen, *Das Bilderverbot: Seine Entstehung und seine Entwicklung im alten Testament*, 2nd ed. (Frankfurt am Main: Athenäum, 1987).

114. Not prohibiting clay, for instance.

115. Cf. Bonfiglio, *Reading Images, Seeing Texts*, 296, to which I am indebted: "What is not clear is whether the spirit of the law also extended to *seeing* images *as* Yahweh."

Is Belief (or Is It Faith?) an Ancient Israelite Notion?

an altogether different affair; their relationship to religious viewing, at least, is a topic best reserved for another time.[116]

Whatever the case, the larger point is that if a visual studies approach has any merit, then we should look for traces of Yhwh (and/or other deities) less in (in)famous-but-debatable objects like Pithos A from Kuntillet ʿAjrud or the Munich terracotta than "in the thousands of seals that have been recovered from ancient Israel/Palestine and Jordan."[117] More than twelve thousand seals have been recovered from controlled excavations; they are being meticulously published by Othmar Keel and others.[118] Hundreds of these seals contain divine images or symbols of one sort or another. Not all of these seals can be imports; many are local products, even if imitations, that come from Israelite sites during the times of Israelite life in the land. Of course, it is entirely possible that such images "represent foreign gods and are thus testimony to heterodox or syncretistic, non-Yahwistic tendencies on the part of certain Israelite populations."[119] But another possibility seems equally likely, namely, "that in some instances such divine figures were stand-ins . . . for Yhwh—ways, that is, that Yhwh was figured even if such figuration was quite malleable, varied, and not standardized. Such 'flexibility' in

116. In fact, one wonders if the point about *seeing as* might have led to a need to gloss the commandment further by explicitly prohibiting *worship* of these received images (as such?).

117. Brent A. Strawn, "Canaanite/Israelite Iconography," in *Behind the Scenes of the Old Testament: Cultural, Social, and Historical Contexts*, ed. Jonathan S. Greer, John W. Hilber, and John H. Walton (Grand Rapids: Baker Academic, 2018), 181.

118. Othmar Keel, *Corpus der Stempelsiegel-Amulette aus Palästina/Israel: Von den Anfängen bis zur Perserzeit; Einleitung* (Fribourg: Academic Press; Göttingen: Vandenhoeck & Ruprecht, 1995); Keel, *Corpus der Stempelsiegel-Amulette aus Palästina/Israel: Von den Anfängen bis zur Perserzeit; Katalog Band I: Von Tell Abu Faraǧ bis ʿAtlit* (Fribourg: Academic Press; Göttingen: Vandenhoeck & Ruprecht, 1997); Jürg Eggler and Othmar Keel, *Corpus der Siegel-Amulette aus Jordanien: Von Neolithikum bis zur Perserzeit* (Fribourg: Academic Press; Göttingen: Vandenhoeck & Ruprecht, 2006); Keel, *Corpus der Stempelsiegel-Amulette aus Palästina/Israel: Von den Anfängen bis zur Perserzeit; Katalog Band II: Von Bahan bis Tel Eton* (Fribourg: Academic Press; Göttingen: Vandenhoeck & Ruprecht, 2010); Keel, *Corpus der Stempelsiegel-Amulette aus Palästina/Israel: Von den Anfängen bis zur Perserzeit; Katalog Band III: Von Tell el-Farʿa Nord bis Tell el-Fir* (Fribourg: Academic Press; Göttingen: Vandenhoeck & Ruprecht, 2010); Keel, *Corpus der Stempelsiegel-Amulette aus Palästina/Israel: Von den Anfängen bis zur Perserzeit; Katalog Band IV: Von Tel Gamma bis Chirbet Husche* (Fribourg: Academic Press; Göttingen: Vandenhoeck & Ruprecht, 2013); Keel, *Corpus der Stempelsiegel-Amulette aus Palästina/Israel: Von den Anfängen bis zur Perserzeit; Katalog Band V: Von Tel el-ʿIdham bis Tel Kitan* (Fribourg: Academic Press; Göttingen: Vandenhoeck & Ruprecht, 2017). See also Keel, *700 Skarabäen und Verwandtes aus Palästina/Israel: Die Sammlung Keel* (Leuven: Peeters, 2020).

119. Strawn, "Canaanite/Israelite Iconography," 181. See Bonfiglio, *Reading Images, Seeing Texts*, 301–7, esp. 302 and n. 243, for the fine line between (re)appropriation and syncretism.

Fig. 10.12. Scaraboid; Beth-Shemesh (Iron Age IIA: 980–940 BCE). Keel and Uehlinger, *Gods, Goddesses, and Images of God in Ancient Israel*, 139, fig. 162c.

Fig. 10.13. Scaraboid; Tel en Nasbeh (Iron Age IIA: 980–940 BCE). Keel and Uehlinger, *Gods, Goddesses, and Images*, 139, fig. 162d.

Fig. 10.14. Scaraboid; Gezer (Iron Age IIA: 980–940 BCE). Keel and Uehlinger, *Gods, Goddesses, and Images of God*, 139, fig. 162b.

divine presentation is, in fact, precisely what one finds in the pages of the Old Testament and in the literary profile of Yhwh, who could be portrayed as a lion roaring from Mount Zion or trammeling humans ... or depicted as master of the animal kingdom, including the unusual ostrich" (see figs. 10.12–14).[120]

The seals are not only numerous; they are also highly mobile: the equivalent of mass communication in premodern periods.[121] The seals are also "by far the most extensively attested image-bearing object from ancient Israel/Palestine," which generally lacks monumental art on the scale of Mesopotamia, Egypt, or Hatti.[122] So, if Yhwh is to be found in the archaeological record, given the sheer amount of seals to consider, the search for Yhwh's (cult) image should begin, if not also end, with the seal corpus.

Conclusion

In sum, the present essay has attempted to show that belief versus faith is a false dichotomy, especially if the two are played off against each other as something cognitive (thinking) versus something more existential (trusting). There is more than one good reason to resist such a bifurcation of belief and faith (see "Defining Belief (or Is It Faith?) in the Hebrew Bible" and "The Place of Cognition: Theological Belief/Faith?" above), one of which is the view afforded by visual studies (see

---

120. Strawn, "Canaanite/Israelite Iconography," 181.
121. See Othmar Keel and Christopher Uehlinger, *Altorientalische Miniaturkunst: Die ältesten visuellen Massenkommunikationsmittel; Ein Blick in die Sammlungen des Biblischen Instituts der Universität Freiburg Schweiz* (Freiburg: Universitätsverlag Freiburg Schweiz; Göttingen: Vandenhoeck & Ruprecht, 1996).
122. Strawn, "Canaanite/Israelite Iconography," 181.

Is Belief (or Is It Faith?) an Ancient Israelite Notion?

"Seeing and/as Believing: The Visual as a Locus for and of Belief/Faith" above). The essay has also tried to demonstrate that artistic remains, especially when "seen" through the lens of visual studies, offers us a great deal of data to ponder when it comes to considering belief/faith in the biblical world. "Seeing is believing," but seeing also *involves* and *reflects* belief/faith (cognition) and is a real site or locus for (facilitating) belief/faith. This is what the artistic data, with the help of visual studies, indicate, and this, in turn, is a signal contribution and substantive addition that the art adds to the literary remains. Indeed, the artistic data not only compliments the epigraphic record, it also quickly outpaces it. The statistics are quite stunning: the corpus of 342 (or so) inscriptions dating from the tenth through the sixth centuries BCE (112 of which come from just one site, Arad) can be contrasted with the more than 12,000 seals found in the seal corpus (to date).[123] By this metric, seals outnumber inscriptions 20 to 1. A further example of this disparity: Jericho has yielded more seals (597) by itself than the entire corpus of significant Hebrew inscriptions (342).[124] Or, to compare data from a single site: Jerusalem has yielded 43 inscriptions but 521 seals.[125] If art is a locus of belief/faith, there is a great amount of material to be sifted and studied; it awaits and deserves more sustained attention from scholars.[126]

---

123. Johannes Renz and Wolfgang Röllig, *Handbuch der althebräischen Epigraphik*, 3 vols. (Darmstadt: Wissenschaftliche Buchgesellschaft, 1995), 1:11–19, 20–22 (though they omit Arad ostraca nos. 105–9, resulting in a total of only 107 ostraca). After Arad, the sites with the most inscriptions are Jerusalem (43), Lachish (36), and Samaria (14); see 1:23–27. Other publications contain somewhat fewer or far more than Renz and Röllig. For the latter, see, G. I. Davies, *Ancient Hebrew Inscriptions: Corpus and Concordance*, 2 vols. (Cambridge: Cambridge University Press, 1991, 2004), though many of the inscriptions collected by Davies are broken and contain only a word or two, or even just part of a word. Another valuable collection is F. W. Dobbs-Allsopp, J. J. M. Roberts, C. L. Seow, and R. E. Whitaker, *Hebrew Inscriptions: Texts from the Biblical Period of the Monarchy with Concordance* (New Haven: Yale University Press, 2005).

124. See Keel, *Corpus V*, 34–275.

125. Renz and Röllig, *Handbuch*, 1:23–24; Keel, *Corpus V*, 277–513.

126. Even if one wishes to restrict oneself to the epigraphic record, there is much to consider in terms of belief/faith. See, e.g., Rainer Albertz, "Personal Names and Family Religion," in Rainer Albertz and Rüdiger Schmitt, *Family and Household Religion in Ancient Israel and the Levant* (Winona Lake, IN: Eisenbrauns, 2012), 245–386, esp. 262–336, for a lengthy discussion of the religious beliefs expressed in 675 Hebrew personal names attested in the epigraphic record. The largest category concerns birth (192 names or 28.4%), with names expressing thanksgiving only slightly smaller in number (164 names, 24.3%), followed by "names of confession" (119 names, 17.6%) (see p. 254). However, since the latter two categories are difficult to disentangle, Albertz argues that they "should be regarded as closely related"; when that is done, these represent 41.9% of all personal names (255). Finally, there is a smaller, not unrelated set of names of praise (7.1%). Here again, there is some overlap, so when all of the "prayer names" are taken together, they

Fig. 10.15. Cult stand (A); Taanach (Iron Age I). Kurt Galling, ed., *Biblisches Reallexikon*, 2nd ed. (Tübingen: Mohr, 1977), 191.

I conclude with one last example of belief/faith and art. In his recent, magisterial treatment of God in ancient Israelite religion, Theodore Lewis offers an extensive analysis of the evidence for Yhwh's "iconography of divinity."[127] After carefully weighing the options, Lewis argues that the best case for theriomorphic imagery used for Yhwh is the bull, not only because of some iconographic evidence but also because of three texts ("literary candidates") from the Hebrew Bible, though none of these texts is especially developed compared to the divine bull imagery present at Ugarit. Lewis's reference to the biblical texts in the course of a discussion of the iconography of divinity reflects the image-text continuum mentioned earlier even as it confirms the importance of preexisting knowledge (or training) in the act of seeing: textual data remain important, *even in art*, though they are not everything, *especially in art*. Lewis next reviews "three serious candidates" for bull iconography drawn from "the archaeological record that have been suggested to depict Yahweh theriomorphically."[128] These objects, too, are not particularly strong in Lewis's opinion because the evidence for each is inconclusive.[129] For example, when it comes to the Taanach cult stand recovered in 1968 (fig. 10.15), "if Yahweh is represented . . . it is more likely to be the sun disk that portrays his divinity, with the animal serving as the beast upon which he is mounted."[130] After

---

"constitute approximately one half of all Hebrew personal names" (255). The content of these prayer names includes things like divine attention, salvation, assistance, and protection; trust in God; and praise for God's greatness, goodness, vitality, and praiseworthiness. It seems impossible to argue that such categories have nothing to do with belief.

127. Lewis, *Origin and Character of God*, 287–426.
128. Lewis, *Origin and Character of God*, 420.
129. Cf. Bonfiglio, *Reading Images, Seeing Texts*, 286, speaking of an even larger dataset: "It is not possible to establish irrefutably that any of these objects were originally meant to depict Yahweh."
130. Lewis, *Origin and Character of God*, 421. On 332–33, Lewis deems it "much easier to see

Is Belief (or Is It Faith?) an Ancient Israelite Notion?

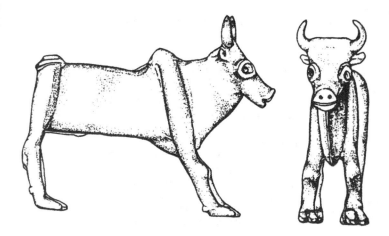

Fig. 10.16. Bronze figurine; east of Dothan (ca. twelfth century BCE). Amiḥai Mazar, "The 'Bull Site'—An Iron Age I Open Cult Place," *BASOR* 247 (1982): 30, figs. 2A–B.

eliminating the figures at Kuntillet 'Ajrud as Bes or Bes-like (see above), Lewis is left with what he deems the "one clear candidate for an example of Yahweh being represented theriomorphically—namely, the exquisite bronze bull figure from the Bull Site" (fig. 10.16).[131]

At the end of the present study, a positive response to Lewis's opinion about the bronze bull can be offered: why not? But such a response is decidedly *not* predicated on the bull's features, careful craftsmanship, or possible ritual function.[132] Nor is it the result of an obvious and overabundance of connections between bovine imagery and Yhwh. Instead (or perhaps additionally), a positive response is possible because of the insights offered by visual studies and religious ways of seeing. To be sure, it is also possible that this bull could represent Baal or El (Lewis's own preference and my own), especially if the piece had been recovered in regions to the far north given the dominance of bull imagery for 'Ilu in the Ugaritic texts (the *text*-image relationship strikes again!).[133] But, per visual studies, why not Yhwh instead of, in addition to, or maybe even at the same time

---

the quadruped as *associated* with Yahweh (it is certainly not an attribute animal) if it were a mature bull rather than a frisky calf or colt."

131. Lewis, *Origin and Character of God*, 421, where he also asks a very good question about the Kuntillet 'Ajrud remains: "Without the inscription, would anyone have labeled the standing figures as being Yahweh and his consort?"

132. Lewis, *Origin and Character of God*, 421; see further 200–202, 322, 332–33.

133. See Lewis, *Origin and Character of God*, 200, 202; cf. 421; Strawn, "Canaanite/Israelite Iconography," 173–75.

as 'Ilu/El?[134] Perhaps the deity in question (whichever it be) is an aniconic rider on the back of the bull-now-become-a-mount, but maybe the deity is the bull itself in full zoomorphic form. Whatever the case, the study of visual culture, aesthetic response, the visual medium of belief, the religious apparatus of sight, and so on and so forth suggest that it is entirely possible that an ancient Israelite viewer might have seen this bull and thought it none other than Yhwh or that it (re)presented Yhwh in some fashion, even if originally, in terms of production, this bull was meant as something else altogether and/or symbolized some entirely different deity (or even no deity at all).[135] Such is the power of sight, especially seeing and/as believing.

Works Cited

Aḥituv, Shmuel, Esther Eshel, and Ze'ev Meshel. "The Inscriptions." Pages 73–142 in *Kuntillet 'Ajrud (Ḥorvat Teman): An Iron Age II Religious Site on the Judah-Sinai Border*. Edited by Ze'ev Meshel. Jerusalem: Israel Exploration Society, 2012.

Ahlström, G. W. "The Bull Figurine from Dhahrat et-Tawile." *BASOR* 280 (1990): 77–82.

Albertz, Rainer. "Personal Names and Family Religion." Pages 245–386 in Rainer Albertz and Rüdiger Schmitt, *Family and Household Religion in Ancient Israel and the Levant*. Winona Lake, IN: Eisenbrauns, 2012.

Allen, James P. *Genesis in Egypt: The Philosophy of Ancient Egyptian Creation Accounts*. New Haven: Yale University Press, 1988.

———. *Religion and Philosophy in Ancient Egypt*. New Haven: Yale University Press, 1989.

Argenton, Alberto. *Art and Expression: Studies in the Psychology of Art*. Edited by Ian Verstegen. London: Routledge, 2019.

---

134. D. Morgan, *Sacred Gaze*, 36: "Images do what their users require of them, which may involve many things at once." But note Ramachandran's important point about visual processing: "There cannot be two overlapping patterns of neural activity simultaneously. Even though the human brain contains a hundred billion nerve cells, no two patterns may overlap. In other words, there is a bottleneck of attention. Attentional resources may be allocated to *only one entity at a time*" (*Brief Tour*, 52, emphasis added).

135. Note the debate over whether the piece (and site) belonged to early Israelite settlers— so A. Mazar, "The 'Bull Site': An Iron Age I Open Cult Place," *BASOR* 247 (1982): 27–42—or if it is the product of a nonindigenous group, so G. W. Ahlström, "The Bull Figurine from Dhahrat et-Tawileh," *BASOR* 280 (1990): 77–82. See Lewis, *Origin and Character of God*, 200. Cf. Bonfiglio, *Reading Images, Seeing Texts*, 292: "The theoretical insights from religious ways of seeing indicate that Israelite viewers may have been led to see or recognize their deity in a variety of art objects *even if those objects were originally intended to display a different subject matter, or indeed, a different god.*"

Is Belief (or Is It Faith?) an Ancient Israelite Notion?

Armstrong, Paul B. *How Literature Plays with the Brain: The Neuroscience of Reading and Art*. Baltimore: Johns Hopkins University Press, 2013.

Arnheim, Rudolf. *Art and Visual Perception: A Psychology of the Creative Eye*. Berkeley: University of California, 1974.

———. *Toward a Psychology of Art: Collected Essays*. Berkeley: University of California, 1966.

———. *Visual Thinking*. Berkeley: University of California Press, 1969.

Assmann, Jan. *Egyptian Solar Religion in the New Kingdom: Re, Amun and the Crisis of Polytheism*. Translated by Anthony Alcock. London: Kegan Paul, 1995.

Barr, James. *The Semantics of Biblical Language*. Oxford: Oxford University Press, 1961.

Barton, Carlin A., and Daniel Boyarin. *Imagine No Religion: How Modern Abstractions Hide Ancient Realities*. New York: Fordham University Press, 2016.

Beck, Pirhiya. "The Drawings and Decorative Designs." Pages 143–204 in *Kuntillet 'Ajrud (Horvat Teman): An Iron Age II Religious Site on the Judah-Sinai Border*. Edited by Z. Meshel. Jerusalem: Israel Exploration Society, 2012.

———. "The Drawings from Ḥorvat Teman (Kuntillet 'Ajrud)." *Tel Aviv* 9 (1982): 3–68.

———. *Imagery and Representation: Studies in the Art and Iconography of Ancient Palestine: Collected Articles*. Tel Aviv: Emery and Claire Yass Publications in Archeology, 2002.

Black, Fiona C., and Jennifer L. Koosed, eds. *Reading with Feeling: Affect Theory and the Bible*. Atlanta: SBL Press, 2019.

Blackwell, Ben C. *Christosis: Engaging Paul's Soteriology with His Patristic Interpreters*. Grand Rapids: Eerdmans, 2016.

Bonfiglio, Ryan P. *Reading Images, Seeing Texts: Towards a Visual Hermeneutics for Biblical Studies*. Fribourg: Academic Press; Göttingen: Vandenhoeck & Ruprecht, 2016.

Borst, Grégoire. "Neural Underpinning of Object Mental Imagery, Spatial Imagery, and Motor Imagery." Pages 74–87 in *The Oxford Handbook of Cognitive Neuroscience*. Edited by Kevin N. Ochsner and Stephen Michael Kosslyn. Oxford: Oxford University Press, 2014.

Boylan, Alexis L. *Visual Culture*. Cambridge: MIT Press, 2020.

Brawley, Robert L. "Generating Ethics from God's Character in Mark." Pages 57–74 in *Character Ethics and the New Testament: Moral Dimensions of Scripture*. Edited by Robert L. Brawley. Louisville: Westminster John Knox, 2007.

Brueggemann, Walter. *Theology of the Old Testament: Testimony, Dispute, Advocacy*. Minneapolis: Fortress, 1997.

Buber, Martin. *Two Types of Faith*. Translated by Norman P. Goldhawk. New York: Syracuse University Press, 2003.

Carasik, Michael. *Theologies of the Mind in Biblical Israel*. New York: Lang, 2006.

Carvalho, John. *Thinking with Images: An Enactivist Aesthetics*. New York: Routledge, 2019.

Chan, Michael J. *The Wealth of Nations: A Tradition-Historical Study*. Tübingen: Mohr Siebeck, 2017.

Childs, Brevard S. *Introduction to the Old Testament as Scripture*. Philadelphia: Fortress, 1979.

Cohen, Mark E. *The Canonical Lamentations of Ancient Mesopotamia*. 2 vols. Potomac, MD: Capital Decisions Limited, 1988.

Cornell, Collin., ed. *Divine Doppelgängers: YHWH's Ancient Look-Alikes*. University Park, PA: Eisenbrauns, 2020.

Cutting, Gary. "Is Belief a Jewish Notion?" *New York Times*, March 30, 2014. http://opinionator.blogs.nytimes.com/2014/03/30/is-belief-a-jewish-notion/?_php=true&_type=blogs&hp&rref=opinion&_r=0.

Damasio, Antonio. *Descartes' Error: Emotion, Reason, and the Human Brain*. New York: Quill, 2000.

———. *Feeling and Knowing: Making Minds Conscious*. New York: Pantheon, 2021.

———. *The Feeling of What Happens: Body and Emotion in the Making of Consciousness*. San Diego: Harcourt, 1999.

Davies, G. I. *Ancient Hebrew Inscriptions: Corpus and Concordance*. 2 vols. Cambridge: Cambridge University Press, 1991, 2004.

DeYoe, E. A., P. Bandettini, J. Neitz, D. Miller, and P. Winans. "Functional Magnetic Resonance Imaging (FMRI) of the Human Brain." *Journal of Neuroscience Methods* 54 (1994): 171–87.

Dobbs-Allsopp, F. W., J. J. M. Roberts, C. L. Seow, and R. E. Whitaker. *Hebrew Inscriptions: Texts from the Biblical Period of the Monarchy with Concordance*. New Haven: Yale University Press, 2005.

Dohmen, Christoph. *Das Bilderverbot: Seine Entstehung und seine Entwicklung im alten Testament*. 2nd ed. Frankfurt am Main: Athenäum, 1987.

Eggler, Jürg, and Othmar Keel. *Corpus der Siegel-Amulette aus Jordanien: Von Neolithikum bis zur Perserzeit*. Fribourg: Academic Press; Göttingen: Vandenhoeck & Ruprecht, 2006.

Eidinow, Esther, Julia Kindt, and Robin Osborne, eds. *Theologies of Ancient Greek Religion*. Cambridge: Cambridge University Press, 2016.

Engel, S. A., D. E. Rumelhart, B. A. Wandell, A. T. Lee, G. H. Glover, E.-J. Chichilnisky, and M. N. Shadlen. "fMRI of Human Visual Cortex." *Nature* 369 (1994): 525.

Esrock, Ellen J. *The Reader's Eye: Visual Imaging as Reader Response*. Baltimore: Johns Hopkins University Press, 1994.

Fink, Sebastian. "Metaphors for the Unrecognizability of God in Balaĝs and Xenophanes." Pages 231–43 in *Mesopotamia in the Ancient World: Impact, Continuities, Parallels; Proceedings of the Seventh Symposium of the Melammu Project*

Held in Obergurgl, Austria, November 4–8, 2013. Edited by Robert Rollinger and Erik van Dongen. Münster: Ugarit-Verlag, 2015.

Gericke, Jaco. *The Hebrew Bible and Philosophy of Religion*. Atlanta: Society of Biblical Literature, 2012.

Goldin, Judah. *Studies in Midrash and Related Literature*. Edited by Barry L. Eichler and Jeffrey H. Tigay. Philadelphia: Jewish Publication Society, 1988.

Greggs, Tom. *Theology against Religion: Constructive Dialogues with Bonhoeffer and Barth*. London: T&T Clark, 2011.

Hankins, Davis. "'Much Madness Is Divinest Sense': The Economic Consequences of Yahweh's Parasocial Identity." *The Bible and Critical Theory* 14 (2018): 17–41.

Harlow, John M. "Recovery from the Passage of an Iron Bar through the Head." *Publications of the Massachusetts Medical Society* 2 (1868): 329–47.

Hazony, Yoram. *The Philosophy of Hebrew Scripture*. New York: Cambridge University Press, 2012.

Helmer, Christine. "Theology and the Study of Religion: A Relationship." Pages 230–54 in *The Cambridge Companion to Religious Studies*. Edited by Robert A. Orsi. Cambridge: Cambridge University Press, 2012.

Heschel, Abraham Joshua. *Moral Grandeur and Spiritual Audacity: Essays*. Edited by Susannah Heschel. New York: Farrar, Straus & Giroux, 1996.

Hofstadter, Albert, and Richard Kuhns, eds. *Philosophies of Art and Beauty: Selected Readings in Aesthetics from Plato to Heidegger*. Chicago: University of Chicago Press, 1964.

Hulster, Izaak J. de. *Iconographic Exegesis and Third Isaiah*. Tübingen: Mohr Siebeck, 2009.

Hulster, Izaak J. de, and Brent A. Strawn. "The Power of Images: Isaiah 60, Jerusalem, and Persian Imperial Propaganda." Pages 197–216 in *Iconographic Exegesis of the Hebrew Bible/Old Testament: An Introduction to Its Method and Practice*. Edited by Izaak J. de Hulster, Brent A. Strawn, and Ryan P. Bonfiglio. Göttingen: Vandenhoeck & Ruprecht, 2015.

Hus, Shih-Wei, and Jaume Llop Raduà, eds. *The Expression of Emotions in Ancient Egypt and Mesopotamia*. Leiden: Brill, 2021.

Jensen, Robin M. "Visuality." Pages 309–43 in *The Cambridge Companion to Ancient Mediterranean Religions*. Edited by Barbette Stanley Spaeth. Cambridge: Cambridge University Press, 2013.

Johnson, Dru. *Biblical Knowing: A Scriptural Epistemology of Error*. Eugene, OR: Cascade, 2013.

———. *Biblical Philosophy: A Hebraic Approach to the Old and New Testaments*. Cambridge: Cambridge University Press, 2021.

Kahneman, Daniel. *Thinking, Fast and Slow*. New York: Farrar, Straus & Giroux, 2011.

Karenga, Maulana. *Maat: The Moral Ideal in Ancient Egypt: A Study in Classical African Ethics*. New York: Routledge, 2004.

Keel, Othmar. *Corpus der Stempelsiegel-Amulette aus Palästina/Israel: Von den Anfängen bis zur Perserzeit; Einleitung.* Fribourg: Academic Press; Göttingen: Vandenhoeck & Ruprecht, 1995.

———. *Corpus der Stempelsiegel-Amulette aus Palästina/Israel: Von den Anfängen bis zur Perserzeit; Katalog Band I: Von Tell Abu Farağ bis 'Atlit.* Fribourg: Academic Press; Göttingen: Vandenhoeck & Ruprecht, 1997.

———. *Corpus der Stempelsiegel-Amulette aus Palästina/Israel: Von den Anfängen bis zur Perserzeit; Katalog Band II: Von Bahan bis Tel Eton.* Fribourg: Academic Press; Göttingen: Vandenhoeck & Ruprecht, 2010.

———. *Corpus der Stempelsiegel-Amulette aus Palästina/Israel: Von den Anfängen bis zur Perserzeit; Katalog Band III: Von Tell el-Far'a Nord bis Tell el-Fir.* Fribourg: Academic Press; Göttingen: Vandenhoeck & Ruprecht, 2010.

———. *Corpus der Stempelsiegel-Amulette aus Palästina/Israel: Von den Anfängen bis zur Perserzeit; Katalog Band IV: Von Tel Gamma bis Chirbet Husche.* Fribourg: Academic Press; Göttingen: Vandenhoeck & Ruprecht, 2013.

———. *Corpus der Stempelsiegel-Amulette aus Palästina/Israel: Von den Anfängen bis zur Perserzeit; Katalog Band V: Von Tel el-'Idham bis Tel Kitan.* Fribourg: Academic Press; Göttingen: Vandenhoeck & Ruprecht, 2017.

———. *700 Skarabäen und Verwandtes aus Palästina/Israel: Die Sammlung Keel.* Leuven: Peeters, 2020.

Keel, Othmar, and Christoph Uehlinger. *Altorientalische Miniaturkunst: Die ältesten visuellen Massenkommunikationsmittel; Ein Blick in die Sammlungen des Biblischen Instituts der Universität Freiburg Schweiz.* Freiburg: Universitätsverlag Freiburg Schweiz; Göttingen: Vandenhoeck & Ruprecht, 1996.

———. *Gods, Goddesses, and Images of God in Ancient Israel.* Translated by Thomas H. Trapp. Minneapolis: Fortress, 1998.

Kellner, Menachem. *Dogma in Medieval Jewish Thought: From Maimonides to Abravanel.* Oxford: Oxford University Press, 1986.

———. *Must a Jew Believe Anything?* Oxford: Littman Library of Jewish Civilization, 2006.

Kipfer, Sara. *Visualizing Emotions in the Ancient Near East.* Fribourg: Academic Press; Göttingen: Vandenhoeck & Ruprecht, 2017.

Klawans, Jonathan. *Josephus and the Theologies of Ancient Judaism.* Oxford: Oxford University Press, 2012.

Kosslyn, Stephen M., William L. Thompson, and Giorgio Ganis. *The Case for Mental Imagery.* Oxford: Oxford University Press, 2006.

Lash, Nicholas. *The Beginning and the End of 'Religion'.* Cambridge: Cambridge University Press, 1996.

———. *Believing Three Ways in One God: A Reading of the Apostles' Creed.* Notre Dame: University of Notre Dame Press, 1993.

LeMon, Joel M., and Brent A. Strawn. "Once More, Yhwh and Company at Kuntillet 'Ajrud." *Maarav* 20 (2013): 83–114.

Levenson, Jon D. *The Hebrew Bible, the Old Testament, and Historical Criticism: Jews and Christians in Biblical Studies*. Louisville: Westminster John Knox, 1993.

Lewis, Theodore J. *The Origin and Character of God: Ancient Israelite Religion through the Lens of Divinity*. Oxford: Oxford University Press, 2020.

Liverani, Mario. *Assyria: The Imperial Mission*. Translated by Andrea Trameri and Jonathan Valk. Winona Lake, IN: Eisenbrauns, 2017.

Maiden, Brett E. *Cognitive Science and Ancient Israelite Religion: New Perspectives on Texts, Artifacts, and Culture*. Cambridge: Cambridge University Press, 2020.

Massironi, Manfredo. *The Psychology of Graphic Images: Seeing, Drawing, Communicating*. Translated by Nicolo Bruno. Mahwah, NJ: Erlbaum, 2002.

Mazar, A. "The 'Bull Site': An Iron Age I Open Cult Place." *BASOR* 247 (1982): 27–42.

McClellan, Daniel O. *Yhwh's Divine Images: A Cognitive Approach*. Atlanta: SBL Press, 2022.

Mendelsund, Peter. *What We See When We Read*. New York: Vintage, 2014.

Miller, Patrick D. *The Religion of Ancient Israel*. Louisville: Westminster John Knox, 2000.

Mitchell, W. J. T. *What Do Pictures Want? The Lives and Loves of Images*. Chicago: University of Chicago Press, 2015.

Moberly, R. W. L. "Knowing God and Knowing about God: Martin Buber's *Two Types of Faith Revisited*." *SJT* 65 (2012): 402–20.

Moran, William L. "The Babylonian Job." Pages 182–200 in *The Most Magic Word*. Edited by Ronald S. Hendel. Washington, DC: Catholic Biblical Association, 2002.

Morgan, David. *The Embodied Eye: Religious Visual Culture and the Social Life of Feeling*. Berkeley: University of California Press, 2012.

———, ed. *Religion and Material Culture: The Matter of Belief*. London: Routledge, 2010.

———. *The Sacred Gaze: Religious Visual Culture in Theory and Practice*. Berkeley: University of California Press, 2005.

———. *Visual Piety: A History and Theory of Popular Religious Images*. Berkeley: University of California Press, 1998.

Morgan, Teresa. *Being 'in Christ' in the Letters of Paul: Saved through Christ and in His Hands*. Tübingen Mohr Siebeck, 2020.

———. *Roman Faith and Christian Faith: Pistis and Fides in the Early Roman Empire and Early Church*. Oxford: Oxford University Press, 2015.

Needham, Rodney. *Belief, Language, and Experience*. Chicago: University of Chicago Press, 1972.

Neubauer, Simon, Jean-Jacques Hublin, and Philipp Gunz. "The Evolution of Modern Human Brain Shape." *Science Advances* 4.1 (2018): 1–8.

Nilsson, Nols J. *Understanding Beliefs*. Cambdrige: MIT Press, 2014.

Nongbri, Brent. *Before Religion: A History of a Modern Concept*. New Haven: Yale University Press, 2013.

Paivio, Allan. *Mental Representations: A Dual Coding Approach*. New York: Oxford University Press, 1986.

Panofsky, Erwin. *Studies in Iconology: Humanistic Themes in the Art of the Renaissance*. New York: Oxford University Press, 1939. Repr., Oxford: Westview, 1972.

Pelikan, Jaroslav. *Credo: Historical and Theological Guide to Creeds and Confessions of Faith in the Christian Tradition*. New Haven: Yale University Press, 2003.

Pelikan, Jaroslav, and Valeire Hotchkiss, eds. *Creeds and Confessions of Faith in the Christian Tradition*. 3 vols. New Haven: Yale University Press, 2003.

Pinker, Steven. *The Blank Slate: The Modern Denial of Human Nature*. New York: Penguin, 2002.

———. *Visual Cognition*. Cambridge: MIT Press, 1985.

Pongratz-Leisten, Beate., ed. *Reconsidering the Concept of Revolutionary Monotheism*. Winona Lake, IN: Eisenbrauns, 2011.

Portuese, Ludovico. *Life at Court: Ideology and Audience in the Late Assyrian Palace*. Münster: Zaphon, 2020.

———. "Toward a (Neuro-)Psychology of Art: Cues for Attention in Mesopotamian Art." *Ash-Sharq* 4 (2020): 157–86.

Ramachandran, V. S. *A Brief Tour of Human Consciousness: From Imposter Poodles to Purple Numbers*. New York: Pi, 2004.

———. *The Tell-Tale Brain: A Neuroscientist's Quest for What Makes Us Human*. New York: Norton, 2011.

Ramachandran, V. S., and W. Hirstein. "The Science of Art: A Neurological Theory of Aesthetic Experience." *Journal of Consciousness Studies* 6.6–7 (1999): 15–51.

Renz, Johannes, and Wolfgang Rölling. *Handbuch der althebräischen Epigraphik*. 3 vols. Darmstadt: Wissenschaftliche Buchgesellschaft, 1995.

Sadoski, Mark, and Allan Paivio. *Imagery and Text: A Dual Coding Theory of Reading and Writing*. 2nd ed. New York: Routledge, 2013.

Scarry, Elaine. *Dreaming by the Book*. New York: Farrar, Straus, & Giroux, 1999.

Schmidt, Brian B. "The Aniconic Tradition: On Reading Images and Viewing Texts." Pages 75–105 in *The Triumph of Elohim: From Yahwisms to Judaism*. Edited by Diana V. Edelman. Grand Rapids: Eerdmans, 1995.

Schniedewind, William. "An Early Iron Age Phrase to Kuntillet 'Ajrud?" Pages 134–45 in *Le-ma'an Ziony: Essays in Honor of Ziony Zevit*. Edited by Frederick E. Greenspahn and Gary A. Rendsburg. Eugene, OR: Cascade, 2017.

Scott, Jack B. "אָמַן." *TWOT* 1:51–53.

Schroer, Silvia. *In Israel gab es Bilder: Nachrichten von darstellender Kunst im Alten Testament*. Freiburg: Universitätsverlag Freiburg Schweiz, 1987.

Sereno, M. I., A. M. Dale, J. B. Reppas, K. K. Kwong, J. W. Belliveau, T. J. Brady, B. R. Rosen, and R. B. Tootell. "Borders of Multiple Visual Areas in Humans Revealed by Functional Magnetic Resonance Imaging." *Science* 268 (1995): 889–93.

Slotnick, S. D., W. L. Thompson, and S. M. Kosslyn. "Visual Mental Imagery Induces Retinotopically Organized Activation of Early Visual Areas." *Cerebral Cortex* 15 (2005): 1570–83.

Smith, Mark S. *God in Translation: Deities in Cross-Cultural Discourse in the Biblical World*. Grand Rapids: Eerdmans, 2010.

———. "Recent Study of Israelite Religion in Light of the Ugaritic Texts." Pages 1–26 in *Ugarit at Seventy-Five*. Edited by K. Lawson Younger Jr. Winona Lake, IN: Eisenbrauns, 2007.

Smith, Wilfred Cantwell. *Believing: An Historical Perspective*. Oxford: Oneworld, 1998.

———. *Faith and Belief*. Princeton: Princeton University Press, 1979.

Sonik, Karen, and Ulrike Steinert, eds. *The Routledge Handbook of Emotions in the Ancient Near East*. New York: Routledge, 2023.

Spencer, F. Scott, ed. *Mixed Feelings and Vexed Passions: Exploring Emotions in Biblical Literature*. Atlanta: SBL Press, 2017.

Strawn, Brent A. "Canaanite/Israelite Iconography." Pages 172–82 in *Behind the Scenes of the Old Testament: Cultural, Social, and Historical Contexts*. Edited by Johnathan S. Greer, John W. Hilber, and John H. Walton. Grand Rapids: Baker Academic, 2018.

———. "The History of Israelite Religion." Pages 86–107 in *The Cambridge Companion to the Hebrew Bible/Old Testament*. Edited by Stephen B. Chapman and Marvin A. Sweeney. Cambridge: Cambridge University Press, 2016.

———. *What Is Stronger Than a Lion? Leonine Image and Metaphor in the Hebrew Bible and the Ancient Near East*. Fribourg: Academic Press; Göttingen: Vandenhoeck & Ruprecht, 2005.

Strawn, Brent A., and Joel M. LeMon. "Religion in Eighth-Century Judah: The Case of Kuntillet 'Ajrud (and Beyond)." Pages 379–400 in *Archaeology and History of Eighth-Century Judah*. Edited by Zev I. Farber and Jacob L. Wright. Atlanta: Society of Biblical Literature, 2018.

Thirion, Bertrand, Edouard Duchesnay, Edward Hubbard, Jessica Dubois, Jean-Baptiste Poline, Denis Lebihan, and Stanislas Dehaene. "Inverse Retinotopy: Inferring the Visual Content of Images from Brain Activation Patterns." *NeruoImage* 33 (2006): 1104–16.

Tobin, Vincent Arieh. *Theological Principles of Egyptian Religion*. New York: Lang, 1989.

Tooteel, R. B. H. "Deoxyglucose Analysis of Retinotopic Organization in Primate Striate Context." *Science* 218 (1982): 902–4.

Tsur, Reuven. *Poetic Conventions as Cognitive Fossils.* Oxford: Oxford University Press, 2017.

Turner, Mark. *Reading Minds: The Study of English in the Age of Cognitive Science.* Princeton: Princeton University Press, 1991.

Tyler, Ann C. "Shaping Belief: The Role of Audience in Visual Communication." *Design Issues* 9 (1992): 21–29.

Uehlinger, Christoph. "Anthropomorphic Cult Statuary in Iron Age Palestine and the Search for Yahweh's Cult Images." Pages 97–155 in *The Image and the Book: Iconic Cults, Aniconism, and the Rise of Book Religion in Israel and the Ancient Near East.* Edited by Karel van der Toorn. Leuven: Peeters, 1997.

Van De Mieroop, Marc. *Philosophy before the Greeks: The Pursuit of Truth in Ancient Babylonia.* Princeton: Princeton University Press, 2016.

Versnel, H. S. *Coping with the Gods: Wayward Readings in Greek Theology.* Leiden: Brill, 2011.

Walker, Justin. *The Power of Images: The Poetics of Violence in Lamentations 2 and Ancient Near Eastern Art.* Leuven: Peeters, 2022.

Westh, Peter. "Illuminator of the Wide Earth; Unbribable Judge; Strong Weapon of the Gods: Intuitive Ontology and Divine Epithets in Assyro-Babylonian Religious Texts." Pages 48–61 in *Past Minds: Studies in Cognitive Historiography.* Edited by Luther H. Martin and Jesper Søresen. London: Equinox, 2011.

Wolf, Maryanne. *Reader, Come Home: The Reading Brain in a Digital World.* New York: Harper, 2018.

Wyschogrod, Michael. "The Impact of Dialogue with Christianity on My Self-Understanding as a Jew." Pages 725–35 in *Die Hebräische Bibel und ihre zweifache Nachgeschichte: Festschrift für Rolf Rendtorff zum 65. Geburstag.* Edited by Erhard Blum, Christian Macholz, and Ekkehard W. Stegemann. Neukirchen-Vluyn: Neukirchener, 1990.

Younger, K. Lawson, Jr. "Gods at the Gates: A Study of the Identification of the Deities Represented at the Gates of Ancient Sam'al (Zincirli) with Possible Historical Implications." *ARAM Periodical* 31 (2019): 317–48.

Zevit, Ziony. *The Religions of Ancient Israel: A Synthesis of Parallactic Approaches.* London: Continuum, 2001.

Zimmerli, Walther. *I Am Yahweh.* Translated by Douglas W. Scott. Atlanta: Knox, 1982.

11

(Be)li(e)ving in a Material World

What Can Ancient Figurines Teach Us about the Modern Study of Religion?

ERIN DARBY

What, if anything, can material culture tell us about ancient "belief"? Over the last several years a number of theories—such as Catherine Bell's notion of ritualization, Pierre Bourdieu's construction of *habitus*, and David Morgan's approach to material religion—have been used to reconstruct ancient conceptions and perceptions, particularly in the study of ancient religion and identity. These theories approach belief and actions as intertwined and embodied. In figurine studies, scholars apply these approaches to figurines in order to hypothesize the thoughts, beliefs, and identities of ancient inhabitants, thus purportedly circumventing a more dated and textually derived picture of religion.

There are downsides, however, related to our inability to reconstruct the way ancient subjects experienced, let alone perceived, ritual objects. To illustrate this point, the following chapter collates examples of theoretical approaches to figurines in ancient Judah, demonstrating some of the weaknesses in their implementation. Instead, the most effective approach to the interpretation of ancient figurines (and other religious material culture) relies upon critical theory while centering the reconstruction of societal infrastructures and economies that gave rise to ancient believers' identities.

ERIN DARBY

Israelite Belief and the Modern Categories of Religion

At its base, ancient Israelite religion and early Judaism pose a fundamental challenge for the modern study of "religion," in so much as neither Hebrew nor Aramaic have a clear correlate for the term, let alone a category of experience that ancient peoples would have defined over and against other areas of life. Nevertheless, Judaism and the religions of ancient Mesopotamia and Egypt played an important role in the creation of the categories ordering the modern study of religion.

In J. Z. Smith's field-defining essay "Religion, Religions, Religious," he traces a genealogy for the scholarly category "religion" following the term's meaning from its original and specific application to Catholic ritual in the Western world through its metamorphosis into a global, cross-cultural category of analysis.[1] What is less-remarked upon in his essay is the varying roles that Judaism and Near Eastern texts played in the creation of the taxonomic system.

In Smith's telling, Edward Brerewood categorized Judaism as a religion alongside "Christianity, Mohametanism, . . . and Idolatry" in his 1614 work *Enquiries Touching the Diversity of Languages and Religions through the Chief Parts of the World* (fig. 11.1 on p. 227). By the 1835 publication of J. Newton Brown's *Encyclopedia of Religious Knowledge*, idolatry had been separated and ranked into its own subcategory, while Judaism remained with Christianity and Islam (fig. 11.2 on p. 227). Proceeding to W. D. Whitney's 1881 categorization, the position of Judaism changed drastically and was now subsumed under "race religion" (fig. 11.3 on p. 227). Not so subtle is the implied contrast with Zoroastrianism, so-called Mohammedanism, Buddhism, and Christianity as "founder religions." As more texts from the ancient world came to light, the position of Judaism grew more complicated. In Cornelius Petrus Tiele's publications from 1876 and 1884, Judaism became a mediating category (fig. 11.4 on p. 228). It had regained a more positive position in the "ethical religions" but remained separate from Islam, Buddhism, and Christianity, which were designated "universalistic nomistic communities." Judaism was the sole member of the ethical religions' "nationalistic religious communities" subcategory. Judaism was also divided from all other ancient Near Eastern traditions, which were relegated to various (lower) categories within "natural religion."

So where does this leave the religion of ancient Israel? Judaism has almost always held an ambiguous position within the classification of religion. In most

---

1. J. Z. Smith, "Religion, Religions, Religious," in *Critical Terms for Religious Studies*, ed. Mark Taylor (Chicago: University of Chicago Press, 1998), 269–84.

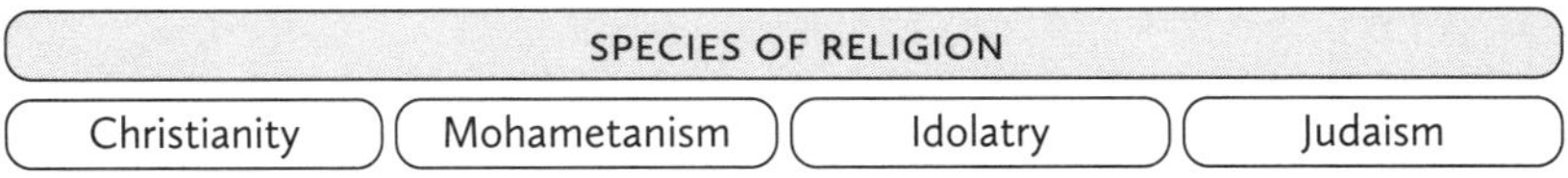

(Be)li(e)ving in a Material World

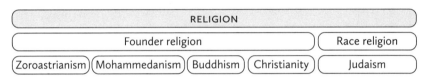

Fig. 11.1. Brerewood's categories of religion, after J. Z. Smith, "Religion, Religions, Religious," 275.

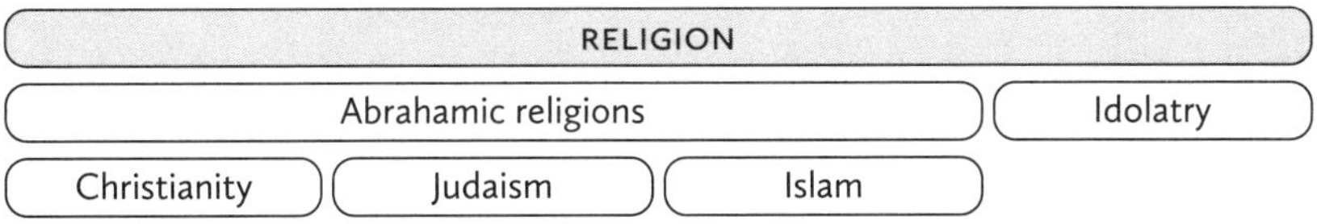

Fig. 11.2. Brown's categories of religion, after J. Z. Smith, "Religion, Religions, Religious," 276.

Fig. 11.3. J. D. Whitney's categories of religion, after J. Z. Smith, "Religion, Religions, Religious," 277–78.

classification systems, texts from the ancient Near East (including the Levant) have been separated from Judaism and placed into even "lower" categories. In this manner, Judaism and ancient Near Eastern religion have formed the fuzzy border region separating higher and lower order traditions. As with all border regions, they have helped protect more well-defined categories, like Christianity, from taxonomic ambiguity.

It should come as no surprise that the study of ancient Israelite religion will, by its very nature, challenge many of the attributes used to demarcate "religion." And the history of scholarship suggests that one of the reasons Judaism and Near Eastern tradition fit so poorly in the taxonomy of religion was the field's fixation on belief, which was largely contrasted with ritual.[2] The more ritualistic a tradition was perceived to be, the lower its evolutionary status. The supremacy of belief in the study of the ancient Near East was further undergirded by the centrality of

---

2. Erin Darby, *Interpreting Judean Pillar Figurines: Gender and Empire in Judean Apotropaic Ritual* (Tübingen: Mohr Siebeck, 2014), 8, 9, 15; Catherine Bell, *Ritual Theory, Ritual Practice* (New York: Oxford University Press, 1992), 30–46; Jonathan Z. Smith, "Great Scott! Thought and Action One More Time," in *Magic and Ritual in the Ancient World*, ed. Paul Mirecki and Marvin Meyer (Leiden: Brill, 2002), 73–91.

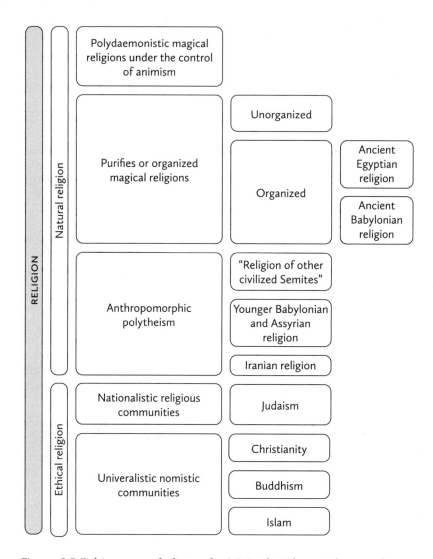

Fig. 11.4. C. P. Tiele's category of religion, after J. Z. Smith, "Religion, Religions, Religious," 278–79.

texts, which were the first sources of information about the ancient Near East to impact Western scholarship. Thus it was not "belief" alone but rather textualized, ratified, and elite beliefs that informed scholarly categories. These fossils could be dehistoricized, analyzed, and abstracted in the project of forming a Linnaeun systed of the world's religious traditions and "religion" more generally.

(Be)li(e)ving in a Material World

The Archaeology of Belief?

What happens if, instead of framing our query by means of textual record, we focus instead on daily life, what contemporary scholars often call "religion on the ground"? One of the primary challenges is that the vast majority of everyday Israelites did not leave a textual legacy of either their thoughts or actions. Instead, scholars turn to nonepigraphic objects from the material record. But what can faunal bones, household architecture, or broken clay figurines tell us about ancient belief?

Over the last several decades the field of religious studies has reconsidered the ranked dichotomy of "belief versus ritual." Indeed, interlocutors have astutely questioned whether they can be separated at all. Scholars like Catherine Bell, building on the work of cultural anthropology and critical theory, have argued that knowing and doing are not only completely integrated but fully embodied. Similarly, knowing can be largely unconscious and often contradictory. Finally, Bell and others have argued that humans are structured by their participation in ritualized action and the *materia* thereof.[3]

One by-product of this more nuanced approach to belief and ritual, what we might call "tradition" or "praxis," is that the object of investigation ceases to be "belief" but "believers." Yet, this critical turn in ritual studies demands more data and greater detail, and it should yield conclusions that take into consideration conflict, contradiction, and continuity. While this engagement with "belief" opens new avenues for study, it also requires far more information, which poses serious challenges for historians and archaeologists. It also requires us to think more broadly about what we include in "belief," particularly for a culture that does not attempt to divide "religious belief" from other types of ideation.

This leaves us with various frameworks through which we might approach material culture as a source of information about ancient believers. None of them are without challenges. Perhaps the easiest approach is to suggest that any evidence of human activity from within an identified ritual space could be the by-product of believers and their belief. The trick is identifying which spaces are ritualized, which has been the subject of much scholarly hand-wringing.[4] Depending on the

---

3. Bell, *Ritual Theory*, 30–46, 98, 107, 184–87, 199–223. Ronald L. Grimes, "Performance Theory and the Study of Ritual," in *Textual, Comparative, Sociological, and Cognitive Approaches*, vol. 2 of *New Approaches to the Study of Religion*, ed. Peter Antes, Armin W. Geertz, and Randi R. Warne (Berlin: de Gruyter, 2004), 132, 134–35.

4. Lars Fogelin, "The Archaeology of Religious Ritual," *Annual Review of Anthropology* 36 (2007): 55–71; Evangelos Kyriakidis, "Archaeologies of Ritual," in *The Archaeology of Ritual*, ed. Evangelos Kyriakidis (Los Angeles: Cotsen Institute of Archaeology, 2007), 289–308. For a survey

status of the ritualized space, and keeping in mind that official space is easiest to identify, the remaining material culture may suggest more about religious personnel or official elite- or state-level praxis than the beliefs of other segments of the population. Moreover, the state of preservation for a ritual space may significantly impede our ability to reconstruct even the physical conditions through which visitors experienced architecture and objects.

Another approach is to focus on symbolic depictions, wherever they are found. In this iconological approach, the focus remains on decoding the meaning of symbols with only secondary consideration of the manner of their creation or the setting in which particular individuals engaged the artifacts.[5] While these objects, like seals, may have been handled by a larger segment of the population, treating them as abstract symbols takes us away from the focus on the discrete "believer," as encouraged by theories of ritualization, and brings us back to beliefs as abstracted entities largely divorced from their interaction with particular creators or viewers.

The work of scholars in the material religion school takes more seriously the interaction between objects and viewers, focusing on multifaceted human experience of religion itself, including various ways of feeling and knowing. Contrasting his approach with a more traditional, textually driven framework, David Morgan notes that "religions consist of feeling, sensation, implements, spaces, images, clothing, food, and all manner of bodily practices."[6] When experienced together, "commonly experienced artifacts become social media that educate the senses and operate as forms of sociality."[7] In making this statement, Morgan argues that a focus on lived religion demands an attentiveness to "the things people do in order to organize their worlds into coherent domains of experience."[8]

While there is little doubt that Morgan's approach comes closest to the complexity of human believers, how do we access the moods and motivations of ritu-

---

of approaches to religion and ritual, see Andrea M. Creel, "Connectivity on the Edge of Empire: Movement, Liminality, and Ritual in the Southern Levantine Drylands" (PhD diss., University of California, Berkeley, 2017), 23–27.

5. Darby, *Interpreting Judean Pillar Figurines*, 303–7, with literature; Ryan P. Bonfiglio, *Reading Images, Seeing Texts: Towards a Visual Hermeneutics for Biblical Studies* (Fribourg: Academic Press/Göttingen: Vandenhoeck & Ruprecht, 2016), 122–65.

6. David Morgan, "The Material Culture of Lived Religions: Visuality and Embodiment," in *Mind and Matter: Selected Papers of the Nordik 2009 Conference for Art Historians*, ed. Johanna Vakkari (Helsinki: Helsingfors, 2010), 16.

7. D. Morgan, "Material Culture of Lived Religions," 17.

8. D. Morgan, "Material Culture of Lived Religions," 18.

(Be)li(e)ving in a Material World

alized participants? Morgan optimistically answers: "I intend instead the study of ways of feeling, forms of sensation, modes of perception. These are not hopelessly subjective and therefore inaccessible phenomena, but may be studied as shared patterns or routines that endure and therefore characterize groups of people as forms of sociality, as the sensuous means of social association and shared imagination."[9] While material religion has provided a number of scholars with theoretical tools to imagine the intersection between humans and things as integrated and entangled, the analysis requires access to the spaces in which humans engage ritual activity, not to mention the testimonies and observable behavior of ritual actors that could be used to inform a reconstruction of feelings and sensations.[10] Without strong data, we could easily fall back on narratives based in biological essentialism about how all humans share common experiences over vast stretches of time regardless of cultural difference.

To summarize the material religion approach, authors often study the formal characteristics of objects and their physical context, which are interpreted in light of their larger cultural context. The method depends upon a theoretical framework explaining how objects and humans interact, that is, how humans perceive or engage with materials and how materials affect humans (more on this point below). The analysis does adopt a more complex view of believers and belief, treating belief as embodied, situational, affective, and interactive. Religious belief is investigated as an integrated aspect of human perception and part of a network of social institutions.

The questions for historians of ancient Israelite believers are manifold. Do we have enough high-quality information? Lacking strong data, do the theoretical approaches we adopt help inform our understanding of religion, or does our already-formed understanding of religion dictate how we interpret materials? If focusing on materials, rituals, and sensory perception should fundamentally change the picture we draw of religion, how do we explain the versions of Israelite religion that remain static?

---

9. D. Morgan, "Material Culture of Lived Religions," 18.

10. See the entire special issue entitled "Key Words in Material Religion," edited by Birgit Meyer, David Morgan, Crispin Paine, and S. Brent Plate in *Material Religion* 7.1 (2011); David Morgan, "Materializing the Study of Religion," *Religion* 46.4 (2016): 640–43; Morgan, *The Sacred Gaze: Religious Visual Culture in Theory and Practice* (Berkeley: University of California Press, 2005); Morgan, *The Embodied Eye: Religious Visual Culture and the Social Life of Feeling* (Berkeley: University of California Press, 2012). See also Creel, "Connectivity on the Edge of Empire," 20–23.

ERIN DARBY

Figurines and Identity as a Proxy for Belief

In order to assess the feasibility of a material religion approach to reconstructing ancient believers, we can use the growing body of literature on figurines and identity, adopting Judean pillar figurines as a lens. Identity in this scholarship has come to accrue the sense of an embodied way of knowing, which could be intertwined with family system, social organizations, religious institutions, and a host of other factors. It is a messy category, but it is one that avoids an overly wooden and simplistic approach to belief.[11] That having been said, it relies on access to strong data with which to reconstruct with some plausibility the thoughts and feelings of an ancient population.

A variety of studies using both texts and artifacts have attempted to reconstruct the rise of Israelite or Judahite "identity." Earlier investigations focused on Israelite identity (variously defined) in the context of the Iron Age I hill country and debates concerning Israelite identity in the ninth or tenth centuries (see below for sources). More recent work has recast the rise of Israelite identity in the context of ninth- and, more properly, eighth-century Judah.[12] Analysis has considered whether political infrastructure preceded or followed a sense of collective identity and the interaction of tribal, ethnic, and national identity as well as how to weigh individual data points in these overall questions. Although scholars rigorously debate the data, the concept of identity remains undertheorized, particularly in figurine studies.

Many scholars working on figurines and identity rely heavily on the early work of Douglass Bailey.[13] Adopting modern theoretical frameworks, Bailey aimed to

11. Most recently see, Avraham Faust, "An Imperial Encounter: The Egyptian Empire in Canaan, Highland Ethnogenesis, and the Transformation of History," in *Power and Identity at the Margins of the Ancient Near East*, ed. Sara Mohr and Shane Thompson (Denver: University Press of Colorado, 2023), 14–41, with literature. Here Faust is most interested in ethnic identity, which he distinguishes from other types of identity. It may be that ethnic identity is easier to identify in the archaeological record, if Faust is correct that a group may elevate particular types of material culture as an outward sign of that identity.

12. See below for sources as well as the literature in Darby, *Interpreting Judean Pillar Figurines*, 367–97; Darby, "Reaction, Reliance, Resistance: Judean Pillar Figurines in the Neo-Assyrian Levant," in *Imperial Peripheries in the Neo-Assyrian Period*, ed. Craig W. Tyson and Virginia R. Herrmann (Boulder: University Press of Colorado, 2019), 128–49; Darby, "Judean Pillar Figurines: Religion and National Identity in Eighth Century Judah," in *Archaeology and History of Eighth Century Judah*, ed. Zev I. Farber and Jacob L. Wright (Atlanta: Society of Biblical Literature Press, 2018), 401–14.

13. Douglass W. Bailey, *Prehistoric Figurines: Representation and Corporeality in the Neolithic* (London: Routledge, 2005).

232

use figurines to reconstruct various aspects of personal and social identity in the Neolithic world. Unfortunately, lacking detailed data, many of Bailey's interpretations were based on universalizing assumptions. For example, Bailey writes that human beings have always had a "universal concern ... about personal identity" and "the desire to correlate external bodily appearance with less tangible components of individual identity may well rest deep within the human psyche."[14] Nevertheless, Bailey also acknowledges that "if we need a more concrete interpretation, then the emphasis must rest on the local, (pre)historical context in particular inequalities of power and status," suggesting that our ability to proceed beyond these broad generalizations is directly dependent on what we can reasonably know about a given local context.[15] Without consideration of these data, we could inadvertently reconstruct the process of ancient identity formation, as if it is similar to our own. Differences would become undetectable.

These challenges are visible in many discussions of Judean pillar figurines (JPFs) from Iron Age–period southern Israel, and a survey of approaches to these objects will illustrate several issues in reconstructing believers in the ancient world. JPFs are small terracotta female figurines from the polity of Judah dating from the eighth through the sixth century BCE. The corpus consists primarily of solid pillar bases with the figurine's hands on or slightly below the breasts. JPFs have two main head styles—handmade specimens with shallow depressions for eyes and mold-made figurines. Mold-made heads tend to have between one and six rows of horizontal curls, are forward-staring, and possess almond shaped eyes and smiling mouths. Some JPFs have an attached turban or turban and sidelocks. While few

Fig. 11.5a. (*above*) Various styles of Judean pillar figurines from Jerusalem in the Israel Museum. Courtesy of Chamberi.

Fig. 11.5b. (*below*) Judean pillar figurine with hand-pinched head, from the Israel Museum, courtesy of Françoise Foliot.

---

14. Bailey, *Prehistoric Figurines*, 75, 82.
15. Bailey, *Prehistoric Figurines*, 195.

figurines have well-preserved paint, there is ample evidence they would all have been painted. A few examples hold a disc or a child (figs. 11.5a–b on p. 233).

JPFs are an interesting test case because, despite their prevalence in the Iron IIB and C, they are never clearly mentioned in any extent textual record, including the Hebrew Bible.[16] They are recovered from most of the population centers in Judah, and the majority are found in association with domestic architecture or neighborhood streets. They seem to have broken easily, but there is no evidence for ritual disposal. Rather, breaks occur predictably at the weakest points: where the heads are attached to the bodies via a clay tang or under the torso where hand-modeled breasts and arms are attached to the pillar base. They are almost always found in secondary or tertiary archaeological context, such as leveling for floors, chinks in walls, fills accumulated in rooms, streets, and even toilets.[17]

Based on the way figurines were described in the ritual texts of contemporaneous cultures like Neo-Assyrian Mesopotamia, it is highly likely JPFs had a ritual function, but they are not clearly associated with the iconography of recognizable goddess. It is just as likely they represent lower-level divine entities or guardian figures. We have no accompanying ritual tablets that indicate how JPFs functioned in specific rituals, who used them, or who made them, and given their archaeological context it is very difficult to use archaeological assemblages to reconstruct these rituals with any real surety.[18] Thus, the pictures of believers and beliefs we reconstruct using JPFs are heavily impacted by the theories we apply to the material culture.

Judean Pillar Figurine Case Studies

One approach to identity is to invoke the concept in general to refer to a way a group thinks or feels but without defining the term. For example, in an influential article Ryan Byrne invokes the concept of identity within imperial systems to argue that Judeans used figurines as a means of resisting Assyrian power. Byrne does not specify a particular theoretical framework, and his article does not discuss the historiographic issues related to how we might measure any encroachment of Assyrian religion or reconstruct the organization of figurine production in Judah.

---

16. Darby, *Interpreting Judean Pillar Figurines*, 259–300.

17. Darby, *Interpreting Judean Pillar Figurines*, 98–180.

18. Darby, *Interpreting Judean Pillar Figurines*, 61–97, 311–63. See also Lauren K. McCormick, "My Eyes Are Up Here: Guardian Iconography of the Judean Pillar Figurine" (PhD diss., Syracuse University, 2023), 179–93.

(Be)li(e)ving in a Material World

In short, the idea of ethnic and religious identity as applied to ancient Judah takes the place of more in-depth discussions of historiographic problems.[19] As a result, in Byrne's reconstruction JPFs prove the centrality of women's procreative function within the context of a national Judean identity without addressing whether we can actually reconstruct (1) the function of figurines; (2) the contexts in which individuals encountered them; (3) the importance of national identity in the conceptions of ancient Judeans; or (4) the thoughts of the average ancient Judean.

Ian Wilson's treatment of figurines and Judean identity has been a much-needed improvement to Byrne's work, given his explicit discussion of theoretical models like hegemony and counter-hegemony. But does Wilson's use of Gramsci's theory of hegemony solve the historiographic problem? Wilson does not focus on the context or modes of production for JPFs, information essential to understanding how and in what ways Judeans actually encountered figurines and the place of figurines in the infrastructure of society at large. However, Wilson employs the concept of counter-hegemony, perhaps inadvertently, to fill in what we do not know.[20] His article seems to use Gramsci's theory as a predictive model to assert that Judeans must have engaged in some form of counter-hegemony. In contrast, one must ask how much material from Gramsci's distinctively modern theory is applicable to non-Western and premodern contexts. Does hegemony or counter-hegemony look the same in eighth-century Judah and twentieth-century Italy?[21]

In an application of concepts from material religion to JPFs at Tel en Nasbeh, Aaron Brody argues that these artifacts provide direct access to women's religious beliefs and their power within domestic religion. In doing so, Brody's invocation of "material religion" comes to stand in for the notion that artifacts affect actors without discussing how and in what ways. Brody focuses on the types of artifacts found in particular architectural contexts, but given Tel en Nasbeh's challenging state of publication he is not able to address the complex data we would need to (1) draw implications for the gender of participants; (2) reconstruct the exact nature of their interactions with the objects; or (3) draw implications for the way human actors would transform their experience with the objects into

19. Ryan Byrne, "Lie Back and Think of Judah: The Reproductive Politics of Pillar Figurines," *NEA* 67.3 (2004): 137–51.

20. Ian Douglas Wilson. "Judean Pillar Figurines and Ethnic Identity in the Shadow of Assyria," *JSOT* 36.3 (2012): 259–78.

21. Antonio Gramsci, *The Prison Notebooks*, ed. and trans. Joseph Buttigieg (New York: Columbia University Press, 2011). For a discussion of applications of Gramsci's theories, see Stuart Hall, "Gramsci's Relevance for the Study of Race and Ethnicity," *Journal of Communication Inquiry* 10.2 (1986): 5–27.

ideations.[22] Given the absence of data, it is not surprising that the majority of scholars adopting a material religion approach focus on the modern or contemporary world. Morgan's thesis requires a high level of knowledge about both the physical conditions under which a given object is viewed and knowledge of the internal workings of viewers.[23]

Other scholars favor theories of embodiment and practice. One example is the work of Kristine Garroway, who employs concepts such as enculturation, socialization, and engendering.[24] Garroway's discussion of these theories is a helpful contribution to the field; however, historiographic problems in the interpretation of figurines receive less attention in her approach. Garroway's adoption of these theories assumes that children are engendered by their interaction with JPFs, but she provides no new data to help interpret their function. While she draws upon her extensive knowledge of childhood studies and focuses on the particularities of childhood in an ancient Israelite context, when she approaches the way children would have engaged with figurines the conversation focuses more on the application of theory. In function, the theory of engendering—largely dependent on the work of Judith Butler—is used by Garroway as a predictive model that assures us children were engendered and then enables speculation as to how. In the process of acknowledging that gender is culturally constructed, do we then stop and ask whether we have enough information to know how and in what ways that process occurred in ancient Israel? Do we even have enough information to understand, in any real sense, how individuals are engendered in the imagined world of the biblical text?[25]

At their base, many of these approaches to identity are indebted to Pierre Bourdieu's theory of *habitus*, which focuses on the way subjects are constructed through the interaction between subjective structures (i.e., how humans perceive

22. Aaron Brody, "Materiality of Religion in Judean Households: A Contextual Analysis of Ritual Objects from Iron II Tell en-Nasbeh," *NEA* 81.3 (2018): 212–21.

23. David Morgan, ed., *Religion and Material Culture: The Matter of Belief* (London: Routledge, 2009); Morgan, "Material Culture of Lived Religions," 14–31. Morgan consistently refers to "sense," "ways of feeling," and "perception." See also Morgan's comments about a variety of historical studies where he notes the importance of historiographic issues, including the ability to reconstruct contexts in which images are viewed, social settings, and human responses, in his article "Visual Religion," *Religion* 30 (2000): 41–53.

24. Kristine Henriksen Garroway, "Enculturating Children in Eighth-Century Judah," in Farber and Wright, *Archaeology and History*, 415–29, esp. 418–20; Garroway, "Children and Religion in the Archaeological Record of Ancient Israel," *Journal of Near Eastern Religions* 17.2 (2017): 116–39; Garroway, *Growing Up in Ancient Israel: Children in Material Culture and Biblical Text* (Atlanta: SBL Press, 2018).

25. Garroway, "Enculturating Children," 419–20.

themselves, the world, and their social relations) and objective structures (i.e., the structures external to their own perceptions). While concepts like *habitus* have found their way into a variety of material culture studies, particularly approaches to Israelite identity, in some cases scholars have overlooked the level of information that Bourdieu found necessary for practice theory.[26] This is a significant loss.

While Bourdieu does aim to identify cross-cultural structures, he takes the following as his starting point: "My entire scientific enterprise is indeed based on the belief that the deepest logic of the social world can be grasped *only if one plunges into the particularity of an empirical reality, historically located and dated,* but with the objective of constructing it as a 'special case of what is possible,' ... that is, as an exemplary case in a finite world of possible configurations."[27] To begin the comparative enterprise Bourdieu has in mind, we must first have access to as much information as possible—but what is the proper threshold?

When Bourdieu discusses comparison, he suggests that structures of *habitus* present in, say, the French educational system, could also characterize Japanese society, but he suggests testing that hypothesis by engaging in a thorough analysis of the Japanese context. He does not suggest using the French system as a predictive model to fill in details we do not know about modern Japan, and he allows that Japan and France could be quite different. In other words, we must have enough information to test whether a given sociocultural context reflects a theory of *habitus* rather than assuming that it does. Ultimately, does our knowledge of ancient Israel rise to this standard?

---

26. E.g., Dermot Anthony Nestor, *Cognitive Perspectives on Israelite Identity* (New York: T&T Clark, 2010); Avraham Faust, "The Emergence of Iron Age Israel: On Origins and Habitus," in *Israel's Exodus in Transdisciplinary Perspective: Text, Archaeology, Culture and Geoscience*, ed. T. E. Levy, T. Schneider and W. H. C. Propp (New York: Springer, 2015), 470–71; David Ilan, "Household Gleanings from Iron I Tel Dan," in *Household Archaeology in Ancient Israel and Beyond*, ed. Assaf Yasur-Landau, Jennie R. Ebeling, and Laura B. Mazow (Leiden: Brill, 2011), 152–53. Some of these authors, like Faust, toggle between Bourdieu's work and Giddens's theory of structuration. Giddens is commonly invoked in discussions of Israelite and Judean nationalism, at least since the early 1990s; e.g., Steven Grosby, "Religion and Nationality in Antiquity: The Worship of Yahweh and Ancient Israel," *European Journal of Sociology* 32.2 (1991): 229–65. For a contrasting perspective, critical of whether archaeology provides enough information to assess habitus (here in a discussion of ethnicity), see Raz Kletter, "In the Footsteps of Bagira: Ethnicity, Archaeology, and 'Iron Age I Ethnic Israel,'" *Approaching Religion* 4.2 (2014): 2–15. For a reevaluation of Giddens's work, including a discussion of its applicability in different social settings, see Ian Craib, *Anthony Giddens* (London: Routledge, 1992).

27. Pierre Bourdieu. "Social Space and Symbolic Space," in *Practical Reason: On the Theory of Action* (Stanford: Stanford University Press, 1998), 2 (emphasis mine).

ERIN DARBY

JUDEAN PILLAR FIGURINES AND THE IDENTIT(IES) OF ANCIENT BELIEVERS

Salience, Subjectivity, and Institutional Infrastructure

An entirely different approach to identity takes place within social scientific research focusing on in-group and out-group behaviors and measuring "salience."[28] The question of salience asks us to evaluate the larger infrastructure of societal relations in order to identify the mechanics of identity formation. Salience requires that we consider the possibility of competing identities, ranked identities, and the way various social networks and geographic contexts impact identity salience. We cannot assume that, even if identity is a cross-cultural concept, that salience of particular identities would remain unchanged overtime. Even though the student of ancient religion will never reach the data benchmarks necessary to address the identity salience of populations we cannot interview and whose self-testimony we do not have, the literature reminds us about the complexity of identity (or identities) situated in differing social, historical, cultural, and economic contexts.

Quite different in method but similar in their mutual demand for specificity are the writings of Foucault and Althusser. Both focus on the particular mechanisms through which subjects are constituted, such as societal institutions. Moreover, within the framework of Marxist critique, both thinkers are prone to see historical ruptures or disjunctions that reflect particular structures of power in particular

---

28. Note that these studies have been criticized as paying too little attention to specificity and diversity even within a modern context. Moreover, almost all applications of this approach to identity require access to the lived testimony of a statistically significant set of participants. Gary R. Weaver and Bradley R. Agle, "Religiosity and Ethical Behavior in Organizations: A Symbolic Interactionist Perspective," *The Academy of Management Review* 27.1 (2002): 77–97; James E. King Jr., "(Dis)Missing the Obvious: Will Mainstream Management Research Ever Take Religion Seriously?" *Journal of Management Inquiry* 17.3 (2008): 214–24; J. C. Turner et al., *Rediscovering the Social Group: A Self-Categorization Theory* (Oxford: Blackwell, 1987); George B. Cunningham, "The Influence of Religious Personal Identity on the Relationships among Religious Dissimilarity, Value Dissimilarity, and Job Satisfaction," *Social Justice Research* 23.1 (2010): 60–76; Diether Gebert et al., "Expressing Religious Identities in the Workplace: Analyzing a Neglected Diversity Dimension," *Human Relations* 67 (2014): 543–63; Vetta Sanders Thompson, "Variables Affecting Racial-Identity Salience among African Americans," *Journal of Social Psychology* 139.6 (2000): 748–61; H. Tajfel and J. C. Turner, "The Social Identity Theory of Intergroup Behavior," in *Psychology of Intergroup Relations*, ed. S. Worchel and W. G. Austin, 2nd ed. (Chicago: Nelson Hall, 1986), 7–24; S. Stryker, *Symbolic Interactionism: A Social Structural Version* (Menlo Park, CA: Benjamin/Cummings, 1980); S. Stryker and R. T. Serpe, "Commitment, Identity Salience, and Role Behavior: Theory and Research Example," in *Personality, Roles, and Social Behavior*, ed. W. Ickes and E. S. Knowles (New York: Springer, 1982), 199–218.

(Be)li(e)ving in a Material World

historical epochs rather than to assume one overarching way subjects are constituted across time and space. Thus, theorists like Foucault and Althusser grounded their theoretical paradigms in the early modern and modern periods and within the geographical context of Europe and America. They contrasted their analysis of modern subject-hood with the premodern and non-Western. It is almost impossible to understand these theories apart from the institutions that they examine, such as modern educational systems, mental hospitals, prisons, criminal justice systems, and religious institutions. We are told that unique modern (and Western) instantiations of "the state" and even the family provide the basis for understanding how modern subjectivity, and thereby identity, is hailed and negotiated.[29]

Ideological criticism of the biblical text or ancient Israel has a relatively long life in modern biblical studies, ranging from Gottwald to Boer and Yee.[30] Nevertheless, even these reconstructions of ancient modes of production, institutions, and ideologies are challenged by the gaps in our knowledge about the past. Without a fairly complete reconstruction of these objective structures, it is all but impossible to understand how and in what ways ancient inhabitants imagine their identities and whether they had what we might call "subjectivities."

Judean Pillar Figurines, Judeans, and Political Economy

Despite the challenges, I would like to argue that any reconstruction of ancient belief or believers must start from a consideration of social institutions and political economy. Moreover, this approach might do more to shift our understandings of ancient believers than have the approaches surveyed above, which, despite their use of a variety of methodological lenses, largely maintain the same interpretation of JPFs—that they are associated with women or fertility. To test this approach, the following section evaluates how our reconstruction of believers changes if we start from the social, political, and economic conditions at the time JPFs became popular.

---

29. Michel Foucault, *Madness and Civilization: A History of Insanity in the Age of Reason*, trans. Richard Howard (New York: Vintage, 1988); Foucault, *Discipline and Punish: The Birth of the Prison*, trans. Alan Sheridan (New York: Vintage, 1995); Foucault, *The History of Sexuality Volume 1: An Introduction*, trans. Robert Hurley (New York: Vintage, 1990); Louis Althusser, *On the Reproduction of Capitalism: Ideology and Ideological State Apparatuses*, trans. G. M. Goshgarian (London: Verso, 2014).

30. Norman K. Gottwald, *The Tribes of Yahweh: A Sociology of Religion of Liberated Israel 1250–1050 B. C. E.* (Maryknoll, NY: Orbis, 1979); Roland Boer, *The Sacred Economy of Ancient Israel* (Louisville: Westminster John Knox, 2015), esp. 41–44; Gale Yee, *Poor Banished Children of Eve: Woman as Evil in the Hebrew Bible* (Minneapolis: Fortress, 2003).

Much of our understanding of household religion in ancient Israel has focused on the role of agriculture in ancient Israel's economic system and daily life, particularly in the eighth century. Authors have also attempted to understand the interplay of agricultural systems and themes in Israelite religion.[31] Many have taken seriously the difficult environmental conditions that marked daily subsistence in ancient Israel. Owing to the realization of these data, some scholars have then hypothesized about the importance of "fertility" in the ancient Israelite hierarchy of needs, likening the fertility of the land to that of the herd and even the family. So the narrative goes, fertility was a principle concern in this harsh landscape, therefore creating the presumed centrality of fertility rituals in the Iron I and II periods.

In a more practical sense, the hypothesis that portrays all of ancient Israel and Judah as subsistence farmers further undergirds the assumption that family size was a driving ritual need, if for no other reason than the economic viability of the family farm. Thus the hypothesized family economy can be used to argue for the prevalence of fertility concerns in family religion.[32]

Of course, once fertility is mentioned, scholarship can barely resist the desire to discuss the endemic clay females holding their breasts found throughout Judah in the eighth through sixth centuries BCE. Owing to typical interpretations of the iconography, scholars commonly connect these figurines with either fertility-inducing rituals or females explicitly, especially in the home.[33] When combined with the difficult landscape and concomitant health concerns related to female

31. David C. Hopkins, "Bare Bones: Putting Flesh on the Economics of Ancient Israel," in *The Origins of the Ancient Israelite States*, ed. Volkmar Fritz and Philip R. Davies (Sheffield: Sheffield Academic Press, 1996), 121–39; Hopkins, "Agriculture," in *Oxford Encyclopedia of Archaeology in the Near East*, ed., Eric M. Meyers (New York: Oxford University Press, 1997), 1:22–30. Carol Meyers, *Discovering Eve: Ancient Israelite Women in Context* (Oxford: Oxford University Press, 1988); Meyers, "Terracottas without Texts: Judean Pillar Figurines in Anthropological Perspective," in *To Break Every Yoke: Essays in Honor of Marvin L. Chaney*, ed. Robert B. Coote and Norman K. Gottwald (Sheffield: Sheffield Phoenix, 2007), 115–30; Meyers, *Rediscovering Eve: Ancient Israelite Women in Context* (Oxford: Oxford University Press, 2013); Avraham Faust, "The Farmstead in the Highlands of Iron Age II Israel," in *The Rural Landscape of Ancient Israel*, ed. A. M. Maeir, S. Dar, and Z. Safrai (Oxford: Archaeopress, 2003), 91–204; Faust, "Households Economics in the Kingdoms of Israel and Judah," in *Household Archaeology in the Bronze and Iron Age Levant*, ed. Assaf Yasur-Landau, Jennifer Ebeling, and Laura Mazow (Leiden: Brill, 2011), 255–73.

32. Meyers, "Terracottas without Texts," 215–30; Meyers, *Rediscovering Eve*, 52, 101–2.

33. Darby, *Interpreting Judean Pillar Figurines*, 55–59; Erin Darby, "Judean Pillar Figurines and the Making of Female Piety in Israelite Religion," in *Gods, Objects, and Ritual Practice*, ed. Sandra Blakely (Atlanta: Lockwood, 2017), 193–214; Erin Darby, "Sex in the City? Judean Pillar Figurines and the Archaeology of Jerusalem," in *Iron Age Terracotta Figurines from the Southern Levant in Context*, ed. Erin Darby and Izaak J de Hulster (Leiden: Brill, 2022), 178–214.

and infant mortality, this constellation of agricultural, economic, and environmental factors seems to justify interpretations focusing on fertility, females, and their offspring.[34]

One response to this problem is to interrogate the particular readings of JPF iconography in such a way that challenges the association between JPFs, females, and fertility, and such a move has been done elsewhere.[35] Once arguments on iconographic grounds are isolated and removed, it becomes apparent that few archaeological data indicate JPFs were used only for fertility or solely by females. Even their location in domestic units cannot be used to argue strongly for this association, unless we assume that only women lived in Israelite houses or that the only thing going on there was sex and child-rearing.

Fertility and Household Economy in Population Centers

Yet another way of approaching the problem is to interrogate the mode of production and household economy that marked the period during which JPFs rise to prominence, namely, the eighth century. While agricultural subsistence hardships are often assumed to characterize the entire Iron I and II period (see below), in reality this period saw some marked shifts in political economy and mode of production. This is not to say that agriculture ceased to be an influence in the lives of Israelites in the eighth through sixth centuries, but this period witnessed significant changes in Judah's imperial and economic contexts.

The Iron IIB and C periods saw further urbanization in Judah, and material culture indicates a shift in the organization of labor in some major cities like Jerusalem.[36] In particular, the rise of seals attesting to various divisions of labor; the development of administrative systems that governed the distribution of agricultural goods, like the *lmlk* and concentric circle handles; biblical texts that attest to a change in land ownership bearing directly on agricultural produce and subsistence; the shift toward the production of cash crops; and Judah's integration in a trade economy (including that of South Arabia) all indicate that the eighth century—the period during which JPFs appear and become popular—differed

---

34. Meyers, "Terracottas without Texts," 215–30; Rüdiger Schmitt, "Elements of Domestic Cult in Ancient Israel," in Rainer Albertz and Rüdiger Schmitt, *Family and Household Religion in Ancient Israel and the Levant* (Winona Lake, IN: Eisenbrauns, 2012), 57–219; cf. Meyers, *Rediscovering Eve*.

35. Darby, *Interpreting Judean Pillar Figurines*, 303–66.

36. Oded Borowski, *Agriculture in Iron Age Israel* (Boston: American Schools of Oriental Research, 2002), 9, 29, 165.

markedly from the general subsistence agricultural model that is often applied to the entire Iron Age.[37]

Here a word about "urban" or "urbanization" is in order. Investigations of settlement types often toggle between biblical terminology and archaeological data.[38]

37. Regarding the divisions of labor, see Joseph Blenkinsopp, "The Family in First Temple Israel," in *Families in Ancient Israel*, ed. Leo G. Perdue et al. (Louisville: Westminster John Knox, 1997), 85; Amihai Mazar, *Archaeology of the Land of the Bible* (New York: Doubleday, 1990), 455–58, 518–20; Nahman Avigad, *Hebrew Bullae from the Time of Jeremiah: Remnants of a Burnt Archive* (Jerusalem: Israel Exploration Society, 1986); Gabriel Barkay, "The Iron Age II–III," in *The Archaeology of Ancient Israel*, trans. R. Greenberg; ed. Amnon Ben-Tor (New Haven: Yale University Press, 1992), 326–27, 350. Concerning the administrative aspects of the seals, see Andrew Vaughn, *Theology, History, and Archaeology in the Chronicler's Account of Hezekiah* (Atlanta: Scholars Press, 1999), 185–219; Oded Lipschits, Omer Sergi, and Ido Koch, "Royal Judahite Jar Handles: Reconsidering the Chronology of the *lmlk* Stamp Impressions," *Tel Aviv* 37 (2010): 3–32; Lipschits, Sergi, and Koch, "Judahite Stamped and Incised Jar Handles: A Tool for Studying the History of Late Monarchic Judah," *Tel Aviv* 38 (2011): 5–41. Regarding land ownership issues and agricultural produce, see Baruch Halpern, "Jerusalem and the Lineages in the Seventh Century BCE: Kinship and the Rise of Individual Moral Liability," in *Law and Ideology in Monarchic Israel*, ed. Baruch Halpern and Deborah W. Hobson (Sheffield: Sheffield Academic, 1991), 59–91; Peter Machinist, "The Fall of Assyria in Comparative Ancient Perspective," in *Assyria 1995: Proceedings of the 10th Anniversary Symposium of the Neo-Assyrian Text Corpus Project Helsinki, September 7–11, 1995*, ed. Simo Parpola and Robert M. Whiting (Helsinki: Neo-Assyrian Text Corpus Project, 1997), 183–86; Kenton L. Sparks, *Ethnicity and Identity in Ancient Israel: Prolegomena to the Study of Ethnic Sentiments and Their Expression in the Hebrew Bible* (Winona Lake, IN: Eisenbrauns, 1998), 201–2, 217. On the shift to cash crops, see Borowski, *Agriculture in Iron Age Israel*, 8, 164. Concerning Judah's integration into a trade economy, see Ryan Byrne, "Early Assyrian Contact with Arabs and the Impact on Levantine Vassal Tribute," *BASOR* 331 (2003): 20; John S. Holladay Jr., "Hezekiah's Tribute, Long-Distance Trade, and the Wealth of Nations ca. 1000–600 BC: A New Perspective," in *Confronting the Past: Archaeological and Historical Essays on Ancient Israel in Honor of William G. Dever*, ed. Seymour Gitin, John E. Wright, and J. P. Dessel (Winona Lake, IN: Eisenbrauns, 2006), 309–31; Israel Finkelstein, "Kadesh Barnea: A Reevaluation of its Archaeology and History," *Tel Aviv* 37 (2010): 121–23.

38. Cf. Faust, "Farmstead in the Highlands of Iron II Israel," 91–204; Baruch A. Levine, "The Biblical 'Town' as Reality and Typology: Evaluating Biblical References to Towns and their Functions," in *Urbanization and Land Ownership in the Ancient Near East*, ed. Michael Hudson and Baruch A. Levine (Cambridge: Peabody Museum of Archaeology and Ethnology, 1999), 421–53; Oded Borowski, *Daily Life in Biblical Times* (Atlanta: Society of Biblical Literature, 2003); Volkmar Fritz, *The City in Ancient Israel* (Sheffield: Sheffield Academic, 1995); C. H. J. de Gues, *Towns in Ancient Israel and in the Southern Levant* (Leuven: Peeters; 2003); Philip Davies, "Urban Religion and Rural Religion," in *Religious Diversity in Ancient Israel and Judah*, ed. Francesca Stavrakopoulou and John Barton (London: T&T Clark, 2010), 104–17; William Dever, *The Lives of Ordinary People in Ancient Israel: Where Archaeology and the Bible Intersect* (Grand Rapids: Eerdmans, 2012); Meyers, "Terracottas without Texts," 215–30; Ziony Zevit, *The Religions of Ancient Israel: A Synthesis of Parallactic Approaches* (London: Continuum, 2001), 250, 265.

(Be)li(e)ving in a Material World

Dever rightly notes many of the relevant texts were recorded after the eighth century, making it difficult to correlate them with the archaeological evidence.[39] To complicate matters further, it has been noted that while עָרִים may refer to walled cities in the biblical text, these centers may exhibit few other characteristics that modern scholars would consider necessary for urbanization.[40] One of the implications of this type of position is the supposition that most household economies were little changed by the location of the household and remained focused on agricultural produce.[41]

As outlined above, the archaeology does in fact indicate shifts in political economy and social organization. The introduction of tribute requirements in the ninth century would certainly have had some effect on the household economy, even if that economy remained primarily agricultural.[42] Now, it might be argued that these shifts characterized capital cities more than sites like Tel en Nasbeh, Lachish, or Beersheba.[43] Still, it is naive to expect that vassalage had no effect on the organization of labor across the country. Moreover, at least in the hill country there is some indication of site specialization, such as wine production and storage at Gibeon, grain at Nasbeh, and a redistribution center at Moza, which may serve as evidence for the increase in agricultural specialization and a shift in distribution.[44]

39. Dever, *Lives of Ordinary People in Ancient Israel*, 50, 72, 102; Francesca Stavrakopoulou, "'Popular' Religion and 'Official' Religion: Practice, Perception, Portrayal," in Stavrakopoulou and Barton, *Religious Diversity in Ancient Israel and Judah*, 48.

40. Meyers, *Rediscovering Eve*, 40–42; Davies, "Urban Religion and Rural Religion," 104–17; Lester L. Grabbe, "Sup-Urbs or Only Hyp-Urbs? Prophets and Populations in Ancient Israel and Socio-Historical Method," in *Every City Shall Be Forsaken: Urbanism and Prophecy in Ancient Israel and the Near East*, ed. Lester L. Grabbe and R. D. Haak (Sheffield: Sheffield Academic, 2001), 95–123.

41. Meyers, *Rediscovering Eve*, 41–42; Volkmar Fritz, "Cities of the Bronze and Iron Ages," in Meyers, *Oxford Encyclopedia of Archaeology in the Near East*, 2:19–25; Phillip J. King and Lawrence E. Stager, *Life in Biblical Israel* (Louisville: Westminster John Knox, 2001), 5.

42. Blenkinsopp, "Family in First Temple Israel," 87–90; Halpern, "Jerusalem and the Lineages," 59–91; Faust, "Households Economics," 255–73).

43. Meyers, *Rediscovering Eve*, 41.

44. Zvi Greenhut and Alon de Groot, "Tel Moẓa in Context," in *Salvage Excavations at Tel Moẓa: The Bronze and Iron Age Settlements and Later Occupations*, ed. Zvi Greenhut, Alon de Groot, and Eldad Barzilay (Jerusalem: Israel Antiquities Authority, 2009), 217; Avraham Faust, "The Impact of Jerusalem's Expansion in the Late Iron Age on the Forms of Rural Settlements in its Vicinity," [Hebrew] *Cathedra* 84 (1997): 53–62; Nurit Feig, "The Environs of Jerusalem in the Iron Age II," [Hebrew] in *The Biblical Period (The History of Jerusalem)*, ed. Shmuel Aḥituv and Amihai Mazar (Jerusalem: Yad Ben Zvi, 2000), 387–409; Yehuda Dagan and Leticia Barda, "Jerusalem, Upper Naḥal Soreq Survey," *Hadashot Arkheologiyot* 121 (2009): https://www.hadashot-esi.

ERIN DARBY

There is no accurate way to predict what effect this shift might have had on the need or desire for family reproduction. One argument might be that the less a family controlled its own land, the less large-scale reproduction was necessary or sustainable.[45] This would depend on the size of land allotments, the amount of the produce families would retain, and the number of mouths to feed. At the same time, the ideal of large families with their own "portion" might live on, despite or even because this ceased to be the reality for many families living in population centers. In general, some biblical ideals celebrate the number of children born to a family as a sign of prosperity and blessing.[46] However, a more nefarious and perhaps realistic set of rules govern under what conditions a head of household may sell household members over to debt servitude, preserving an alternate reality that probably affected an increasing number of families as socioeconomic disparity increased.[47]

In sum, many scholars have addressed the household economy of the Iron I and II periods as a monolithic entity largely based on the assumption that household economy, whether in walled or unwalled settlements, remained relatively stable. Other scholars have recognized the impact of settlement type and political economy on households. Yet, few scholars have explored the significance of these shifts on the place of fertility rituals in the household and the rise of JPFs. It is to that end that we now turn.

Judean Pillar Figurines and Institutions in "Urban" Contexts

Urban Families and Household Economy

Current data suggest that JPFs were prominent in walled population centers, that they correspond to the population density at a given site, and that they appear much more intensively in such environments than in remote village settlements. Again, this could be an accident of preservation, but in these same cities, like Je-

---

org.il/Report_Detail_Eng.aspx?id=1222; Raphael Greenberg and Gilad Cinamon, "Stamped and Incised Jar Handles from Rogem Gannim and Their Implications for the Political Economy of Jerusalem: Late 8th–Early 4th Centuries B. C. E.," *Tel Aviv* 33 (2006): 229–43, Lipschits, Sergi, and Koch, "Royal Judahite Jar Handles," 18–21; Jeffrey R. Zorn, "Tell en Nasbeh: A Reevaluation of the Architecture and Stratigraphy of the Early Bronze Age, Iron Age, and Later Periods" (PhD diss., University of California, Berkeley, 1993), 251–54, 256.

45. Meyers, *Rediscovering Eve*, 41–42; Faust, "Households Economics," 255–73.

46. Borowski, *Daily Life in Biblical Times*, 81–83; Meyers, "Terracottas without Texts," 115–30; Meyers, *Rediscovering Eve*, 158; Hopkins, "Bare Bones," 484.

47. Meyers, *Rediscovering Eve*, 101–2; Blenkinsopp, "Family in First Temple Israel," 55–56.

(Be)li(e)ving in a Material World

rusalem and the surrounding area, we do have evidence for the division of labor and the diversified management of agricultural production.

In fact, if we arrange JPFs with known provenience along a hierarchy of sites, we see that figurines are most prominent in walled settlements with monumental structures with some evidence of city planning.[48] This makes it rather odd that some have discussed these objects in the context of village or rural religion.[49] That having been said, the question remains: who might have been using JPFs in these urban contexts? The answer to this question depends in large part on who was living in these population centers. In Joseph Blenkinsopp's opinion, "In identifying the typical household as an agrarian unit, we should add that we know practically nothing about the urban family during the Israelite monarchy."[50] Moreover, Oded Borowski says that "what differentiates the Israelite city from other types of settlement is its concentration of a large population and its lack of dependence on agriculture for its livelihood."[51] Complicating this point, scholarly characterizations of cities have sometimes underrepresented segments of the population, such as tradesmen or day laborers.[52] These scholars have claimed that inhabitants of cities were largely affiliated with temple and palace, particularly upper-class citizens, suggesting that the shift to nonagricultural functions in cities caused most inhabitants to vacate urban areas and consequently move into the countryside.[53]

In contrast, to take Jerusalem as an example, there is little evidence for a contraction in size until the seventh century.[54] In fact, the city continued to grow throughout the eighth century, during the time when such a shift toward

48. Borowski, *Daily Life in Biblical Times*, 14; Raz Kletter, *The Judean Pillar-Figurines and the Archaeology of Asherah* (Oxford: Tempus Reparatum, 1996), fig. 16.

49. E.g., Borowski, *Daily Life in Biblical Times*, 24–25.

50. Blenkinsopp, "Family in First Temple Israel," 54.

51. Borowski, *Daily Life in Biblical Times*, 43, 55.

52. E.g., the characterization of Borowski, *Daily Life in Biblical Times*, 13, 54; Fritz, *City in Ancient Israel*; Fritz, "Cities of the Bronze and Iron Ages," 19–25 ; Ze'ev Herzog, *Archaeology of the City: Urban Planning in Ancient Israel and Its Social Implications* (Tel Aviv: Emery and Claire Yass Archaeology Press, 1997). Regarding tradespeople and day laborers in particular, note Blenkinsopp "Family in First Temple Israel," 54; Borowski, *Daily Life in Biblical Times*, 30, 55–56.

53. Borowski, *Daily Life in Biblical Times*, 44; Herzog, *Archaeology of the City*, 276.

54. Israel Finkelstein, "Environmental Archaeology and Social History: Demographic and Economic Aspects of the Monarchic Period," in *Biblical Archaeology Today, 1990: Proceedings of the Second International Congress on Biblical Archaeology*, ed. Amiran Biran and J. Aviram (Jerusalem: Israel Exploration Society and the Israel Academy of Sciences and Humanities, 1993), 56–66; Finkelstein, "The Archaeology of the Days of Manasseh," in *Scripture and Other Artifacts: Essays on the Bible and Archaeology in Honor of Philip J. King*, ed. Michael D. Coogan, J. Cheryl Exum, and Lawrence E. Stager (Louisville: Westminster John Knox, 1994), 169–86; Alon de Groot and Hannah Bernick-Greenberg, eds., *Area E: Stratigraphy and Architecture: Text*, vol. 7A of *Ex-*

centralization and reorganization in bureaucratic management would be taking place.[55] Furthermore, while portions of "urban" populations might have been affiliated with temple or royal personnel (e.g., Area G of the City of David), scholars should not discount the presence of other occupants. For example, the capital city domestic quarters include what we presume to be nonelites, particularly on the southwestern hill.[56] Nonelites have also been associated with Area E of the City of David.[57] These neighborhoods might be comparable to structures in other cities, like Nasbeh and Gibeon.[58] This implies that not all urban citizens were elite occupants, arguing not for a middle class per se but rather something between the city's elites and the rural peasants, as William Dever has suggested.[59]

In the case of Jerusalem, JPFs are found in neighborhoods of all economic types, suggesting little correlation to status.[60] Once again, their presence in most population centers throughout Judah seems to indicate that they correlate with population density. The earliest possible fragments also arise in population centers, undergirding the hypothesis that population centers were important for the rise of JPFs.[61] Given the current state of excavation and publication for outlying settlements, it is difficult to compare and contrast JPF frequency in these sites with the patterns in population centers. Indeed, fragments are known from unwalled settlements as well, though certainly less numerous.[62] In sum, the com-

---

cavations at the City of David, 1978–1985: Directed by Yigal Shiloh (Jerusalem: Hebrew University of Jerusalem Press, 2012), 162.

55. De Groot and Bernick-Greenberg, *Excavations at the City of David*, 159–60.

56. Hillel Geva, "Western Jerusalem at the End of the First Temple Period in Light of the Excavations in the Jewish Quarter," in *Jerusalem in Bible and Archaeology*, ed. Andrew G. Vaughn and Ann E. Killebrew (Atlanta: Society of Biblical Literature, 2003), 206–7; Geva, "The Settlement on the Southwestern Hill of Jerusalem at the End of the Iron Age: A Reconstruction Based on the Archaeological Evidence," *ZDPV* 122 (2006): 140–50; cf. Avraham Faust, "The Settlement of Jerusalem's Western Hill and the City's Status in Iron Age II Revisited." *ZDPV* 121 (2005): 97–118.

57. De Groot and Bernick-Greenberg, *Excavations at the City of David*, passim.

58. For Nasbeh, see Chester Charleton McCowan, *Tell en-Nasbeh Excavated under the Direction of the Late William Frederic Badè*, vol. 1 (Berkeley: The Palestine Institute of Pacific School of Religion and the American Schools of Oriental Research, 1947). For Gibeon, see James Bennett Pritchard, *The Water System of Gibeon* (Philadelphia: University Museum, University of Pennsylvania, 1961); Pritchard, *Gibeon: Where the Sun Stood Still; The Discovery of the Biblical City* (Princeton: Princeton University Press, 1962).

59. Dever, *Lives of Ordinary People in Ancient Israel*, 233–38, 322

60. Darby, *Interpreting Judean Pillar Figurines*, 151–75.

61. Darby, *Interpreting Judean Pillar-Figurines*, 213–23.

62. Kletter, *Judean Pillar-Figurines*; Darby, *Interpreting Judean Pillar Figurines*, 230–39.

bined knowledge of JPF provenience resulting from over a century of study argues against relegating the figurines to rural agricultural settlements.

It may also be possible to see the diversification of labor in urban centers reflected in the pantheon and the divine entities invoked by JPFs. This would first require us to expand our idea of what "figure" the figurines represent. While major goddesses of the pantheon have been the targets of scholarly hypotheses, lower-level divine entities are excluded almost entirely.[63] Again, the figurines are not labeled with the name of any goddess, and most naked female images stretching back to the Old Babylonian period remain unidentified. The premises associating JPFs with major goddesses are twofold. First, any anthropomorphic depiction from Judah must represent an important deity (unless textual evidence suggests otherwise, as in the case of Bes). Second, free-standing anthropomorphic images represented the entity supplicated in any accompanying rituals.

Both of these assumptions remain unsupported. There is a plethora of evidence for lower-level divine entities both in texts and iconographic objects in the Levant.[64] Given the lack of implements, headdresses, and the horns of divinity on JPFs, there is nothing in the iconography to suggest any association with an important female deity.[65] Furthermore, coterminous figurine rituals from elsewhere in the Neo-Assyrian empire suggest that main deities of the pantheon are usually the recipients of supplications in figurine rituals and not the entity represented by the figurine itself.[66] In Late Bronze Ugarit, El is actually attributed with creating a clay female image (Shatiqatu) to heal King Kirtu, but the clay female is only a mediatrix, and the healing is attributed to El.[67]

If the JPFs are a lower-level deity or a protective image, akin to Shatiqatu in the Ugaritic corpus, then perhaps there is some correlation between the increase of bureaucratic positions and the popularization of mid-level bureaucratic deities. Lowell Handy has shown, in fact, that at the same time when more individuals found themselves being supported somewhere between the royal house and the farm, so, too, a host of lower-level deities arose who also performed medial functions between high gods and humans.[68] Thus, the popularization of JPFs in these

63. Darby, *Interpreting Judean Pillar Figurines*, 44–46, 311–63. Cf. most recently McCormick, "My Eyes Are Up Here," 164–96.

64. E.g., Mark Smith, *The Memoirs of God: History, Memory, and the Experience of the Divine in Ancient Israel* (Minneapolis: Augsburg, 2004), 86–119; Zevit, *Religions of Ancient Israel*, 651.

65. Meyers, "Terracottas without Texts," 115–30.

66. Darby, *Interpreting Judean Pillar Figurines*, 81–97.

67. Darby, *Interpreting Judean Pillar Figurines*, 337, 362, with literature.

68. Lowell K. Handy, *Among the Host of Heaven: The Syro-Palestinian Pantheon as Bureaucracy* (Winona Lake, IN: Eisenbrauns, 1994), 162–63.

same contexts might be tied to changing conceptions about lower-level divine entities and the ability to use these protective images in domestic spaces rather than shrine spaces.

Reframing JPFs in this way complicates the narrative that undergirds the presumed need for family fertility to run the family farm. The JPFs arise in urban contexts during a time when at least some of the cities' inhabitants were no longer supporting themselves solely by subsistence agriculture. Even if we presume that agriculture and fertility were strongly embedded in Judean values—regardless of whether numerous children were necessary[69]—this situation is quite different and deserves examination in its own right as a crystallized value at odds with the necessary conditions of city life.

Urban Potters

Furthermore, focusing our attention on JPFs as part of Judean urbanization and economic differentiation may lead to a more particular investigation of the institutions responsible for navigating daily life. I have argued elsewhere that we lack any clear support that JPFs were produced by the state or by state-run workshops.[70] The ceramic production industry in urban centers is, however, worthy of more serious investigation. While some pottery items could be produced in each home (e.g., particularly unfired objects), evidence from sites like Jerusalem indicates that the ceramics industry was already professionalized by the eighth century, with potters working in population centers and sometimes exporting their wares to other sites in Judah.[71] Additionally, many southern sites during the eighth century saw the introduction of the fast wheel and mass production.[72]

If JPFs are affiliated with a ceramics industry, the same vagaries that affect the professionalization of that gild and their role at individual sites would also

69. Borowski, *Daily Life in Biblical Times*, 81.

70. Darby, *Interpreting Judean Pillar Figurines*, 189–200.

71. Alon de Groot and Hannah Bernick-Greenberg. "The Pottery of Strata 12–10," in *Area E: The Finds*, ed. Alon de Groot and Hannah Bernick-Greenberg, vol. 7B of *Excavations at the City of David, 1978–1985: Directed by Yigal Shiloh* (Jerusalem: Hebrew University of Jerusalem Press, 2012), 57–198; Nava Panitz-Cohen, "The Pottery Assemblage," in *Yavneh 1: The Excavation of the 'Temple Hill' Repository Pit and the Cult Stands*, ed. Raz Kletter, Irit Ziffer, and Wolfgang Zwickel (Fribourg: Academic Press; Göttingen: Vandenhoeck & Ruprecht, 2010), 110–45.

72. Margreet Steiner, "Stratigraphical Analysis, Architecture and Objects of the Phases," in *The Iron Age Extramural Quarter on the South-East Hill*, ed. Hendricus J. Franken and Margreet L. Steiner, vol. 2 of *Excavations in Jerusalem 1961–1967* (Oxford: Oxford University Press, 1990), 3–60; Hendricus J. Franken, *A History of Pottery and Potters in Ancient Jerusalem* (London: Equinox, 2005).

affect the creation and distribution of figurines. This would tie the production and popularization of JPFs to a different organization of labor that reflected the increased importance and diversification of tradesmen and, presumably, their families. It also suggests that potters and craft specialists, as believers in their own right, deserve more consistent attention.[73]

Urban Apotropaic Religious Officials

Furthermore, figurine count might also correlate with the multiplication of ritual officials in population centers who can perform figurine rituals. In comparison, both Assyrian and Egyptian figurine rituals spanning from the Late Bronze through the Iron II period were led by a variety of religious officials, many of which also had strong ties to temples. Figurines were regularly used for many different concerns, including illness and danger in the home.[74] Once more, regardless of where figurine rituals related to illness and protection took place, many texts suggest that professionals associated with the temple were involved.

In comparison, from the end of the seventh century the City of David Area G, where copious figurines were found, housed elites possibly connected with the temple and royal house.[75] In this same period, some of the ritual officials performing magicomedical, exorcistic, and apotropaic rituals in Assyrian centers were also scribes.[76] In fact, Area G produced evidence for a variety of ritual officials, including one seal belonging to "a healer" in the House of the Bullae corpus.[77] Christopher Rollston has hypothesized that Area G "was an area of substantial epigraphic activity" adding that some royal and temple officials could have been literate as well.[78] This is not to presume that we know who performed JPF rituals or that JPFs functioned the same as figurine rituals elsewhere, but rather that

---

73. Darby, *Interpreting Judean Pillar Figurines*, 183–212; David Ben-Shlomo and Erin Darby, "A Study of the Production of Iron Age Clay Figurines from Jerusalem," *Tel Aviv* 41 (2014): 180–204. Note also Erin Darby, "From Material Symbols to Symbolic Materials: A Production Approach to Ancient Near Eastern Iconography," in *Through the Eyes of the Ancient Near East: Othmar Keel's Symbolism of the Biblical World Fifty Years Later*, ed. Ryan Bonfiglio, Brent Strawn, and Joel LeMon (Göttingen: Vandenhoeck & Ruprecht, forthcoming).

74. Darby, *Interpreting Judean Pillar Figurines*, 61–97, with literature.

75. Darby, *Interpreting Judean Pillar Figurines*, 151–60, 176–83, 209.

76. Darby, *Interpreting Judean Pillar Figurines*, 61–97, with literature.

77. Yair Shoham, "A Group of Hebrew Bullae from Yigal Shiloh's Excavations in the City of David," in *Ancient Jerusalem Revealed*, ed. Hillel Geva (Jerusalem: Israel Exploration Society, 1994), 58.

78. Christopher Rollston, *Writing and Literacy in the World of Ancient Israel: Epigraphic Evidence from the Iron Age* (Atlanta: Society of Biblical Literature, 2010), 119, 129–30, 131, 132.

we cannot automatically assume figurines belonged to some household sphere of religious identity that was necessarily separated from other levels of religious experience or cultic personnel.

Furthermore, it could be that we need to readjust our idea of the function of figurines. What type of needs might have arisen uniquely in population centers that had more cosmopolitan populations than the village hinterland?[79] As has been demonstrated, fertility for the family farm would not necessarily explain this pattern. One answer might be the deadly pestilence, noted as the gravest concern in the biblical text.[80] In fact, the Assyrian center experienced a number of plagues in the ninth through the eighth centuries, and some of the figurine rituals from Iron II Assyria that deposited protective guardians in the home were meant to combat illness.[81] As the empire saw the increase of population movement due to trade, warfare, and urbanization, perhaps urban landscapes presented unique conditions for the spread of disease and challenges for public health that might require a variety of responses.

Conclusions

As expected, the study of belief and believers in ancient Judah poses a great many challenges. Belief has always been a thorny taxonomic category for Judaism and the ancient Near East. In the attempt to avoid an abstracted, text-centered, elite, and disembodied approach to belief, the field of religious studies has adopted a variety of modern theoretical approaches that treat belief and believers as complex, embodied, contradictory, and contextualized entities. These newer approaches take into consideration the way humans across varying socioeconomic statuses can be structured by institutions and environments, spaces and objects.

While most of these theories are meant as heuristic devices for understanding subject formation and praxis in modern and contemporary settings, scholars of ancient Israel, including figurine specialists, have attempted to apply them to the ancient world, often under the rubric of "identity." This application poses particular challenges given the paucity of information about how ancient communities encountered ritual spaces and artifacts as well as the institutions that enabled daily life. It runs the risk of transforming analytical tools into predictive models

79. See also Davies, "Urban Religion and Rural Religion," 109.

80. Meyers, *Rediscovering Eve*, 54; Borowski, *Agriculture in Iron Age Israel*, 158–61; Borowski, *Daily Life in Biblical Times*, 77–78.

81. Darby, "Reaction, Reliance, Resistance," 128–49, with literature.

(Be)li(e)ving in a Material World

that are then used to fill in what we do not know about ancient Israel. In so doing, we may inadvertently ignore significant differences in the way believers operated that might differ from our own modern and contemporary settings. One casualty of that risk is that scholars adopting a wide variety of theoretical approaches to JPFs all roughly portray beliefs about figurines and figurine users the same way, an interpretation that has been little changed since the early twentieth century.

In contrast, this chapter has argued that the best way for historians and archaeologists to access ancient believers is to begin with an attentiveness to the objective structures that governed daily life, including political economies and social institutions. Historiography will likely always fall short of the amount of information required for a complete reconstruction that reflects total cultural specificity, but the approach can be used to test our reconstructions of the past and to highlight the complexity of ancient believers' competing, contested, and complimentary identities.

When seen in this light, whatever interactive relationship JPFs shared with believers was likely dictated by changes in the urban household economy, any concomitant impacts on the structure of households, the diversification of labor roles in population centers, the rise of craft guilds and the professionalization of ceramic producers in urban settings, and the interaction between household units and ritual specialists, particularly at times when the participants were in need of protection from sickness or other dangers common in dense settlements connected throughout the broader region. To the extent that JPFs structured and were structured by Judean believers in the Iron IIB and C period, they likely served as a node at the intersection of various institutional systems and related identities.

Were more known about the environmental conditions through which any given believer viewed the objects, or even the appearance of the figurines themselves when complete with whitewash and paint, more might be posited about the interaction between the believers and the objects. Nor can we say how the figurines were manipulated in ritual, who would have held them, or where they were stationed during the ritual intervention. In the absence of those details, it is unlikely we will be able to reconstruct the complexity of how different houses, neighborhoods, or population centers were variously structured by their interactions with figurines.

Works Cited

Althusser, Louis. *On the Reproduction of Capitalism: Ideology and Ideological State Apparatuses.* Translated by G. M. Goshgarian. London: Verso, 2014.

Bailey, Douglass W. *Prehistoric Figurines: Representation and Corporeality in the Neolithic*. London: Routledge, 2005.

Barkay, Gabriel. "The Iron Age II–III." Pages 302–73 in *The Archaeology of Ancient Israel*. Translated by Raphael Greenberg. Edited by Amnon Ben-Tor. New Haven: Yale University Press, 1992.

Bell, Catherine. *Ritual Theory, Ritual Practice*. New York: Oxford University Press, 1992.

Ben-Shlomo, David, and Erin Darby. "A Study of the Production of Iron Age Clay Figurines from Jerusalem." *Tel Aviv* 41 (2014): 180–204.

Blenkinsopp, Joseph. "The Family in First Temple Israel." Pages 48–103 in *Families in Ancient Israel*. Edited by Leo G. Perdue, Joseph Blenkinsopp, John J. Collins, and Carol Meyers. Louisville: Westminster John Knox, 1997.

Boer, Roland. *The Sacred Economy of Ancient Israel*. Louisville: Westminster John Knox, 2015.

Bonfiglio, Ryan P. *Reading Images, Seeing Texts: Towards a Visual Hermeneutics for Biblical Studies*. Fribourg: Academic Press; Göttingen: Vandenhoeck & Ruprecht, 2016.

Borowski, Oded. *Agriculture in Iron Age Israel*. Boston: American Schools of Oriental Research, 2002.

———. *Daily Life in Biblical Times*. Atlanta: Society of Biblical Literature, 2003.

Bourdieu, Pierre. "Social Space and Symbolic Space." Pages 1–13 in *Practical Reason: On the Theory of Action*. Stanford: Stanford University Press, 1998.

Brody, Aaron. "Materiality of Religion in Judean Households: A Contextual Analysis of Ritual Objects from Iron II Tell en-Nasbeh." *NEA* 81.3 (2018): 212–21.

Byrne, Ryan. "Early Assyrian Contact with Arabs and the Impact on Levantine Vassal Tribute." *BASOR* 331 (2003): 11–25.

———. "Lie Back and Think of Judah: The Reproductive Politics of Pillar Figurines." *NEA* 67.3 (2004): 137–51.

Craib, Ian. *Anthony Giddens*. London: Routledge, 1992.

Creel, Andrea M. "Connectivity on the Edge of Empire: Movement, Liminality, and Ritual in the Southern Levantine Drylands." PhD diss., University of California, Berkeley, 2017.

Cunningham, George B. "The Influence of Religious Personal Identity on the Relationships Among Religious Dissimilarity, Value Dissimilarity, and Job Satisfaction." *Social Justice Research* 23.1 (2010): 60–76.

Dagan, Yehuda, and Leticia Barda. "Jerusalem, Upper Naḥal Soreq Survey." *Hadashot Arkheologiyot* 121 (2009): http://www.hadashot- esi.org.il/report_detail_eng.asp?id= 1222&mag_id=115.

Darby, Erin. "From Material Symbols to Symbolic Materials: A Production Approach to Ancient Near Eastern Iconography." In *Through the Eyes of the Ancient Near*

East: *Othmar Keel's Symbolism of the Biblical World Fifty Years Later*. Edited by Ryan Bonfiglio, Brent Strawn, and Joel LeMon. Göttingen: Vandenhoeck & Ruprecht, forthcoming.

———. *Interpreting Judean Pillar Figurines: Gender and Empire in Judean Apotropaic Ritual*. Tübingen: Mohr Siebeck, 2014.

———. "Judean Pillar Figurines and the Making of Female Piety in Israelite Religion." Pages 193–214 in *Gods, Objects, and Ritual Practice*. Edited by Sandra Blakely. Atlanta: Lockwood, 2017.

———. "Judean Pillar Figurines: Religion and National Identity in Eighth Century Judah." Pages 401–14 in *Archaeology and History of Eighth Century Judah*. Edited by Zev I. Farber and Jacob L. Wright. Atlanta: Society of Biblical Literature Press, 2018.

———. "Reaction, Reliance, Resistance: Judean Pillar Figurines in the Neo-Assyrian Levant." Pages 128–49 in *Imperial Peripheries in the Neo-Assyrian Period*. Edited by Craig W. Tyson and Virginia R. Herrmann. Boulder: University Press of Colorado, 2019.

———. "Sex in the City? Judean Pillar Figurines and the Archaeology of Jerusalem." Pages 178–214 in *Iron Age Terracotta Figurines from the Southern Levant in Context*. Edited by Erin Darby and Izaak J. de Hulster. Leiden: Brill, 2021.

Davies, Philip. "Urban Religion and Rural Religion." Pages 104–17 in *Religious Diversity in Ancient Israel and Judah*. Edited by Francesca Stavrakopoulou and John Barton. London: T&T Clark, 2010.

Dermot, Anthony Nestor. *Cognitive Perspectives on Israelite Identity*. New York: T&T Clark, 2010.

Dever, William. *The Lives of Ordinary People in Ancient Israel: Where Archaeology and the Bible Intersect*. Grand Rapids: Eerdmans, 2012.

Faust, Avraham. "The Emergence of Iron Age Israel: On Origins and Habitus." Pages 467–82 in *Israel's Exodus in Transdisciplinary Perspective: Text, Archaeology, Culture and Geoscience*. Edited by Thomas E. Levy, T. Schneider, and William H. C. Propp. New York: Springer, 2015.

———. "The Farmstead in the Highlands of Iron Age II Israel." Pages 91–204 in *The Rural Landscape of Ancient Israel*. Edited by Aaron M. Maeir, S. Dar, and Z. Safrai. Oxford: Archaeopress, 2003.

———. "Households Economics in the Kingdoms of Israel and Judah." Pages 255–73 in *Household Archaeology in the Bronze and Iron Age Levant*. Edited by Assaf Yasur-Landau, Jennifer Ebeling, and Laura Mazow. Leiden: Brill, 2011.

———. "The Impact of Jerusalem's Expansion in the Late Iron Age on the Forms of Rural Settlements in its Vicinity." [Hebrew] *Cathedra* 84 (1997): 53–62.

———. "An Imperial Encounter: The Egyptian Empire in Canaan, Highland

Ethnogenesis, and the Transformation of History." Pages 14–41 in *Power and Identity at the Margins of the Ancient Near East*. Edited by Sara Mohr and Shane Thompson. Denver: University Press of Colorado, 2023.

———. "The Settlement of Jerusalem's Western Hill and the City's Status in Iron Age II Revisited." *ZDPV* 121 (2005): 97–118.

Feig, Nurit. "The Environs of Jerusalem in the Iron Age II." [Hebrew] Pages 387–409 in *The Biblical Period (The History of Jerusalem)*. Edited by Shmuel Aḥituv and Amihai Mazar. Jerusalem: Yad Ben Zvi, 2000.

Finkelstein, Israel. "The Archaeology of the Days of Manasseh." Pages 169–86 in *Scripture and Other Artifacts: Essays on the Bible and Archaeology in Honor of Philip J. King*. Edited by Michael D. Coogan, J. Cheryl Exum, and Lawrence E. Stager. Louisville: Westminster John Knox, 1994.

———. "Environmental Archaeology and Social History: Demographic and Economic Aspects of the Monarchic Period." Pages 56–66 in *Biblical Archaeology Today, 1990: Proceedings of the Second International Congress on Biblical Archaeology*. Edited by Amiran Biran and J. Aviram. Jerusalem: Israel Exploration Society and the Israel Academy of Sciences and Humanities, 1993.

———. "Kadesh Barnea: A Reevaluation of its Archaeology and History." *Tel Aviv* 37 (2010): 111–25.

Fogelin, Lars. "The Archaeology of Religious Ritual." *Annual Review of Anthropology* 36 (2007): 55–71.

Franken, Hendricus J. *A History of Pottery and Potters in Ancient Jerusalem*. London: Equinox, 2005.

Fritz, Volkmar. "Cities of the Bronze and Iron Ages." Pages 19–25 in vol. 2 of *Oxford Encyclopedia of Archaeology in the Near East*. Edited by Eric M. Meyers. New York: Oxford University Press, 1997.

———. *The City in Ancient Israel*. Sheffield: Sheffield Academic, 1995.

Foucault, Michel. *Discipline and Punish: The Birth of the Prison*. Translated by Alan Sheridan. New York: Vintage, 1995.

———. *The History of Sexuality Volume 1: An Introduction*. Translated by Robert Hurley. New York: Vintage, 1990.

———. *Madness and Civilization: A History of Insanity in the Age of Reason*. Translated by Richard Howard. New York: Vintage, 1988.

Garroway, Kristine Henriksen. "Children and Religion in the Archaeological Record of Ancient Israel." *Journal of Near Eastern Religions* 17.2 (2017): 116–39.

———. "Enculturating Children in Eighth-Century Judah." Pages 415–29 in *Archaeology and History of Eighth-Century Judah*. Edited by Zev I. Farber and Jacob L. Wright. Atlanta: SBL Press, 2018.

———. *Growing Up in Ancient Israel: Children in Material Culture and Biblical Text*. Atlanta: Society of Biblical Literature, 2018.

Gebert, Diether, Sabine Boerner, Eric Kearney, James E. King Jr., Kai Zhang, and Lyndia Jiwen Song, "Expressing Religious Identities in the Workplace: Analyzing a Neglected Diversity Dimension." *Human Relations* 67 (2014): 543–63.

Geva, Hillel. "The Settlement on the Southwestern Hill of Jerusalem at the End of the Iron Age: A Reconstruction Based on the Archaeological Evidence." *ZDPV* 122 (2006): 140–50.

———. "Western Jerusalem at the End of the First Temple Period in Light of the Excavations in the Jewish Quarter." Pages 183–208 in *Jerusalem in Bible and Archaeology*. Edited by Andrew G. Vaughn and Ann E. Killebrew. Atlanta: Society of Biblical Literature, 2003.

Gottwald, Norman K. *The Tribes of Yahweh: A Sociology of Religion of Liberated Israel 1250–1050 B. C. E.* Maryknoll, NY: Orbis, 1979.

Grabbe, Lester L. "Sup-Urbs or Only Hyp-Urbs? Prophets and Populations in Ancient Israel and Socio-Historical Method." Pages 95–123 in *Every City Shall Be Forsaken: Urbanism and Prophecy in Ancient Israel and the Near East.* Edited by Lester L. Grabbe and R. D. Haak. Sheffield: Sheffield Academic, 2001.

Gramsci, Antonio. *The Prison Notebooks.* Edited and translated by Joseph Buttigieg. New York: Columbia University Press, 2011.

Greenberg, Raphael, and Gilad Cinamon. "Stamped and Incised Jar Handles from Rogem Gannim and Their Implications for the Political Economy of Jerusalem: Late 8th–Early 4th Centuries B. C. E." *Tel Aviv* 33 (2006): 229–43.

Greenhut, Zvi, and Alon de Groot. "Tel Moẓa in Context." Pages 213–31 in *Salvage Excavations at Tel Moẓa: The Bronze and Iron Age Settlements and Later Occupations.* Edited by Zvi Greenhut, Alon de Groot, and Eldad Barzilay. Jerusalem: Israel Antiquities Authority, 2009.

Grimes, Ronald L. "Performance Theory and the Study of Ritual." Pages 109–38 in *Textual, Comparative, Sociological, and Cognitive Approaches.* Vol. 2 of *New Approaches to the Study of Religion.* Edited by Peter Antes, Armin W. Geertz, and Randi R. Warne. Berlin: de Gruyter, 2004.

Groot, Alon de, and Hannah Bernick-Greenberg, ed. *Area E: Stratigraphy and Architecture: Text.* Vol. 7A of *Excavations at the City of David, 1978–1985: Directed by Yigal Shiloh.* Jerusalem: Hebrew University of Jerusalem Press, 2012.

———. "The Pottery of Strata 12–10." Pages 57–198 in *Area E: The Finds.* Edited by Alon de Groot and Hannah Bernick-Greenberg. Vol. 7B in *Excavations at the City of David, 1978– 1985: Directed by Yigal Shiloh.* Jerusalem: Hebrew University of Jerusalem Press, 2012.

Grosby, Steven. "Religion and Nationality in Antiquity: The Worship of Yahweh and Ancient Israel." *European Journal of Sociology* 32.2 (1991): 229–65.

Gues, C. H. J. de. *Towns in Ancient Israel and in the Southern Levant.* Leuven: Peeters, 2003.

Hall, Stuart. "Gramsci's Relevance for the Study of Race and Ethnicity." *Journal of Communication Inquiry* 10.2 (1986): 5–27.

Halpern, Baruch. "Jerusalem and the Lineages in the Seventh Century BCE: Kinship and the Rise of Individual Moral Liability." Pages 11–107 in *Law and Ideology in Monarchic Israel*. Edited by Baruch Halpern and Deborah W. Hobson. Sheffield: Sheffield Academic, 1991.

Handy, Lowell K. *Among the Host of Heaven: The Syro-Palestinian Pantheon as Bureaucracy*. Winona Lake, IN: Eisenbrauns, 1994.

Herzog, Ze'ev. *Archaeology of the City: Urban Planning in Ancient Israel and Its Social Implications*. Tel Aviv: Emery and Claire Yass Archaeology Press, Institute of Archaeology, Tel Aviv University, 1997.

Holladay, John S., Jr. "Hezekiah's Tribute, Long-Distance Trade, and the Wealth of Nations ca. 1000–600 BC: A New Perspective." Pages 309–31 in *Confronting the Past: Archaeological and Historical Essays on Ancient Israel in Honor of William G. Dever*. Edited by Seymour Gitin, John E. Wright, and J. P. Dessel. Winona Lake, IN: Eisenbrauns, 2006.

Hopkins, David C. "Agriculture." Pages 22–30 in vol. 1 of *Oxford Encyclopedia of Archaeology in the Near East*. Edited by Eric M. Meyers. New York: Oxford University Press, 1997.

———. "Bare Bones: Putting Flesh on the Economics of Ancient Israel." Pages 121–39 in *The Origins of the Ancient Israelite States*, Edited by Volkmar Fritz and Philip R. Davies. Sheffield: Sheffield Academic, 1996.

Ilan, David. "Household Gleanings from Iron I Tel Dan." Pages 133–54 in *Household Archaeology in Ancient Israel and Beyond*. Edited by Assaf Yasur-Landau, Jennie R. Ebeling, and Laura B. Mazow. Leiden: Brill, 2011.

King, James E., Jr. "(Dis)Missing the Obvious: Will Mainstream Management Research Ever Take Religion Seriously?" *Journal of Management Inquiry* 17.3 (2008): 214–24.

King, Phillip J., and Lawrence E. Stager. *Life in Biblical Israel*. Louisville: Westminster John Knox, 2001.

Kletter, Raz. "In the Footsteps of Bagira: Ethnicity, Archaeology, and Iron Age I Ethnic Israel." *Approaching Religion* 4.2 (2014): 2–15.

———. *The Judean Pillar-Figurines and the Archaeology of Asherah*. Oxford: Tempus Reparatum, 1996.

Kyriakidis, Evangelos. "Archaeologies of Ritual." Pages 289–308 in *The Archaeology of Ritual*. Edited by Evangelos Kyriakidis. Los Angeles: Cotsen Institute of Archaeology, 2007.

Levine, Baruch A. "The Biblical 'Town' as Reality and Typology: Evaluating Biblical References to Towns and Their Functions." Pages 421–53 in *Urbanization and*

Land Ownership in the Ancient Near East. Edited by Michael Hudson and Baruch A. Levine. Cambridge: Peabody Museum of Archaeology and Ethnology, Harvard University, 1999.

Lipschits, Oded, Omer Sergi, and Ido Koch. "Judahite Stamped and Incised Jar Handles: A Tool for Studying the History of Late Monarchic Judah." *Tel Aviv* 38 (2011): 5–41.

———. "Royal Judahite Jar Handles: Reconsidering the Chronology of the *lmlk* Stamp Impressions." *Tel Aviv* 37 (2010): 3–32.

Machinist, Peter. "The Fall of Assyria in Comparative Ancient Perspective." Pages 179–95 in *Assyria 1995: Proceedings of the 10th Anniversary Symposium of the Neo-Assyrian Text Corpus Project Helsinki, September 7–11, 1995*. Edited by Simo Parpola and Robert M. Whiting. Helsinki: Neo-Assyrian Text Corpus Project, 1997.

Mazar, Amihai. *Archaeology of the Land of the Bible*. New York: Doubleday, 1990.

McCormick, Lauren K. "My Eyes Are Up Here: Guardian Iconography of the Judean Pillar Figurine." PhD diss., Syracuse University, 2023.

McCowan, Chester Charleton. *Tell en-Nasbeh Excavated under the Direction of the Late William Frederic Badè*. Vol. 1. Berkeley: The Palestine Institute of Pacific School of Religion and the American Schools of Oriental Research, 1947.

Meyer, Birgit, David Morgan, Crispin Paine, and S. Brent Plate, eds. "Key Words in Material Religion." *Material Religion* 7.1 (2011): 1–162.

Meyers, Carol. *Discovering Eve: Ancient Israelite Women in Context*. Oxford: Oxford University Press, 1988.

———. *Rediscovering Eve: Ancient Israelite Women in Context*. Oxford: Oxford University Press, 2013.

———. "Terracottas without Texts: Judean Pillar Figurines in Anthropological Perspective." Pages 115–30 in *To Break Every Yoke: Essays in Honor of Marvin L. Chaney*. Edited by Robert B. Coote and Norman K. Gottwald. Sheffield: Sheffield Phoenix, 2007.

Morgan, David. *The Embodied Eye: Religious Visual Culture and the Social Life of Feeling*. Berkeley: University of California Press, 2012.

———. "The Material Culture of Lived Religions: Visuality and Embodiment." Pages 14–31 in *Mind and Matter: Selected Papers of the Nordik 2009 Conference for Art Historians*. Edited by Johanna Vakkari. Helsinki: Helsingfors, 2010.

———. "Materializing the Study of Religion." *Religion* 46.4 (2016): 640–43.

———, ed. *Religion and Material Culture: The Matter of Belief*. London: Routledge, 2009.

———. *The Sacred Gaze: Religious Visual Culture in Theory and Practice*. Berkeley: University of California Press, 2005.

———. "Visual Religion." *Religion* 30 (2000): 41–53.

Panitz-Cohen, Nava. "The Pottery Assemblage." Pages 110–45 in *Yavneh 1: The Excavation of the 'Temple Hill' Repository Pit and the Cult Stands*. Edited by Raz Kletter, Irit Ziffer, and Wolfgang Zwickel. Fribourg: Academic Press; Göttingen: Vandenhoeck & Ruprecht, 2010.

Pritchard, James Bennett. *Gibeon: Where the Sun Stood Still; The Discovery of the Biblical City*. Princeton: Princeton University Press, 1962.

———. *The Water System of Gibeon*. Philadelphia: University Museum, University of Pennsylvania, 1961.

Rollston, Christopher. *Writing and Literacy in the World of Ancient Israel: Epigraphic Evidence from the Iron Age*. Atlanta: Society of Biblical Literature, 2010.

Schmitt, Rüdiger. "Elements of Domestic Cult in Ancient Israel." Pages 57–219 in Rainer Albertz and Rüdiger Schmitt, *Family and Household Religion in Ancient Israel and the Levant*. Winona Lake, IN: Eisenbrauns, 2012.

Shoham, Yair. "A Group of Hebrew Bullae from Yigal Shiloh's Excavations in the City of David." Pages 55–61 in *Ancient Jerusalem Revealed*. Edited by Hillel Geva. Jerusalem: Israel Exploration Society, 1994.

Smith, Mark. *The Memoirs of God: History, Memory, and the Experience of the Divine in Ancient Israel*. Minneapolis: Augsburg, 2004.

Smith, Jonathan Z. "Great Scott! Thought and Action One More Time." Pages 73–91 in *Magic and Ritual in the Ancient World*. Edited by Paul Mirecki and Marvin Meyer. Leiden: Brill, 2002.

———. "Religion, Religions, Religious." Pages 269–84 in *Critical Terms for Religious Studies*. Edited by Mark Taylor. Chicago: University of Chicago Press, 1998.

Sparks, Kenton L. *Ethnicity and Identity in Ancient Israel: Prolegomena to the Study of Ethnic Sentiments and Their Expression in the Hebrew Bible*. Winona Lake, IN: Eisenbrauns, 1998.

Stavrakopoulou, Francesca. "'Popular' Religion and 'Official' Religion: Practice, Perception, Portrayal." Pages 37–58 in *Religious Diversity in Ancient Israel and Judah*. Edited by Francesca Stavrakopoulou and John Barton. London: T&T Clark, 2010.

Steiner, Margreet. "Stratigraphical Analysis, Architecture and Objects of the Phases." Pages 3–60 in *The Iron Age Extramural Quarter on the South-East Hill*. Edited by Hendricus J. Franken and Margreet L. Steiner. Vol. 2 of *Excavations in Jerusalem 1961–1967*. Oxford: Oxford University Press, 1990.

Stryker, S. *Symbolic Interactionism: A Social Structural Version*. Menlo Park, CA: Benjamin/Cummings, 1980.

Stryker, S., and R. T. Serpe. "Commitment, Identity Salience, and Role Behavior: Theory and Research Example." Pages 199–218 in *Personality, Roles, and Social Behavior*. Edited by W. Ickes and E. S. Knowles. New York: Springer, 1982.

Tajfel, H., and J. C. Turner. "The Social Identity Theory of Intergroup Behavior." Pages

7–24 in *Psychology of Intergroup Relations*. Edited by S. Worchel and W. G. Austin. 2nd ed. Chicago: Nelson Hall, 1986.

Thompson, Vetta Sanders. "Variables Affecting Racial-Identity Salience among African Americans." *Journal of Social Psychology* 139.6 (2000): 748–61.

Turner, J. C., M. A. Hogg, P. J. Oakes, S. D. Reicher, and M. S. Wetherell. *Rediscovering the Social Group: A Self-Categorization Theory*. Oxford: Blackwell, 1987.

Vaughn, Andrew. *Theology, History, and Archaeology in the Chronicler's Account of Hezekiah*. Atlanta: Scholars Press, 1999.

Weaver, Gary R., and Bradley R. Agle. "Religiosity and Ethical Behavior in Organizations: A Symbolic Interactionist Perspective." *The Academy of Management Review* 27.1 (2002): 77–97.

Wilson, Ian Douglas. "Judean Pillar Figurines and Ethnic Identity in the Shadow of Assyria." *JSOT* 36.3 (2012): 259–78.

Yee, Gale. *Poor Banished Children of Eve: Woman as Evil in the Hebrew Bible*. Minneapolis: Fortress, 2003.

Zevit, Ziony. *The Religions of Ancient Israel: A Synthesis of Parallactic Approaches*. London: Continuum, 2001.

Zorn, Jeffrey R. "Tell en Nasbeh: A Reevaluation of the Architecture and Stratigraphy of the Early Bronze Age, Iron Age, and Later Periods." PhD diss., University of California, Berkeley, 1993.

Contributors

Edward Armstrong is a research associate of the British School at Athens and a visiting fellow with the Australian National University. After completing his PhD at the University of St Andrews in 2023, he held the Jacobi Fellowship at the Kommission für Alte Geschichte und Epigraphik des Deutschen Archäologischen Instituts in Munich, Germany.

Erin Darby is an associate professor in the Department of Religious Studies at the University of Tennessee. Erin is an active field archaeologist and specialist in the archaeology of religion, ancient iconography, and the literatures and cultures of the southern Levant. Her work *Interpreting Judean Pillar Figurines*, coedited volume *Iron Age Terracotta Figurines from the Southern Levant in Context*, and several related publications explore the religious and figural world of ancient Judah and the ancient Near East.

Stefano De Feo is a postdoctoral researcher at the Institute for New Testament Studies at the Faculty of Theology of the University of Bern. He earned a degree in philosophy from the University of Milan and completed his PhD in theology at the University of Bern (2024). His doctoral dissertation focused on the significance of eschatology in ancient philosophical and religious traditions.

Michael Anthony Fowler is Assistant Professor of Art History in the Department of Art and Design at East Tennessee State University. He completed a PhD in art history and archaeology at Columbia University in 2019, specializing

CONTRIBUTORS

in ancient Greece and West Asia. In his research and scholarship, Fowler focuses on topics related to material religion, iconography, gender, violence, and classical reception.

Thomas Harrison is Keeper of the Department of Greece and Rome at the British Museum and a specialist in archaic and classical Greek culture. His publications include *Divinity and History: The Religion of Herodotus, The Emptiness of Asia: Aeschylus' "Persians" and the History of the Fifth Century*, and *Writing Ancient Persia*. He is currently completing a monograph on classical Greek religious belief.

David J. Johnston has held various academic positions, is a fellow at the Higher Education Academy, and completed his doctoral thesis at the University of St Andrews, Scotland, in which he argued that the law of Romans 7 is the law as preached by Paul's opponents. His research draws on themes of contingency and coherence and the location of Paul within apocalyptic and Jewish perspectives, while presenting a detailed exegesis of the argument of Paul's letters.

Theodore J. Lewis is Blum-Iwry Professor of Near Eastern Studies at Johns Hopkins University. He is the author of *The Origin and Character of God: Ancient Israelite Religion through the Lens of Divinity* (Oxford), which received the Frank Moore Cross Award from the American Society of Overseas Research, the Award for Excellence in the Study of Religion: Historical Studies from the American Academy of Religion, and the Biblical Archaeology Society Biennial Publication Award for the Best Book Relating to the Hebrew Bible. Lewis is the general editor of the series Writings from the Ancient World and past editor of the journal *Near Eastern Archaeology*.

Teresa Morgan is McDonald Agape Professor of New Testament and Early Christianity at Yale University. Among her numerous books in ancient biblical history and early Christian studies, she is currently finishing a four-volume historical and theological study of early Christian faith.

Camilla Recalcati is currently a Golda Meir Postdoctoral Fellow at the Hebrew University of Jerusalem and a postdoctoral researcher at Bar-Ilan University. She earned her PhD from the Faculty of Theology and Religious Studies at the Université Catholique de Louvain, Belgium, where her dissertation explored Egyptian influences on the lexical elements of the Septuagint. Her research interests include the Septuagint, Greek lexicography, and Hellenistic Judaism in Egypt.

Contributors

Matthew T. Sharp is Lecturer in New Testament Studies at the University of St Andrews, UK. He gained his PhD from the University of Edinburgh in 2021. His first book, *Divination and Philosophy in the Letters of Paul*, was a recipient of the 2023 Manfred Lautenschläger Award for Theological Promise.

Brent A. Strawn is D. Moody Smith Distinguished Professor of Old Testament and Professor of Law at Duke University. He has edited over thirty volumes to date, including the award-winning *The Oxford Encyclopedia of the Bible and Law* (2015). He has authored over 250 articles, essays, and contributions to reference works as well as six books, most recently *The Incomparable God: Readings in Biblical Theology* (2023). Strawn is ordained in the United Methodist Church and has served as a translator and editor for the Common English Bible (2011) and the New Revised Standard Version Updated Edition (2022).

Index of Authors

Page numbers in italics refer to figures.

Adcock, Frank E., 8n6
Agle, Bradley R., 238n28
Aḥituv, Shmuel, 202n91, 243n44
Ahlström, G. W., 216n135
Albertz, Rainer, 122n26, 213n126, 241n34
Alcorta, Candace, 102n15
Alexandridou, Alexandra, 151n19
Allen, James P., 189
Althusser, Louis, 238, 239
Amesbury, Richard, 90n42
Anderson, Michael J., 150n17
Ando, Clifford, 42–45, 48
Argenton, Alberto, 193n52
Armstrong, Paul B., 193n53
Armstrong, Ruth, 95n52
Arnheim, Rudolf, 192, 193–94, 196
Assmann, Jan, 36n45, 187–92, 201n90
Avery, Harry C., 16n32
Avigad, Nahman, 129n40, 242n37
Ayres, Lewis, 76n8, 88n35

Badian, Ernst, 11n15
Bailey, Douglass W., 232–33

Barkay, Gabriel, 242n37
Barnes, Jonathan, 13n24
Barrett, Louise, 102n15
Baven, T. J. van, 75n5
Beatrice, Pier Franco, 29n23
Beck, Pirhiya, 202, 204
Becker, Matthias, 37n49
Becking, Bob, 113n3, 114
Bell, Catherine, 225, 227n2, 229
Bielby, James, 75n5, 83n23
Bies, Robert, 83n22
Black, Fiona C., 187n28
Blackwell, Ben C., 182n12
Blenkinsopp, Joseph, 113, 115n11, 242n11, 243n42, 244n47, 245
Bloch, Ernst, 23
Bockmuehl, Markus N. A., 51n29
Bodel, John, 122n26
Boer, Roland, 239
Boespflug, Mark, 81n17
Bonfiglio, Ryan P., 191n46, 196, 197, 198n72, 199nn79–80, 199n82, 200,

INDEX OF AUTHORS

201nn88–90, 206n101, 206n104, 207n106, 208n109, 210, 211n119, 214n129, 230n5, 249n73

Bonnechere, Pierre, 142n1, 146n11

Boone, Mark J., 75n5

Borowski, Oded, 241n36, 242nn37–38, 244n46, 245, 248n69, 250n80

Borst, Grégoire, 194n56

Bosworth, Albert B., 18n43

Bourdieu, Pierre, 225, 236, 237

Boylan, Alexis L., 195n62, 196n64

Braithwaite, R. B., 100n8, 101n13

Brandl, Baruch, 125n34, 126n35

Brawley, Robert L., 180n5

Brelich, Angelo, 142n1

Bremmer, Jan N., 24n4, 30n28, 142n1

Brody, Aaron, 235, 236n22

Brooten, Bernadette J., 50n26

Brothers, Doris, 95n53

Brown, Raymond E., 64n25, 65n25

Brueggemann, Walter, 190n45

Buber, Martin, 179, 180, 181, 182, 183, 184, 186

Bukina, Anastasia G., 149n15

Bundrick, Sheramy D., 154n30

Burkert, Walter, 8n8, 9, 12nn19–20, 14n26, 15n29, 52n33

Byrne, Brendan, 60

Byrne, Ryan, 234, 235, 242

Cacitti, Remo, 25n6, 30, 34n42, 37n47

Cambitoglou, Alexander, 156n38, 158n39

Campbell, Douglas A., 62nn15–16, 63n16, 67n33, 68, 69

Carasik, Michael, 187n28

Carvalho, John, 193n52

Chan, Michael J., 201n90

Chapman, Suzanne, 149n14, 152n22, 154

Childs, Brevard S., 205

Cohen, Mark E., 189n35

Cohn, Leopold, 31n30

Conybeare, Catherine, 94n51

Cook, Robert M., 115, 156nn35–36

Cornelius, Izak, 74n1, 120n21, 121n23, 127n36

Cornell, Collin, 190n45

Craib, Ian, 237n26

Crane, Gregory, 8n7, 13n22

Creel, Andrea M., 230n4, 231n10

Cunningham, George B., 238n28

Cutting, Gary, 177n1

d'Agostino, Bruno, 151n21

Damasio, Antonio, 186

Darby, Erin, 227n2, 230n5, 232n12, 234nn16–18, 240n33, 241n35, 246nn60–62, 247, 248n70, 249nn73–76, 250n81

Davies, G. I., 213n123

Davies, Philip, 240n31, 242n38, 243n40, 250n79

Dever, William, 242, 246, 246n59

DeYoe, E. A., 194n56

Dixon, Norman F., 106n23

Dobbs-Allsopp, F. W., 213n123

Dohmen, Christoph, 210n113

Dowden, Ken, 149

Downing, F. G., 34n39

Duhn, Friedrich von, 156

Dunbar, Robin, 102n15

Dunn, James, 49n22

Durand, Jean-Louis, 146n11, 159n46

Easterling, P. E., 102n16

Eggler, Jürg, 211n118

Eidinow, Esther, 8n9, 12n20, 16nn30–31, 103

Eklund, Timothy, 76n6

Ellis, Anthony, 103n18

Elster, Jon, 101, 105nn21–22, 106, 108

266

Index of Authors

Engberg-Pedersen, Troels, 46n13
Engel, S. A., 194n56
Eshel, Esther, 202n91
Esrock, Ellen J., 193n54
Eyl, Jennifer, 43n6, 44n7, 46n14

Fahr, Wilhelm, 36n46
Faust, Avraham, 232n11, 237n26, 240n31, 242n38, 243, 244n45, 246n56
Fensham, F. Charles, 114
Fernández Marcos, Natalio, 166n6
Festinger, Leon, 101–2, 104
Festugière, André-Jean, 28n20
Fink, Amir S., 129n39
Fink, Sebastian, 189n35
Finkel, Irving L., 115n11, 245n54
Finley, John H., 10n13
Fischer, Nick, 16n33
Fischer, J. B., 168n14
Flower, Michael A., 144n6, 145n7, 160n48
Flowerree, Amy, 76n6
Fogelin, Lars, 229n4
Fontinoy, Charles, 144n5
Ford, James C., 25n5
Fortin, Jean-Pierre, 75n5
Foucault, Michel, 238, 239
Fowler, Michael Anthony, 9n10
Fox, Matthew A., 26n10
Fox, P. T., 194n56
Fredriksen, Paula, 62–64
Freedberg, David, 196n62
Frend, William H. C., 29n24
Fritz, Volkmar, 240n31, 242n38, 243n41, 245n52
Furley, William D., 7–9
Furtwängler, Adolf, 156n38, 158n40

Gabba, Emilio, 108n34
Gallarte, Israel Muñoz, 43n6
Galzerano, Manuel, 25n7, 33n39

Ganis, Giorgio, 193n52, 194n55
Gebert, Diether, 238n28
Georgi, Dieter, 32n35
Georgoudi, Stella, 148n13, 149n13, 150n17
Gericke, Jaco, 189n39
Gibson, C. L., 116n12
Gilibert, Alessandra, 116n12, 119n18, 123n28, 128n38, 130n42
Glassner, Jean-Jacques, 115n11
Goldin, Judah, 191n47
Gottwald, Norman K., 239, 240n31
Gould, John, 102–3
Grabbe, Lester L., 115n11, 243n40
Graf, Fritz, 45
Gramsci, Antonio, 235
Grassi, Giulia Francesca, 125n33
Greggs, Tom, 181n9
Greschat, Katharina, 89n40
Grimes, Ronald L., 229n3
Grosby, Steven, 237n26
Gruen, Erich S., 113–14
Gues, C. H. J. de, 242n38
Gunz, Philipp, 187n29
Gupta, Nijay K., 44n7, 54n36

Hafemann, Scott J., 61n9
Hall, Stuart, 235n21
Hällström, Gunnar af, 78n14
Halpern, Baruch, 242n37, 243n42
Hampshire, Stuart, 100n8
Hankins, Davis, 180n5
Hardin, Russell, 84n26
Harlow, John Martyn, *185*, 186n23
Harrison, Carol, 75n5, 91n43
Harrison, Thomas, 8n8, 18n40
Hasnain, M. K., 194n56
Hay, David M., 54
Hazony, Yoram, 189n39
Heath, Malcolm, 17n36

INDEX OF AUTHORS

Helmer, Christine, 178n3

Henkelman, Wouter F. M., 113n2

Henrichs, Albert, 142n1, 143n3

Henriksen Garroway, Kristine, 236

Herrmann, Virginia R., 119n18, 124n33, 130n43, 232n12

Heschel, Abraham Joshua, 181n8

Hirsch-Luipold, Rainer, 31n31

Hirstein, W., 194n58

Hofstadter, Albert, 192n49

Hogan, James C., 11n16

Holloway, Steven W., 135n46

Hölscher, Tonio, 153n29

Hopkins, David C., 240n31, 244n46

Hornblower, Simon, 7–9, 11n17, 18n39, 18nn41–42, 19

Horowitz, Alexandra, 196n62

Horsley, Richard A., 32n35

Hotchkiss, Valerie, 183n15

Hublin, Jean-Jacques, 187n29

Hughes, Dennis, 143n2

Hughes, Jessica, 107n29

Hulster, Izaak J. de, 136n48, 209n111, *210*, 240n33

Hunt, Peter, 12n18

Hus, Shih-Wei, 187n28

Hutter, Manfred, 114n9, 125n33

Huttunen, Niko, 49n23

Ilan, David, 237n26

James, Jesse, 18n43

Japhet, Sara, 115n11

Jenkins, Tim, 101n11

Jensen, Robin M., 196n65

Jewett, Robert, 48n20, 66n28

Jiménez, Miguel Requena, 43n3

Johnson, Dru, 189n39

Johnson, Marshall D., 59n2

Jong, Albert de, 112, 113n2, 137

Jordan, Boromir, 9nn10–11, 18n43

Jung, Carl G., 27n14

Kahneman, Daniel, 186n26

Kallet, Lisa, 13n22

Karenga, Maulana, 189n37

Kazantzidis, George, 13n22, 16n33

Keel, Othmar, 190n45, 204nn94–95, 211, 212, 213nn124–125

Keil, Carl F., 113n6

Kellner, Menachem, 180–81n8

Kenney, John Peter, 75n5

Kindt, Julia, 8n9, 9n11, 192n48

King, Charles, 26n9

King, James E., Jr., 238n28

Kipfer, Sara, 187n28

Kitzler, Petr, 31n32

Klein, Isabelle, 194n56

Kletter, Raz, 237n26, 245n48, 246n62, 248n71

Kluiver, Jeroen, 150n16

Koch, Ido, 242n37, 244n44

Koosed, Jennifer L., 187n28

Kooten, George H. van, 43n6, 47n16, 49nn23–24

Kosslyn, Stephen M., 193n53, 194n55–56

Kruse, Colin G., 66

Kuhns, Richard, 192n49

Kujanpää, Katja, 61, 62n12

Kundhi, Gubhinder, 95n52

Kwon, Yong-Gyong, 53n34

Kyriakidis, Evangelos, 229n4

Labendz, Jenny R., 37n48

Lampe, Peter, 59n2

Lang, Andrew, 107n31

Lanzillotta, Lautaro Roig, 30n28

Lash, Nicholas, 181

Lateiner, Donald, 13n22

LeMon, Joel M., 202n91, 203, 204,

Index of Authors

205n100, 206nn102–103, 208n108, 249n73

Lessing, G. E., 55n40

Levenson, Jon D., 179

Levieils, Xavier, 25, 27n13, 31n31

Levine, Baruch A., 242n38

Lewicki, Roy J., 83n22

Lewis, Theodore J., 117n13, 119nn18–19, 121n24, 133n45, 135n46, 190n45, 195n60, 214–15, 216n135

LiDonnici, Lynn R., 107n28, 108, 109nn36–38

Lilla, Salvatore R. C., 77n12

Lim, Timothy H., 165n3

Lipschits, Oded, 115n11, 165n3, 168n12, 242n37, 244n45

Lissarrague, François, 147n11, 150n17, 159n46

Liverani, Mario, 189n37

Llop Raduà, Jaume, 187n28

Lloyd-Jones, Hugh, 12n19, 15–16, 17n37

Long, A. G., 52n33

Longenecker, Richard N., 62, 65n25

Loraux, Nicole, 148n13

Löwith, Karl, 25n6

Luhrmann, T. M., 106n27

Lycett, John, 102n15

Machinist, Peter, 242n37

Mackey, Jacob L., 44n7

Mackey, Luis H., 87n34

Macleod, Colin, 18n43

Maiden, Brett E., 187, 195n61

Mangieri, Anthony, 148n13, 158n44, 159n46

Marinatos, Nanno, 9n10

Martyn, J. Louis, 62n15

Massironi, Manfredo, 193n52

Masson, Émilia, 125n33

Mazar, Amihai, *215*, 216n135, 242n37, 243n44

McAllister, Daniel J., 83n22

McClellan, Daniel O., 187n28

McCormick, Lauren K., 234n18, 243n63

McDonald, Denys N., 63n20

McNiven, Timothy J., 153n28

Mehl, Véronique, 150n17

Meier, John P., 64n25

Mendelsund, Peter, 193n53

Meshel, Ze'ev, 202, 203, 204n95, *207*, *208*

Meyers, Carol, 240nn31–32, 241n34, 242n38, 243, 244nn45–47, 247n65, 250n80

Mihalios, Stefanos, 32n33

Miller, Patrick D., 190n45

Minear, Paul S., 59n2

Mininger, Marcus A., 49n25, 51n29

Mitchell, W. J. T., 196

Moberly, R. W. L., 179n5, 180n5, 181, 182, 182nn12–13, 183, 184, 185, 186

Moltmann, Jürgen, 23

Moo, Douglas, 58n1, 59n3, 60n5, 65n26, 67n35, 69n43

Moran, William L., 89n35

Moret, Jean-Marc, 156n38

Morgan, David, 196n66, 197, 198, 199, 200, 201n88, 206n105, 216n134, 225, 230, 231, 236

Morgan, Teresa, 43nn5–6, 54n38, 76n6, 77n11, 84nn24–25, 85n28, 90n41, 95n52, 180n7, 182n12, 183n16, 184n20

Morris, Leon, 50n28

Muir, J. V., 102n16

Mylonopoulos, Ioannis, 146n11, 150n17, 151n20, 152, 153n29, 156n38, 158n41, 159n46

INDEX OF AUTHORS

Naerebout, Frederick G., 99n4
Naiden, Fred S., 107n29, 108n13
Nanos, Mark D., 60n4, 63n18, 66nn31–32
Needham, Rodney, 100, 101n13, 191n47
Neer, Richard, 147n12, 158n41
Nestor, Dermot Anthony, 237n26
Neubauer, Simon, 187n29
Niehr, Herbert, 119n18, 129n41, 136nn47–48
Nongbri, Brent, 43n5, 190n40
Novenson, Matthew V., 52n32

Obbink, Dirk, 28n16
Oost, Stewart I., 9n10
Ornan, Tallay, 121n22
Osborn, Eric, 77n12
Owusu, Adobea Y., 95n52

Paivio, Allan, 192n51
Papalexandrou, Nassos, 158n42
Pardee, Dennis, 124n33
Parise Badoni, Franca, 159n47
Parker, Robert, 44n6, 99–100
Passoni-Dell'Acqua, Anna, 165n3, 171n19, 172nn23–24, 173n28
Payne, Annick, 123n30
Pelikan, Jaroslav, 181n9, 183n15
Petridou, Georgia, 46n11
Pfeiffer, Stefan, 166n5
Pifer, Jeanette Hagen, 44n7
Pinker, Steven, 193n53, 195n60
Pirenne-Delforge, Vinciane, 143n4
Pongratz-Leisten, Beate, 190n45
Portuese, Ludovico, 194, 195, 196, 207n107
Pouillon, J., 101n13
Pouzadoux, Claude, 156n38
Powell, C. Anton, 16n30
Prag, A. John N. W., 154n33
Pucci, Marina, 119n18, 130n42

Rahe, Paul, 7–8, 18n43
Ramachandran, V. S., 194, 195, 216n134
Reed, Baron, 76n6
Reichold, Karl, 156n38, 158n40
Reiter, Siegfried, 31n30
Renz, Johannes, 213n123, 213n125
Rhodes, P. J., 108n35
Ritter, Adolf M., 29n25
Roberts, J. J. M., 213n123
Robertson, Paul, 46n13
Rollens, Sarah E., 46n11
Röllig, Wolfgang, 213
Rösel, Martin, 168n12
Rosenthal, M. A., 27n12
Roubekas, Nickolas P., 24n2
Roy, Olivier du, 75n5
Rüpke, Jörg, 26n9

Sadoski, Mark, 192n51
Sanders, E. P., 65n27
Sanders, Seth, 118n14, 125n33
Sandvoss, Ernst, 36n44
Sass, Benjamin, 125n34, 126, 129n40
Satterfield, Susan, 43n3
Scarry, Elaine, 193n53
Scheid, John, 26n9
Schiesaro, Alessandro, 33n39, 34n40
Schloen, J. David, 129n39
Schlosser, Joel Alden, 13n22
Schmidt, Brian B., 204, 205
Schoedel, William R., 25n8
Schreiner, Thomas R., 59n4
Schrimpton, Gordon S., 10n14
Schroer, Silvia, 210n112
Schultz, Celia E., 50n27
Schwarz, Gerda, 150n17, 152n22
Schwenn, Friedrich, 142n1
Schwiderski, Dirk, 116n12, 129n40
Scrutton, Anastasia, 94n51
Seow, C. L., 213n123

Index of Authors

Sereno, M. I., 194n56
Sergi, Omer, 136n48, 242n37, 244n44
Serling, Richard E., 95n52
Serpe, R. T., 238n28
Sevinç, Nurten, 158n41
Sharp, Matthew T., 46nn14–15
Simpson, Adelaide D., 28
Slotnick, S. D., 194n56
Small, Jocelyn Penny, 145n8
Smit, Peter-Ben, 32n34
Smith, H. S., 172n22
Smith, Jonathan Z., 226, 227, *228*
Smith, Mark S., 190n45, 191n47
Smith, Morton, 28n20
Smith, Tyler Jo, 150n16
Smith, Wilfred Cantwell, 179, 182n13
Smith, William Robertson, 99
Sonik, Karen, 187n28
Sosis, Richard, 102n15
Sourvinou-Inwood, Christiane, 8n8, 9
Sparks, Kenton L., 242n37
Spatharas, Dimos, 13n22, 16n33
Spek, R. J. van der, 115n11
Spencer, F. Scott, 187n28
Stampolidis, Nicholas Chr., 144n6
Stansbury-O'Donnell, Mark D., 152, 153
Star, Christopher, 34n29
Steinert, Ulrike, 187n28
Stern, Gaius, 50n27
Stransbury, Mark D., 152–53
Strawn, Brent A., 178n3, 202n91, 203, 204,
  205n100, 206nn102–103, 208n108, *210*,
  211, 212, 215n133, 249n73
Struck, Peter T., 52n30
Stryker, S., 238n28
Studer, Basil, 83n23

Tajfel, H., 238n28
Tamur, Ehran, 126n36
Tenkorang, Eric Y., 95n52

TeSelle, Eugene, 73n1, 75n5
Thiessen, Matthew, 48n18, 69n44
Thirion, Bertrand, 194n56
Thompson, Vetta Sanders, 238n28
Thompson, William L., 193n53
Thür, Gerhard, 167n8
Timmer, Daniel, 36n45
Tobin, Vincent Arieh, 189n37
Toit, David S. du, 50n28
Tootell, R. B. H., 193
Touchefeu-Meynier, Odette, 150n17
Tov, Emanuel, 171n20
Tremlin, Todd, 102n14, 107n30
Trendall, Arthur D., 156n38, 158
Tropper, Josef, 116n12
Troxel, Ronald, 168n15
Tsiafakis, Despoina, 152n25
Tsur, Reuven, 193n53
Turner, Eric G., 166n4
Turner, J. C., 238n28
Turner, Mark, 193n53
Twining, Louisa, 92n47
Tyler, Ann C., 196n65, 198, 199n77
Tzetzes, John, 148n12

Uehlinger, Christoph, 190n45, 196n62,
  204nn94–95, 209n110, 212

Van De Mieroop, Marc, 189n39
Van Essen, D. C., 194n56
Van Fleteren, Frederick, 75n5
Vaughn, Andrew, 242n37, 246n56
Vermeule, Emily, 149n14, 152n22, 154
Vernant, Jean-Pierre, 146
Versnel, Henk S., 98n1, 102, 192n48
Veyne, Paul, 106n26
Voos, Joachim, 128n38

Walker, Justin, 193n53, 194n56, 207n106
Walsh, Joseph J., 30n29
Walters, Henry B., 148n12

INDEX OF AUTHORS

Watson, Francis, 59n2
Weaver, Gary R., 238n28
Wendt, Heide, 44, 48n18, 52n33, 55n39
West, Martin L., 144n5
Westh, Peter, 187n28
Whitaker, R. E., 213n123
White, Joel R., 53n34
Whitmarsh, Tim, 8n7, 24n4, 28n15,
  28n20, 30nn27–28, 36nn45–46
Wiesehöfer, Josef, 113n2
Williamson, Hugh G. M., 115n11
Williamson, Timothy, 76n6
Wilson, Ian Douglas, 235
Winiarczyk, Marek, 24, 25n6, 27n13
Witherington, Ben, III, 61

Wittgenstein, Ludwig, 100
Woldorff, M. G., 194n66
Wolf, Maryanne, 193n53
Wyschogrod, Michael, 177, 178, 180,
  181n8, 185, 188, 189

Yadin, Yigael, 125n34
Yakubovich, Ilya, 124n33
Yarbro Collins, Adela, 50n28
Yee, Gale, 239n30
Younger, K. Lawson, Jr., 119n18, 123,
  124nn32–33, 125, 126n35, 191n47, 198

Zambon, Marco, 31n31
Zevit, Ziony, 204n97, 242n38, 247n64
Zimmerli, Walther, 182n14

Index of Subjects

Achilles, 142–43, 145–47, 149–51, 156, 158–60

Agamemnon, 11

agnostic, 137–38

Ahaz, 116

Ajax, 15, 47

Alcibiades, 19

Alexander, 35

Alexandria of Egypt, 5, 165, 175

Aphrodite, 101

Apollo, 11–12, 17, 20, 52, 158

Arameans, 116, 124

Archidamus, 11

Archilochus, 107

Asclepius, 35, 107–8

Asia Minor, 30, 35

atheism, 23–31, 36–37

atheists, 23, 25–26, 28, 30, 34–37

Athenagoras, 31

Athens, 10, 17–18, 36, 104, 108

Atreus, 15

Augustine, 73–95

Aulis, 143

Babylon, 115–16

Balbus, 45

baptism, 50, 74, 88, 91, 94

Bar Rakib, 112–37

belief: as assent 80, 82, 85, 88, 92; and cognitive religion, 8; as content one accepts as true, 32, 34, 37, 44, 45, 55, 81, 89, 113, 118, 143, 167, 170, 172, 174, 188, 206, 237; disbelief, 24n4, 26n10; in divine action, 12, 17, 105; in divine justice, 12, 15, 17, 19, 107; and faith 51, 54, 73–74, 179–82, 184–87, 191–92, 195, 212–13; and *fides qua*, 75–76, 90; in fortune, 16; as framework of understanding, 102–3; in god(s), 11, 36n45, 112, 114, 116, 136–37, 165, 171, 201; and Judaism, 177–78, 180; opposite atheism, 25n6; opposite unbelief/atheism, 23; as orientation toward something, 145; as part of a system of religious life, 10, 14, 20, 43, 99–100, 109, 115, 166, 229, 234–35, 239, 250–51; and practice, 9, 101, 104, 225, 227, 230; and reason,

INDEX OF SUBJECTS

77–78, 92; and social systems, 106, 122, 164, 173, 175, 231–32; and trust, 84, 86, 91, 183n16; and visuality, 196n65, 197–99, 205, 214, 216

Cecilius, 33–34
Christianity, 44, 54, 75, 77–78, 179–81, 188, 226–28; Catholic Christianity, 74, 80; Jewish Christianity, 64n25; Protestant Christianity, 179; Roman Christianity, 64n25; Western Christianity, 75
Chrysippus, 52
Cicero, 45, 48
circumcision, 61, 62n16, 63, 63n18, 63n19, 69–70
Clement of Alexandria, 77–78
cognition, 76n7, 178, 184–86, 192, 198, 213
cognitive, 77, 81, 179, 183–88, 191–95, 201, 206–7, 212; content, 183–84; dissonance, 102, 105
cognitive science, 107, 187, 191
conversion, 46, 62n16, 64, 69n44, 74, 80, 86, 112–14
Corinthians, 44–48
cosmos, 9, 20, 25n7, 31, 47, 160, 189n37
Cotta, 45, 48
creed, 44, 49, 54, 99, 181, 183n15, 198; Nicene Creed, 74
cult: aniconic, 49; of Asclepius, 35; funerary, 118; of Hellenistic kings, 164–66, 175; of Ishtar, 121; image of Yhwh, 209–12; Jewish, 60; of Kubaba, 126; of Marduk, 115; Roman, 31, 36–37, 45–46
Cyrus, 112–16, 136–37

Delium, 2, 9, 11–12, 14, 19–20
Democritus, 27
divination, 35, 42, 46, 51–52, 104, 106

divine intervention, 12–13, 16, 107–8; divine favor, 12, 14–15, 47; providence, 24, 26–27, 29, 37, 78; representation, 119–20
doctrine, 27, 31, 44, 46, 54, 75, 99

Egypt, 5, 165, 169, 172, 187–91, 195, 212
emotion, 83–85, 94, 151, 153, 155n34, 158, 183–87, 194
empiricism, 42–49, 51–55, 237
Epicurus, 27–29, 34–35
Epidaurus, 107–8
eschatology, 23–24, 29–33, 36, 55, 60–64, 68–69
ethics, 62, 62n16
ethnicity, 44, 58–61, 67–70, 232, 232n11, 235, 237n26
Euripides, 11, 17, 167
existence of god(s), 10–11, 14, 24–25, 26n11, 28, 29, 77n10, 115n11
Ezra, 112, 114, 137–38

faith, 51–54, 68–70, 75–77, 81–94, 178–88, 191–98, 212–14; concept of, 180n6; content of, 76n8, 182; definition of, 93; the faith, 74, 94; faith in, 81, 109, 113, 180; rule of, 76n8; weak in, 58, 60, 65–67, 70
fortune, 12–14, 16, 16n30, 20, 103

Galatians, 47, 68

Hadad, 118, 120–22, 124, 127, 131–32
Hector, 47
Hecuba, 17
Herodotus, 104, 167
Hesiod, 143
Holy Spirit, 88, 91
Homer, 143, 152
Honoratus, 80, 84
hope, 12–20, 51–55, 74, 76–77, 84, 90, 92

Index of Subjects

iconography, 192, 201n90, 208n109, 214, 234, 240–41, 247

immorality, 48n19

impiety, 14, 25, 28, 31n31, 36, 48–49

Iphigenia, 143

Ishtar, 120–21

Ismene, 16

Israel, 60–64, 166, 169, 182, 190, 210, 212

Istros, 144–45

Jesus, 44, 50–54, 65, 87, 89, 91, 199–200, 209

Judaism, 44, 60, 66, 77, 177–80, 180n8, 226–28, 250

Julius Proculus, 45

justice, 10–20, 51, 90, 129, 239

Justin Martyr, 31

knowledge: of God (γνῶσις), 78–79, 91–92, 184

Kubaba, 124–26

Kulamuwa, 119–23, 127–32, 136

Livy, 42, 50

Lucian of Samosata, 24, 30, 35

Marduk, 115–16

Melos, 17–18

Messiah, 32, 44, 59n4, 60–61, 65, 70, 113

Minucius Felix, 33–34

morality, 10–11, 14–15, 18, 75, 107, 109, 143, 146. *See also* immorality

myth, 103, 143–46, 149, 152–54, 156, 160

Neoptolemos, 147, 155–56, 158

Nestor Pylios, 149

Nicias, 13–14, 16, 19

Oedipus, 16

oracle, 16n35, 17, 17n35, 42–43, 46, 52n30, 55, 103–4, 182. *See also* prophecy

Ördekburnu, 125–26

Origen, 78, 92, 93

pagan, 30–35, 37, 62–63, 92, 114

Pagondas, 11–12

Panamuwa I, 119–21, 132–33

Panamuwa II, 116–18, 124, 127, 132

pantheon, 63n18, 113n2, 114, 119, 124, 129, 247

Patroklos, 143, 145, 156

Paul, 44–55, 59–60, 62–70, 89–90

Pausanias, 11

Persians, 104

Philo of Alexandria, 31, 188

philosophy, 24, 27, 34, 74–75, 94, 189

Phoinix, 149–50, 152–54, 156–59

Plataea, 9–11, 19–20

Plutarch, 28, 48, 52

politics, 8, 24, 36–37, 123

Polycarp, 30–31

Polymestor, 11

Polyxena, 144–46, 149, 151–52, 156, 158–60

Porphyry, 37

practice: as behavior, 75n4, 77, 79, 90, 94, 129n39, 180; concurrent with belief/faith, 89, 92, 178, 191; distinct from belief/faith, 8–9, 15, 178–79

practice, religious, 60–63, 99, 201, 230, 236–37

prayer, 11, 42, 74, 89, 94, 199, 213–14

prophecy, 52n30, 81, 85. *See also* oracle

Ptolemy II Philadelphus, 165

Ptolemy III, 171

Rakib-El, 118, 120, 122, 125–27, 129, 131–34, 136

religion, 102–3, 195, 197, 226, 228, 230, 231; ancient, 98–99, 105, 122, 196n62,

275

225, 226–28, 238; Aramean/Assyrian, 234; biblical, 119, 119n19, 171; Christian, 187; cognitive, 8; Egyptian, 189n37, 191, 226; Greek, 7–10, 12, 14, 17–20, 28, 98–100, 102, 105; Israelite, 119, 178, 185, 190, 214, 226–27, 229, 232, 235–36, 240, 245; and politics, 36–37; Roman, 26, 42–45, 51–52, 55, 133

ritual, 8–9, 15, 26, 47–48, 117–18, 144–46, 227, 234–49; vis-à-vis belief, 98–102, 227, 229–30

Rome, 29, 32, 42, 45, 47, 59–62, 69–70

Romulus, 45

sacrifice, 15, 20, 100, 102, 142–60

Salamis, 103–4, 143

salvation, 32n35, 52, 65, 214n126

sanctuary, 12, 14–15, 19–20

Sappho, 105

Sicily, 19, 105

Socrates, 36, 142

Sophocles, 15–17

Sparta, 10–13

spirit/spiritual, 46, 88, 91, 112, 197, 199

Stoic, 26, 31, 34, 45

symbolism, 15, 117, 120–22, 128–31, 133–34, 158, 198, 200, 230

synagogue, 66

temple, 10, 11, 15, 107, 112, 245–46, 249

Tertullian, 31–32, 91, 93

Themistokles, 143

Thucydides, 7–20, 105

Tiglath-Pileser III, 116–17, 134

Troy, 47, 149

trust, 11–12, 14, 53–55, 73–78, 82–95, 180–83, 186

truth, 47–49, 77–81, 83–84, 86–90, 94, 143, 179

worship, 74, 94, 99; of Greco-Roman gods, 28–29, 36–37, 49, 101–2, 105; of Israel's God, 60–63, 69–70, 208; of Marduk, 116; of Romulus, 45; of Yaho, 114

Xenophon, 105–6, 167

Yȧdiya, 118–24

Yahweh, 112–14, 201, 214–15

Zincirli, 120, 123–27, 131, 133, 137, 198

Index of Scripture

HEBREW BIBLE

Genesis

15	168
15:2	167, 168
15:8	167, 168
24:7	114
32:10	171
32:13	173
49:24	169, 169n16

Exodus

1:20	171
3:10	166n7
6:6	169, 169n16
19	166n7
32:32	173n27
34:7	173, 174

Numbers

1:48	174
1:53	173–75
10:29	171
10:32	171, 171n18
14:18	173, 174
14:19	173n27
16:22	174n32

Deuteronomy

1:34	174n32
3:24	168n13
7:9	86n31
9:7–8	174n32
9:26	168n13
32:4	86n31

1 Samuel

2:12	182

2 Kings

16:9	116
16:10–18	117

2 Chronicles

36:23	114

Ezra

1:1	112
1:2	112, 114, 116

Nehemiah

1:5	114

Job

13:15	169

Psalms

136:26	114
144(145):13	86n31

Proverbs

29:25	169

Isaiah

1:24	168
3:1	168
7	116
10:33	168
41:2–4	113
44:28	113
45:1–7	113
45:13	113
46:10–11	113
48:14–15	113

INDEX OF SCRIPTURE

Jeremiah

1:6	169
4:10	169
15:11	169
22:16	182

Daniel

3:1–30	169
3:37	169
9:8	169
9:15	169
9:16	169
9:19	169
11:32	182

Jonah

4:3	168

Habakkuk

2:4	68n37

NEW TESTAMENT

Matthew

7:7	89n38
12:24	81n19

Mark

1:15	29, 32
3:22	81n19
9:34	81n19

Luke

11:9	89n38
11:15	81n19
18	89

John

20:29	178

Acts

1:3	32
1:6–8	32
8:37	91n45
17:31	33

Romans

1:18	48, 50
1:19–21	49
1:20	49
1:21–23	49
1:23	49
1:24–31	49
1:27	50
3:3	68n31
3:20	69
3:21	50, 51
3:21–26	50, 51n29
3:24	50
3:25	50, 51
3:25–26	51
3:26	50, 68
3:27–28	68
6:1–11	50
6:14	69
7	68n42
7:8	68
8:2	62
8:11	53
8:18	52
8:20–23	52
8:23	53, 53n34
8:24–25	51–53
8:31–39	32
9–11	65
9:3	65
10:9	45
14	68n42, 69
14:1	59–60, 67, 67n36
14:1–15:7	61, 61n8, 62
14:1–15:13	58–60, 67
14:2	60
14:13	66n31
14:14	60
14:22	67
14:23	59, 67, 67n36, 68n42, 69
15:1	60, 67n34
15:7–9	70
15:8	61
15:9–12	60, 61, 64, 64n24, 70
15:14–21	62

1 Corinthians

2:4–5	46, 47
2:6	29, 32
4:3–5	32
6:2	32
7:29–31	29
10:2–4	48
10:11	32
10:11b	29
11:27–30	47
11:29–30	52
11:32	47
12:7–11	46
12:12	46
13:12	52
15:2	25
15:3–8	44
15:6	45n10
15:11	45
15:18–19	46
15:20	53
15:23	32
15:23–26	29
15:35–57	53n34

278

Index of Scripture

15:50–57	52, 55	**1 Thessalonians**		**Sirach**	
15:51	32	4:14	53	23:1	168
16:22b	32	4:15–18	55	34:1	168
		4:16	32	36:1	168
2 Corinthians		5:24	86n31	46:1	169
1:18	86n31			46:5	169
1:22	53	**2 Thessalonians**			
4–5	54n36	1:5	52n31	**2 Maccabees**	
4:13–14	53			3:24	169
4:13–5:10	51, 52	**Hebrews**		5:20	169
4:16	52, 54	1:12	29, 32	6:14	169
4:17–18	52	11:1	178	12:15	169
4:18	51			12:28	169
5:4	52	**1 Peter**		15:3	169
5:5	53, 53n34	1:5	32	15:4	170
5:6	53			15:22	168
5:7	51, 53, 54	**2 Peter**		15:23	170
5:10	52	3:3–16	55	15:29	170
Galatians		**Revelation**		**3 Maccabees**	
2:16	68	18:1–10	32	2:2	169
3:3–5	47	20:4–6	32	2:3	170
3:5	47	20:11–15	32	5:51	170
5:6	182			6:39	170
		DEUTEROCANONICAL			
Ephesians		**WORKS**			
3:14–17	87				
		Tobit			
Philippians		8:17	168		
1:27–30	52n31	**Judith**			
3:9	68				
3:10–21	52	5:20	168		
3:19–21	52	9:12	168		

Index of Other Ancient Sources

Aeschylus

Persae
169   167n8

Aristotle

Poetica   13n23, 13n24

Arnobius

Adversus nationes
2.8   78n15

Athanasius

Epistula festalis
10.6   93n50

Athenagoras

Legatio pro Christianis
4   31

Augustine

Confessionum libri XIII
6.5.7   86

6.10.6	86
9.10.24	82
10.5.7	86

Contra Academicos
3.20.43   90n42

De fide et symbolo
10.26   91n44

De fide rerum quae non videntur

1.2–2.3	87
2–4	86

De libero arbitrio
2.5   82n20

De magistro

11.36	80, 87
11.37	87
11.38	87

De ordine

1.2.32	82n20
1.8.23–24	86n30
2.1.1	82n20
2.5.15	42n90

2.9.26	90n42
3.15.42	79

De Trinitate

4.18.24	88, 90
13.2.5	74–75
14.15.21	86n32

De utilitate credendi

1.2	80
8.20	83
9.22	83
10.23	83, 84
10.24	84
12.26	84
17.35	81, 85

De vera religione

24.45	86n30, 88n37
25.46	81n18
25.47	81n18

De vita beata

1.4	85n29
2.10	82n20

Enarrationes in Psalmos
32.3–4   94

Index of Other Ancient Sources

Enchiridion de fide, spe, et caritate

31.117	89n38

Epistulae

120.2	90n42
120.3–4	90n42

Sermones

29.6	89n30
56.1	91n44
65.1	89, 93n50
75.4	89n39
90.4	93n50
115.1	89
144.2	89n38

Soliloquiorum libri II

1.2.4	86n30
1.2.13	86n30
1.2.23	86n30

Cassius Dio

Historia romana

6.71.14	30n28
52.36	25n6

Chromatius

In Matthaeum

18.4.1–2	93n50

Cicero

De divinatione

1.7	48
2.130	52

De natura deorum

1.1.2	26n10

1.43.121	26n10
1.116	48
2.6	45
3.11–13	45

De republica

2.17–20	45n9

Clement of Alexandria

Stromateis

1.6.27	77
1.7.38	77
2.2	77
2.2.9	77n13
2.3.13	77
2.4.12	77n13
2.4.14–15	77
2.4.48	77
2.9–12	77
2.9.45	77
2.11.48–49	77
2.22.125	78
4.151.1	93n50
5.1	77
5.1.1–6	77
7.10.55	78

Cyprian

Epistulae

5.1–2	93n50
7.5	93n50
10.1	93n50

Cyril of Alexandria

Commentariorum in Lucam, homiliae

113	89n39

Demosthenes

In Stephanum ii

43.66	14n26

Dio Chrysostom

Rhodiaca

13	48

Dionysius of Halicarnassus

Antiquitates romanae

2.56.1–6	45n9
2.63.3	45n9

Epicurus

Epistula ad Menoeceum

123	28n16

Euripides

Bacchae

313–314	15n29
386–394	13

Electra

624–627	15n29

Hecuba

35–44	145
1127b	11

Hercules furens

771–773	15

Hippolytus

88	167n9

Troades

612–613	17

INDEX OF OTHER ANCIENT SOURCES

Eusebius

Historia ecclesiastica
5.1.9   31

Gregory of Nyssa

In Ecclesiasten homiliae
8   93n50

Oratio catechetica magna
24   93n50

Herodotus

Historiae
1.91   167n8
3.122–123   15n29
7.140–144   103
8.51–53   104
8.144.2   9n11
9.61–62   15

Homer

Ilias
3.275–280   14n26
7.84–90   152
11.727–729   15n29
11.760–761   15n29
11.772–775   15n29
13.815–823   47
23.175–177   143
23.176   143n2
23.245   152

Odyssea
24.80–84   152

Irenaeus

Adversus haereses
3.12.8   91n45

Jerome

Commentariorum in Epistulam ad Galatas libri III
2.3.11   93n50

John Chrysostom

Epistulae
1.2   91n47

Homiliae in epistulam ad Hebraeos
19.2   91n47

Homiliae in Genesim
65.19   89n39

Homiliae in Joannem
26.2   91n47

Justin Martyr

Apologia i
6   31
13   31
25   31

Leo

Sermones
38.5   93n50

Livy

Ab urbe condita
1.16.1–8   45n0

22.57.2–3   50
22.57.4–6   42
22.57.6   50

Lucian

Alexander (Pseudomantis)
25   24, 30, 35
38   24, 30, 36

Minucius Felix

Octavius
5   29n22
11   33
34   34

Origen

Commentarium in evangelium Matthaei
11.5   89n39

Contra Celsum
1.4–5   78
1.6   78
1.11   78
1.20–21   78
1.31   78
1.55   78
2.3–4   78
2.11.30–31   79
2.11.32–33   79
3.39   78
5.3   78
6.13   78

In Canticum canticorum
3.5   93n50

Index of Other Ancient Sources

Pelagius

Epistula ad Claudium

19	93n50

Philo of Alexandria

De aeternitate mundi

15	31

De fuga et inventione

136	77n9
152	77n9

De migratione Abrahami

43–44	77n10

De mutatione nominum

182	77n9
201	77n9

De specialibus legibus

4.176	77n9

De virtutibus

46	77n9

Quis rerum divinarum heres sit

96	77n10

Plato

Apologia

26c	36n46

Leges

10	24n5
698a	167n8
888c	9n11
729e	14n26
757a	167n8

Respublica

391b	142

Pliny the Younger

Epistulae

6.20	33n38

Plutarch

Amatorius

757b–c	26n11

De defectu oraculorum

420b	29n22

De Pythiae oraculis

402e	37n49
404c–d	52n30
404e	52

De superstitione

165b	28
165c	28n19

Quaestiones romanae et graecae

291c	48

Romulus

27–28	45n9

Polycarp

To the Philippians

10.1	93n50

Quintus Smyrnaeus

Posthomerica

14.324–338	145
14.396	148n12

Sophocles

Ajax

666–667	15
709–712	15
837–842	15
925–932	15

Oedipus coloneus

385–386	16
387	16
413	17
1584	17

Philocrates

1031–1036	15n29

Suetonius

Divus Augustus

94–95	47

Vespasianus

5.2–3	47

Tertullian

Apologeticus

10	31
10.2	29n21
18.6	32
47.12	33

Thucydides

Historia belli peloponnesiaci

2.71–78	9
2.74.2	11
2.89.10	16
3.52–68	9

INDEX OF OTHER ANCIENT SOURCES

3.56.4	16	5.103.1	13	**Xenophon**	
3.58.1–2	10	5.104	12		
3.58.2	10	5.112	12, 17	*Anabasis*	
4.76–78	9	5.116.3–4	13	3.2.1–13	100
4.88	18	6.8–81	9	3.2.13	167n9
4.89–101	9	6.32.1–2	18	*Cyropaedia*	
4.92.6–7	12	7.61.3	16	8.8.7	48
4.92.7	11	7.63.4	13	*Memorabilia*	
4.93.1	12	7.72	16	1.3.1	14n26
4.98.2	15, 15n29	7.77	105	4.3.16	14n6
5.84–116	9	7.77.3	14		
5.90	12, 17, 18	7.77.4	15, 18		